FIVE THOUSAND AMERICAN FAMILIES—
PATTERNS OF ECONOMIC PROGRESS

VOLUME IV

Family Composition Change and Other Analyses of the First Seven Years of the Panel Study of Income Dynamics

Edited by Greg J. Duncan and James N. Morgan

With Contributions by Jay Cherlow, Richard D. Coe, Michael Conte, Richard T. Curtin, Greg J. Duncan, Daniel Hill, Martha Hill, Saul Hoffman, John Holmes, James N. Morgan, Sandra J. Newman, and Nripesh Podder

Conducted Under Contracts with the Office of Economic Opportunity (Responsibility for this project has been transferred to the Office of the Assistant Secretary for Planning and Evaluation, Department of Health, Education, and Welfare)

ISR   SURVEY RESEARCH CENTER
INSTITUTE FOR SOCIAL RESEARCH
THE UNIVERSITY OF MICHIGAN

165570

ISR Code No. 3819

Permission is hereby granted for the quotation of this publication without prior specific permission for purposes of criticism, review, or evaluation, subject only to the "fair use" provisions of the Resolution on Permissions of the Association of American University Presses, including citation of the source.

Five Thousand American Families — Patterns of Economic Progress, Volume IV
Library of Congress Catalog Card No. 74-62002
ISBN 0-87944-196-8 paperbound
ISBN 0-87944-197-6 clothbound

Published by the Institute for Social Research
The University of Michigan, Ann Arbor, Michigan 48106

Published 1976
Manufactured in the United States of America

CONTENTS

Preface

This fourth volume of findings from the Panel Study of Family Income Dynamics makes use of seven years of data collected in the first parts of 1968 through 1974. It contains three main sections. First, there are five chapters dealing with change in family composition, dividing the analysis according to the initial family situation of the individuals studied. This focus follows naturally from our finding in Volume III that most changes in economic status result from changes in family composition.

In the second section there are three chapters on the impact of inflation on commuting and driving costs, on food expenditures, and on housing costs. Finally, there are some special studies on sex discrimination, the anatomy of inequality, and summaries of work going on elsewhere with the panel data to the extent we have been able to keep up with it.

Proper credit to initiators and early participants in analysis of this study has appeared in previous volumes of this series. We are continuingly indebted to the thousands of respondents who graciously answer our questions and keep in touch with us when they move. We remain impressed by the persistence of our hundreds of interviewers in finding and talking with people, and by the patience of scores of editors and coders in making sense of the answers and converting them to digits. To our expert and loyal research staff (none has left) we have added another computer specialist, Paula Pelletier, and another graduate research assistant, Richard Coe. Linda Stafford and Elizabeth Brater edited this volume.

We are grateful to a number of readers of earlier versions of this manuscript whose suggestions have improved its substance and its clarity. Among them are Jonathan P. Lane, our chief contact at the Office of the Secretary for Planning and Evaluation, U. S. Department of Health, Education, and Welfare, the sponsor of this study; Paul Glick, U. S. Census Bureau; Ernest R. Berndt, University of British Columbia; William C. Birdsall, University of Michigan; Wilbur J. Cohen, University of Michigan; James Cramer, University of California at Davis; Peter de Janosi, Ford Foundation; Robert Ferber, University of Illinois; Arland Thornton, Survey Research Center; Susan H. Cochrane, University of South

Carolina; Thomas Glennan, National Academy of Sciences; Edward Gramlich, Cornell University; C. Russell Hill, University of South Carolina; Carol Jones, Urban Institute; Jan Kmenta, University of Michigan; Isabell Sawhill, Urban Institute; Janet Peskin, Department of Health, Education and Welfare; and Milton Moss, National Bureau of Economic Research.

Greg J. Duncan
James N. Morgan
Ann Arbor

PART I

FAMILY COMPOSITION CHANGE

AND

ECONOMIC WELL-BEING

Chapter 1

INTRODUCTION AND OVERVIEW

Greg J. Duncan and James N. Morgan

Introduction

The main purpose of the Panel Study of Income Dynamics has been to investigate factors that affect the changes in economic well-being of families over time. By this seventh year of the study, it has become increasingly apparent that families themselves undergo fundamental changes and that these changes are among the principal causes of changes in economic status. To quote the summary of the first volume in this series, "Decisions about marriage, bearing children, and encouraging older children and other adults to stay in the household or leave it seem to be the main individual decisions that affect one's status . . ."[1]

We have chosen, therefore, to devote a considerable portion of this volume of findings to a systematic look at several of the more important changes in family composition and at the relationship between these changes and changes in economic well-being.

---

[1]Morgan et al. (1973), p. 337.

2

By the seventh year of the panel (1974), fewer than one-third of the families had the same composition as in the first year, and over one-third were headed by someone who had not been the head of the same family in 1968. In this study, members of the original families were followed when they left their households, and intertemporal analysis using the family unit became increasingly difficult as the number of these newly formed families increased. Although the new families could be compared with the original households from which one or more of their members came, interpretation became complicated.

In the analysis described in the first part of this volume, therefore, we used the *individual* rather than the *family* as the analysis unit to study the cause and effects of family composition change, although we retained *family* income and *family* income relative to needs (income/needs) as measures of economic well-being.

Some 16,000 individuals were members of the original sample of families in early 1968. Properly weighted to allow for differential sampling, response, and panel loss rates, they were (and continue to be) representative of the population of the continental United States.[2] Since families with low incomes were oversampled, information about the individuals in modest economic circumstances is somewhat more reliable than in a more balanced total sample of the same size.

For any point in time, each individual in our sample could be classified according to his or her relationship to the head of a family. The following chapters deal separately with groups of individuals who in the first year of the study (1968) were: (1) married household heads and their wives, (2) unmarried household heads, (3) children 10 years of age and older, (4) other family members 10 and older, and (5) all sample members under 10 years of age.[3] These groups of individuals were represented in our sample according to the following

---

[2] Some of the individuals died, went into institutions, or were lost to the panel. In appropriate chapters, we give information on the frequency and initial economic position of these nonresponse individuals.

[3] We excluded children born to panel members after the Spring 1968 interview. They are part of a long-term panel, but it is difficult to think of comparing 1974 situations with situations before they were born.

percentages:

Relation to Head in 1968

Married Male Household Heads in 1968	21.0%*
Wives of Household Heads in 1968	22.3%*
Unmarried Male Household Heads	2.0%
Unmarried Female Household Heads	6.2%
Children 10-18 years of age	19.7%
Children 19-29 years of age	5.3%
Children, Grandchildren, etc., 1-10 years of age	22.1%
Others over 10 years of age	1.4%

*There are more former wives than former husbands left in the panel because of differential mortality and other panel losses.

Over a period of time, changes in family composition could have involved any of the individuals. Married heads and wives could have divorced, separated, or become widowed. The unmarried heads (those who were single, divorced, separated, or widowed) could have married. Children could have split off from their families to establish households of their own. Other kinds of changes were also possible.

Not all family composition changes were equally important or interesting. Some, such as widowhood, may have exerted a greater impact but may have also involved a large random component determined by forces totally outside the control of the family members. Other changes, such as the splitting off of children, may appear to be inevitable life-cycle progressions unless it is realized that their *timing* could have been altered by people's decisions in ways systematically related to variables of interest.

The analysis of the *effects* of family composition change on economic well-being presented here is largely descriptive. Using family composition change as an independent variable, we have determined how often the various changes occurred among our groups of sample individuals over the seven years of the panel and have related these changes to a variety of measures of change in economic status. An overview of these descriptive findings is given in the following section of this chapter.

We have also treated family composition change as a *dependent* variable and have investigated the three most important kinds of change within a common theoretical framework. These changes—divorce or separation, marriage or remarriage, and splitting off—often resulted in dramatic changes in economic status and, more importantly, each may have been affected by the purposes, desires, and environments of the individuals involved. We were particularly interested in learning whether determinants of family composition change include variables that might be affected by public policy. Proper estimates of the effects of important factors

which are amenable to policy influence, however, could be made only when all causal
variables were taken into account. We have used the same basic theoretical model
to investigate each of the family composition changes. An overview of the theoretical framework is given in the second section of this chapter, followed by a
summary of findings and a conclusion.

Analysis

I. AN OVERVIEW OF CHANGES IN FAMILY COMPOSITION AND IN FAMILY ECONOMIC WELL-BEING

We began our analysis simply by comparing changes in economic status, particularly flows into and out of poverty, with various kinds of family composition
change experienced by the individuals in the sample. This is shown in Table 1.1.
All sample individuals were categorized first by their relationship to the head of
a household in the initial year of the panel, and second, by the major changes in
the composition of their families over the seven panel years. We have defined
"poverty" as being the bottom fifth of the income/needs distribution.[4] The table
shows for each group of individuals (1) the fraction of those who were initially
poor who had climbed out of poverty by 1973, and (2) the fraction of those who had
not been poor initially who had fallen into poverty by 1973.[5]

We examined, for example, the family and economic changes experienced by
the women who began the panel period as wives. They comprised 22.3 percent of
all sample individuals. Most (85 percent) of them remained married throughout.
Among the always-married women, 45 percent of those who had been poor at the beginning of the panel period became nonpoor, while about 6 percent of those who began
above the poverty line eventually fell below it.[6] Using this always-married group
as a comparison, we can now turn to those who had been divorced and remarried by
the seventh year. This group was small (constituting 2.3 percent of all initially
married women) and differed little from the maritally stable group. For the initially poor among these women, the chance of climbing out of poverty was somewhat

---

[4]Families are ranked not by income but by the ratio of their income to an estimate
of their needs based on family size and composition. See Glossary.

[5]A table showing the fraction of *all* individuals in these groups who climbed out
of or fell into poverty is given in the appendix to this chapter.

[6]This 45 percent figure reflects the remarkably high turnover rate in much of
the poverty population. For a more complete description, see Chapter 1 of
Volume I of this series.

TABLE 1.1 (Sheet 1 of 2)

Major Family Composition Changes and Change in
Poverty Status by 1968 Relation to Household Head
(All Sample Individuals)

1968 Family Status and Change	Percent of All Sample Individuals	Percent of Group	Proportion of Poor in 1967 Who Were Nonpoor in 1973	Proportion of Nonpoor in 1967 Who Were Poor in 1973
Married Male Household Heads	21.0%		.46	.06
Married throughout		89.9%	.45	.06
Divorced,Remarried		3.2	.74*	.05
Divorced		4.0	.67	.13
Wives of Household Heads**	22.3		.42	.08
Married throughout		84.8	.45	.06
Divorced,Remarried		2.3	.56*	.07
Widowed		6.8	.33	.24
Divorced		5.7	.26	.33
Unmarried Male Household Heads	2.0		.39	.14
Stayed Unmarried		64.2	.23	.20
Married		35.7	.95*	.06
Unmarried Female Household Heads	6.2		.36	.17
Stayed Unmarried		80.6	.37	.18
Married		14.9	.88	.08
Children 10-18 Years of Age in 1968	19.7		.49	.11
Stayed in Household		60.8	.37	.06
Split, Became Single Heads		9.9	.43	.39
Split, Married		25.8	.78	.12
Split, Married and Divorced		2.1	.39	.39
Children 19-29 Years of Age in 1968	5.3		.72	.06
Stayed in Household		16.8	.41	.05
Split, Became Single Heads		13.3	.68	.15
Split, Married		62.5	.83	.04

*Estimate based on fewer than 25 observations.

**There are more former wives than former husbands left in the panel because of differential mortality and other losses.

TABLE 1.1 (Sheet 2 of 2)

1968 Family Status and Change	Percent of All Sample Individuals	Percent of Group	Proportion of Poor in 1967 Who Were Nonpoor in 1973	Proportion of Nonpoor in 1967 Who Were Poor in 1973
Children, Grandchildren, Nieces, Nephews, and Others 1-10 Years of Age in 1968	22.1%		.44	.17
Children, No Family Change		32.9%	.45	.09
Children, Change in Family Other than Head or Wife		45.7	.50	.18
Children, Went with Divorced Mother		6.8	.13	.27
Children, One Parent Died		2.0	.25*	.36
Children, Single Parent Married		5.3	.71	.19
Other, No Change		1.3	.36	.55
Other, Change in Head or Wife		3.1	.49	.37
Other--Older than 10 Years	1.4		.53	.17
All	100.0%			

NOTE: Only changes that involve 50 or more of the sample individuals are listed. "Percent of Group" percentages do not necessarily ad to 100 due to omitted groups.

Poverty is defined as the lowest quintile of the family income/need distribution.

*Estimated based on fewer than 25 observations.

higher than for those who were stably married--56 percent versus 45 percent.[7]
Their chances of falling into poverty were virtually the same--7 percent and 6 percent, respectively. The initially married wives who became widowed or divorced and
did not remarry, however, fared much worse. Fewer than one-third of the women in
these two groups who began in poverty managed to climb out. More dramatic was the
fact that 24 and 33 percent, respectively, of those women who became widowed or
divorced and who began above the poverty line eventually fell below it. These
percentages were four times as great as those for women who remained stably married.

The other groups of sample individuals--particularly those consisting of
women--showed a similar relationship between economic status and family composition change. Some highlights:

● *Married male household heads.* A little over one-fifth of the sample were in
this group at the beginning of the panel period. Their situation was much less
clearly tied to marital status change than was true for their wives. Those who
began out of poverty were twice as likely to fall into poverty if they got divorced and did not remarry, compared with those who experienced no change in marital status. Of those who began in poverty, both groups of divorced husbands
(those who did and those who did not remarry) had a greater chance of climbing
out than did those who remained married throughout.

● *Unmarried male household heads.* For the few individuals who began in this
group, marriage was associated with a higher probability of climbing out of poverty for those who were initially poor and with a lower probability of falling
into poverty for the initially nonpoor.

● *Unmarried female household heads.* Women in this group who then married
experienced benefits similar to those of their male counterparts. The vast majority (88 percent) of these women who began poor and who then married became nonpoor.
Among those who began *above* the poverty line, marriage decreased the chances of
falling below it from 18 percent to 8 percent.

● *Children over 10 years of age.* For children 10-18 years old who began in
nonpoor families, those who departed from the parental home were much more likely
to fall into poverty, particularly when the child either left and did not marry
or left, married, and then divorced. Among the children who began the panel
in poor families, those who split off were generally less likely to end up poor;
this was particularly true for those who split and then married. Similar patterns

---

[7]This finding should be treated cautiously because it is based on fewer than 25
observations.

were found among the groups of older children (19-29 years old), although their
economic status was not as closely tied to these changes.

● *Children under 10 years of age*. The young children in the sample had no control over family composition changes and yet were greatly affected by them. Overall, almost 45 percent of the initially poor children ended up nonpoor and 17 percent of those who began above the poverty line ended up below it. Only about
one-eighth of those who went with the mother after a divorce climbed out of poverty,
and over one-quarter of those who began nonpoor ended up poor. The children in
families where one parent died and the surviving spouse did not remarry fared even
worse: More than one-third of these children who began above the poverty line
had fallen below it by the seventh year.

But just as divorce or death decreased the chance of climbing out of poverty,
marriage increased it. Over 70 percent of the initially poor children in families
where an unmarried head became married had climbed out of poverty by the seventh
year of the panel.

● *"Others" under 10 years of age*. A small fraction of the sample was made up
of very young grandchildren, nieces, nephews, and other relatives of the household
heads. These individuals, regardless of the changes in their families, fell into
poverty at a high rate.[8]

Our findings consistently showed that an individual's chances of falling into
or climbing out of poverty were closely related to changes in the composition of
his or her family. Detailed discussions of this relationship are presented for
several panel subgroups in the following chapters.

II. A GENERAL APPROACH TO ANALYSIS OF FAMILY COMPOSITION CHANGE

Our approach to the analysis of family composition change has centered on
the *economic* aspects of current and alternative living arrangements. In a way
it seems quite natural to include economic explanatory factors because the family
composition changes have such important effects on the economic status of families.
We omitted, however, many obviously important psychological and sociological mo-
tives, such as love and societal pressures, which play a significant role in
causing people to incur and maintain family obligations. In many cases, these
factors are probably more important determinants of change than economic ones.
It is not surprising, then, that we find that economic variables are able to explain only a small fraction of the variation in family composition changes.

---

[8]These groups do not exhaust the set of possible changes. Table 1.1 is restricted
to changes for which there were at least 50 observations. Finer detail is presented in each of the appropriate chapters.

Our choice of an economic model can be defended in several ways. First, some explanatory variables may account for a great deal of interpersonal difference but either do not change over time or do not change in the same way for substantial groups of people. For example, personalities clash, divergent family backgrounds cause trouble, some behavior patterns may make parents eager to have their children leave home. Such variables may have little power in explaining aggregate changes, even though they help our clinical understanding of individual behavior. A number of the economic variables can, on the other hand, change in the same direction at the same time for many people, or be changed by public policy, so that their effects do not average out in the aggregate.

A second reason is that our primary interests here concern the effects of policy-relevant economic variables on family composition changes. Whether the omission of important psychological variables affects our estimates of these relationships depends upon the correct causal ordering of economic and psychological variables. We estimated a model containing mostly economic variables:

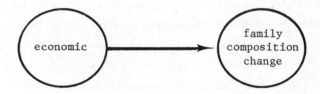

and we hypothesized that the economic variables *cause* the family composition changes.

If the economic variables are causally prior to the omitted psychological ones, then the latter were termed *intervening* variables and can be represented as follows:

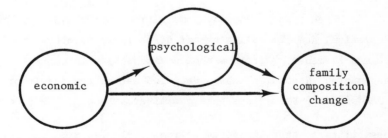

In this case, our estimates of the relationship between economic variables and family composition changes would still be correct. By omitting the psychological

10

variables, we were unable to estimate the extent to which the effects of economic factors operate *through* psychological measures as opposed to operating *independently* of them.

If, on the other hand, economic and psychological variables operate on the same causal level,

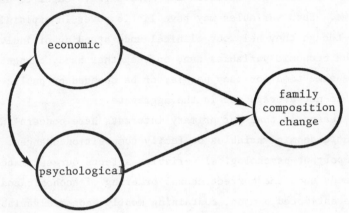

omitting the psychological variables *may* bias the estimated relationship between economic variables and family composition change. This is the classic problem of omitted variables, with positive associations among the three sets of variables leading to an *overestimate* of the importance of economic factors. If psychological variables exist that belong at the same causal level as economic ones and are interrelated with both the economic variables and the family composition changes, then our results may be misleading.[9]

In sum, the model of family composition change that we discuss in this volume is an economic one. It does not explain these changes completely, but we do expect it to provide correct estimates of the relationship between economic variables of interest and changes in family composition.

The Model

Each of the three types of family composition change--marriage/remarriage, divorce or separation, and the splitting off of children or other family members--involve two common elements. First, a choice exists between current and alternative living arrangements. Second, a change decision may be the result of how *both an individual and others involved* evaluate the alternatives.[10] We hypothesized that

---

[9] A final possibility is that the psychological variables are logically prior to the intervening economic ones. Previous volumes in this series have presented evidence that none of our psychological measures seem to affect economic status.

[10] These decisions, of course, are not necessarily made within the calm, rational setting implied by the economic interpretation given here.

certain objective measures of the alternatives would relate systematically to the change decisions made by the individuals in the sample.

Since these family composition changes were *joint* decisions on the part of an individual *and* his current or potential family, it was necessary for us to be aware of factors that may have been important to both groups. If a certain variable affected an individual's and others' desires for a certain change in opposing directions, then estimating the relationship between that variable and family composition change required particular care, and it was important that the analytical framework allow for this simultaneity of differing interests.

Our general approach to the analysis of family composition change was quite similar to the conventional economic analysis of markets. In the conventional analysis, depicted in Figure 1.1, a demand schedule for a commodity is ascertained by asking potential buyers to specify the amounts they would be willing to buy at different prices. The less expensive the commodity, the greater the desired purchase. Thus, the demand curve in Figure 1.1 slopes downward. Desired supply, on the other hand is an increasing function of price, and a supply schedule can be obtained in a manner similar to that used for the demand schedule—that is, by asking potential suppliers their willingness to sell different amounts of the commodity at different prices. The amount of a commodity that is marketed per unit of time and its price are determined jointly by these supply and demand schedules.

FIGURE 1.1

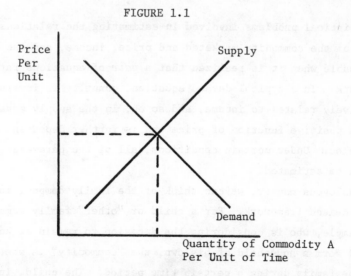

Although price is a key determinant of the quantity bought and sold, it is not the only one. The position of the demand schedule may depend upon the prices of other commodities, income, tastes and preferences, and so on, while supply may

vary with changes in production conditions (for example, temperature and rainfall
with agricultural commodities). Changes in these other variables *shift* the demand
and supply schedules and change the market equilibrium quantity and price. If desired demand depends upon income, for example, we might have two demand schedules,
as shown in Figure 1.2--one for a market with a low level of income, the other with
a higher income level. The quantity and price of the marketed commodity are both
higher in the market with the higher income level.

FIGURE 1.2

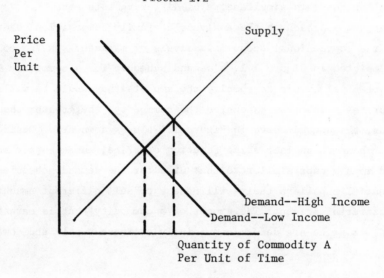

The statistical problems involved in estimating the relationship between
the quantity of the commodity marketed and price, income, and the other factors
become manageable when it is realized that a *pair* of equations rather than a single
one are at work. In a typical demand equation, quantity is inversely related to
price, positively related to income, and so on; in the supply equation, however,
quantity is a positive function of price and is further dependent upon the other
supply variables. Under certain conditions, all of the parameters in these two
equations can be estimated.

In an analogous manner, we can think of the family composition changes within
a supply and demand framework. For a child or "other" family member in the household, for example, who is considering the decision to remain at home or else to
split off and form a household of his own, the "commodity" is whether or not he
remains in the family during a certain time period. The child, in this case, is
the demander, while other household members (particularly the head and wife) are
the suppliers. For any particular individual, this "quantity" of current arrangements must either be all or nothing (either he chooses to split off from the family

in that time period or he does not). For a group of individuals, however, some *fraction* would remain in the current arrangements, and the commodity could be interpreted as the *probability* that the current arrangements would be chosen.

The analogue to commodity price is the relative contribution made to the household by the individual considering the change. The concept is not a new one—George Levinger and others have theorized about the various emotional as well as more concrete contributions each party brings to a relationship. Clearly, people with different affective needs have some advantage in "trading" with one another, and their contribution relative to others in the house will play a part in the family arrangements that are made.

The only component of individual contribution that is sufficiently quantitative to compare across individuals is their contribution of time—either in earning money or doing housework or child care. For children and "others" in the household, the "price" (called here the *net transfer position*) is calculated as the ratio of the sum of the labor market and housework hours contributed by the individual to the per capita market and housework hours for *all* family members. Individuals who earn nothing and do little housework receive a net *subsidy* from their family and would have a small net transfer score. Those working extensively at home and/or in the labor market contribute more than they receive and would thus be in a large net transfer position. Just as the demand and supply schedules for a commodity relate to price in opposite ways, so too would the demand and supply schedules for current living arrangements relate in opposite ways to this net transfer price. With other factors such as educational status being held constant, a child receiving a large subsidy from his family would theoretically want to remain within the current arrangements more than a child who heavily subsidizes his family. The demand schedule for current arrangements, in other words, would be downward sloping with respect to this "price," as shown in Figure 1.3. The *supply* of current arrangements to the individual from his family would be an increasing function of the net transfer position. Other factors being equal, a family would be more willing to supply the current arrangements to a child if he "produces" more than he consumes.

It is difficult, of course, to think of family situations such as this with "other factors" being equal. A family is probably more willing to supply current arrangements to a subsidized family member if he is disabled and requires extra care or is completing the education that they planned for him. We hypothesized that these "other factors" would shift the demand and supply schedules, just as income, other prices, and production variables shift the schedules in the analysis of more conventional commodities.

14

FIGURE 1.3

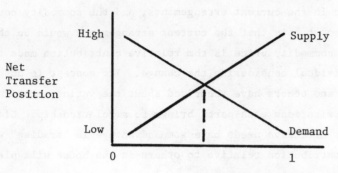

Quantity of Current Arrangements--
Probability that No Family Composition
Change Will Occur

A further analogy to the analysis of commodity markets is the way in which
the net transfer position variable equilibrates supply and demand, just as commodity price does in conventional markets. If, for example, the commodity price
is higher than its equilibrium level, then desired supply will exceed desired demand, and market forces will be at work to drive the price down to its equilibrium level. It is plausible that similar forces may take place within the household. If a child is contributing much more than he consumes and thus wants to
split off much more than his family wants him to, they might be willing to have
him do less housework, contribute a smaller fraction of his earnings to the family, or both. His net transfer position would fall and this "market" would equi-
librate at one quantity of current arrangements (i.e., at a single probability
that no change would occur).

The supply and demand framework can be extended to the other kinds of family
composition changes as well. For spouses contemplating divorce or separation,
the "commodity" is the probability that the marriage would be kept intact during
the course of the panel period.[11] The "price" is similar to the net transfer
position variable of the potential splitoff. For wives, we have defined the
price variable as the wife's fraction of the total labor market and housework
time of both husband and wife. Thus, if both spouses work full time (2,000 hours
each) and the wife works an extra 500 hours at home, her net transfer position
would be 2500 ÷ 4500, or .56. The husband's net transfer position in this example would be simply 1-.56, or .44.

[11]Our analysis focuses on transitions from 1968 to 1974. We could have analyzed
pooled year-to-year changes, such as getting divorced even if the person remarried. Such analysis is still worthwhile though our data do not reveal
changes which were reversed within one year.

We did not value time differently for the two spouses, partly because self-selection biases make it incorrect to rely on market wages, or imputed market wages in the case of the wife not currently working for money, and partly because people tend to marry people with similar backgrounds, education and tastes so that we might be introducing differential bias in estimating the wife's wage rate rather than genuine differences between the value of husband's and wife's time. The estimation of a wage rate for wife would have to deal with the self-selection by which those relatively better at raising children than at earning money tend to work less, have less job seniority, and earn less. Such a woman's time may be far more valuable to the family and to her spouse than her current market wage would indicate. Indeed, the residual discrimination against women added to the effects of their interrupted work experience makes their market wage almost certainly an underestimate of the value of their contributions to the household per hour.

With the price variable thus defined, it is possible to discuss the supply and demand schedules for the current arrangments (that is, for keeping marriage intact). Without any loss in generality, we treat the wife as the demander of the current arrangements and the husband as supplier. The wife's demand for the current arrangements should be inversely related to her net transfer position. A working wife who spends as much or more time than her husband working at home and in the labor market should be less willing to remain married than a wife who does little work and is heavily subsidized by her husband. Other things being equal, a husband may be less willing to "supply" current arrangements when the net transfer position of his wife is very low.

For spouses considering marital breakup, as for children considering the decision to split off from the parental household, "other things" are never equal, and we recognized that a host of other factors needed to be included in a complete model of the divorce or separation decision. The effects of these other factors, we expected, would be to shift the supply and demand schedules. Wives with more education and labor market experience, for example, would be better able to support themselves and thus be more willing to dissolve the marriage. Both members of a couple living in a small town may be less willing to divorce because of stricter norms against divorce that generally prevail in smaller communities. Thus, although the basis of this analysis framework is economic, various sociological and psychological factors could be included within it as variables that shift either the supply or the demand schedules, or both.

The marriage/remarriage decision for those who were unmarried (i.e., divorced, separated, widowed, or single) could also be put into this framework with some modifications. Rather than considering the demand and supply of *current* arrange-

ments as a function of net transfer position, it is more useful to think of the
supply and demand of alternative arrangements (i.e., marriage) as a function of
potential net transfer position.[12] This potential position variable was estimated
by matching the characteristics of unmarried individuals with those of currently
married persons and then equating the *potential* net transfer position of the former with the *actual* net transfer position of the latter. As with the two other
family composition changes, the unmarried panel members' demand schedule was expected to relate inversely with the net transfer position while supply would have
a positive association with it.

Additional variables were included in these supply and demand equations. We
were particularly interested in whether the receipt of Aid to Families with Dependent Children (AFDC) income affected the demand for remarriage on the part of unmarried mothers with dependent children.

Although the supply and demand framework did not fit all family composition
changes equally well, we found it useful because it pointed out the problems of
simultaneity inherent in all of the decisions. If this simultaneity had not been
recognized and taken into account, the empirical estimates of relationships between independent variables and the family composition change dependent variables
would have been biased or inconsistent. A general discussion of statistical considerations and procedures is given in Appendix B.

III. A GENERAL SUMMARY

Two broad generalizations seem to be warranted regarding the relationship
between family composition changes and changes in economic status. First, the
economic status of men was affected far less by family composition change than
was that of women. Second, changes brought about by marriage and remarriage that
resulted in two-parent families were the most beneficial, while such changes as
divorce, separation, splitting off, and widowhood which resulted in a family with
an unmarried household head were generally detrimental. These two findings were
remarkably consistent for all groups of individuals that formed our sample. Both
were the product of several obvious facts of contemporary society: Women earn less
than men partly because of discrimination and partly because of their less regular
pattern of labor force participation. In addition, two-parent families often have

---

[12] It might be possible to create more elaborate models which have separate equations for the supply and demand both of the current situation and of the most
attractive possible alternatives, but this multiplies the number and overlap of
variables represented by proxies. We chose instead to deal with the most obvious and crucial simultaneity and introduce possible differences in alternative
opportunities as part of the set of explanatory characteristics. One could also
look at living together as a case of bilateral bargaining with a wide range of
relative contributions acceptable to both parties, in the spirit of Edgeworth's
contract curve.

two earners while single-parent families do not.[13] And finally, dependents are much more likely to go with the mother than the father after a marital disruption.

IV. EVIDENCE ON POLICY-RELEVANT VARIABLES

Since economic welfare is closely tied to changes in family composition, it is important to be aware of the factors that may affect these changes, particularly when they are amenable to alteration through public policy. Our approach has focused on the *economic* aspects of current and alternative living arrangements. Few sociological variables and virtually no psychological measures were available, although both are certainly a necessary part of a complete explanation of these changes. The validity of both our approach to the analysis of the data and the policy discussion presented here depends upon the assumption that economic factors, in part, *cause* changes in family composition--an assumption which we, as economists, are willing to make.

We have evidence on two types of policy-relevant variables. The first set consists of directly alterable variables such as AFDC support levels, local labor market conditions, and so on. The second group is a more general one and includes economic variables possibly related to family composition changes and to other kinds of public policies.

It was hypothesized that the receipt of AFDC income might encourage divorce and separation among low-income married couples or discourage remarriage among unmarried female household heads with children, or both. In fact, we did find some evidence of an effect on divorce and separation. Low-income couples living in states with the highest levels of AFDC payments were generally less likely to remain intact during the panel period. The difference in the incidence of divorce or separation between these couples and those with otherwise similar characteristics living in states with low AFDC payments was about 12 percentage points. Regarding a possible discouraging effect of AFDC income on remarriage, however, we found virtually *no* evidence that such a relationship existed. The unmarried female heads with children who received AFDC income differed very little from women in similar circumstances who did not receive it.

Variables measuring environmental conditions were also of interest. We found weak evidence that they affected the timing of the decision of children to split off from parental homes. Male children living in the most densely populated areas were less likely to leave home over a given time period than those from rural

---

[13]Of course, the definition of needs assumes economies of living together, and the results flow partly from the estimated size of those economies.

areas. Female children from depressed areas were more likely to leave home than
those where employment possibilities were more favorable.

On a more general level, we found some significant associations between family composition changes and the economic aspects of current and alternative living
arrangements. Unmarried female heads, for example, were significantly less likely
to marry if they had high potential earnings. Married couples were most likely
to divorce or separate if the wive was in the labor force, and this effect was
even more marked if her work hours were extensive. This relationship may not be
completely causal since wives could have begun working in response to an unsatis-
factory marriage or in anticipation of a divorce.

Measures of income and assets also related to these change decisions. Both
home ownership and high savings levels were deterrents to divorce. Higher income
levels were associated with lower remarriage rates among the initially unmarried
women in our sample. Finally, we found evidence that the split decisions of both
sons and daughters were retarded in cases where various indications of high housing
quality were found.

V. CONCLUSIONS

Our findings have policy relevance in several ways. First, a substantial number of young children were affected in major ways by the decisions made by their
parents and other relatives concerning family arrangements. Children cannot be
expected to do anything about family changes and yet many public policies directed at adults change families and affect children.

A second point concerns the role of AFDC income in marital status changes.
We have found that high levels of AFDC payments may have encouraged divorce and
separation but did not seem to affect remarriage. The AFDC-divorce relationship
has also been found by others using more aggregate data. While we would expect
higher AFDC payments to increase divorce rates (if, of course, other sources of
income do not also increase), we are not saying that the proper policy should be
to lower the payments in order to discourage divorce. If income maintenance programs favor single-parent families *vis a vis* two-parent families with children,
and if it is approved public policy to encourage stable marriages, then the solution may well be to improve the treatment of two-parent families rather than
reduce the level of AFDC payments to single-parent families.[14]

Third, the volatility of family composition raises questions about the impact

---

[14] The redistribution aspects of one alternative method of income maintenance is
given in Chapter 3 of Volume III of this series.

of other public policies on the family. Since we have been concerned mostly with established national policies, or other policies which do not vary much from one county or state to another, we have no natural experiment or even statistical procedure for estimating potential effects of changed rules, policies, or programs. Although policy-related assessments should always be approached with caution, it would appear credible, for example, that the rules of both tax and income maintenance programs may encourage or discourage reliance on extended family help patterns, marriage or remarriage, parenthood, or cohabitation for economic reasons, such as to share housing costs and provide mutual assistance. The income tax law, for example, is now regarded as generally favorable to single people rather than married couples.[15] It is quite possible that the standards of income maintenance may incorporate such extreme assumptions about economies of scale in living together (and attempt to recapture them) that they encourage splitting up rather than mutual help and cooperation. For example, the current standard allows approximately $1,800 plus $800 per person, or $5,000 for a family of four. But if the individuals declared themselves to be two families of two people each, each smaller family would be allowed $3,200, for a total of $6,400. Furthermore, the supply of different types of dwellings and the allocation of housing supports may well affect the timing of children's decisions to leave home, get married, and start having their own children.

In sum, the definitions of "family," "household," and "income" used in the various tax, income maintenance, and subsidy programs are far more than administrative details. While these definitions certainly affect the current operation of a particular program, they may also change the composition of families and, ultimately, the long-term results of these programs. Quantitatively, the family is still the principal income maintenance program.

References

Levinger, George. "Marital Cohesiveness and Dissolution: An Integrative Review," Journal of Marriage and the Family, February, 1965.

Morgan, James N. et al. Five Thousand American Families--Patterns of Economic Progress. Volume I. Ann Arbor: Institute for Social Research, 1974.

---

[15]This depends upon the relative incomes of the married couples.

Appendix 1.1

Appendix Table A1.1 shows a type of poverty flow statistic which differs
from that presented in the text. Here, a calculation has been made of the proportion of all sample individuals in a particular family composition change group who
(1) were below the poverty line in 1967 and above it in 1973 and (2) who were above
the poverty line in 1967 and below it in 1973. Each of these proportions is the
product of two probabilities. The first (given in the third column of the table)
is the percentage of individuals in the group who were poor in 1967 times the percentage of those who became nonpoor by 1973. The second (in the fourth column) is
the percentage of nonpoor in 1967 times the percentage of those who had fallen
into poverty by 1973.

The resulting proportions are useful in thinking about aggregate impacts.
The difference between the two proportions is the *net* increase or decrease in the
proportion who were poor. Any of these proportions can be multiplied by the number
of individuals in that group to estimate how many million people were involved.
The aggregate number of individuals in any group (row) of the table is a product
of the proportion of sample individuals in the main group times the proportion of
them in the subgroup, times the number of individuals in the population.

For instance, line nine shows that of the wives of household heads who got divorced and did not remarry, 21.4 percent fell into poverty while 3.8 percent climbed
out, so that 17.6 percent more of them were poor in 1973 than in 1967. They represent 5.7 percent of the married women, who were 22.3 percent of all individuals,
so they represent 5.7 x 22.3 or 1.27 percent of all individuals. There were
approximately 200 million individuals in the resident population in 1968, so that
1.27 percent represents some 254,000 individuals. Of these, 21.4 percent or 54,366
fell into poverty, 3.8 percent or 9.652 climbed out, for a net increase in poor
individuals of 17.6 percent of 254,000 or 44,700 individuals. This assumes, of
course, that our remaining panel members were still representative of the population; that is, that the individuals who were lost to the panel were not substantially different from those who remained, but our examination has shown that at
least their initial condition did not differ appreciably from the rest.[16]

---

[16]
Initial income and income/needs of the panel losses are given in each chapter
of this section.

TABLE A1.1 (Sheet 1 of 2)

Major Family Composition Changes and Change in
Poverty Status by 1968 Relation to Household Head
(All Sample Individuals)

1968 Family Status and Change	Percent of All Individuals	Percent of Group	Proportion Poor in 1967 and Nonpoor in 1973	Proportion Nonpoor in 1967 and Poor in 1973
Married Male Household Heads	21.0%		.050	.056
Married throughout		89.9%	.046	.055
Divorced, Remarried		3.2	.085	.047
Divorced		4.0	.103	.109
Wives of Household Heads	22.3		.050	.072
Married throughout		84.8	.045	.055
Divorced, Remarried		2.3	.123	.056
Widowed		6.8	.094	.173
Divorced		5.7	.038	.214
Unmarried Male Household Heads	2.0		.094	.109
Stayed Unmarried		64.2	.055	.140
Married		35.7	.146	.053
Unmarried Female Household Heads	6.2		.135	.103
Stayed Unmarried		80.6	.103	.111
Married		14.9	.295	.053
Children 10-18 Years of Age in 1968	19.7		.118	.089
Stayed in Household		60.8	.083	.045
Split, Became Single Head		9.9	.098	.301
Split, Married		25.8	.193	.087
Split, Married and Divorced		2.1	.149	.237
Children 19-29 Years of Age in 1968	5.3		.106	.047
Stayed in Household		16.8	.110	.154
Split, Became Single Head		13.3	.128	.123
Split, Married		62.5	.109	.033

TABLE A1.1 (Sheet 2 of 2)

1968 Family Status and Change	Percent of All Individuals	Percent of Group	Proportion Poor in 1967 and Nonpoor in 1973	Proportion Nonpoor in 1967 and Poor in 1973
Children, Grandchildren Nieces, Nephews, and Others 1-10 Years of Age in 1968	22.1		.071	.089
Children, No Family Change		32.9	.047	.057
Children, Change in Members Other than Head or Wife		45.7	.071	.072
Children, Went with Divorced Mother		6.8	.032	.249
Children, One Parent Died		2.0	.049	.144
Children, Single Parent Married		5.3	.195	.079
Other, No Change in Family Head or Wife		1.3	.132	.238
Other, Some Change in Head or Wife		3.1	.171	.181
Other--Over 10 Years of Age	1.4		.146	.128
All	100.0%			

NOTE: Only changes that involve 50 or more of the sample individuals are listed. "Percent of Group" percentages do not necessarily add to 100 due to omitted groups.

Poverty is defined as the lowest quintile of the family income/need distribution.

Chapter 2

HUSBANDS, WIVES, AND DIVORCE

Saul Hoffman and John Holmes

Introduction

Research on marital instability has occupied the energies of social scientists and policy makers for several decades. This interest reflects concern over the rapid increase in divorce rates (they have nearly tripled since 1958) which affects all levels of American society. At the same time, statistical profiles show the disproportionate representation of households headed by women in the poverty population. Analysis based on the first five years of the Panel Study of Income Dynamics (1968-1972) and reported in Volumes I and II of this series confirmed this strong link between marital instability and poverty status. Even after adjusting for demographic and environmental variables, female-headed families with children were shown to be two and one-half times as likely to be temporarily poor[1] and twice as likely to be persistently poor as similar families headed by married couples.[2]

In this chapter we focus on changes in marital status. The population considered here consisted of all persons who were married at the outset of the panel study (1968). We discuss the changes in economic well-being of these husbands and wives over the panel period and present a more detailed analysis of the most frequent marital status change, divorce or separation. In Section I, we consider briefly the experiences of initially married men. A more detailed analysis of their wives follows in Section II. In the last section we shift our attention to divorce or separation as a dependent variable. We have used the structural equations approach outlined in Chapter 1 as the basis for predicting marital instability.

Analysis

I.   MARRIED MEN AND THE EFFECTS OF MARITAL INSTABILITY

Married couples in the initial year (1968) either remained intact during the panel period or else underwent some kind of marital status change. Although some of the changes may represent inevitable life-cycle occurrences such as the death of a spouse, the greatest incidence of change in marital status was separation or divorce. Throughout this chapter, we do not attempt to distinguish between divorce and separation. The emphasis here is on the decision to terminate

---

[1]Morgan et al. (1974), p. 26.

[2]Ibid., p. 30.

the current living arrangement, whether or not the marriage was finally dissolved by a court decree. This section focuses on the experiences of men who were initially married in 1968, with particular emphasis on their associated marital and economic status through 1974.

Classification of initially married men by their marital status in the final year alone would mask some changes which occurred during the interim years and prevent any multiple changes in marital status from being detected. Thus each change in marital status has been recorded and the corresponding path taken by each person has been noted to capture the dynamics of family composition change. As depicted in Figure 2.1, the vast majority of these men remained married—at least during the panel period. Nearly nine out of every ten initially married men remained with their spouses through 1974.

Two types of involuntary separation can be identified. The more frequent type, death of a spouse, was experienced by slightly under 3 percent of the initially married men. Nearly 75 percent of this small group remained widowed for the duration of the study. A second category of involuntary separation included those instances in which one spouse was temporarily confined in an institution at some time during the panel period. Since this small group of men (only seven recorded cases) may have differed systematically from the other subgroups, it has been isolated in a separate path.

The most frequent change in marital status was associated with a *voluntary* termination of the initial living arrangement. Roughly 1 out of every 14 initially married men was divorced or separated during the seven-year period. It is interesting to note that half of this group had remarried by 1974. A few, less than 0.5 percent, were divorced more than once. As in earlier studies, a substantial racial difference in the incidence of voluntary marital dissolution was observed in the panel data. The proportion of initially married nonwhite men reporting a divorce or separation after 1968 was nearly double that of their white counterparts (12.0 percent versus 6.7 percent; see Figures A2.1a and A2.1b).

To assess the impact of family composition change on the economic well-being of initially married men, the seven-year changes in family money income and income/needs were calculated for the different groups and are presented in Table 2.1. The largest group, those with intact marriages throughout the panel period, experienced increases in family real money income and in income/needs of slightly more than 3 percent per annum.[3] This was substantially less than increases re-

---

[3] The percentage changes are based on the proportionate increase in mean income for 1973 versus 1967. The ending year values are deflated by the increase in the CPI Index since 1967.

26

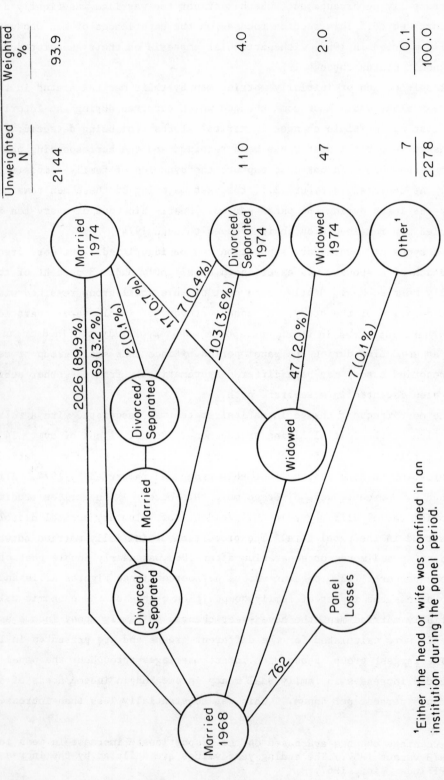

FIGURE 2.1

Married Men in 1968 and Their Associated Status Through 1974
(Entire Sample)

	1974 Marital Status	
	Unweighted N	Weighted %
Married 1974	2144	93.9
Divorced/Separated 1974	110	4.0
Widowed 1974	47	2.0
Other[1]	7	0.1
	2278	100.0

2026 (89.9%)

69 (3.2%)

2 (0.1%)

17 (0.2%)

7 (0.4%)

103 (3.6%)

47 (2.0%)

7 (0.1%)

762

[1]Either the head or wife was confined in an institution during the panel period.

NOTE: For each path, the unweighted number of cases and the corresponding weighted percentages are included.

TABLE 2.1

Change in Economic Well-Being by Change in Marital Status[1]
(All Married Men in 1968)

Change in Marital Status	Unweighted N	Mean 1967 Family Income	Percent Change in Mean Real Income 1967-1973	Mean 1967 Family Income/Needs	Percent Change in Mean Real Family Income/Needs 1967-1973
Married Throughout	2026	$10,250	21.8%	2.89	20.8%
Divorced or separated[2,3]	110	9,000	-10.6	2.48	30.0
Divorced and Remarried[3]	69	9,800	36.9	2.62	41.5
Widowed (No Remarriage)	47	7,750	- 4.5	2.39	4.8
Average		$10,150	20.7%	2.85	21.4%
Panel Losses	762	$ 8,950		2.63	

---

[1]Excluded from the above table are the following: (1) 17 men who were widowed and subsequently remarried, (2) 7 cases where either the head or wife was confined in an institution, and, (3) 2 cases with multiple divorces when the final status is married.

[2]Includes 7 cases with multiple divorces during the panel period.

[3]The percentage change in mean real income and income/needs does not include any obligations for child support and/or alimony payments. After deducting from income *all* contributions to dependents outside the family unit, the percentage change in mean real income and income/needs is reduced to 26.9 percent and 30.8 percent respectively for men who were divorced and later remarried. The corresponding figures for men who remained divorced are -19.2 percent and 16.5 percent respectively.

ported by men who were divorced and later remarried. The latter group had changes
in real income and income/needs which were nearly double those of couples who
stayed married. Although men who remained divorced or separated showed a deline
of 10 percent in real money income from 1967-73, the accompanying reduction in
needs more than offset the loss in income. This resulted in a 30 percent increase in this group's real income/needs. The final subgroup, widowers who did
not remarry, showed a virtually unchanged position on both money income and in-
come/needs after adjusting for inflation.

Some indication of the bias due to panel losses can be seen by comparing
the initial economic status of the nonresponse cases with the rest of the sample.
Nearly a third of initially married men (762 cases; see Figure 2.1) were lost
from the panel after 1968. The overall mean 1967 family money income and income/
needs of these nonresponse cases was only slightly below that for persons remaining with the panel.

After reviewing the subsequent economic fortunes of 133 panel couples whose
marriages had been disrupted, Hampton noted that "...the economic status of
former husbands improves while that of the former wives deteriorates."[4] While
there does appear to have been some association between changes in marital and
economic status, the relationship for initially married men was not nearly as
strong as it was for their *wives*. This is not surprising since the extra responsibilities associated with caring for children often restrict the wife's
earning opportunities. In the next section, we focus on the experiences of
these wives in greater detail.

II. MARRIED WOMEN AND THE EFFECTS OF MARITAL INSTABILITY

Previous studies of the relationship between marital status and economic
status have usually focused on women, and especially on those women who head
families. It is by now well-known that female-headed families are disproportionately poor. For example, in Volume III of this monograph series it was
shown that while families headed by women accounted for only 16 percent of all
families, they comprised 44 percent of the families whose incomes were less
than their needs. Moreover, female-headed families tended to be among the persistently poor, accounting for 52 percent of all families whose incomes were
less than their needs every year from 1967 to 1973.[5]

In this section we focus in greater detail on the relationship between the

---

[4]Duncan and Morgan (1975), p. 185.

[5]Ibid., p. 36.

marital status and economic status of women, and changes in both. We begin by looking at all women who were married in 1968 and then trace the various changes which occurred in their marital status from 1968 through 1974. We use these marital status changes to explain changes in economic well-being from 1967 to 1973, and we give special attention to economic differences between women who have experienced different changes in marital status.

Changes in Economic Status and Marital Status

The sample consisted of 2,422 women who were married in 1968 and for whom we have seven years of information. Of these, 672 are nonwhites.[6] Figure 2.2 classifies these women according to their 1974 marital status and their changes in status from 1968 to 1974. Nearly 85 percent remained married throughout the period, 8 percent were divorced or separated at least once, and 7 percent were widowed. After the initial interviewing year, 640 married women were lost from the panel. Since the 1967 economic status of these nonresponse families was similar to those remaining with the study (see Table 2.2), the results of this analysis should not be affected substantially.

Table 2.2 shows the seven-year percentage change in mean real income and income to needs for each of the major categories of marital status change. The findings are rather striking. Those who remained married not only started at a higher average income level in 1967 than those who were subsequently divorced, separated, or widowed, but they also enjoyed a sizeable increase in both income measures. Those who were divorced and remarried experienced even greater increases in economic well-being. However, this group included only 54 women and exhibited tremendous variation in income change, so the results should be interpreted with caution.[7] Finally, for the women whose 1974 status was divorced, separated, or widowed, real income fell about 30 percent. The ratio of income to needs also fell, though not so sharply, since family size also declined with these changes in marital status.

When we look at the mean percentage changes in income rather than the percentage changes in mean income, we note essentially the same pattern. All

---

[6]The weighted frequencies are 90.2 percent and 9.8 percent for whites and non-whites.

[7]For example, almost 28 percent of these women had seven-year increases in real income/needs of more than 100 percent, while 8 percent suffered declines of more than 50 percent, and 7.5 percent moved onto welfare from 1967 to 1973.

30

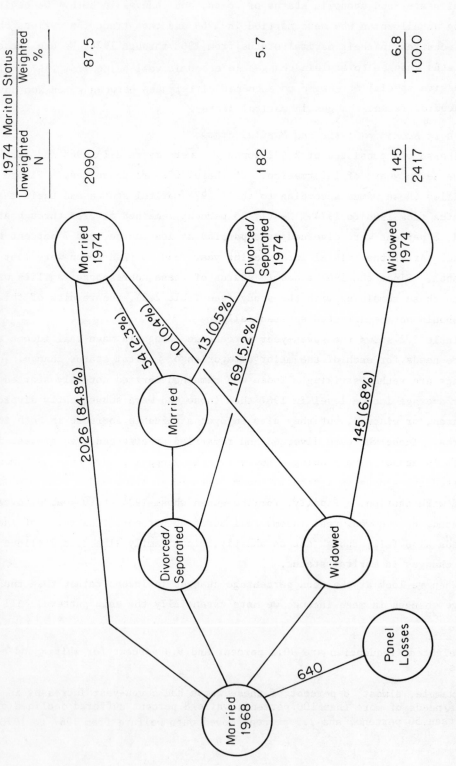

FIGURE 2.2

Seven-Year Change in Marital Status for Married Women in 1968

NOTE: For each path, the unweighted number of cases and the corresponding weighted percentages are included.

TABLE 2.2

Seven-Year Change in Economic Status by Change in Marital Status[1]
(All Married Women in 1968)

Change in Marital Status	Number of Cases	Weighted Percentage	1967 Income	Percent Change in Real Income 1967-1973[2]	1967 Income/ Needs	Percent Change in Real Income/Needs 1967-1973[2]
Married Throughout	2026	84.8%	$10,257	21.7%	2.88	20.8%
Divorced or Separated	182	5.6	9,205	−29.3	2.24	− 6.7
Divorced and Remarried	54	2.3	7,601	89.4	2.21	75.1
Widowed (No Remarriage)	145	6.8	6,970	−33.3	2.33	−12.4
All	2407		$ 9,906	17.7	2.80	18.3
Panel Losses	640		$ 9,246		2.69	

[1]Ten women who became widowed and then remarried have been omitted from the table.

[2]1973 Income and Income/Needs have been deflated.

groups showed considerable variation in income change.[8] Nevertheless, while almost 35 percent of the women who remained married suffered declines in real in-
income/needs, nearly 60 percent of the women who were divorced, separated, or
widowed in 1974 had experienced a decline in economic status. Indeed, nearly
15 percent of these women had decreases of more than 50 percent, compared to only
4 percent of the always-married women. It is interesting to note that there were
virtually no differences with respect to the bivariate distribution between
those women who were widowed and those who were divorced or separated. (See
Table A2.1a for the complete distributions.)

Although marital status change seems to be a significant factor in explaining changes in the economic status of women, it is surely not the only important
factor. To the extent that changes in marital status represent the effect of
other relevant variables, the simple bivariate relationship presented above
would be misleading. Consequently, we look at the effects of marital status
change in a multivariate context.[9] The dependent variable in this analysis is
the percentage change in real income/needs for each individual. The complete
results are presented in Appendix A2.1b. Here, we focus on marital status change
and contrast the bivariate and multivariate results, as given by the unadjusted
and adjusted mean changes in income/needs. These results are summarized in Table
2.3. Table 2.4 lists the predictors according to their relative importance in
the multivariate analysis (Beta^2) and in a bivariate analysis (Eta^2).

Change in marital status did have systematic and statistically significant
effects on individual changes in income. The results, shown in Table 2.3, were
roughly similar to those presented earlier for mean income changes, except that
the average income change for all groups was positive.[10] Looking at the multivariate results, we found that those who remained married increased their real
income/needs by an average of 35 percent, while for those who were divorced or

_____

[8]Individuals almost always exhibit far greater variability in income than aggregates or group means tend to reveal. Sometimes these changes are genuinely
misleading, especially if the base year--1967 in this case--is unrepresentative
for any reason. For some individuals, large percentage changes simply reflect
a random component of income which distinguishes a good year from a bad one.
For others, large percentage changes in income correspond to life-cycle stages,
particularly for young persons at the beginning of their careers and for older
persons near the end of theirs.

[9]The analysis was performed using a statistical program, MCA, which is equivalent to multiple regression with dummy variable predictors.

[10]Presumably, this is partly due to the effect of large positive percentage increases outweighing smaller percentage declines in income/needs.

TABLE 2.3

Effect of Change in Marital Status on Seven-Year Percentage
Change in Real Family Income/Needs
(All Married Women in 1968)

Change in Marital Status	Number of Cases	Weighted Percentage	Unadjusted Mean[1]	Adjusted Mean[2]
Married Throughout	2018	85.0	35.9	35.4
Divorced or Separated	177	5.6	13.3	7.5
Divorced and Remarried	52	2.3	112.1	100.3
Widowed	141	6.7	11.4	26.0
Widowed and Remarried	10	0.4	68.2	66.5
TOTAL	2398	100.0	34.8	--

Summary Statistics for Change in Marital Status

Bivariate Analysis	Multivariate Analysis
$Eta^2 = .026$	$Beta^2 = .019$
$F = 16.0^{**}$	$Partial\ R^2 = .019$
	$F = 9.36^{**}$

**Significant at .01 level.

[1]Based on a bivariate analysis with seven-year change in marital status as the independent variable.

[2]Results were obtained from a multivariate analysis which included race, age, and education of wife, city size, and region as additional independent variables. Cases where the percentage change in income/needs was more than five standard deviations above the mean were excluded. Complete results are presented in Appendix Table A2.2.

TABLE 2.4

Gross and Net Explanatory Power of Predictors
of Percentage Change in Real Income/Needs
(All Married Women in 1968)

Variable	Eta^2	$Beta^2$
Age	.033	.033
Change in Marital Status	.026	.019
City Size (1974)	.007	.006
Wife's Education (1968)	.005	.004
Region (1974)	.005	.002
Race	.002	.001

MTR #7512

separated in 1974, real income/needs rose by only 7.5 percent. These averages have been adjusted for the effects of other variables. Widows exhibited the smallest increases in the bivariate analysis, but much of this was due to the age of both themselves and their former husbands. In the multivariate analysis, they fared much better than divorced or separated women, though not so well as those who remained married. While change in marital status was not the most important predictor of income change (age of wife had that distinction, as shown in Table 2.4), it was a statistically significant predictor in both bivariate and multivariate analysis.

Patterns of Work and Welfare

Although the preceding discussion has highlighted certain aspects of the association between changes in marital status and changes in economic status, it has obscured some other elements of the relationship. One such element is the composition of family income. A divorced woman, for example, may return to the labor force, thereby replacing her former spouse's income with her own. For other women, transfer income--either welfare or alimony--may increase. We take a closer look now at changes of this kind, with special emphasis on the women who were divorced or separated in 1974, and we also examine differences between whites and nonwhites.

Table 2.5 classifies women according to the change in their labor force and welfare status between 1967 and 1973. Column two confirms the well-known fact that, in general, nonwhite women participated in the labor market more regularly than white women. More than 40 percent of the nonwhite women worked in both 1967 and 1973, while only about 25 percent of the white women did. However, for women who were divorced or separated in 1974, the opposite was true--a greater percentage of white than nonwhite women worked in both years.

The last two columns of Table 2.5 contrast entry into the labor market with going onto welfare. Much has been written about the alleged welfare dependence of the female-headed family, and particularly those families headed by a black woman. These data both confirm and provide a reinterpretation of this popular notion. Divorced or separated women of *any* race were more likely to be on welfare than women in more stable families. Six percent of the divorced or separated white women who were not receiving welfare in 1967 were receiving it in 1973, compared to only one-half of 1 percent for women who remained married. For nonwhite women, the percentages were still higher: 16.4 percent compared to 5 percent.

However, as column three makes clear, many more women moved into the labor market than onto welfare in response to a change in marital status. The figures

TABLE 2.5

Seven-Year Change in Labor Force and Welfare Status
by Change in Marital Status
(All Married Women in 1968)

	Number of Cases	Percent Working in 1967 and 1973[1]	Probability of Being Employed in 1973, if not Employed in 1967[1]	Probability of Receiving Welfare in 1973, if not Receiving Welfare in 1967
Married Throughout				
White	1491	24.6%	22.8%	0.5%
Nonwhite	535	40.7	23.5	5.0
Divorced or Separated				
White	90	50.5	63.8	6.0
Nonwhite	92	37.8	53.7	16.4
All				
White	1740	26.1	24.3	0.8
Nonwhite	667	40.4	26.0	5.8

[1]Defined as 250 or more hours in labor force in 1967 or 1973.

NOTE: The figures for ALL also include women who were widowed and those who were divorced and remarried.

MTR # 7512

shown in column three are conditional probabilities; they reflect the probability of working in 1973, given that a woman did not work in 1967. More than 60 percent of the white women who were married and not working in 1967 and who were divorced or separated in 1974 were working in that final year. For nonwhites, the comparable figure was over 50 percent. Figure 2.3 compares the percentage of all divorced or separated women who were working with the percentages on welfare in 1974.

Finally, the actual act of divorce or separation seemed to affect the welfare status of white women more strongly than that of blacks. Black families--whether headed by a married couple or by a single female--tended to have lower incomes and higher welfare rates than did white families. But the differences by race in welfare rates were much greater for married women than for women who were divorced or separated. For a white woman, the conditional probability of receiving welfare income in 1973 if she did not receive it in 1967 increased twelvefold--from 0.5 percent to 6.0 percent--if she became divorced or separated. But for a black woman, the probability--while higher than for a white woman--was about three times greater for a divorced or separated woman than for a married woman.

Changes in Sources of Income

The total changes in real income noted earlier in this section were very much the product of these changes in labor force and welfare status. We focus here on seven-year changes in total income, in transfer income (including Social Security), and in the woman's labor income.

As shown in Table 2.6, there were substantial differences both between the women who remained married throughout the period and those who became and remained divorced or separated and between whites and nonwhites who underwent similar changes in marital status.

Married women of both races experienced real income increases of over $2,000, with the largest share of the increase coming from the husband's labor income. For nonwhites, increases in the income of others in the family unit was second in importance; for whites, the increase in transfer income was next in importance. In contrast, women who became and remained divorced or separated suffered a decline in real income over the period. This occurred in spite of substantial increases in the labor income of these women--over $1,800 for whites and nearly $1,950 for nonwhites.

More striking, however, were the differences by race between the women who became divorced or separated during the period. For the whites, real income fell by more than $3,000; for the nonwhites, the decline was only $230. While

FIGURE 2.3

1973 Employment and Welfare Rates
(All Initially Married Women Who Were Divorced or Separated in 1974)

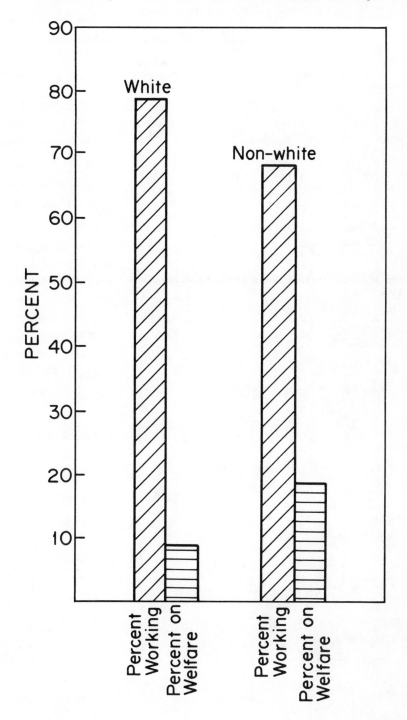

TABLE 2.6

Seven-Year Change in Real Family Income
by Source of Income and Change in Marital Status
(All Married Women in 1968)

	Number of Cases	Total Change in Income	Change in Woman's Labor Income	Change in Transfer Income	Change in Income of Others	Change in Spouse's Income
Married Throughout						
White	1491	$ 2239	$ 210	$ 471	$ 374	$1187
Nonwhite	535	2066	309	301	434	1023
Divorced or Separated						
White	90	-3177	1833	948	646	-6602
Nonwhite	92	- 230	1946	1450	1819	-5445
All						
White	1740	1761	305	529	396	535
Nonwhite	667	1704	472	416	559	257

NOTE: The figures for ALL also include women who were widowed and those who were divorced or separated.

MTR #7512

transfer income rose in real terms by nearly $950 for whites, it increased 50 percent more for nonwhite women. The largest difference--more than $1,100--was in the increase in the income of others. Apparently, family living arrangements involving multiple earners were more common for nonwhites than for whites.[11] In all, changes in these three sources of income--the woman's labor and transfer income and the income of others--accounted for 96 percent of the loss in spouse's earnings due to dissolution of the marriage for nonwhites and about 50 percent for whites.

The effects of these various changes become apparent when we compare the composition of 1973 income for the women who remained married throughout with that for those who were divorced or separated. Table 2.7 exhaustively decomposes total income for whites and nonwhites into four basic components--taxable and transfer income of the woman and her spouse (if present) and the taxable and transfer income of others.

Again, there were considerable differences both by marital status and by race. For the married women, taxable income amounted to about 85 percent of the total income for both whites and nonwhites, compared to only about 60 percent for white divorced or separated women and about 40 percent for nonwhites. Transfer income accounted for an average of 20 to 25 percent of the total income of these women. The greatest difference by race was in the taxable income of others. Nonwhite divorced or separated women derived more than a quarter of their support from this source; for whites, the income of others accounted for only one-sixth of total income. In all, while white divorced or separated women earned more than 60 percent of their total income, nonwhites received about 55 percent as some kind of transfer--their own transfer income and the transfer and taxable income of others in the family unit.

The nature and composition of transfer income itself varied widely among these groups. A simple distinction can be drawn between transfer programs which are at least partially contributory and those which are essentially redistributive. Social Security and pensions are typical of the first kind of program. AFDC is the most prominent transfer program in the second category, though it is by no means the only one. Intermediate to these categories is alimony and child support, where redistribution occurs between individuals known to each other. Table 2.8 shows total 1973 transfer income and the average amounts from

_____

[11]One indication of this is that there was on average 1.65 adults older than 18 living in households headed by nonwhite divorced or separated women. For white divorced or separated women, there were only 1.32 adults in the household.

TABLE 2.7

Composition of 1973 Income
by Source of Income and Seven-Year Change in Marital Status
(All Married Women in 1968)

Change in Marital Status	Number of Cases	Taxable Income of Woman and Spouse (if any)	Transfer Income of Woman and Spouse (if any)	Taxable Income of Others	Transfer Income of Others	Total	Mean 1973 Income
Married Throughout							
White	1491	87.0%	6.6%	5.9%	0.3%	100.0%	$16,964
Nonwhite	535	84.7	6.5	7.7	1.0	100.0	13,236
Divorced or Separated							
White	90	62.0	20.8	16.1	1.0	100.0	8,695
Nonwhite	92	43.3	26.7	28.6	1.4	100.0	8,509
All							
White	1740	85.0	7.9	6.4	0.6	100.0	15,890
Nonwhite	667	80.7	8.6	9.4	1.3	100.0	12,190

NOTE: The figures for All also include women who were widowed and those who were divorced and remarried.

MTR #7512

welfare and alimony for child support for each of the major marital status groups. (See Tables A2.1c and A2.1d for more complete details.)

Table 2.8 shows that while both groups received a considerable amount of transfer income, these two categories of transfer income were important only for those women who were divorced or separated in 1974. While these two kinds of transfer income accounted for over two-thirds of the transfer income for these white women and for over 50 percent for nonwhites, the relative importance varied significantly by race. Alimony or child support alone amounted to 60 percent of the total transfer income for the white divorced or separated women, while welfare provided, on average, only 8 percent. For nonwhites, however, the proportions were nearly equal—about a quarter of transfer income each. It may well be the case that welfare and alimony or child support operate as crude substitutes. Thus, where alimony or child support is not adequately provided, for whatever reasons, public assistance is a necessary alternative. In this connection, it is interesting to note that while the average annual alimony or child support payment for nonwhites was $500 less than for whites, the addition of welfare reduced this difference to an average of only $75.

Finally, we look only at those women who actually received welfare, alimony, or child support. As shown in Table 2.9, less than half of all divorced or separated women were receiving any alimony or child support. A greater percentage of whites than blacks received this kind of income, and in amounts that were 50 percent greater than for blacks. Over six times as many divorced or separated white women and twice as many nonwhites reported income from alimony or child support than reported income from welfare.

A summary measure of many of the changes we have examined in this section is shown in Table 2.10. It compares income/needs in 1967 and 1973 for each of

TABLE 2.10

1967 and 1973 Income/Needs as a Fraction
of Income/Needs of Always-Married Women
(All Married Women in 1968)

Change in Marital Status	White		Nonwhite	
	1967	1973	1967	1973
Divorced or Separated	.82	.60	.76	.69
Divorced and Remarried	.78	1.13	.64*	.92*
Widowed	.86	.61	.55*	.47*

*Less than 30 observations

TABLE 2.8

Composition of 1973 Transfer Income by Source
and Seven-Year Change in Marital Status
(All Married Women in 1968)

Change in Marital Status	Number of Cases	Total Transfer Income	AFDC	Alimony/Child Support
Married Throughout				
White	1491	$1124	$ 6	$ 6
Nonwhite	535	860	97	0
Divorced or Separated				
White	90	1811	150	1083
Nonwhite	92	2275	588	570
All				
White	1740	1257	17	65
Nonwhite	667	1053	153	55

NOTE: The figures for ALL also include women who were widowed
and women who were divorced and remarried.

MTR #7512

TABLE 2.9

Annual Income Per Recipient, 1973, from Welfare and Alimony/Child Support
(All Married Women in 1968)

	Married Throughout		Divorced or Separated	
	White	Nonwhite	White	Nonwhite
Percent Receiving Welfare Payments	1.0%	5.6%	7.1%	17.1%
Average Welfare Payments	$1650	$1729	$2530	$3442
Percent Receiving Alimony/Child Support			46.3%	36.7%
Average Alimony/Child Support Payments			$2351	$1554

MTR #7512

the main categories of marital status change to that of the group of women who
remained married throughout. The group of always-married women were better off
even in 1967--when all the women in the sample were married--than were the women
in the other major groups we have considered. By 1973, in spite of the increases
in labor force activity, in transfer income, and in the income of others in the
family unit, this differential had widened for the women who were divorced, separated, or widowed. Thus, in 1973, white divorced or separated women had an income to needs ratio which was 60 percent of that for married women; in 1967,
their income/needs ratio had averaged 82 percent of that of always-married women.
Widows fared even worse, falling from 86 percent to 61 percent of the figure for
always-married women. While the relative decline in income to needs was less
for nonwhites, their ratios also fell, from 76 percent to 69 percent and from 55
percent to 47 percent, respectively, for divorced or separated women and for
widows.

Summary

This section has examined the relationship between the economic well-being
and marital status of initially married women. Where previous studies have documented the cross-sectional relationship between economic status and marital
instability, this analysis has focused on change over seven years among a group
of more than 2,400 women. Because the study began when all these women were
married and before many of them became divorced, separated, or widowed, it provides a rare look at the ways in which changes in economic status occur.

Two basic findings have emerged in our analysis. First, *changes* in economic status were related to *changes* in marital status. Women who remained married
throughout the seven-year period fared far better than did those who were divorced, separated, or widowed in 1974. Even after adjusting for the effects of
other relevant variables, we found that the always-married women achieved percentage increases in real family income/needs which were five times as large as
those for women who were divorced or separated in 1974. This resulted from a
sharp drop in the income of divorced or separated women compared to the always-
married group. In 1967, their income was just under four-fifths that of the
always-married women; by 1974, this fraction had fallen to just over three-fifths.

Second, changes in marital status led to a series of changes in economic
activity. There was certainly no firm and inevitable progression from divorce
or separation to welfare dependence. Some women did, of course, go onto welfare,
but many more took employment, and some coped with financial problems by moving
in with friends or relatives. Six percent of the white divorced or separated
women began receiving welfare income, while 16 percent of the nonwhite women did

so. By comparison, among the always-married women, less than 0.5 percent of the white women and 5 percent of the nonwhite women started receiving welfare income. But even for the nonwhite divorced or separated women, transfer income amounted on average to just over a quarter of 1973 income.

By far the more frequent change in economic activity was in labor force participation. Nearly 80 percent of the women who were still divorced or separated by 1974 reported working in 1973; of these, almost 30 percent had not been working in 1967. More of the white divorced or separated women worked than did non-whites, but even for the nonwhites almost four times as many worked as were on welfare in 1973.

Finally, we have noted the role of alimony or child support and of changes in family living arrangements. Whites were more likely to receive alimony or child support if they were divorced or separated than were nonwhites, and when they did receive alimony or child support, they averaged 50 percent more than did nonwhites. For nonwhites, the increase in the number of family living arrangements involving multiple income earners was most significant. For the divorced or separated nonwhites, the seven-year real increase in the income of others in the family unit was over $1,800 and in 1973 this income source accounted for nearly 30 percent of their total income.

III. THE MODEL OF MARITAL INSTABILITY

In the previous two sections we have looked at the ways in which changes in marital and economic status were related. We have seen that the relationship was a strong one, particularly for wives, and one in which marital instability led to a substantial deterioration in economic well-being. In this section, we shift our attention from the *effects* of marital instability to its *causes* and focus on the most studied of all changes in marital status, divorce or separa-tion.[12]

The model we used to analyze marital instability is explained in general terms in Chapter 1. The model builds on much of the previous research on divorce and separation but extends that analysis in two basic directions. First, many previous studies have emphasized simple correlations between marital instability and the various socioeconomic or demographic characteristics of the couples who are divorced or separated. In the cases where the characteristic in question is itself correlated with other variables, this analysis may be mis-

---

[12] We do not distinguish between divorce and separation in our analysis.

leading. Consequently, we have used multivariate analysis, which has enabled us to consider the effects of any single variable of interest after adjusting for the effects of all other variables.

Second, and more fundamentally, our model explicitly recognizes the fact that divorce or separation is necessarily a joint decision. Dissolution of a marriage can, of course, be initiated by either spouse and, as George Levinger notes in his summary of research on marital instability, there is no reason to assume that the effects of socioeconomic factors are identical for husbands and wives.[13] Hence, the decision to dissolve a marriage should logically be a function of the desires of *both* spouses. Previous research has, virtually without exception, concentrated solely on *overall* effects. Most of this research focused on outcomes (who got divorced or separated) rather than on the decision-making process which resulted in the dissolution. The overall effect of a variable on divorce rates may be quite different from its effect on each spouse. Indeed, it is possible to construct examples where the effects on each spouse are large and in opposite directions, so that the overall effect is negligible.

The analysis we have used acknowledges this "jointness" by applying a simultaneous equations model to this decision. The likelihood of maintaining the marriage is seen as the interaction between the desire or "demand" of one spouse for retaining the current arrangement and the willingness of the other to continue to "supply" these arrangements. The equilibrating mechanism for adjusting differences in the desire for maintaining the marriage is the relative time contribution of each partner in market and nonmarket activities. This pseudo price variable operates to adjust these differences much as the more familiar price variable equates supply and demand in commodity markets.

We are, of course, *not* suggesting that this price variable alone determines whether a marriage will end in divorce or separation. The sociological literature abounds with examples of other factors which are associated with higher than average likelihoods of divorce. Our model focused on some of these--race, education, income, urban residence, age at marriage, and dissimilarity of backgrounds--in great detail. One striking advantage of this structural equations approach is that it facilitates quantification of the magnitudes and directions of these variables as they affect *each* spouse's desire to maintain the marriage. Although either spouse could be viewed as demanding or supplying the present living arrangement, the convention here is to regard the wife in the former role and the husband as the supplier. Thus the model can be summarized as follows:

---

[13]Levinger (1965).

DEMAND: $Q_D = \alpha + \beta P + \eta X_1 + \varepsilon$ (1)

SUPPLY: $Q_S = \gamma + \delta P + \theta X_2 + \nu$ (2)

where   P denotes the equilibrating mechanism, the price
        variable,

X_1, X_2 are the sets of other socioeconomic factors
(not necessarily distinct) influencing the desire
of each spouse to remain married,

Q_S, Q_D, represent the probability of supplying/de-
manding the present living arrangement (intact
marriage), and

ε, ν are the disturbance terms.

The pivotal element--the "price" variable--is discussed in greater detail in the
following section, together with the rationale for including other factors,
X_1 and X_2, which influence the desire of either spouse to terminate the marriage.

The Price Variable

The price variable was measured by the relative *hours* contributed in the
labor market and on housework by each spouse. It might be argued that the price
variable should include a measure of the *quality*, as well as the *quantity*, of
the contribution of each partner. That is, the inputs of each spouse should be
weighted by the *value* of their time, where, ideally, this valuation would represent the opportunity cost of each spouse's time. The decision to use a more
egalitarian measure, based on an equal valuation of the hours contributed by
each spouse, was motivated by both theoretical and empirical considerations.
First, we would argue that the hours--*not the dollars*--contributed by each spouse
best reflect the view of the other spouse regarding equal sacrifice. Second,
the relatively low labor force participation of wives made it difficult to value
the time contributions of women who worked only at home.[14] This problem was
further compounded by an inherent self-selection process: women who worked may,
in fact, face different opportunity sets than similar women who chose not to
work. Although some shadow price could undoubtedly be assigned to their time
inputs in the home, any such imputation would be ultimately arbitrary. In any
event, we did experiment initially, using a half-sample, with a procedure which
valued all housework at a uniform wage rate. The results were consistently un-
successful and the specific rate which we applied to housework hours was very

---

[14]Only 40 percent of all married women worked more than 250 hours in the labor
market in 1967.

difficult to justify.

The variable *hours net transfer* was constructed by dividing the wife's annual labor market and housework hours by the combined contribution of both spouses. We hypothesized that, other things being equal, an inverse relationship should exist between the relative contribution of the wife and her desire for maintaining the present living arrangement. That is, wives with a low contribution of labor market and housework hours relative to their husbands, *ceteris paribus*, should be more inclined to continue the marriage. Hence, a downward sloping demand curve was predicted ($\beta < 0$ in equation [1]). In contrast, a relatively high contribution of total hours by the husband would diminish his desire to supply the present living arrangement. Thus, an upward sloping supply curve ($\delta > 0$ in equation [2]) should result if this framework captures the dynamics of marital instability.

The value of the hours net transfer variable is *jointly* determined by the interaction of the desires of both the husband and wife to maintain the current living arrangement. At any given level of this pseudo price variable, any differences in the willingness to remain married should create incentives for an adjustment toward the equilibrium value. For example, if at some level of hours net transfer the husband's desire to remain married exceeds his wife's inclination for continuing with the present living arrangement, he should be able to remedy this situation by increasing either his labor market hours or time spent on housework. In a similar fashion, the wife could lower her hours net transfer position by working less either in the home or in the labor market. Thus, the value of this pseudo price variable is determined *within* the system. In contrast, the sets of socioeconomic variables, X_1 and X_2, which influence the desire of each spouse to maintain the current living arrangement are determined *outside* the system. That is, the level of these *exogenous* factors are independent of the process described by the above equation system, while the value of *endogenous* variable--hours net transfer--is determined *jointly* and *simultaneously* by the socioeconomic variables and the disturbances set forth in equations (1) and (2).

The sets of socioeconomic variables can be classified into six general areas:

1. Adjustments to the Price Variable

2. Attractiveness of Alternatives

3. Dissimilarity of Background

4. Effects of Children

5. Assets

6. Other Demographic Variables

Some of these variables are common to *both* equations and were expected to have the same directional effect for both husband and wife. Any differential in the *magnitude* of these adjusting factors would be of some interest. Each set of variables is discussed separately in the following sections.

Adjustments to the Price Variable

As noted above, we hypothesized that wives with a low price position (that is, with a low contribution of market and nonmarket hours relative to their husbands) would be expected to want to continue the present living arrangement. However, the hours net transfer variable must reflect the notion that beyond some threshold further contributions in the market place by the husband would not increase the desire of the wife to maintain the marriage. The "career" man whose single-minded devotion to his job keeps him absent from home would not, in general, be adding to his wife's marital satisfaction by working additional hours. Therefore, we used the average number of hours worked on the main job in 1969 to capture this discontent. A response of 60 hours or more per week was used as the threshold for this "excess hours" effect.[15] A similar variable was constructed for those few wives who worked 60 hours or more a week in the labor market.[16] A negative relationship was expected between both of these variables and the desire of the other spouse to continue the marriage.

The persistence of labor market problems of the husband should increase the wife's desire for dissolving the marriage. As Burgess and Cottrell have noted, the security of income seemed to be more important than absolute income.[17] Included in the panel study was an index of the employment problems experienced by the head of the household over the past years.[18] A high score on this index, representing severe difficulties in the labor market, should diminish the wife's inclination for remaining married. Thus, a negative relationship was expected between this measure of the "security" of income and marital stability.

Attractiveness of Alternatives

In some marriages, the only deterrent to divorce on the part of the wife is

---

[15] Nearly 1 out of every 11 heads of households reported working an average of 60 hours or more per week on their main job. All farmers are coded zero for this variable, regardless of their reported hours.

[16] Only 0.4 percent of *all* women reported working an average of 60 or more hours per week.

[17] See Burgess and Cottrell (1939).

[18] This measure includes such things as losing a job, frequent job turnover, unemployment, or a recent illness or accident of a serious nature.

her inability to support herself--and perhaps her children as well--in a separate household. For other women, this presents no problem. It would seem reasonable then to suggest, as Levinger does, that "the more readily she (the wife) can support herself outside the marital relationship or can be assured of such support from other means . . . the more ready she would be to break the marriage."[19]

Since a large proportion of the women were not in the labor force, an estimate of *potential* earnings was used to measure the extent of financial independence. Variables from the human capital wage determination model were used to construct this estimate of a wife's earning capacity. The level of educational attainment of the wife, when coupled with estimates of years of labor market experience, should be an adequate predictor of her hourly wage.[20] There should be an inverse relationship between a wife's financial independence and her desire for continuing with the marriage.

Past research on divorce and separation has noted a persistent negative association between marital instability and family income. Since our model includes direct measures of some of the variables for which income may be a proxy (home ownership, savings, and employment problems of the husband), no direct measure of family income was included. Instead, the husband's wage rate was included on the supply side to represent his alternative situation. We expected it to affect his decision to remain married in the same way that the wife's potential financial independence affects her decision.

For some wives whose potential earnings capacity would fall far short of their financial needs in a separate household, some form of public assitance, usually AFDC, may be the only alternative to continuing with the present situation. Since the level of these categorical assistance payments is directly controlled by laws and administrative rulings, its influence on marital instability is of interest. We expected the alternative of public assistance programs to have its greatest impact on families with low incomes.[21] Accordingly, the average AFDC payment per recipient[22] for the state of residence in 1969 was combined

---

[19]Levinger, op. cit., p. 26.

[20]See Mincer (1974).

[21]For example, Honig (1974, p. 321) argues that "increases in the level of support of AFDC families, without concurrent increases in the earnings of low-income families, are likely to lead to increases in the proportion of families headed by a female."

[22]Estimates of average AFDC payments per recipient by state are based on 1970 City-County Data Book. Only 18 out of 45 states reported payments exceeding $45.

with 1968 family income/needs to form the following pattern variable:

Family Income/Needs--AFDC Interaction

		Average AFDC Payment	
		Low (<$45)	High (≥$45)
Income/Needs	Low (≤1.5)	1	2
	High (>1.5)	4	3

Three variables are formed from cells 1, 2, and 3 of the pattern variable (the fourth was eliminated because of statistical considerations). Because we were interested in whether the marital stability of any of these groups differed from the rest of the sample (and not from some omitted group), we applied a simple transformation of variables which enabled us to express the resulting coefficients as deviations from the overall mean.[23] The variable of greatest interest represents cell #2, that is, families with low income/needs who live in states with the highest AFDC levels. The incentive for divorce or separation was expected to be greatest for these families and we therefore expected a significant negative difference in marital stability between this group and the overall mean.

Dissimilarity of Background

Sociologists and, more recently economists,[24] have argued that dissimilarity of background between marriage partners is instrumental in leading to divorce or separation. This is especially so for differences in education and religious preference. However, because information on religious affiliation was obtained only for the head of the household, we concentrated on differential

---

[23]This is accomplished by constraining the estimated dummy variable coefficients to sum to zero and then rewriting the dummy variables as deviations from the omitted group. Thus, rather than estimating

$$Y = \alpha + \beta_1 X_1 + \beta_2 X_2 + \beta_3 X_3 + \varepsilon,$$

where X_1, X_2, and X_3 represent the three interactions of interest and X_4 is the omitted group, we estimated the equation as follows:

$$Y = \alpha + \beta_1 (X_1 - X_4) + \beta_2 (X_2 - X_4) + \beta_3 (X_3 - X_4) + \varepsilon.$$

[24]See Becker (1973).

educational attainment of spouses as the measure of dissimilar social status.
The educational level of each spouse was classified according to the following
scale:

1. 0-5 grades

2. 6-11 grades

3. High school graduate

4. Attended college or holds college degree.

The absolute value of the difference in this variable for the partners was used
to measure dissimilarity. Since higher values of this variable indicate greater
dissimilarity, an inverse relationship was expected between this variable and the
desire of each spouse to continue the marriage.

The Effects of Children

The presence of children in a family may affect marital stability in several
ways. Young children require an extensive time commitment and thereby severely
restrict the employment options of the spouse--almost always the wife--who cares
for them. Children are also a considerable financial obligation for the family.
At the same time, they can be regarded as both a cause and result of marital satisfaction. That is, children may themselves be a primary source of marital satisfaction or they may reflect and reinforce some previous level of satisfaction
with the marriage. In either case, it has long been known that childless couples
are more prone to divorce.[25] Thus, we included a measure of whether there were
any children in the family and we further distinguished those families with children younger than two years of age in 1969 from the rest.[26] We expected that both
spouses would be less likely to seek a divorce or separation where children were
involved, and especially when there were very young children.

Our analysis also included two variables reflecting the couple's future intentions concerning their children: whether the couple expected to have more
children, and whether the couple expected their children to receive a college education. Both variables suggest the nature of the couple's future commitments to
their marriage and to their family, and both were expected to be negatively related to the likelihood of divorce or separation.

Assets

One of the most persistent findings of previous research on divorce and

---

[25] See Monahan (1955) and Jacobson (1959).

[26] We initially considered defining this variable in terms of the presence of
pre-school age children. However, divorce/separation rates differ substantially
between families with children younger than age two and all other families.

separation has been the inverse relationship between marital instability and the social status of the family. Part of the effects of status may be captured by some of the variables we have already discussed such as wage rates and education. Another component of status, however, is wealth, and we included in our analysis two measures of wealth--whether the couple owned a home and whether they had savings equal to at least two months' income. Home ownership may contribute to the stability of family life as well. Not only does home ownership contribute to the consumption satisfaction of marriage, but, also in the event of marital discord, the community ties and complications involved in dividing property may deter some couples from seeking a divorce or separation. We expected that each wealth variable would increase the desires of both spouses to remain married.

Other Demographic Variables

Although marital instability is prevalent in all levels of American life, it has been particularly associated with blacks[27] and with those who marry young.[28] The finding in previous studies of a racial difference in divorce rates may be attributed to the omission of some socioeconomic factors which are correlated with race. Because of the abundance of literature detailing a differential incidence of divorce between whites and nonwhites, the effect of the variable "whether black" on the desire of each spouse to remain married is of considerable interest. The effect of early marriage was captured by the variable "whether married by age twenty." This factor, along with "whether a previous marriage," were hypothesized to have an inverse relationship with marital stability. Ideally, the latter should reflect a previous marriage by *either* husband or wife. However, questions on age at marriage and whether there was a previous marriage were asked only of the head of the household and therefore were included only on the supply side.

Commonly cited deterrents to marital dissolution are frequent church attendance[29] and residence in a small community.[30] The latter reflects the expectation that social pressures in a small community may impede the partners from considering divorce. Although information on the frequency of church attendance

---

[27]Bernard (1966), Cutright (1971) and Udry (1966) reported blacks having substantially more marital dissolution than whites using the 1960 Census data.

[28]In a multivariate framework Bumpass and Sweet (1972) and Sweet and Bumpass (1973) found age at marriage has an important impact on marital instability even when other variables are controlled.

[29]Locke (1951) reported less marital dissolution among frequent church attenders.

[30]See Carter and Plateris (1963).

was available only for the husband, we also included it on the demand side since most husbands who attend church do so with their wives. City size was expected to influence the desires of both partners and was included as both a supply and a demand variable.

The last set of factors included in this group are the presence of a disability and the age of each spouse. We defined disability as being any affliction which limited the *type or amount* of work each spouse could do. In some cases the disability of a spouse imposes an added burden on the other partner. The necessity of providing additional care for the disabled spouse may affect the other's desire for continuing the marriage. Although feelings of devotion may override the inconvenience caused by the added burden of caring for an afflicted spouse, some may come to resent this added intrusion and seek to dissolve the marital relationship. Hence, no unequivocal statement can be made regarding the influence of a disability on the desire of the other spouse to continue the marriage. Finally, the age of the husband and wife respectively, were included in the supply and the demand equations. The age of each partner reflects, in part, the availability of potential marriage partners. Since availability declines with age, marital stability and age were expected to be positively related.

Omitted Variables

One prominent set of variables on which we have virtually no information is the level of marital satisfaction. This may seem like a rather glaring omission and, indeed, the social science literature is filled with models which rely on some index of marital satisfaction as the key indicator of marital instability. However, if the variables we have included are causally *prior* to marital satisfaction--that is, if they determine the level of marital satisfaction--then the absence of direct measures of marital satisfaction does not invalidate our approach. As Goode has argued, "...the economic factor does not act directly but is mediated through other factors, mainly sociological."[31] Thus, although we are not able to measure the effects of interpersonal conflicts directly, the overall impact of the purely economic factors does provide some useful insight into the study of marital discord.

Dependent Variable, Sample Restrictions, and Estimation Procedures

The dependent variables in our analysis of marital discord--Q_D and Q_S--represent the probability of continuing with the present living arrangement. Both are dichotomous variables,[32] coded zero if a divorce or separation occurs after 1969

---

[31] Goode (1956).

[32] Estimation with a dichotomous dependent variable introduces the econometric

and one otherwise.[33] The sample was restricted to men who were younger than age
56 in 1969 and their spouses. This was done because the wife would be in a relatively high hours net transfer position if the husband was no longer in the labor
force. In cases where the husband was retired, the price variable was not expected to operate in the normal fashion.

A two-stage estimating procedure, two-stage least squares,[34] was used to take
explicit account of the simultaneity of the decision to divorce or separate. Our
approach involved using a random half-sample for some preliminary experimentation
in specifying an appropriate model. This was limited primarily to determining
the best formulation for some dummy variables and to discovering whether some
variables for which we had limited theoretical justification had any effect at
all. The resulting model was then tested on an independent half-sample which
provided a valid statistical test of the model, as well as some indication of the
sensitivity of the parameter estimates to the data.[35] Finally, the whole sample
was used to give the best estimates of parameter values.

IV. ANALYSIS RESULTS

The results of the full sample are presented in Table 2.11. Also included
in the table are the overall effects of the variables in our analysis as given
by the quantity reduced form equation.[36] The reduced form estimates most closely
parallel previous sociological analyses of marital instability. The results of
the two half-sample regressions are presented in the Appendix in Table A2.1e.
Finally, Appendix Table A2.1f shows the estimation of the full sample quantity
reduced form equation using MCA dummy variable regression. The weighted and unweighted distribution of the sample together with unadjusted and adjusted mean
marital dissolution rates are shown for each category in that table.

Price Variable

The full sample results (Table 2.11) indicated that the inclination of each
spouse to continue with the marriage was quite responsive to the endogenous hours

---

problem of heteroskedasticity. That is, the variance of the disturbance term
is not constant over all units. The conventional correction for heteroskedasticity involves dividing each observation by its estimated standard error.
However, this correction was not made in the above model.

[33]Since the 1968 survey did not ask about hours spent on housework, this necessi-
tated restricting the sample to couples who were married in 1968 and 1969.

[34]See Appendix B for details on this estimating procedure.

[35]See Five Thousand American Families, Volume I, for an example of this procedure.

[36]See Appendix B for details on this procedure.

TABLE 2.11

Regression Results for Predicting Marital Stability[1]
(Entire Sample)

	Two Stage Least Squares Estimation of Demand Equation	Two Stage Least Squares Estimation of Supply Equation	Ordinary Least Squares Estimation of Reduced Form[3] Equation
Endogenous:			
Hours Net Transfer[2]	-.458 (.242)	.471* (.190)	
Exogenous:			
Age of Wife	.005** (.001)		
Education (Wife)	-.011 (.011)		.002 (.010)
Labor Market Experience (Wife)	-.003 (.003)		-.003 (.003)
Experience Squared (Wife)	.72E-4 (.98E-4)		.57E-4 (.96E-4)
Whether Husband Works ≥ 60 Hours/Week	-.100** (.030)		-.060** (.021)
Whether Family Income/Needs ≤ 1.5 and High AFDC[4]	-.055* (.023)		-.066** (.022)
Whether Family Income/Needs ≤ 1.5 and Low AFDC[4]	.072** (.021)		.056** (.019)
Whether Family Income/Needs ≥ 1.5 and High AFDC[4]	.004 (.014)		.016 (.013)
Whether Child ≤ Age 2 (1969)	.061* (.026)	.053* (.026)	.056* (.025)
Whether Child > Age 2 (1969)	.34E-5 (.020)	-.007 (.019)	-.004 (.020)
Whether Expect More Children	.025 (.021)	.053** (.021)	.037 (.020)
Dissimilarity of Education	-.007 (.012)	-.016 (.012)	-.012 (.012)
Whether Expect College for Children	.021 (.016)	.023 (.016)	.020 (.016)
Whether Home Owner	.058** (.016)	.058** (.016)	.056** (.016)

	Two Stage Least Squares Estimation of Demand Equation	Two Stage Least Squares Estimation of Supply Equation	Ordinary Least Squares Estimation of Reduced Form[3] Equation
Whether City Size > 50,000	-.022 (.016)	-.030* (.015)	-.024 (.015)
Whether Employment Problems (Husband)	-.018* (.009)	-.015 (.009)	-.015 (.009)
Whether at Least Two Months Savings	.049** (.015)	.056** (.015)	.051** (.014)
Whether Attend Church	.034* (.014)	.025 (.014)	.028* (.014)
Whether Previous Marriage		-.030 (.021)	-.030 (.021)
Age of Husband		.005** (.001)	.006** (.001)
Whether Wife Works ≥ 60 Hours/Week		-.474** (.097)	-.425** (.093)
Whether Wife Works 20-59 Hours/Week		-.058** (.018)	-.024 (.015)
Wage of Husband		.004 (.003)	-.89E-5 (.003)
$\bar{R}^2$	.057	.064	.101
Mean Dependent Variable	.912		
Sample Size	1732		

*Significant at 5% level.

**Significant at 1% level.

NOTE: Estimated coefficients are shown with standard errors enclosed in parentheses.

The demand equation relates independent variables to the wife's demand for maintaining the current arrangements; the supply equation refers to the husband's supply of the current arrangements.

---

[1]Restricted to couples aged 16-55 in 1968. The dependent variables--Q_D and Q_S-- are zero if a divorce or separation occurs after 1969; and one otherwise.

[2]Hours Net Transfer = $\dfrac{\text{Wife's Market + Housework Hours}}{\text{Husband's and Wife's Market + Housework Hours}}$.

[3]Reduced form equation for the "quantity"--whether the initial living arrangement is maintained for the duration of the panel study.

[4]The level of AFDC payments per recipient for the state of residence in 1969 is dichotomized--high denoting payments ≥ $45 (18 states) and low denoting payments < $45.

net transfer variable. The supply coefficient was statistically significant, while the estimated coefficient in the demand equation just failed to attain significance at the .05 level. Both coefficients had the expected sign and indicated that as the relative time contribution of the wife increased by 10 percentage points the wife's (husband's) desire for maintaining the marriage decreased (increased) by nearly 5 percentage points. Similar results were obtained in both half-samples; however, the price variable was statistically significant only in the wife's (demand) equation for the second half-sample.

Adjustments to the Price Variable

The hypothesized inverse relationship between marital stability and excessive working hours by either spouse was confirmed by our findings. As shown in Table 2.11, husbands or wives who worked 60 hours or more a week were *substantially* more likely to undergo a divorce or separation than were other couples. This excess-hours effect persisted in both half-samples as well (see Table A2.1e). It should be noted, however, that this commitment to one's job may reflect previous marital discord. Hence, it may be a symptom of earlier discontent and not the cause of the subsequent divorce. A similar but much weaker association was noted for wives who were employed at least half-time but less than the above threshold.[37]

The employment problems index, representing the security of income, had the expected negative sign in both equations. However, it is statistically significant only in the demand equation.

Attractiveness of Alternatives

Our specification of the possible effects of welfare benefit levels on marital instability focused on the interaction between welfare benefit levels and family income/needs. We found a consistent and significantly negative effect of high welfare benefit levels on the marital stability of families with a low level of income/needs. The overall impact of this policy variable, as reflected by the quantity reduced form estimate (see Table 2.11), showed that families in that category were, on average, about 6 percent *more* likely to dissolve their marriage. Even more striking was the comparison with low-income families who differed only by residing in a state with low welfare benefit levels. These families were about 6 percent *less* likely to divorce or separate. Thus, among families with

---

[37] Since this set of variables reflects elements of the price variable, no similar measure was included for the husband. The low labor force participation of the wives allowed inclusion of this dummy variable without severe stability problems. It was felt that some adjustment to the price variable was necessary for the husbands. Hence, only the excess hours effect was retained in the final formulation.

low income/needs, the presence of high welfare benefit levels appeared to decrease marital stability by 12 percent. Since both variables were significant at conventional levels of statistical significance, the relationship appeared to be quite strong.[38] These results are consistent with Honig's contention that public assistance programs which primarily restrict assistance to female-headed families increase female-headship rates.[39]

Although proxies for the potential wage of wives--educational attainment and years of labor market experience--had the expected sign, they were not significant in any sample. Similarly, the results for the hourly wage of the husband were insignificant.

Dissimilarity of Background

Dissimilarity of background did not have a notable effect on marital stability. The estimated coefficients were negative as predicted but, except for the initial half-sample, they were small and only equal to their standard errors. It should be noted, however, that our measure of dissimilarity related only to differences in educational attainment. It may well be that if information on family background and on differences in religious affiliation had been available and incorporated in the analysis, the observed effect of dissimilarity would have been stronger.

Effects of Children

The predicted effect of young children on marital instability was confirmed in our analysis. Both the husband and the wife were more inclined to continue their marriage if they had a child younger than age two. It is interesting that the presence of a young child affected both spouses about equally. However, this did not apply to parents of older children. Whether or not there were any children older than age two in the household had no significant effect on either husband or wife, nor did any effects show up in the reduced form. In particular, there seems to have been no discernible difference between *childless* couples and couples whose youngest child was *older* than age two. It seems likely, then, that young children act to sustain marriages primarily by being a responsibility which parents find difficult to ignore. Undoubtedly, children are a continuing source of satisfaction in many marriages. But the sharp distinction we found between

---

[38] We also tested the relationship using family income/needs and welfare benefit levels as continuous variables along with a single interaction term for the low income/needs-high welfare benefits group. The estimated coefficient for the interaction term was negative and significant at the .01 level.

[39] Honig, op. cit., p. 321.

couples with children younger than age two and those with older children suggests that this satisfaction was not sufficient to preserve an otherwise unsatis-
factory marriage. Rather, it seems that as the child grew older and required
less care, the parents no longer viewed divorce or separation as necessarily
harmful to the child.

Families that expected to have more children were more stable during the
panel period than families which did not. Surprisingly, the effect was weak and
statistically insignificant for the wife, but strongly positive and significant
for the husband. However, the question on expectation of more children was asked
only of the husband. Thus, this variable may not adequately reflect the wife's
intentions.

The measure of whether or not a family expected its children to receive a
college education was less successful in predicting marital stability. The differential importance of these two expectational measures may reflect planning
horizon differences between the short run (expecting more children) and the longer
run (college). It is also true that the connection between marital instability
and the expected educational attainment of the children is much less direct than
that between marital instability and the expectation of having more children.
One reason for this is that the ability and intentions of the child, as well as
the stability of the marriage, are important factors in determining educational
attainment. Consequently, the effect of this variable might reasonably be weaker
than the expectation of having more children.

Assets

Our analysis also confirmed the inverse relationship between divorce or separation and economic status. The two wealth measures, home ownership and whether
the couple had savings equal to at least two months' income, both had strong positive effects on marital stability. They were about equally important and their
effect on both spouses was equally strong. A couple with a home of their own and
savings of two month's income was 10 percent less likely to be divorced or separated during the period.

Other Demographic Variables

In Volume III of this series, Hampton reported finding no evidence that marital instability was higher for blacks than whites.[40] After adjusting for the
effects of other variables, he concluded that black families were more stable than
similar white families. Although our model differed significantly from his and
included an extra year of data, the results of our analysis reinforce his conclu-

----

[40] See _Five Thousand American Families_, Volume III, Chapter 4.

sion. In the preliminary model-building phase, a dummy variable for race was found to be uniformly insignificant irrespective of other variables included in the analysis. Consequently, we eliminated race from any further consideration.

Two other variables, age at marriage and the measures of disability, had very weak effects and were also eliminated from our analysis. Only variables such as these, which were consistently smaller than their standard errors and for which there was no strong theoretical reason for inclusion, were excluded from further analysis.

Our analysis did confirm some earlier findings. A husband who had been married previously was more likely to become divorced or separated than were other husbands. Also, families who attended church regularly had more stable marriages. Similarly, increased age had a stabilizing effect on marriage. A ten-year increase in age reduced both spouses' desires for divorce or separation by 5 percent.[41] Finally, the effects of residence in a large community (greater than 50,000) were mixed. This variable had the predicted negative sign and was statistically significant in the full sample supply equation. However, the results were not uniformly strong in the half-samples.

Summary

1. Changes in marital status did have a strong and systematic effect on the economic status of women. When we compared the seven-year percentage increase in income/needs for women who were married in 1968 and adjusted for the effects of other variables, we found that those who remained married throughout had increases five times as great as those who were divorced or separated.

2. For women who were divorced or separated, there were accompanying changes in economic activity. Some began receiving welfare income, but many more took employment. Of those not working in 1967, more than 60 percent of the whites and 50 percent of the nonwhites were working in 1973. By contrast, among those not receiving welfare in the initial year, only 6 percent of the whites and 16 percent of the nonwhites were receiving it in 1973. There were also changes in family living arrangements, with multiple income earners more common among divorced or separated women.

3. For married men in 1968, subsequent changes in marital status had only

---

[41]This means only that older couples have more stable marriages than do younger couples. It does not necessarily mean that as a couple ages its marriage will become more stable.

mild effects on their economic well-being. Men who were divorced or separated in 1974 suffered a decline in real income over the panel period, but when the ratio of income to needs was considered, their economic status showed substantial improvement. This largely reflected the decline in their needs since the children generally remained with the mother.

4. A structural equation model was applied to the analysis of marital instability. It was based on the notion that divorce or separation was inherently a joint decision and that a conventional supply and demand model could be used to capture this simultaneity. The results of this analysis were encouraging. The price variable, measured by the relative contribution of the spouses in market and nonmarket activities, had the expected sign in all samples. The full sample results, which gave the best estimates of the parameters of the model, showed estimated price coefficients well in excess of their standard errors.

5. The effects of several socioeconomic and demographic variables on marital stability were investigated in detail. The presence of very young children was found to be significant in deterring *both* spouses from seeking a divorce or separation. However, no discernible difference was observed between childless couples and those with children over age two. The two wealth variables, home ownership and whether the couple had savings equal to two months' income, further confirmed the well-reported inverse relationship between marital instability and economic status. As in the findings reported in Volume III, there is no evidence that black families are less stable than similar white families. When either spouse worked an excessive number of hours in the labor market, that couple was more likely to be divorced or separated during the panel period. Finally, the analysis lends further credence to previous findings that public assistance programs which primarily restrict assistance to female-headed families increase female headship rates.

References

Becker, Gary S. "A Theory of Marriage: Part 1," Journal of Political Economy, 81 (July/August 1973).

Bernard, Jessie. "Marital Stability and Patterns of Status Variables," Journal of Marriage and The Family, November, 1966.

Bumpass, Larry L. and Sweet, James A. "Differentials in Marital Instability: 1970," American Sociological Review, December, 1972.

Burgess, Ernest W., and Cottrell, Leonard S, Jr. Predicting Success or Failure in Marriage. New York: Prentice-Hall, Inc., 1939.

Carter, Hugh and Plateris, Andrew. "Trends in Divorce and Family Disruption,"
    HEW Indicators, September, 1963.

Cutright, Phillips. "Income and Family Events: Marital Stability," Journal
    of Marriage and The Family, May, 1971.

Duncan, Greg J. and Morgan, James N., eds., Five Thousand American Families--Patterns
    of Economic Progress. Volume III. Ann Arbor: Institute for Social
    Research, 1975.

Goode, William J. Women in Divorce. New York: The Free Press, 1956.

Honig, Marjorie. "AFDC Income, Recipient Income, and Family Dissolution,"
    Journal of Human Resources, Summer, 1974.

Jacobson, Paul H. American Marriage and Divorce. New York: Rinehart, 1959.

Levinger, George. "Marital Cohesiveness and Dissolution: An Integrative Review,"
    Journal of Marriage and The Family, February, 1965.

Locke, Harvey J. Predicting Adjustment in Marriage: A Comparison of A Divorced
    and Happily Married Group. New York: Holt, 1951.

Monahan, Thomas P. "Is Childlessness Related to Family Stability?" American
    Sociological Review, August, 1955.

Morgan, James N. et al. Five Thousand American Families--Patterns of Economic
    Progress. Volume I. Ann Arbor: Institute for Social Research, 1974.

Mincer, Jacob. Schooling, Experience, and Earnings. New York: NBER, 1974.

Sweet, James A. and Bumpass, Larry L. "Differentials in Marital Instability
    of the Black Population: 1970," Discussion Paper. Institute for Research
    on Poverty, 1973.

Thornton, Arland D. "Marital Instability and Fertility." An unpublished PhD.
    Dissertation at the University of Michigan, 1975.

Udry, J. Richard. "Marital Instability by Race, Sex, Education, and Occupation
    Using 1960 Census Data," The American Journal of Sociology, September, 1966.

Appendix 2.1

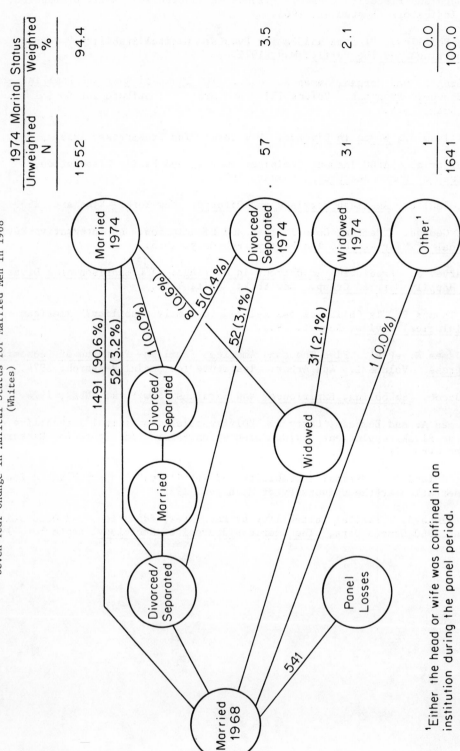

FIGURE A2.1a

Seven-Year Change in Marital Status for Married Men in 1968
(Whites)

	1974 Marital Status	
	Unweighted N	Weighted %
	1552	94.4
	57	3.5
	31	2.1
	1	0.0
	1641	100.0

[1]Either the head or wife was confined in an institution during the panel period.

NOTE: For each path, the unweighted number of cases and the corresponding weighted percentages are included.

MTR #6042

FIGURE A2.1b

Seven-Year Change in Marital Status for Married Men in 1968
(Nonwhites)

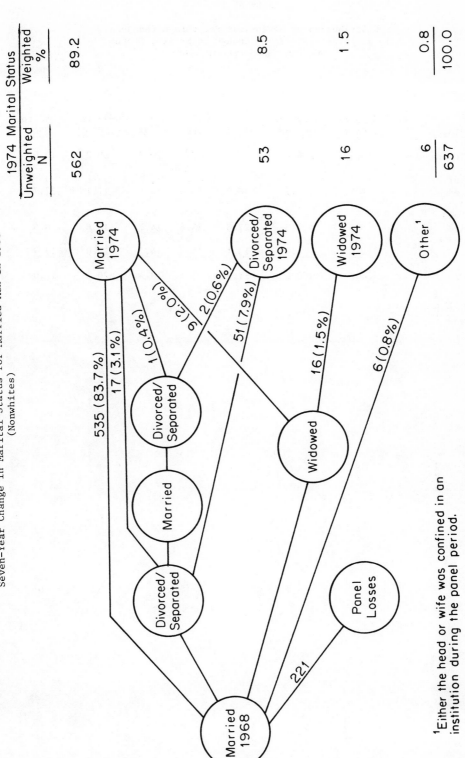

	1974 Marital Status	
	Unweighted N	Weighted %
Married 1974	562	89.2
Divorced/Separated 1974	53	8.5
Widowed 1974	16	1.5
Other[1]	6	0.8
	637	100.0

[1]Either the head or wife was confined in an institution during the panel period.

NOTE: For each path, the unweighted number of cases and the corresponding weighted percentages are included.

MTR # 6042

TABLE A2.1a

Distribution of Seven-Year Percentage Change
in Real Income/Needs By Change in Marital Status
(All Married Women in 1968)

Change in Marital Status	Number of Cases	Weighted Percent	>100%	25-100%	0-25%	-25 to 0%	-50 to -25%	<-50%
Married Throughout	2026	84.8	11.5	33.3	20.3	20.2	10.6	4.1
Divorced or Separated	182	5.7	8.0	18.0	14.4	17.1	27.7	14.8
Divorced and Remarried	54	2.3	27.8	25.6	14.7	17.6	6.5	7.8
Widowed	145	6.8	13.1	15.3	14.3	23.0	19.9	14.3
Average	2407	100.0	11.8	31.1	19.4	20.1	12.0	5.5

MTR #7512

TABLE A2.1b

Seven-Year Percentage Change in Real Family Income/Needs
(All Married Women in 1968)

Variable	Number of Cases	Weighted Percentage	Eta^2	Beta^2	Unadjusted Mean	Adjusted Mean
Race			.0015	.0011		
White	1732	90.2			33.7	33.8
Nonwhite	666	9.8			45.4	44.0
Age of Wife (1968)			.033	.033		
< 25	344	13.3			51.6	48.0
25-34	610	23.0			35.6	35.8
35-44	640	25.3			47.7	48.9
45-54	429	18.6			36.2	37.1
55-64	265	13.6			2.6	2.0
65-74	94	5.3			9.7	9.5
>74	16	1.0			19.0	25.0
Wife's Education (1968)			.0053	.0044		
0-5 grades	117	3.3			44.9	49.0
6-8	393	13.4			24.6	32.9
9-11	505	17.4			34.5	32.7
12	691	31.9			33.7	31.5
12+	269	12.7			29.7	29.7
College, no degree	228	11.2			43.2	41.8
College, BA	115	6.1			48.3	49.4
BA +	31	1.7			40.5	43.0
NA	32	1.3			35.5	42.3
City Size (1974)			.0072	.0061		
>500,000	766	31.8			24.6	25.4
100,000-499,999	499	21.4			38.8	37.2
50,000-99,999	292	12.5			38.8	37.2
25,000-49,999	163	7.1			31.9	35.3
10,000-24,999	263	11.6			41.5	41.5
< 10,000	415	15.6			44.0	43.9
Region (1974)			.0054	.0020		
Northeast	415	23.4			26.0	31.2
North Central	600	29.3			37.8	37.7
South	1022	30.8			42.0	38.4
West	361	16.5			28.9	28.4
Change in Marital Status			.026	.019		
Married Throughout	2018	85.0			35.9	35.4
Divorced	177	5.6			13.3	7.5
Divorced and Remarried	52	2.3			112.1	100.3
Widowed	141	6.7			11.4	26.0
Widowed and Remarried	10	0.4			68.2	66.5

R^2 (Adjusted) = .057
Mean of Dependent Variable = 34.8

68

TABLE A2.1c

Composition of 1973 Transfer Income
By Source and Seven-Year Change in Marital Status
(White Married Women in 1968)

Change in Marital Status	Number of Cases	Total Transfer Income	AFDC	Alimony/ Child Support	Social Security or Other Retirement Income	Other Transfer Income
Married Throughout	1491	$1124	$ 6	$ 6	$ 989	$ 122
Divorced or Separated	90	1811	150	1083	95	487
Divorced and Remarried	42	1162	112	162	672	215
Widowed	117	2410	0	4	2208	198
All	1740	$1257	$ 17	$ 65	$1026	$ 149

TABLE A2.1d

Composition of 1973 Transfer Income
By Source and Seven-Year Change in Marital Status
(Nonwhite Married Women in 1968)

Change in Marital Status	Number of Cases	Total Transfer Income	AFDC	Alimony/ Child Support	Social Security or Other Retirement Income	Other Transfer Income
Married Throughout	535	$ 860	$ 97	$ 0	$ 609	$ 154
Divorced or Separated	92	2275	588	570	172	944
Divorced and Remarried	12	217	144	0	51	23
Widowed	28	1887	220	0	1432	235
All	667	$1053	$153	$ 55	$ 614	$ 232

MTR #7512

TABLE A2.1e

Regression Results for Predicting Marital Stability[1]

(Married Couples in 1968 and 1969)

	Demand			Supply			Reduced Form[3]		
	First Half Sample	Second Half Sample	Entire Sample	First Half Sample	Second Half Sample	Entire Sample	First Half Sample	Second Half Sample	Entire Sample
Endogenous:									
Hours Net Transfer[2]	-.236 (.328)	-.731* (.358)	-.458 (.242)	.408 (.261)	.345 (.252)	.471* (.190)			
Exogenous:									
Age of Wife	.007** (.002)	.004** (.001)	.005** (.001)						
Education (Wife)	-.014 (.016)	-.010 (.018)	-.011 (.011)				-.005 (.015)	.014 (.015)	.002 (.010)
Labor Market Experience of Wife	-.006 (.004)	-.29E-3 (.004)	-.003 (.003)				-.006 (.004)	-.003 (.004)	-.003 (.003)
Experience Squared (Wife)	.23E-3 (.14E-3)	-.91E-4 (.14E-3)	.72E-4 (.98E-4)				.22E-3 (.14E-3)	-.99E-4 (.14E-3)	.57E-4 (.96E-4)
Whether Husband Works ≥ 60 Hours Per Week	-.080* (.038)	-.122** (.048)	-.100** (.030)				-.059* (.029)	-.047 (.031)	-.060** (.021)
Whether Family Income/Needs ≤ 1.5 and High AFDC[4]	-.064 (.035)	-.057 (.031)	-.055* (.023)				-.078* (.033)	-.060* (.030)	-.066** (.022)
Whether Family Income/Needs ≤ 1.5 and Low AFDC[4]	.052 (.029)	.099** (.030)	.072** (.021)				.043 (.028)	.071** (.026)	.056** (.019)
Whether Family Income/Needs > 1.5 and High AFDC[4]	.013 (.021)	-.007 (.020)	.004 (.014)				.021 (.020)	.010 (.018)	.016 (.013)

TABLE A2.1e (Sheet 2 of 3)

	Demand			Supply			Reduced Form[3]		
	First Half Sample	Second Half Sample	Entire Sample	First Half Sample	Second Half Sample	Entire Sample	First Half Sample	Second Half Sample	Entire Sample
Whether Child ≤ Age 2 (1969)	.110** (.039)	.021 (.037)	.061* (.026)	.085* (.039)	.035 (.036)	.053* (.026)	.096** (.037)	.024 (.036)	.056* (.025)
Whether Child > Age 2 (1969)	.053 (.029)	-.055 (.030)	.34E-5 (.020)	.021 (.029)	-.031 (.027)	-.007 (.019)	.039 (.028)	-.045 (.028)	-.004 (.020)
Whether Expect More Children	.074* (.030)	-.023 (.030)	.025 (.021)	.089** (.029)	.015 (.030)	.053* (.021)	.078** (.029)	-.003 (.028)	.037 (.020)
Dissimilarity of Education	-.034* (.017)	-.020 (.017)	-.007 (.012)	-.036* (.017)	.009 (.017)	-.016 (.012)	-.035* (.017)	.009 (.016)	-.012 (.012)
Whether Expect College For Children	.040 (.024)	.003 (.023)	.021 (.016)	.036 (.024)	.008 (.022)	.023 (.016)	.038 (.024)	.003 (.022)	.020 (.016)
Whether Home Owner	050* (.023)	.065** (.024)	.058** (.016)	.046* (.023)	.072** (.023)	.058** (.016)	.042 (.023)	.074** (.023)	.056** (.016)
Whether City Size > 50,000	-.026 (.024)	-.009 (.022)	-.022 (.016)	-.030 (.022)	-.029 (.020)	-.030* (.015)	-.021 (.024)	-.023 (.020)	-.024 (.015)
Whether Employment Problems (Husband)	-.011 (.014)	-.025* (.013)	-.018* (.009)	-.010 (.013)	-.020 (.012)	-.015 (.009)	-.011 (.013)	-.019 (.012)	-.015 (.009)
Whether at Least Two Months Savings	.056** (.021)	.035 (.023)	.049** (.015)	.052* (.021)	.059** (.022)	.056** (.015)	.054** (.021)	.048* (.020)	.051** (.014)
Whether Attend Church	.038 (.021)	.026 (.019)	.034* (.014)	.028 (.020)	.023 (.019)	.025 (.014)	.033 (.020)	.021 (.019)	.028* (.014)
Whether Previous Marriage				-.050 (.030)	-.009 (.030)	-.030 (.021)	-.053 (.030)	.28E-4 (.030)	-.030 (.021)
Age of Husband				.008** (.001)	.003 (.001)	.005** (.001)	.008** (.002)	.004** (.001)	.005** (.001)
Whether Wife Works ≥ 60 Hours Per Week				-.373** (.124)	-.584** (.158)	-.474** (.097)	-.336** (.118)	-.550** (.157)	-.425** (.093)

TABLE A2.1e (Sheet 3 of 3)

	Demand			Supply			Reduced Form[3]		
	First Half Sample	Second Half Sample	Entire Sample	First Half Sample	Second Half Sample	Entire Sample	First Half Sample	Second Half Sample	Entire Sample
Whether Wife Works 20-59 Hours Per Week				-.039 (.026)	-.067** (.024)	-.058** (.018)	-.012 (.023)	-.039 (.021)	-.024 (.015)
Wage of Husband				.005 (.005)	.003 (.004)	.004 (.003)	.25E-3 (.005)	-.29E-3 (.004)	-.89E-5 (.003)
R^2	.088	.055	.057	.106	.057	.064	.127	.101	.101
Mean Dependent Variable	.906	.917	.912	.906	.917	.912	.906	.917	.912
Sample Size	858	874	1732	858	874	1732	858	874	1732

*Significant at 5% level.

**Significant at 1% level.

NOTE: Estimated coefficients are shown with standard errors enclosed in parentheses.

---

[1] Restricted to couples aged 16-55 in 1968. The dependent variables--Q_D and Q_S--are coded zero if a divorce of separation occurs after 1969; one otherwise.

[2] Hours Net Transfer = $\dfrac{\text{Wife's Market + Housework Hours}}{\text{Husband's and Wife's Market + Housework Hours}}$.

[3] Reduced from equation for the "quantity"--whether the initial living arrangement is maintained for the duration of the panel study.

[4] The level of AFDC payments per recipient for the state of residence in 1969 is dichotomized--high denoting payments $\geq$ $45 (18 states) and low denoting payments < $45.

TABLE A2.1f

MCA Results for Regression Analysis of Divorce/Separation[1]
(Entire Sample)

Independent Variable	Number of Observations	Weighted Percent	Unadjusted Mean	Adjusted Mean
Home Ownership		$\eta^2=.027$		$\beta^2=.007$
No	698	32.0	.155	.122
Yes	1002	68.0	.056	.071
Age of Youngest Child		$\eta^2=.008$		$\beta^2=.003$
No children under 18	305	21.7	.091	.088
< 2	263	14.5	.095	.052
2-5	525	27.1	.118	.098
6-13	468	27.8	.069	.098
14-17	139	8.9	.034	.079
Age at Marriage		$\eta^2=.005$		$\beta^2=.011$
< 20	284	15.0	.089	.069
20-24	803	49.6	.098	.108
25-29	274	17.2	.052	.083
30+	118	6.8	.053	.112
Not First Marriage	221	11.4	.111	.016
Race		$\eta^2=.001$		$\beta^2=.001$
White	1231	92.1	.085	.090
Black	469	7.9	.118	.054
Whether Husband Disabled		$\eta^2=.001$		$\beta^2=.002$
No	1458	87.0	.090	.093
Yes	242	13.0	.072	.054
Dissimilarity of Education		$\eta^2=.001$		$\beta^2=.001$
0 (No Difference)	902	53.9	.083	.083
1	729	42.7	.091	.093
2	67	3.2	.131	.103
3 (College, Grades 1-5)	2	0.0	.000	.000
Years Labor Market Experience (Wife)		$\eta^2=.006$		$\beta^2=.002$
0	513	26.6	.068	.071
1-4	405	25.9	.101	.098
5-9	348	20.9	.111	.098
10-14	168	9.7	.110	.098
15 +	266	16.9	.056	.080
Age of Head		$\eta^2=.031$		$\beta^2=.021$
< 25	179	10.4	.150	.126
25-34	482	28.1	.139	.134
35-44	575	34.7	.081	.083
45-55	464	26.8	.018	.031

TABLE A2.1f (Sheet 2 of 4)

Independent Variable	Number of Observations	Weighted Percent	Unadjusted Mean	Adjusted Mean
Education of Wife		$\eta^2=.003$		$\beta^2=.002$
0-5 Grades	54	1.6	.065	.084
6-8 Grades	207	7.6	.070	.080
9-11 Grades	388	18.2	.103	.100
Completed High School	541	36.2	.083	.084
12 + Nonacademic Training	210	14.2	.107	.107
Some College	171	12.0	.080	.081
BA Degree	83	6.6	.073	.062
Advanced Degree	22	1.9	.059	.072
NA	24	1.6	.112	.060
Whether Husband's First Marriage		$\eta^2=.002$		$\beta^2=.015$
No	230	12.2	.118	.180
Yes	1470	87.8	.083	.075
Church Attendance (Husband)		$\eta^2=.014$		$\beta^2=.004$
Infrequent	969	56.2	.114	.100
Several Times/Month	169	7.7	.097	.104
Once/Week	451	29.7	.045	.067
More Than Once/Week	111	6.4	.038	.051
Whether Expect More Children		$\eta^2=.015$		$\beta^2=.004$
No	930	51.7	.101	.101
Yes	344	22.6	.119	.064
Inap, Wife $\geq$ Age 45	316	19.7	.025	.089
NA/DK	110	6.0	.060	.053
Whether Wife Disabled		$\eta^2=.004$		$\beta^2=.003$
No	1653	98.0	.086	.086
Yes	43	1.8	.112	.125
NA	4	0.2	.531	.443
Educational Expectation For Children		$\eta^2=.011$		$\beta^2=.005$
College	597	40.5	.056	.075
High school	481	21.2	.091	.073
Doubt if High School	54	1.4	.185	.188
Inap, no Children Under 25	530	35.8	.117	.105
NA/DK	38	1.1	.102	.140
City Size		$\eta^2=.014$		$\beta^2=.014$
500,000 +	594	35.3	.104	.113
100,000-499,999	339	21.4	.071	.069
50,000-99,999	196	11.6	.102	.090
25,000-49,999	88	5.0	.055	.057
10,000-24,999	182	11.5	.088	.069
< 10,000	300	15.2	.067	.071

TABLE A2.1f (Sheet 3 of 4)

Independent Variable	Number of Observations	Weighted Percent	Unadjusted Mean	Adjusted Mean
Employment Problems (Husband)	$\eta^2=.009$		$\beta^2=.005$	
None	783	59.0	.071	.074
1	617	30.4	.105	.106
2	222	7.8	.095	.090
3+	78	2.8	.217	.174
Husband's Hourly Wage	$\eta^2=.019$		$\beta^2=.012$	
No Labor Income	48	2.0	.150	.031
< $1.00	54	1.6	.009	.000
1.00-1.49	118	4.5	.205	.145
1.50-1.99	176	6.9	.081	.049
2.00-2.49	199	9.4	.120	.102
2.50-2.99	224	12.3	.100	.066
3.00-3.99	355	22.1	.092	.081
4.00-5.99	378	28.5	.082	.118
6.00+	148	12.7	.019	.062
Hours Work/Week (Husband)	$\eta^2=.019$		$\beta^2=.021$	
None	42	1.6	.191	.248
1-19	16	0.9	.310	.283
20-34	39	2.3	.103	.107
35-39	68	4.6	.116	.125
40	722	37.7	.092	.076
41-47	279	17.5	.062	.065
48	93	5.8	.018	.031
49-59	253	16.9	.059	.073
60+	168	11.6	.128	.142
NA	20	1.2	.205	.196
Hours Work/Week (Wife	$\eta^2=.023$		$\beta^2=.020$	
None	772	44.3	.061	.064
1-19	108	6.4	.062	.069
20-34	137	8.7	.119	.136
35-39	92	6.3	.089	.097
40	455	26.6	.109	.100
41-47	61	3.7	.149	.152
48	15	0.7	.071	.017
49-59	30	1.7	.154	.110
60+	9	0.5	.522	.491
NA	21	1.0	.004	.026
Whether Two Months Income Saved	$\eta^2=.025$		$\beta^2=.015$	
No	505	33.2	.118	.101
Yes	670	48.2	.044	.057
Inap, No Savings	521	18.2	.150	.145
NA	4	0.4	.000	.000

TABLE A2.1f (Sheet 4 of 4)

Independent Variable	Number of Observations	Weighted Percent	Unadjusted Mean	Adjusted Mean
AFDC Per Capita and Income/Needs[2]	$\eta^2=.013$		$\beta^2=.009$	
Low AFDC & Low Inc/Needs	356	8.8	.056	.038
Low AFDC & High Inc/Needs	145	5.7	.198	.160
High AFDC & Low Inc/Needs	597	38.4	.101	.106
High AFDC & High Inc/Needs	602	47.0	.069	.073

[1]Dependent variables coded one if a divorce or separation occurs after 1969 and zero otherwise. Restricted to couples aged 16–55 in 1968.

[2]The average AFDC payment per recipient for the state of residence in 1969 is combined with 1968 family income/needs to form this pattern variable:

	Income/Needs	AFDC Payments
Low	≤ 1.5	< $45
High	> 1.5	45+

Chapter 3

UNMARRIED HEADS OF HOUSEHOLDS AND MARRIAGE

Greg J. Duncan

Introduction

Families consisting of husband and wife and their children, if any, comprise the households most commonly found in the population. However, a substantial minority of households are headed by an unmarried adult who either lives alone or with other family members and who may or may not have been married previously. Included among the households headed by unmarried men and women are, among others, young single adults living alone, the divorced or separated, sometimes with children, and--mostly at the upper end of the age spectrum--widows and widowers.[1] The initially unmarried household heads in our sample and the principal family composition change they faced--marriage--are the subject of this chapter.

Since the population of unmarried household heads was so diverse, it is useful to begin with a few descriptive facts about them. As Table 3.1 shows, three times as many of these families were headed by females than were headed by males.[2] This imbalance was caused by a number of factors, among them the higher remarriage and death rates among males. A practical result of this imbalance was that the larger number of observations on households with unmarried female heads (1,018 versus 208 for males) permitted more elaborate analysis and greater precision in statistical results for them.[3] Table 3.1 shows that the male household heads were much more likely to be single, much less likely to be widowed, and were more heavily concentrated among the younger age brackets than were female heads of households.

Analysis

I. CHANGES IN MARITAL STATUS

During the seven years of the study, many of the initially unmarried heads

---

[1] By single we mean never married, as distinguished from divorced, separated, or widowed.

[2] As shown in Table 3.1, 24.4 percent of these families were headed by males and 75.6 percent by females. Somewhat higher panel losses among the initially unmarried men make these figures exaggerate the actual proportion. When the nonresponse cases were added, the proportions became 29.2 and 70.8 percent. These numbers compared with 1970 Census figures of 28.3 and 71.7 percent, respectively. See U.S. Bureau of the Census (1975), Table 9.

[3] These numbers did not produce the 75.6 percent-24.4 percent distribution mentioned above because they were *unweighted* numbers of observations, while the percentages were based on weighted frequencies.

TABLE 3.1

Sex, Marital Status and Age Distribution
of Unmarried Heads of Households in 1968

Sex	Number of Observations	Weighted Percentage
Male	208	24.4%
Female	1018	75.6

Marital Status	Men	Women
Single	47.1%	20.6%
Widowed	17.9	48.2
Divorced	18.6	17.7
Separated	10.8	10.6
Other or N.A.	5.5	2.8
	100.0%	100.0%

Age		
< 25	21.4%	9.8%
25-34	13.6	13.9
35-44	12.8	14.3
45-54	18.3	17.5
55-64	14.3	21.5
65-74	13.4	15.9
over 75	6.3	7.0
	100.0%	100.0%

MTR 2074

had married and some of them had subsequently separated or become divorced or widowed (see Figures 3.1 and 3.2). About a fifth of the women married.[4] Of these, 15 percent were later divorced or separated and about 5 percent became widowed. Over a third of the men married and virtually all stayed that way.

Panel losses were especially heavy among the men. Of the 364 unmarried male heads interviewed in 1968, 156 were lost, leaving the 208 observations shown in Figure 3.2. Nonresponse accounted for 286 of the 1,304 initially unmarried female heads.[5]

II. MARITAL STATUS CHANGE AND CHANGE IN ECONOMIC STATUS

The simple relationship between the various paths of marital status change and change in economic well-being is shown in Table 3.2 for the female heads and in Table 3.3 for the males. The beginning level and seven-year change in both family income and family income relative to needs comprise the columns of the tables.

There was a strong relationship between marital status change and change in economic status. Regardless of sex, those who married during the panel period just about doubled their family income.[6] Those females who remained unmarried averaged a very modest positive income change, while males who remained unmarried averaged a slight negative income change.

Even when changed family size was accounted for with division of income by a poverty needs standard, the gains for those who married were impressive. Women who remarried averaged an 85 percent gain in real income/needs; the men who married had a mean income/needs increase of 46.2 percent. These gains compared with 15 and 1 percent increases, respectively, in income/needs for the women and men who did not marry.

The remainder of those who began as unmarried heads of households in 1968

---

[4]That these marriage rates are somewhat lower than those given by the Census Bureau is puzzling. One possible explanation is that remarriage rates for nonresponse women were considerably higher than those for women remaining in the panel. A check on 41 of the 113 nonresponse women who began the panel as divorced or separated, however, showed that only *3* had definitely remarried by the third year of the study while 32 definitely had *not* remarried during that time. For the remaining 6, final marital status was impossible to ascertain. It is not likely, then, that differences can be explained by differential nonresponse.

[5]A more complete accounting of the nonresponse cases is given in Table A3.1.

[6]"Marriage" refers both to first marriages and remarriages.

FIGURE 3.1

1968-1974 Family Composition Changes
for Unmarried Female Household Heads in 1968

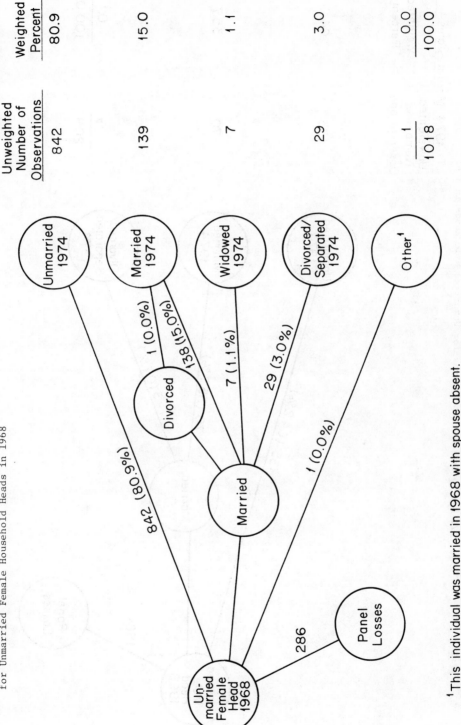

1974 Marital Status

	Unweighted Number of Observations	Weighted Percent
Unmarried 1974	842	80.9
Married 1974	139	15.0
Widowed 1974	7	1.1
Divorced/Separated 1974	29	3.0
Other[1]	1	0.0
	1018	100.0

[1]This individual was married in 1968 with spouse absent. Spouse returned in 1969 and remained until 1974.

FIGURE 3.2

1968-1974 Family Composition Changes for Unmarried Male Heads in 1968

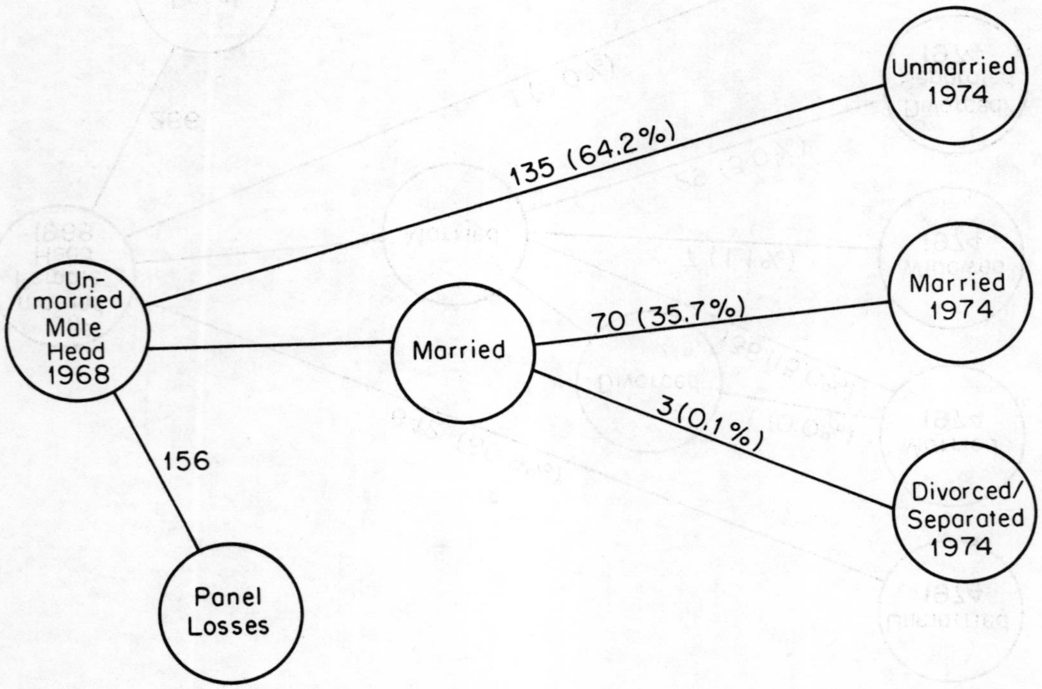

1974 Marital Status

	Unweighted Number of Observations	Weighted Percent
	135	64.2
	70	35.7
	3	0.1
	208	100.0

MTR #2082

TABLE 3.2

Change in Economic Status by Change in Marital Status
(All Unmarried Female Heads of Households in 1968)

Change in Marital Status	Unweighted Number of Observations	Weighted Per-cent	Average 1967 Family Income	Percent Change in Average Real Income 1967-1973	Average 1967 Family Income/ Needs	Percent Change in Average Real Family Income/Needs 1967-1973
Unmarried throughout	842	80.9	$4564	9.5%	1.94	14.7%
Married	138	15.0	5060	134.7	1.82	84.6
Married, then widowed	7	1.1	4288	45.4	1.93	19.5
Married, then divorced or separated	29	3.0	6217	21.7	2.26	-2.7
Married, then divorced, then remarried	1	0.0	5271	67.4	1.61	-4.3
Other	1	0.0	5158	31.1	1.57	-25.4
All	1016	100.0%	$4685	30.6%	1.93	24.1%
Lost to panel	286		$4338		1.93	

MTR 2082

TABLE 3.3

Change in Economic Status by Change in Marital Status
(All Unmarried Male Heads of Households in 1968)

Change in Marital Status	Unweighted Number of Observations	Weighted Per-cent	Average 1967 Family Income	Percent Change in Average Real Income 1967–1973	Average 1967 Family Income/ Needs	Percent Change in Average Real Family Income/Needs 1967–1973
Unmarried throughout	135	64.2%	$6610	−0.2%	2.93	0.8%
Married	70	35.7	6794	98.2	2.86	46.2
Married, then divorced	3	0.1	2875	119.9	1.28	36.8
All	208	100.0%	$6672	35.6%	2.91	16.7%
Lost to panel	156		$5178		2.30	

MTR 2082

experienced more complex changes, but only one change was sufficiently frequent to provide enough observations for a reliable look at associated changes in economic well-being. Three percent of the women (29 observations in all) married and then divorced or separated. At the end of the panel period, these women had higher family incomes (by about 20 percent) but, perhaps because of additional dependents, had a slightly *lower* average level of income relative to needs.

Calculations of 1967 average income and income relative to needs for those lost to the panel (listed at the bottom of Tables 3.2 and 3.3) showed that the nonresponse males were less representative than the nonresponse females. Both measures of income were substantially *lower* for the 156 unmarried men who became nonresponse than for the men who remained in the panel. Nonresponse women averaged slightly lower initial income but showed identical income to needs ratios when compared with the women remaining in the panel.

A final observation, shown in Tables 3.2 and 3.3, concerns the average level of economic well-being for the families of unmarried household heads. The 1967 average family income of the unmarried female heads ($4,685) was considerably less than the average of all families (about $9,000 in 1967).[7] Because the female-headed families often had dependent children, a comparison of well-being using the income/needs measure produced an even more dramatic differential. The average ratio of 1967 income to needs was less than two for the female-headed families and close to three for the families with unmarried male heads. The average ratio for *all* sample families was about halfway between these two numbers (2.58), so that the unmarried male heads were as much above the overall average income/needs level as the female heads were below it.

It is important to keep the absolute levels of well-being in mind when looking at the percentage change numbers. Although women who married, for example, averaged an 84.6 percent increase in income/needs compared to a 46.2 percent increase for men, the differences between the *absolute* increase in income/needs for the two groups was much smaller, and the resulting 1973 *level* of income/needs continued to be higher for the men than for the women.

Regression Analysis of Change in Economic Well-Being

Because we found a strong *bivariate* association between change in marital status and change in economic well-being, it became important to see whether the association was maintained when the effects of various life cycle and environmental variables were taken into account. To take a somewhat extreme example, change in marital status for men may coincide with their retirement decisions.

---

[7]From Morgan et al. (1974), Vol. 1, p. 39.

Failure to account for differences in the age distribution of the men would lead
to an overestimate of the effect of marital status on change in economic well-
being. To adjust for the intercorrelations between marital status change and
basic demographic variables, a dummy variable regression (MCA) was run with the
percentage change in real income/needs as a dependent variable[8] and with marital
status change and the demographic variables as independent variables.[9] The
unadjusted and adjusted mean changes in income/needs by marital status change are
shown in Table 3.4. Table 3.5 gives a complete listing of the net explanatory
power (β^2) of all predictor variables. The complete details of the regressions
are presented in Table A3.2.

In brief, the regression analysis showed that marital status change was the
most important predictor of change in economic status for women, but it was the
least important variable for men. In other words, the important bivariate relationship between change in marital status and change in well-being documented
earlier was almost completely independent of the levels of the demographic variables for women but was closely related to them for men. The detail of the adjustment is given in Table 3.4. Without taking the effects of other predictors into
account, the average increase in real income/needs for women who married was
128 percent and was 34 percent for those who remained unmarried.[10] The comparable unadjusted numbers for men who married and men who remained unmarried followed the same pattern--108 percent and 30 percent, respectively. For women, the
regression adjusted means were quite similar to the unadjusted means--those who
married had an average adjusted increase of 110 percent, compared to 38 percent
for those who did not. For men, on the other hand, the adjusted mean increase
for those who married was actually *less* than the adjusted mean increase for men
who remained unmarried--52 percent versus 61 percent. For the unmarried male
household heads, then, we can conclude when the effects of demographic variables
such as age are taken into account that marital status change had virtually no
association with change in economic well-being. For the women who began the panel

---

[8] Note that in this regression analysis, a percentage change number was calculated
for each individual and then averaged. In the previous tables of this chapter,
percentage changes were calculated from the average level of income/needs for
all individuals.

[9] The demographic variables include age, city size, region, education, race, and
initial marital status.

[10] As noted in footnote 8, these unadjusted numbers differ from those given in
Tables 3.2 and 3.3 because these are averages of percentage changes, while
those of Tables 3.2 and 3.3 are percentage change calculation of averages.

TABLE 3.4

Unadjusted and Adjusted[a] Mean Change in Real
Income/Needs by Change in Marital Status
(Unmarried Household Heads in 1968)

Marital Status Change	Female			Male		
	Number of Observations	Unadjusted Mean	Adjusted Mean[a]	Number of Observations	Unadjusted Mean	Adjusted Mean[a]
Unmarried throughout	841	33.6%	37.7%	135	30.3%	61.4%
Married	136	128.3	110.5	70	108.1	51.9
Married, then divorced	7	58.5	73.9	--	---	--
Married, then divorced or separated	28	24.6	-6.2	3	36.7	56.3
Married, then divorced, then remarried	1	-4.3	12.7	--	---	--
Total	1013	47.4%	--	208	58.0%	--
Eta^2		.104			.068	
F		28.1**			6.0**	
Beta^2			.069			.001
Partial R^2			.062			.001
F			12.8**			0.5

[a]The means are adjusted by regression for the effects of age, city size, region, education, race, and initial marital status. Complete regression results are presented in Table A3.2.

**Significant at .01 level.

Note: Cases where the percentage change in income/needs was more than five standard deviations above the mean were excluded

MTR 2074

TABLE 3.5

Gross (Eta^2) and Net (Beta^2) Explanatory Power of Predictors
of Percentage Change in Real Income/Needs
(Unmarried Household Heads in 1968)

Variable	Female			Male		
	Eta^2	Beta^2	Rank (by Beta^2)	Eta^2	Beta^2	Rank (by Beta^2)
Change in Marital Status	.104	.069	1	.068	.001	7
Age	.093	.048	2	.367	.251	1
City Size	.003	.009	5	.072	.057	2
Region	.002	.001	7	.015	.030	4
Head's Education	.036	.023	3	.212	.033	3
Race	.006	.003	6	.024	.021	5
Initial Marital Status	.040	.018	4	.100	.014	6

Note: See glossary for an explanation of Eta^2 and Beta^2.

MTR 2074

period as unmarried household heads, however, marital status change was very important, with those who married experiencing three times the percentage increase in income/needs of those who remained unmarried.

III. MARRIAGE AS A DEPENDENT VARIABLE

In this section, the marriage decision is considered within the same general analytic framework used for the other family composition changes. At the heart of the model is the simple notion that the chance that a marriage (or remarriage) will occur is a function of both the panel individual's desire for marriage (demand for a spouse) and of his or her eligibility (supply of potential spouses). Both demand and supply relate, in opposite ways, to a "price" of marriage—defined here as the fraction of total labor market and housework hours that the individual can expect to contribute if married.

While the economic analysis of commodity markets may seem to be a strange vehicle for understanding the marriage decision, writers from other disciplines have sometimes used supply and demand concepts in their own analyses of this decision. For example, in Remarriage: A Study of Marriage, Jessie Bernard has organized a discussion of factors affecting remarriage decisions in precisely those terms:

> Thus far we have been discussing the people who want to remarry and the opportunities they have for meeting future mates. We have, so to speak, taken the point of view of the seeker ... but people must be desirable as well as desiring; they must attract as well as pursue; they must be eligible—literally, chooseable—as well as choosing. Let us now consider, therefore, the question of eligibility.[11]

Other writers have evoked supply and demand arguments for the possible effects of single explanatory variables. James Sweet, for example, in discussing the relationship between remarriage and the number of children born to a woman, has used the demand argument that "women with children, particularly those with several children, ought to be under greater economic pressure to remarry than those with no children."[12] And he also noted supply effects: "The most important factor may, however, be the woman's position in the marriage market. A previously married woman with no children is likely to be regarded, in general, as a more attractive marriage partner than one with one or more children."[13] The conse-

----

[11]Bernard (1956), p. 141.

[12]Sweet (1973), p. 17.

[13]Sweet (1973), p. 18.

quence of these arguments is the expectation that the presence of children should increase the demand for remarriage but decrease the supply of potential spouses.

Our analysis of the marriage decision, then, was not generally different from previous work. In many ways it merely formalized some past analyses and gave proper regard to the statistical problems associated with the supply and demand framework.

The Price Variable

Central to the marriage model is the "price" variable, the concept and measurement of which requires some explanation. As in the divorce and separation analysis, price is defined as the fraction of total housework and labor market hours of both spouses that is contributed by one of them. For unmarried household heads contemplating marriage, the price variable equals the fraction of total hours they would expect to contribute if they were to get married. The higher this fraction, the less desirable is marriage. Stated somewhat differently, the demand for marriage should have a negative relationship with the expected fraction of hours to be contributed. In addition to this demand schedule of the unmarried head, we hypothesized that there exists a supply schedule for marriage from potential spouses of the unmarried head. The supply of marriage possibilities should also relate to the expected fraction of total hours contributed by the unmarried household head--but in a positive, rather than a negative direction. Potential spouses, in other words, should want to marry more if they expect to contribute a smaller fraction of total hours.

Operationalizing and measuring this price variable was difficult because we had no direct information on what the unmarried heads expected their contribution of hours would be if they were to marry nor similar information for potential spouses. In the absence of this information, we were forced to assume that the allocation of labor market and housework hours between the unmarried head and potential spouse would be similar to the *actual* allocation for a currently married person with similar characteristics. An example may help to illustrate this point. Suppose that we are concerned with the remarriage decision faced by a 30-year-old woman who is divorced, has a high school education, and has no children. To estimate her fraction of the total housework and labor market hours if she remarried, we look at the *actual* fraction for a married woman who is a 30-year-old high school graduate with no children. We then equate the *potential* fraction of the former with the *actual* fraction of the latter. These estimated fractions are based on dummy variable regressions run on the population of married spouses in 1968. The dependent variable in the regression is the fraction of total initial-year housework and labor market hours contributed by one spouse, and independent variables include age, education, number of children, years of labor market experience, and whether the individual is disabled. The results of the regression (for females) is given in Appendix Table A3.3.[14,15]

Other Explanatory Variables

With the price variable explained, it becomes necessary to discuss and defend the inclusion of other explanatory variables in the model of the marriage decision. The end result of the discussion would be a demand and a supply equation of the following form:

$$\text{Demand:} \quad Q = \alpha_1 + \beta_1 \text{Price} + \beta_2 X_1 + \beta_3 X_2 + e_1$$

$$\text{Supply:} \quad Q = \alpha_2 + \beta_4 \text{Price} + \beta_5 X_1 + \beta_6 X_3 + e_2$$

> where Q is the probability that an unmarried head of household will marry over the course of the seven panel years
>
> "Price" is the estimated hours allocation variable discussed in the previous section
>
> X_1, X_2 and X_3 are other explanatory variables measured in the initial panel year
>
> and e_1 and e_2 are stochastic error terms.

In statistical terms, the price variable is an *endogenous* variable (determined *within* the two equation system), while X_1, X_2 and X_3 are *exogenous* variables (determined *outside* the system). Note that some of the X variables may appear in *both* the supply and demand equations. In the following section we have explained and estimated two models of remarriage, one for the unmarried female household heads and the second for the unmarried male heads.

IV. THE MARRIAGE MODEL FOR UNMARRIED FEMALE HEADS OF HOUSEHOLDS

Income Variables

Of greatest interest is the set of income related variables--in particular, the amount of AFDC income received by the unmarried female heads of households.

---

[14] Since there were so few observations on unmarried male heads, the price variable was constructed only for female heads using information from initially married wives.

[15] Although some of the variables included in these regressions were the same as those which were used to explain the remarriage decision itself, exceptionally high multicollinearity was avoided by collapsing each variable into a relatively small (usually ten) number of categories and then making assignments based on estimated coefficients for each category.

In general, the less adequate the current sources of income, the greater the demand for marriage. This relationship should be especially strong for female
heads, since most of their potential spouses would be in the labor market. Labor
force participation rates for wives, on the other hand, average about half those
of their husbands, so we would expect to find fewer male heads of households who
marry solely for the income of their wives.

Several different sources of income have been included as variables in the
analysis. The amount of AFDC income is the most interesting because it is the
only policy variable subject to direct manipulation which may affect remarriage
rates. A measure of the amount of this income reported during the calendar year
1967 was used to form two dummy variables: (1) whether AFDC income was between
$1 and $2,000 and (2) whether AFDC income was greater than $2,000. By including
these two dichotomous variables and omitting a variable for those who reported
no AFDC income, we obtained estimated coefficients on the dichotomous variables
which showed the extent to which the probability of marriage for those who received these two levels of AFDC income differed from those who received none at
all. Alimony and child support payments are also sources of transfer income for
female heads who were divorced or separated. A measure of this (in thousands of
dollars) was also included. A third current income variable is the sum of non-
transfer money income from all other family sources. This includes mostly labor
income but also the income from capital that may have been recieved in 1967.[16]
A measure of the adequacy of the financial resources available to the homeowning
unmarried female heads is the amount of equity they had built up in the home.
Thus, a variable measuring the imputed rental value of the home (equal to 6 percent of the net equity) was also included.

Each of these different income variables should have a negative effect on
the *demand* for marriage because, with other things equal, the greater the level of
any of them, the less the financial incentive for marriage. We would expect some,
but not all of these income variables, to have an effect on the *supply* of potential spouses. In general, a *positive* relationship should exist between income
and supply. Sweet's reasoning for men should hold equally well for women: "Clearly, a man with a relatively large income would be in a better market position to

---

[16] The amount of rent, dividend, and interest income was tried out as a separate
variable, but its estimated coefficient failed to exceed its standard error in
every case.

attract a potential spouse than one who earns very little."[17,18] But the attractiveness of income should not apply to the sources of income that would be lost
if a remarriage occurs. Thus, the AFDC and alimony-child support variables were
not added on the supply side, and only the equity and family income net of transfer payments were listed as supply variables.[19]

Closely related to these measures of current resources is the labor market
earnings potential of the unmarried female heads. *Potential* earnings, rather
than actual current income, may be a better measure of the ability of the female
head to support herself and other family members because current income levels
often contain a substantial transitory component. Variables measuring years of
education and labor market experience were included as demand variables. The
higher the level of each, it was hypothesized, the less desirable would marriage
be.

Number of Children

Several writers have recognized that dependent children may either increase
or decrease a woman's chances of marriage. To the economic pressure explanation
quoted above, Sweet has added the following demand arguments: "In addition, they
(women with children) are responsible for the full day-to-day care of their children as well as holding a full-time job in the majority of cases. Finally, they
are exposed to a culture which tells them that it is important for children of
either sex to have a 'father' in the household."[20] For all of these reasons, then,
number of children was entered as a demand variable and was expected to increase
the demand for marriage.

Supply considerations argue for an expected *negative* relationship between
number of children and the supply of marriage. The prospect of additional
dependents is not an attractive one for many potential spouses. Sweet has presented the case as follows: "On sheer economic grounds, the woman with children
is more expensive. In addition, she is less likely to want to work than a woman
with no children. It has also been suggested that children inhibit usual court-

---

[17] Sweet (1973), p. 12.

[18] The same argument has been extended to include wealth variables as well. As
Bernard (1956) notes, "Ownership of property may help to overcome many handicaps
in personal appeal, and in any event, it is doubtless an advantage to women . . .
in the remarriage market." (p. 143)

[19] Although most alimony payments stopped with remarriage, most child support payments did not. Unfortunately, it was not possible to separate these two income
sources.

[20] Sweet (1973), p. 18.

ship processes and that potential spouses may not be willing to accept the prospect of a preexisting family."[21]

Variables measuring the number of children under 18 years of age in the household were entered on both the demand and supply sides. As with the AFDC income,
two dummy variables were constructed. The first variable was coded one if the
family contained one or two children, and zero otherwise; the second was coded
one if there were three or more children, and zero otherwise. Coefficients on
these variables show the extent to which marriage probabilities for these groups
differ from the group of unmarried female heads without children. These two dummy
variables were used rather than a single continuous variable measuring the number
of children because it has been argued that the effect of the first child may be
quite different from the effect of additional ones: "Although arithmetically
zero differs from one or more only in degrees, psychologically and sociologically,
a situation with no children is qualitatively different from one with one child
or more."[22]

Additional Supply Variables

Two additional variables were included in the supply equation. The first,
age of the unmarried female head, was expected to have a negative association
with the supply of potential spouses. This is due, in part, to the tendency of
men to marry women younger than themselves and to the increasing ratio of women
to men in higher age brackets. This negative age-remarriage relationship has
been discussed and documented by several writers.[23]

The second supply variable was a crude measure of physical appearance. The
obvious expected effect was for the supply of potential spouses to be greater for
the most attractive persons. As Bernard has stated it, "Whether they are young
or old, people must be attractive enough to win a mate if they are to marry. The
standards of attraction may be low or high, romantic or practical--but they must
be met."[24] The measure included in the panel study data was motivated by reasons
related to job rather than marriage: It is an interviewer assessment of whether
the respondent had "any obvious disfigurements or habits that could make it dif-

---

[21]Sweet (1973), p. 18.

[22]Bernard (1956), p. 14. This statement also implies that the effect of other
variables may depend upon whether there are dependent children involved. A
regression was run separately for the group of unmarried female heads with
children.

[23]See, for example, Goode (1956) p. 279, and Williams and Kuhn (1973) p. 5.

[24]Bernard (1956), p. 142.

ficult for him or her to get a job."

Other Demographic Variables

A trio of basic demographic variables were included in both the supply and demand equations: race, marital status, and city size.

Sweet found that blacks had lower remarriage rates than whites, especially for women whose first marriage was terminated before age 40.[25] This difference persisted when other demographic variables were taken into account. Since this effect could come from either the supply or the demand side, the race variable was included in both equations.

Previous marital status may also have an effect on remarriage rates, and two dichotomous variables--whether widowed and whether single--were included in the regression. Since the omitted group consists of the divorced and separated, coefficients on the two included dummy variables show the extent to which remarriage rates of individuals in these groups differ from the group of divorced and separated household heads. Sweet argued that the remarriage rates of widows should be lower than those of the separated and divorced because the latter "have had conflict in their previous marriage. They may have few, if any, strong loyalties to their former spouse." The widowed, on the other hand, have "experienced a period of grief. They may remain loyal in some sense to their former spouse. Indeed, there are norms regarding remarriage which tell the widowed . . . that [they] should not remarry too quickly." In addition, he argued that "a significant proportion (of the divorced and separated) have experienced disruption precisely because they have found another person . . . . To the degree that they marry that person, their remarriage rates should be higher."[26] The first argument relates to demand, the second to supply, and both lead to the expectation that remarriage probabilities of the widowed would be *less* than those of the divorced and separated. Other factors, however, may mitigate these effects. Conflict in a previous marriage may cause a negative attitude toward marriage and a reluctance to remarry. Since the divorced and separated are much more likely to have experienced conflict than the widowed, the demand for remarriage may be *higher* for the widowed.

The final demographic variable--city size--could be expected to have opposite effects in the supply and the demand equations. On the supply side, the number of potential mates should be higher in the larger cities, and so increased city size

---

[25] Sweet (1973), p. 16.

[26] Sweet (1973), p. 8.

should have a positive relationship with the supply of marriage probabilities.
On the demand side, on the other hand, norms against remaining unmarried are
stronger in smaller communities than in large cities, and so increased city size
could have a negative effect on the *demand* for marriage.[27]

In summary, our marriage model for the unmarried female heads contained
both supply and demand equations. The *endogenous* variable reflects the "price" of
marriage and was measured by the probable ("expected") fraction of total hours
that the unmarried head would contribute if she were to marry. Of the exogenous
variables, age of the household head and whether she is disfigured are unique
to the supply equation, while measures of AFDC income, child support and alimony
payments, education, and labor market experience are unique to the demand equation. Additional variables common to both sides include 1968 total family income
less welfare income, imputed rental income, number of dependent children, race,
marital status, and city size. The procedure used to estimate the system of two
equations—two-stage least squares—is described in Appendix B.

V. ANALYSIS RESULTS FOR UNMARRIED FEMALE HEADS OF HOUSEHOLDS

The estimated coefficients and standard errors of variables in the marriage
model are detailed in the three columns of Table 3.6. Coefficients in the first
column are from estimates of the *demand* equation using the two-stage least squares
technique. The second column shows the results when the procedure is applied to
the *supply* equation. The third column gives estimated coefficients of the *reduced
form* equation. These coefficients reflect the *overall* effect of the exogenous
variables on the marriage rates and tell nothing about how this overall effect
relates to the structural demand and supply effects. Two additional sets of
regression results are given in the appendix. The first, in Table A3.4, is the
estimated reduced form using the MCA dummy variable regression technique for both
the entire population of unmarried female heads and for only the female heads
with children. In addition to presenting both unadjusted and adjusted mean marriage rates for each category of each independent variable, the table also shows
the weighted and unweighted *distribution* of the sample across the categories. Ordinary least squares estimation results for the supply and the demand equations
are presented in Table A3.5.

---

[27]In addition to these income and demographic variables, two social psychological
measures were included—indexes of efficacy-future orientation and trust-hos-
tility. Both were quite insignificant.

TABLE 3.6

Regression Results for Independent Variables
Predicting Marriage/Remarriage
(All Unmarried Female Household Heads)

	Two-Stage Least Squares Estimation of Demand Equation	Two-Stage Least Squares Estimation of Supply Equation	Ordinary Least Squares Estimation of Reduced Form Equation
Endogenous:			
Potential Net Transfer Position (Price)	-1.92^{**} (.189)	$-.034$ (.447)	
Exogenous:			
Age		$-.012^{**}$ (.003)	$-.012^{**}$ (.001)
Whether Disfigurement		$-.037$ (.023)	$-.034$ (.023)
AFDC $1-$2000	$-.123^{*}$ (.061)		$-.107$ (.056)
AFDC > $2000	$-.017$ (.078)		$-.022$ (.071)
Alimony-Child Support (in Thousands of Dollars)	$-.015$ (.025)		$-.013$ (.023)
Imputed Rental Income (in Thousands of Dollars)	$-.040$ (.030)	$-.027$ (.028)	$-.028$ (.027)
Family Income (Less Transfers) (in Thousands of Dollars)	$-.010^{**}$ (.004)	$-.0002$ (.004)	$-.001$ (.003)
Education	$-.013^{**}$ (.004)		.0008 (.003)
Experience	$-.0006$ (.0007)		$-.0002$ (.0006)
1-2 Children	$-.011$ (.036)	$-.031$ (.033)	$-.018$ (.033)
3 + children	$-.013$ (.047)	$-.071$ (.041)	$-.042$ (.044)

TABLE 3.6 (Sheet 2 of 2)

	Two-Stage Least Squares Estimation of Demand Equation	Two-Stage Least Squares Estimation of Supply Equation	Ordinary Least Squares Estimation of Reduced Form Equation
Whether Black	-.061 (.036)	-.090** (.033)	-.094** (.033)
Whether Single	.077 (.039)	.077 (.039)	-.003 (.037)
Whether Widowed	.052 (.036)	.075** (.031)	.064* (.033)
City Size	-.008 (.007)	-.008 (.006)	-.009 (.006)
R^2	.118	.224	.229

$\bar{Y}$ = .180

N = 986

*Significant at .05 level.

**Significant at .01 level

NOTE: Numbers in parentheses are standard errors.

The demand equation relates independent variables to the unmarried female head's demand for remarriage. The supply equation refers to supply of remarriage possibilities from potential spouses. For an explanation of two-stage least squares, see Appendix B.

Price

The two-stage estimates for the endogenous price variable showed that the un-married female head's demand for marriage was quite responsive to price in the ex-pected negative direction, while supply of potential spouses was quite unresponsive to it. The demand coefficient was highly significant and indicated that as the fraction of expected total hours contributed by the potential wife increased by ten percentage points (from, say, .50 to .60), the demand for marriage dropped by almost 20 percentage points.[28,29]

Income

As expected, all of the income components had a negative effect on the demand for remarriage, although many of these coefficients were not large enough to attain statistical significance. Of greatest interest is the effect of AFDC income on marriage, and the results showed very weak support for the hypothesized negative effect. For those who received less than $2,000 of AFDC income, the demand prob-abilities were 12.3 percentage points less than the probabilities for those who did not receive any of this type of income. This difference was large enough to be significant at the 5 percent level. Although a larger amount of AFDC income might be expected to have a greater negative effect on the demand for marriage, it in fact did not. For those who received more than $2,000 of AFDC income, the estimated demand probabilities were only 1.7 percentage points lower than for those who had no AFDC income, and this coefficient was a small fraction of its standard error. Estimated coefficients in the reduced form equation showed that the *overall* effect of AFDC income on marriage rates (and not just the struc-tural demand effect) followed the same pattern, with those who received some AFDC income having lower marriage rates than those who received much more. Neither of these coefficients were significant, so we cannot reject the hypothesis that AFDC income had no effect on marriage rates. Even more striking is the lack of relationship between marriage rates and AFDC income in the MCA results detailed in the appendix. Figure 3.3 shows the adjusted mean marriage rates by six broad AFDC income categories both for all unmarried female heads and for those with children. If anything, remarriage rate tended to *increase* at higher AFDC income levels.

Only one of the other income measures, total family money income less wel-

---

[28]Unless otherwise noted, the probability level dividing significant and insig-nificant coefficients is 5 percent.

[29]Recall that the quantity of remarriage is interpreted as a probability that remarriage will occur.

FIGURE 3.3

Adjusted Mean Probability of Remarriage
By Amount of AFDC Income

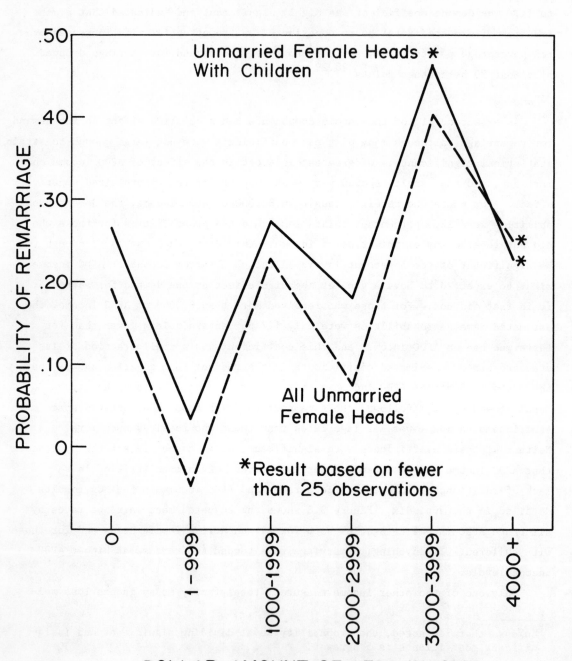

fare, showed a significant effect on the demand for marriage. An extra thousand dollars of this income was estimated to have reduced the demand probability by 1.0 percent.

Of the two measures of *potential* economic status, education and labor force experience, both had the expected negative sign, but only the coefficient on education had statistical significance. An additional year of education was associated with a 1.3 percent decline in the demand probability of marriage. Interestingly, the reduced form coefficient on education was totally insignificant, so this education effect on demand was discovered only when the structural equations were estimated separately.

Coefficients for the two income measures that were also included as supply variables, total family income and imputed rental income, failed to exceed their standard errors. Contrary to the hypothesized positive effect of these income sources of supply, both were negative.

Children

The presence of children showed no significant effect in either demand or supply equations. The demand coefficients on the two dummy variables were quite small and, contrary to expectations, they were negative. The supply effects were larger, with initially unmarried household heads with one or two children estimated to have supply probabilities 3.1 percent lower than for those with no children, and unmarried heads with three or more children had a 7.1 percent lower supply probability. This latter number was significant at the 10 percent but not the 5 percent level. From the reduced form equation it can be seen that the overall effects of children on marriage rates during the panel period were small, negative, and statistically insignificant.

Other Supply Variables

The two additional supply variables--age of the female household head and whether she had a disfigurement--both showed negative effects. The age effect was strong and significant, and each additional year was associated with a 1.2 percentage point decline in the supply probability of marriage. Disfigurement also had a negative effect, but its estimated coefficient was not significant.

Other Demographic Variables

Of the four additional demographic measures included in both supply and demand equations, only city size failed to show up as a significant variable.

Overall, the regression adjusted marriage rates for black women were 9.4 percent lower than for white women. The race effects in the structural equations were stronger for the supply side than for demand. The remarriage *supply* probabilities were 9.0 percentage points less for blacks--a statistically significant result. The estimated *demand* probabilities were 6.1 percent less for blacks, but this coefficient was not significant at the 5 percent level.

The estimated coefficients on the two marital status variables--whether single and whether widowed--showed the extent to which these groups differed from the divorced and separated. It was found that being single significantly *increased* the demand for marriage while the widowed had higher demand, supply, and overall marriage rates. This latter result was generally contrary to our expectations, which were that widows would have *lower* remarriage rates than the divorced and separated. A clue to the puzzle was obtained by examining the unadjusted differences (given in Table A3.4). Here the hypothesis was confirmed: Only 9 percent of the widows remarried, while 18 and 28 percent of those who were initially divorced or separated, respectively, remarried during the seven-year period. But when the effects of other variables were taken into account (most notably age), the widows were shown to have *higher* remarriage rates than the divorced and separated. Of further interest is the result that the higher remarriage rates of widows were significant in the *supply* but not the *demand* equation.

In sum, the estimated coefficients of most variables in the marriage model had the expected signs, although few were large enough to be statistically significant. Regarding the possible effect of AFDC income on remarriage, we found a weak and inconsistent relationship. Other income variables did, however, reduce the demand for remarriage. Both total family income and education (interpreted here as a measure of *potential* earnings) had significant negative coefficients in the demand equation. Of the remaining demand variables, only the marital status measure of "whether single" was significant, with the never-married women having a greater demand for marriage than the divorced and separated.

Of the supply variables, age was the most powerful. Each additional year was associated with a 1.2 percent decline in the supply probability of marriage. Race was also significant, with blacks having a 9 percentage point lower supply probability than whites. This supply effect of race was considerably larger than the demand effect. The final significant supply variable was "whether widowed," with the supply probability of remarriage for widowed women estimated to be 7.5 percent higher than for the divorced and separated.

VI. THE MARRIAGE MODEL FOR UNMARRIED MALE HEADS OF HOUSEHOLDS

Since the economic aspects of the marriage decision were expected to apply equally well to both men and women, the model that was estimated for the initially unmarried men was quite similar to that for the unmarried women. One important difference was that the small number of observations for the men made results from estimation of separate supply and demand equations much less reliable. Only the reduced form estimates relating the *overall* effects of exogenous variables on re- marriage rates were used and no attempt was made to trace the overall effects back through the structural equations.[30]

Most of the variables in the female marriage model could be used for males. Current and potential income sources were expected to decrease the desirability of marriage but increase the supply. Dependent children, it was hypothesized, would increase demand but decrease supply. Age, physical appearance, and the other demographic variables were expected to relate to marriage for males as they did for females.

Some variable differences, however, did exist. For example, some of the in- come sources that were available for females were not generally available for males. Thus, AFDC and alimony/child support income variables were not included in the model for males. Alimony and child support *payments,* on the other hand, may be important because these obligations may have decreased eligibility. As Bernard has stated it, "Financial obligations to a first wife and to children of a first marriage may render ineligible men who would otherwise be eminently eligible."[31] A variable measuring the dollar amount contributed to outside dependents in 1967 was thus included and was expected to have a negative effect on remarriage.

We also included measures of two additional behavioral traits which might have affected eligibility. Bernard argued that "[Not] all the available men are also desirable. The never-married, the too elderly, the invalided, the always late, the too deeply engrossed in profession or business, the niggardly, the ex- ploiting, the drinker, and the philanderer--none of these all too common types is 'husband material,' and so the field is highly restricted."[32] Of this list of traits, the first and second were captured in the "whether single" and age vari- ables, respectively. Three of the remaining factors could be measured (some more precisely than others): disability, employment commitment, and alcohol expendi- tures. The panel study measures of disability, dollar amounts of alcohol expen- ditures, and frequency of bar attendance had virtually no effect on the male remar- riage rates, so these variables were not included in the final model. Two mea-

---

[30]For an explanation of reduced form and structural equations, see Appendix B.

[31]Bernard (1956), p. 144.

[32]Bernard (1956), p. 144.

sures of employment commitment, however, did have moderate effects. The first was whether the male head reported working more than 50 hours per week; the second was based on responses to the question, "Were there times when you didn't get to work at all, even though you were not sick?" "No" responses were coded one and the "yes" responses were coded zero.

Two additional changes in the variable list were made. Since so few (6.4 percent) of the unmarried male heads had dependent children living with them, a *single* dummy variable (rather than the two used for female heads) measuring the presence of any children was included. Second, because age, education, and work experience were so highly intercorrelated for men, the work experience variable was not included in this model; the age variable was expected to pick up some of the effects of experience.

VII. ANALYSIS RESULTS FOR UNMARRIED MALE HEADS OF HOUSEHOLDS

The reduced form coefficient estimates (and their standard errors) for the unmarried male heads are given in the first two columns of Table 3.7. For purposes of comparison, the coefficients and standard errors for females are listed in the third and fourth columns, respectively, of the table.

In general, many of the variables that were found to affect the marriage rates of females had similar effects for the unmarried male heads. The age effect for both groups, for example, was negative, significant, and quite similar. An additional year of age decreased male marriage rates by 1.4 percent and female rates by 1.2 percentage points. The disfigurement variable had a negative but insignificant effect for females. For males it was also negative and it was large enough to be statistically significant.

Although none of the income-related variables was important for males, the measure of financial obligations to dependents was significant. Its sign, however, was *positive* rather than negative. Each additional thousand dollars of such payments was associated with an 8.3 percent *increase* in the probability of remarriage. This may be a demand effect, with those obligated to children from a past marriage more anxious to have or be with children in a future one.

The presence of dependent children decreased remarriage chances by 21.5 percentage points. However, the number of observations on this result was too small to make this a significant coefficient.

Of the other demographic variables included in the model, several had coefficients larger than those estimated for females. Most of them, however, were insignificant—due, in part, to the smaller sample size for men. The estimated

TABLE 3.7

Regression Results for Reduced Form Marriage Models
(Unmarried Household Heads in 1968)

Variable	Men Coefficient	Standard Error	Women Coefficient	Standard Error
	Men		Women	
Age	-.014**	(.003)	-.012**	(.001)
Whether disfigured	-.118*	(.057)	-.034	(.023)
AFDC $1-$2000			-.107	(.056)
AFDC >$2000			-.022	(.071)
Alimony-child support (in thousands of dollars)			-.013	(.023)
Imputed rental income (in thousands of dollars)	-.021	(.078)	-.028	(.027)
Family income (in thousands of dollars)	-.0076	(.0057)	-.001	(.003)
Contribution to outside dependents (in thousands of dollars)	.0830*	(.0405)		
Education	.0058	(.0091)	.0008	(.003)
Experience			-.0002	(.0006)
Whether children	-.215	(.129)		
1-2 children			-.018	(.033)
3 or more children			-.042	(.044)
Whether black	-.145	(.095)	-.094**	(.033)
Whether single	-.227*	(.090)	-.003	(.037)
Whether widowed	-.091	(.094)	.064	(.033)
City size	-.0035	(.0178)	-.009	(.006)
Whether work more than 50 hours per week	-.089	(.085)		
Whether never skip work	.079	(.095)		
R^2	.309		.229	
Number of observations	203		986	
$\bar{Y}$	.362		.180	

*Significant at .05 level

**Significant at .01 level

remarriage rate for black males, for example, was 14.5 percent less than for white males, a difference that was not significant at the 10 percent probability level. The black-white difference for females was smaller (9.4 percent), but the larger sample size made this difference highly significant.

The only significant other demographic variable for men was the "whether single" measure. The single men had regression-adjusted remarriage rates that were 22.4 percentage points lower than those for the men who began the panel period as divorced or separated.

The final two variables were included as measures of job commitment. Excessive job commitment (working more than 50 hours per week) decreased chances of marriage; modest commitment (whether the respondent never skips work) increased it. Neither of these coefficients, however, were statistically significant.

These results for the unmarried male heads were less engaging than those for the females, both because the small number of observations on the men did not permit the separate estimation of supply and demand equations and because there was no policy-relevant variable like AFDC income whose possible effects were of extraordinary interest.

Of the set of variables common to both men and women, two had quite similar effects. Both age and race ("whether black") were associated with reduced marriage rates. Two additional variables were uniquely important for the men. Those who made payments in support of dependents outside the household had *higher* rates of remarriage—a somewhat puzzling result. Finally, both the single and widowed had *lower* marriage rates than the divorced or separated, with the differences between the former and latter large enough to attain statistical significance.

Summary

1. For the group of initially unmarried household heads, family composition changes were relatively frequent and were associated with large changes in economic well-being. About one-fifth of the women married (or remarried), and those who stayed married experienced the greatest increases in income. Over one-third of the men married. The association between marriage and increased economic well-being for them, however, was much weaker than for women, especially after the effects of demographic variables had been taken into account.

2. A model of marriage was developed and estimated separately for the men and women. Factors affecting marriage were classified by whether they affected an individual's *demand* for marriage or the *supply* of potential spouses, or both.

3. Of greatest policy interest is the effect of AFDC income on the marriage rate of women with dependent children. We found virtually *no* evidence of a consistent relationship between the two variables.

4. Other factors did, however, have significant effects on the marriage rates of the initially unmarried female heads. Measures of current and potential income had significant negative associations with the *demand* for marriage. Age and race ("whether black") had significant *supply* effects, also in the negative direction.

5. For the initially unmarried *male* household heads, it was not possible to estimate separate supply and demand effects--rather, only the *overall* effects of variables on remarriage rates were estimated. Age and race had deterrent effects for males similar to those for females.

References

Bernard, Jessie. Remarriage: A Study of Marriage. New York: Dryden Press, 1956.

Goode, William J. Women in Divorce. New York: Free Press, 1956.

Morgan, James N. et al. Five Thousand American Families--Patterns of Economic Progress. Volume I. Ann Arbor: Institute for Social Research, 1974.

Sweet, James A. "Differentials in Remarriage Probabilities." Working Paper 73-29. University of Wisconsin: Center for Demography and Ecology, 1973 (mimeograph).

U.S. Bureau of the Census. Current Population Reports. Series P-20, No. 279. "Population Profile of the United States: 1974." Washington, D.C.: U.S. Government Printing Office, 1975.

Williams, Kristen M. and Kuhn, Russell P. "Remarriages," Vital and Health Statistics, series 21, No. 25, 1973.

Appendix 3.1

TABLE A3.1

Frequency and Income Data on Nonresponse Cases
for Initially Unmarried Household Heads

	Number of Observations	Weighted Percent	Average 1967 Family Income	Average 1967 Family Income/Needs
Male				
Single	60	41.2	$4989	2.17
Widowed	41	31.4	5020	2.49
Divorced/Separated	55	27.4	5644	2.28
All	156	100.0	$5178	2.30
Female				
Single	55	19.2	$4970	2.32
Widowed	118	54.0	3614	1.79
Divorced/Separated	113	26.8	5343	1.93
All	286	100.0	$4338	1.93

TABLE A3.2 (Sheet 1 of 2)

MCA Results on Seven-Year Percent Change in Family Real Income/Needs
(All Unmarried Heads of Households in 1968)

Variable	Men				Women			
	Number of Observations	Weighted Percent	Unadjusted Mean	Adjusted Mean	Number of Observations	Weighted Percent	Unadjusted Mean	Adjusted Mean
Age	η^2=.367		β^2=.251		η^2=.093		β^2=.048	
< 25 years	38	21.4	223.9	194.2	95	9.8	130.5	99.9
25–34	32	13.6	23.7	23.7	193	13.9	61.7	57.7
35–44	32	12.8	12.3	16.2	218	14.3	61.0	67.0
45–54	46	18.3	20.4	27.5	219	17.5	40.1	44.2
55–64	32	14.3	-1.0	4.0	171	21.5	23.3	27.1
65–74	20	13.4	11.7	39.6	82	15.9	19.5	23.8
75 +	8	6.3	4.2	5.7	34	6.7	31.1	37.5
N.A.	--	--	--	--	1	0.3	21.0	32.0
City size	η^2=.072		β^2=.057		η^2=.003		β^2=.009	
> 500,000	78	33.2	74.3	78.0	524	39.4	48.6	43.7
100,000–499,999	47	27.3	91.8	78.7	204	21.7	45.5	44.1
50,000–99,999	21	12.1	32.9	3.9	81	8.9	45.5	42.6
25,000–49,999	22	9.4	10.5	50.7	47	7.5	43.7	50.5
10,000–24,999	13	5.9	93.9	99.1	57	8.4	34.2	35.5
< 10,000	27	12.1	-18.1	-3.3	98	14.1	58.3	71.4
Outside U.S.	--	--	--	--	2	0.0	-41.9	36.7
Region	η^2=.015		β^2=.030		η^2=.002		β^2=.001	
Northeast	35	19.0	27.3	19.4	173	24.5	40.0	43.5
North central	46	29.5	51.6	51.4	263	29.7	53.0	50.1
South	85	27.4	74.7	92.3	404	27.8	46.5	47.8
West	42	24.1	71.2	57.6	171	17.9	50.0	47.9
Other	--	--	--	--	2	0.0	-41.9	-41.9
Education	η^2=.212		β^2=.032		η^2=.036		β^2=.023	
0 years	15	3.3	21.4	55.8	39	2.8	9.8	27.0
1–5 grades	15	4.2	46.0	96.0	49	5.0	18.5	32.7
6–8	54	23.3	10.5	45.1	241	21.8	42.4	55.6
9–11	25	9.7	-17.8	24.3	284	20.6	38.8	38.0
12	20	13.6	27.0	59.4	159	14.8	43.4	44.0
12 plus nonacademic	8	5.7	48.9	53.0	99	12.0	60.9	52.7
Some college	42	23.6	169.0	90.1	82	12.3	91.3	77.3
B.A.	19	11.0	44.0	19.3	42	7.4	43.5	32.4
Advanced degree	9	5.0	79.1	89.3	17	3.2	28.5	17.0
N.A.	1	0.6	-80.0	57.9	1	0.2	-45.3	-87.2

TABLE A3.2 (Sheet 2 of 2)

Variable	Men				Women			
	Number of Observations	Weighted Percent	Unadjusted Mean	Adjusted Mean	Number of Observations	Weighted Percent	Unadjusted Mean	Adjusted Mean
Race	$\eta^2=.024$		$\beta^2=.021$		$\eta^2=.006$		$\beta^2=.003$	
White	136	83.6	9.1	61.8	455	80.1	46.2	45.9
Black	63	12.4	-52.7	34.0	539	18.0	52.9	53.6
Spanish-American	5	2.6	-41.4	92.5	7	0.8	105.2	79.6
Oriental	2	0.9	32.3	74.0	8	0.8	-15.9	6.8
N.A.	2	0.5	-66.8	-203.1	4	0.3	55.1	89.3
Marital Status	$\eta^2=.100$		$\beta^2=.014$		$\eta^2=.040$		$\beta^2=.018$	
Single	95	47.1	105.2	67.9	188	20.6	81.5	57.9
Widowed	39	17.9	3.4	37.4	352	48.2	32.0	48.6
Separated	34	18.6	17.2	39.4	182	17.7	35.6	33.9
Divorced	32	10.8	20.7	82.6	267	10.6	71.1	61.3
Married, spouse absent	7	4.7	47.6	44.3	22	2.5	48.9	-21.4
N.A.	1	0.8	21.8	117.2	2	0.3	28.9	13.6
Change in Marital Status	$\eta^2=.068$		$\beta^2=.001$		$\eta^2=.104$		$\beta^2=.069$	
Unmarried throughout	135	64.2	30.3	61.4	841	81.1	33.6	37.7
Married	70	35.7	108.1	51.9	136	14.7	128.3	110.5
Married, then widowed	--	--	--	--	7	1.1	58.2	73.9
Married, then divorced	3	0.1	36.7	56.3	28	3.0	24.6	-6.2
Married, then divorced, then married	--	--	--	--	1	0.2	-4.3	12.7
$\overline{R}^2$			.360				.161	
$\overline{Y}$			58.0				47.4	
σ_Y			143.6				104.6	

TABLE A3.3

MCA Predicting Fraction of Total Work Hours Contributed by Wife
(All Wives in 1968)

Independent Variable	Number of Observations	Weighted Percent of Sample	Unadjusted Mean Fraction	Adjusted Mean Fraction
Number of children	$\eta^2=.037$		$\beta^2=.011$	
0	707	37.5%	.58	.53
1	407	18.5	.52	.54
2	418	18.7	.51	.55
3	326	12.4	.50	.54
4	187	6.2	.55	.59
5	128	3.2	.52	.55
6	94	2.0	.58	.59
7	43	0.8	.58	.62
8	18	0.3	.61	.63
9	10	0.1	.67	.68
10	11	0.2	.52	.58
>10	5	0.1	.56	.59
Age of wife	$\eta^2=.141$		$\beta^2=.131$	
< 25 years	282	10.8	.51	.54
25–34	588	23.2	.50	.51
35–44	640	25.4	.51	.51
45–54	433	18.7	.52	.51
55–64	298	15.3	.59	.59
65–74	96	5.6	.75	.74
over 75	17	1.0	.85	.83
Education of wife	$\eta^2=.072$		$\beta^2=.032$	
0	17	1.0	.53	.55
1-5 years	111	3.2	.66	.62
6-8	378	13.0	.63	.59
9-11	495	17.3	.55	.55
12	684	32.3	.52	.54
12 plus nonacademic	269	13.0	.53	.53
Some college	226	11.2	.49	.50
College degree	113	6.1	.48	.49
Advanced degree	31	1.8	.48	.47
N. A.	30	1.2	.67	.60
Disabled or requires extra care	$\eta^2=.007$		$\beta^2=.006$	
Yes, disabled	55	1.9	.64	.57
Yes, requires extra care	27	1.2	.50	.43
No	2267	96.8	.54	.54
N. A.	5	0.2	.40	.45
Labor Market Experience	$\eta=.024$		$\beta^2=.018$	
0 years	559	22.5	.55	.53
1-5 years	423	17.9	.52	.52
6-10	405	16.9	.51	.52
11-15	306	13.1	.52	.54
16-20	204	8.9	.55	.56
20 +	413	19.2	.59	.58
N. A.	44	1.4	.55	.51

$\overline{Y} = .54$

$\sigma_Y = .179$

$\overline{R}^2 = .186$

TABLE A3.4 (Sheet 1 of 3)

MCA Results for Regression Analysis of Remarriage
(Unmarried Female Heads of Household and Unmarried Female Heads with Children)

Independent Variable	All Female Heads of Households				Female Heads of Households with Children			
	Number of Observations	Weighted Percent	Unadjusted Mean	Adjusted Mean	Number of Observations	Weighted Percent	Unadjusted Mean	Adjusted Mean
Age of head	η^2=.244		β^2=.286		η^2=.121		β^2=.200	
< 25 years	92	9.5	.65	.68	41	5.8	.57	.68
25-34	184	13.2	.38	.39	152	27.0	.39	.40
35-44	214	14.2	.20	.23	171	30.6	.21	.26
45-54	215	17.8	.07	.08	121	23.4	.10	.02
55-64	171	22.2	.09	.07	0	--	--	--
65-74	82	16.4	.04	.01	40	9.9	.08	.04
75 +	33	6.7	.00	.00	5	3.3	.00	-.06
Disfigurement	η^2=.008		β^2=.004		η^2=.015		β^2=.008	
No	886	89.7	.19	.19	457	88.7	.25	.24
Yes, qualified	56	5.0	.15	.11	32	6.7	.24	.28
Yes	49	5.3	.04	.11	23	4.6	.00	.07
AFDC income	η^2=.009		β^2=.014		η^2=.024		β^2=.027	
$0	813	92.0	.18	.18	365	76.7	.24	.25
1-999	43	2.6	.07	-.05	40	7.5	.08	.03
1000-1999	53	2.3	.28	.22	51	7.0	.28	.26
2000-2999	43	1.3	.10	.07	40	3.9	.10	.17
3000-3999	25	0.9	.45	.39	22	2.7	.48	.45
4000 and over	14	0.9	.28	.24	12	2.3	.20	.22
Alimony-child support	η^2=.004		β^2=.013		η^2=.008		β^2=.042	
$0	883	89.8	.18	.19	434	73.2	.24	.25
1-499	26	1.7	.19	.12	22	4.4	.23	.16
500-999	31	2.9	.21	.04	27	7.3	.17	.09
1000-1999	23	1.9	.20	.17	22	5.8	.20	.20
2000-2999	16	2.1	.33	.31	15	6.4	.33	.38
3000-4999	5	0.7	.05	-.03	4	1.3	.08	-.33
N.A.	7	0.8	.11	-.09	6	1.7	.17	.15

TABLE A3.4 (Sheet 2 of 3)

Independent Variable	All Female Heads of Households				Female Heads of Households with Children			
	Number of Observations	Weighted Percent	Unadjusted Mean	Adjusted Mean	Number of Observations	Weighted Percent	Unadjusted Mean	Adjusted Mean
Number of children	$\eta^2=.029$		$\beta^2=.008$		$\eta^2=.047$		$\beta^2=.017$	
0	449	67.3	.15	.17	0	—	—	—
1	120	9.7	.15	.16	120	29.9	.14	.21
2	134	10.2	.34	.26	134	31.4	.34	.27
3	97	5.6	.19	.15	97	17.4	.19	.17
4	67	2.7	.21	.15	67	8.3	.21	.17
5	54	2.4	.37	.24	54	7.4	.37	.31
6	35	1.1	.20	.15	35	3.5	.20	.27
7	22	0.6	.02	.00	22	1.8	.24	.09
8	1	0.1	.00	.13	1	0.4	.00	.41
9	12	0.3	.37	.34	0	—	—	—
City size	$\eta^2=.020$		$\beta^2=.003$		$\eta^2=.020$		$\beta^2=.033$	
500,000 +	533	39.6	.17	.16	347	51.5	.26	.22
100,000-499,999	186	20.4	.23	.19	94	18.7	.30	.34
50,000-99,999	67	8.4	.22	.23	32	9.6	.12	.18
25,000-49,999	45	7.3	.14	.21	11	4.0	.19	.08
10,000-24,999	58	9.3	.26	.18	16	6.5	.10	.08
1-9999	102	15.1	.08	.18	30	9.7	.20	.34
Race	$\eta^2=.003$		$\beta^2=.006$		$\eta^2=.025$		$\beta^2=.027$	
White	442	80.2	.19	.19	128	63.9	.28	.28
Black	530	17.8	.14	.12	391	34.2	.16	.15
Other	19	1.9	.11	.11	11	1.9	.01	.05
Education	$\eta^2=.070$		$\beta^2=.025$		$\eta^2=.061$		$\beta^2=.045$	
0 years	38	2.6	.02	.14	20	1.9	.08	.19
1-5	48	5.0	.11	.20	21	3.7	.17	.37
6-8	239	22.4	.06	.15	121	17.5	.08	.18
9-11	275	20.2	.17	.14	181	30.6	.24	.15
12	156	14.7	.17	.16	105	21.2	.23	.26
12 plus nonacademic	96	11.9	.25	.19	47	11.6	.30	.28
Some college	81	12.5	.34	.26	25	8.3	.48	.44
B.A.	40	7.3	.28	.24	8	3.9	.20	.35
Advanced degree	17	3.2	.18	.18	2	1.4	.46	.23
N.A.	1	0.2	1.00	1.14	0	—	—	—

TABLE A3.4 (Sheet 3 of 3)

Independent Variable	All Female Heads of Households				Female Heads of Households with Children			
	Number of Observations	Weighted Percent	Unadjusted Mean	Adjusted Mean	Number of Observations	Weighted Percent	Unadjusted Mean	Adjusted Mean
Marital status	$\eta^2=.089$		$\beta^2=.037$		$\eta^2=.046$		$\beta^2=.027$	
Single	180	20.0	.32	.06	73	6.6	.19	.10
Widowed	352	49.6	.09	.21	119	33.6	.17	.27
Divorced	182	18.3	.18	.17	115	31.4	.24	.23
Separated	267	10.7	.28	.21	214	24.6	.27	.19
Single, married previously	10	1.4	.70	.58	9	3.7	.65	.51
Years of work experience	$\eta^2=.091$		$\beta^2=.010$		$\eta^2=.055$		$\beta^2=.024$	
0	157	16.6	.20	.18	81	14.5	.29	.30
1-4	134	14.4	.40	.24	76	17.6	.35	.30
5-9	139	14.6	.26	.19	88	19.5	.29	.22
10-14	115	10.8	.16	.16	78	17.5	.24	.18
15-19	104	9.4	.10	.12	62	10.0	.08	.12
20-24	82	6.5	.01	.10	45	5.3	.03	.12
25-29	79	6.9	.05	.14	40	5.0	.05	.24
30 +	181	20.6	.09	.20	60	10.5	.20	.31
Money income less transfers	$\eta^2=.007$		$\beta^2=.013$		$\eta^2=.036$		$\beta^2=.055$	
$1-$999	160	9.4	.15	.13	105	11.8	.19	.15
1000-1999	205	17.5	.14	.18	92	12.5	.23	.32
2000-2999	192	17.5	.19	.24	100	16.5	.20	.28
3000-3999	133	10.7	.18	.13	82	10.7	.20	.15
4000-4999	77	9.1	.24	.22	39	6.9	.22	.16
5000-7499	133	19.0	.18	.14	73	23.8	.20	.17
7500-9999	43	7.5	.17	.15	22	8.9	.26	.25
10,000 +	48	9.5	.22	.24	17	8.9	.48	.48
Imputed rental income	$\eta^2=.035$		$\beta^2=.005$		$\eta^2=.017$		$\beta^2=.021$	
0	688	53.6	.24	.19	425	63.9	.26	.25
1-999	149	18.0	.10	.18	66	16.8	.20	.22
1000-1999	108	19.0	.12	.20	31	15.1	.22	.26
2000 +	46	9.3	.07	.10	8	4.2	.00	-.05

$\overline{Y} = .179 \qquad \overline{R}^2 = .314$

$\overline{Y} = .234 \qquad \overline{R}^2 = .317$

TABLE A3.5

Regression Results for Independent Variables Predicting
Marriage/Remarriage (For All Unmarried Female Heads)

	Demand		Supply		Reduced Form
Endogenous:	Ordinary Least Squares	2-Stage Least Squares	Ordinary Least Squares	2-Stage Least Squares	
Potential net transfer position	-.675** (.131)	-1.92** (.189)	.615** (.167)	-.034 (.447)	
Exogenous:					
Age			-.017** (.001)	-.012** (.003)	-.012** (.001)
Whether disfigurement			-.036 (.022)	-.037 (.023)	-.034 (.023)
AFDC $1-$2000	-.107 (.058)	-.123* (.061)			-.107 (.056)
AFDC > $2000	-.014 (.075)	-.017 (.078)			-.022 (.071)
Alimony-child support (in thousands of dollars)	-.021 (.024)	-.015 (.025)			-.013 (.023)
Imputed rental income (in thousands of dollars)	-.081** (.028)	-.040 (.030)	-.013 (.027)	-.027 (.028)	-.028 (.027)
Family income (less transfers) (thousands of dollars)	-.003 (.004)	-.010** (.004)	.004 (.003)	-.0002 (.004)	-.001 (.003)
Education	.003 (.004)	-.013** (.004)			+.0008 (.003)
Experience	-.002 (.0006)	-.0006 (.0007)			-.002 (.0006)
1-2 children	.064 (.033)	-.011 (.036)	-.038 (.032)	-.031 (.033)	-.018 (.033)
3+ children	.061 (.045)	-.013 (.047)	-.087* (.039)	-.071 (.041)	-.042 (.044)
Whether black	-.075* (.034)	-.061 (.036)	-.105** (.032)	-.090** (.033)	-.094** (.033)
Whether single	.106** (.037)	.077* (.039)	-.016 (.036)	.007 (.039)	-.003 (.037)
Whether widowed	-.028 (.033)	.052 (.036)	.074* (.031)	.075** (.031)	.064* (.033)
City size	-.004 (.007)	-.008 (.007)	-.008 (.006)	-.008 (.006)	-.009 (.006)
R^2	.150	.118	.236	.224	.229

$\overline{Y}$ = .180

N = 986

*Significant at .05 level.

**Significant at .01 level.

Chapter 4

OLDER CHILDREN AND SPLITTING OFF

Daniel H. Hill and Martha S. Hill

Introduction

The departure of children from their parents' households is the most univer-
sal type of family composition change. Most children do, of course, leave their
parents eventually, but the timing of this event varies greatly among families,
and sometimes separation is only achieved piecemeal in a series of departures and
returns. About half of all young women are still in their parents' homes by age
20, and over half of all young men are still there by age 21. Five years pass
before almost all of them move out. Women are consistently about one year younger
than men when they leave, probably in part because of the tendency of women to
marry men who are a year or two their seniors.

The timing of this departure is frequently important, since the sharing of
household resources between parents and children can be an economic benefit or
necessity for either generation or both. This chapter examines this type of
change in family composition, its effect on the economic well-being of the family
and the children, and some of the factors that influence its timing.

Analysis

I. DEFINITION OF A SPLITOFF

Precise identification of the time when children separate from their parents
is difficult due to ambiguity in the definition of a household. Two characteristics commonly associated with a household—that members live together in a
dwelling unit and that they share resources—have been used in this study as the
basis for determining whether or not a child has established a household separate from that of his or her parents. For the purposes of this analysis, children
who had established separate households were termed "splitoffs." They are defined
as children who were living in the parental family or only temporarily away from
it in 1968 when the study began and who subsequently moved out either to get
married or to start their own households as single adults. The term "own household" means anywhere the splitoff lives other than with his or her original family
and other than institutional housing.[1]

---

[1] Also included in this category as splitoffs were: children who married and continued living in the parental dwelling but in a clearly separate unit of the
dwelling, college students living in off-campus housing who were clearly self-
supporting, and students or members of the armed forces who were married and
living in married housing provided by the relevant institution.

II. AGE, SEX, AND HOUSEHOLD MEMBERSHIP

Most children left the parental household between the ages of 18 and 25, and daughters tended, on the average, to split about one year earlier than sons. The relationship between household status and age of splitting indicated that the age distribution of the percent who split tended to conform to a type of curve known as a Gompertz curve.[2] When the percentage who had become either a household head or wife was graphed on the vertical axis, and age on the horizontal axis, a flattened S-shaped curve resulted.[3] The slope of the curve was always positive and at first increased and then decreased. This Gompertz curve pattern appears to hold both in the cross section and longitudinally, as is shown by Figures 4.1 and 4.2. In Figure 4.1, the portion of children in each age group who had become heads or wives by the final year is plotted as a function of the age in the final year.[4] This graph shows that females, as a group, began leaving home at an earlier age than males by about a year. In 1974, some daughters aged 16 became splitoffs, but no sons under age 17 had yet become splitoffs.[5] In fact, in any age group, larger percentages of daughters than of sons became splitoffs.[6] The steepest increases in the percentage

---

[2] The Gompertz curve is similar to a logistic curve. However, plotting the growth increments of a logistic curve results in a symmetrical curve shaped like a normal curve, whereas plotting the growth increments of the Gompertz curve results in a curve skewed to the right. A Gompertz curve is produced when the growth increments in the logarithms of the dependent variable decrease with time by a constant proportion. The curve is S-shaped and has both upper and lower asymptotes, the lower asymptote being zero. It is characterized by a stage of increasing increments per unit of time followed by a stage of decreasing increments. An additional characteristic is a continuous decrease in the percentage change between successive unit periods of time. See Shryock and Siegel (1971), pp. 381-82.

[3] The lower boundary of the curve is zero. The upper asymptote of the curve is almost 100; the curve never reaches the 100 percent mark since a small percentage of individuals never split from parental households.

[4] The horizontal axis in Figure 4.1 represents age in 1968 + 6, which is approximately age in the final year, 1974. This method of age accounting has been chosen to facilitate investigation of the longitudinal distribution of age cohorts.

[5] The absence of younger splitoffs is in part due to instructions issued to interviewers concerning identification of splitoffs. SRC interviewers have been instructed to classify children under age 18 as splitoffs only under special circumstances. Originally, a child under age 18 could be classified as a splitoff only if he had left home to get married. In later years of the panel study, however, children under age 18 who had left home and were clearly on their own could also be classified as splitoffs.

[6] Although the graph indicates that in the group of 27-year-olds a larger percentage of males than of females became splitoffs, this result has been discounted since it was based on a sample of only 51 females and 70 males.

120

FIGURE 4.1

Percentage of Children in 1968 Who Became Heads
or Wives by 1974, by Age

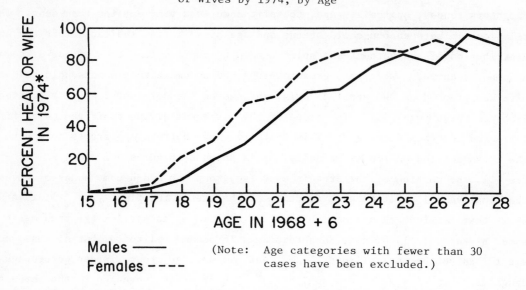

Males ——   (Note: Age categories with fewer than 30
Females – – – –   cases have been excluded.)

FIGURE 4.2

Percentage of Two Age Cohorts of Children in 1968
Who Became Heads or Wives in Successive Years

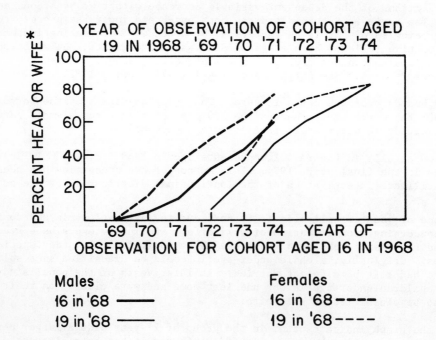

Males	Females
16 in '68 ——	16 in '68 – – – –
19 in '68 ——	19 in '68 – – – –

*This is a weighted percent.

of splitoffs occurred between about ages 17 and 20 for females and between 18 and 21 for males. These tended to level off at an earlier age for daughters than for sons (at about 23 or 24 for daughters as opposed to about 25 or 26 for sons). Approximately half of the females established separate households by age 20, whereas even at 21 less than half of the males had done so.[7]

Figure 4.2 provides a longitudinal view of the progression of separation from the parental household for two separate age cohorts--those aged 16 in 1968 and those aged 19 in 1968. This graph exhibits the same tendencies as Figure 4.1, thus indicating that the longitudinal and cross-sectional relationships between age, sex, and splitting were quite similar.[8]

Among those who became either a household head or wife during the prime ages for splitting, marriage appears to have played a more important role in the split decision for females than it did for males. As Table 4.1 shows, the percentage of splitoffs who were single was much lower for daughters than for sons. Very few daughters split to become heads of single households.

TABLE 4.1

1974 Marital Status of Splitoffs Aged 16-25, By Sex

Sex	Percent Single	Percent Married	Percent Separated, Divorced Widowed	All	Number of Cases
Male	29.8%	64.8%	5.4%	100.0%	473
Female	24.0	70.2	5.8	100.0	631

NOTE: Age is Age in 1968 + 6.

III. CHANGES IN HOUSEHOLD MEMBERSHIP

The relationship between changes in household membership and age deserves

---

[7]As Figure 4.1 shows, the age groups from about age 15 to 25 were well represented in terms of numbers of cases. However, above age 25 for males and 24 for females the number of cases in each age-sex group fell below 100, which made the implications obtainable for these groups somewhat questionable. In order to substantiate the findings, more comprehensive age distributions based on the 1970 Census 1/1000 survey (15 percent Public Use Survey) were plotted. They showed that the age distributions of percentages of heads or wives from the Panel Study were likely to be quite representative of the U. S. population of young adults.

[8]The levels of the percentages of heads or wives for the 19-year-old cohort tended to be lower than for the 16-year-old cohort at the same age since this graph excludes any individuals who had already split by age 19 in 1968.

further attention. Figures 4.3 and 4.4 outline the seven-year household membership experiences of two different groups of children. Because children aged 18
and under were likely to be just entering the split decision phase while those aged
19 and over were already well into it, the sample was subdivided into these two
age groups.[9] The younger group contained approximately five times as many children
as the older group. Household membership status in the seventh panel year was
comprised of the following categories: children; single heads; married heads or
wives; divorced, separated, or widowed heads; returners; and others (grandchildren,
brothers, nieces, etc.).[10]

As might be expected, larger percentages of the younger cohort than the older
cohort were still in the parental home after seven years. Over 60 percent of the

---

[9]Preliminary analysis indicated that the results for the topics described in this
and the next section were quite similar for males and females, so further subdivision based on sex was deemed unnecessary. The major relevant sex differences
were a tendency in the younger groups for more males than females to remain at
home and for more females than males to become married splitoffs and a tendency
in just the opposite direction in the older group.

[10]The term "returners" needs some explanation. In the Panel Study, once an individual became a splitoff, the new household of that individual was added to the
sample and was treated as a separate household even if the individual (and members of the new household) reunited with the parental household. However, such
a subfamily could be identified. Subfamilies received a particular code on the
family composition variable. (That code is "other.") Any splitoff who was part
of a subfamily was potentially a splitoff who had returned to the parental household (a returning splitoff). In order to identify those splitoffs who had actually returned to parental families, the interviews of the splitoffs in subfamilies had to be examined. Additionally, some arbitrary rules had to be made
concerning the classification of such individuals as returning splitoffs. The
following rules were the guidelines used.

A splitoff individual in a subfamily was classified as a returning splitoff if
the interview indicated that:

1. That person was residing in the parents' residence on more than
    a very temporary basis or was residing in the dwelling of a rela-
    tive other than a parent or in-law, and

2. The individual did not appear to be self-supporting.

In Figures 4.3 and 4.4, returning splitoffs are shown as the individuals represented by arrows going from either the "split" or "marry" circles back to the
"child 1968" circle and those represented by the 1974 "returned to parental
household" circles. Returning splitoffs represented in the latter fashion were
"returners"; they were returning splitoffs present in parental households in
1974.

For "returners," and returning splitoffs in general, complete information concerning the parental or substitute parental household to which they belong was
not necessarily available. So, for such individuals, the family information
used in the analysis in this chapter pertains only to the subfamily members.

FIGURE 4.3

Seven-Year Change in Household Membership Status
for Children Aged 10-18 in 1968

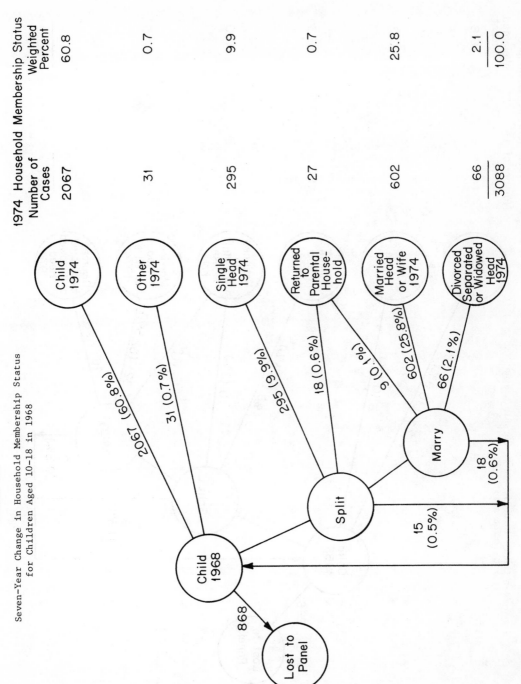

124

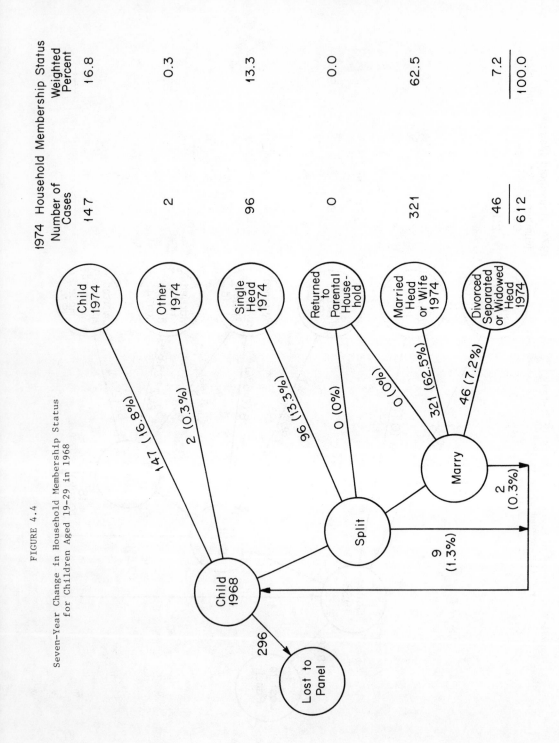

FIGURE 4.4

Seven-Year Change in Household Membership Status
for Children Aged 19-29 in 1968

1974 Household Membership Status

	Number of Cases	Weighted Percent
Child 1974	147	16.8
Other 1974	2	0.3
Single Head 1974	96	13.3
Returned to Parental Household	0	0.0
Married Head or Wife 1974	321	62.5
Divorced Separated or Widowed Head 1974	46	7.2
	612	100.0

children in the younger cohort still lived with their parents in 1974, while only about a sixth of the older cohort did. For those who did split, marriage was the most common means of establishing a household separate from that of the parents. Over 70 percent of the younger splitoffs and nearly 85 percent of the older ones had married by 1974. Since the overall frequency of marriage was higher among the older age cohort than among the younger one, it was not surprising that the frequency of becoming a divorced, separated, or widowed head was also higher among the older than among the younger age cohort. The frequency of splitting off to become a single head, however, was about the same (10 percent) regardless of age, at least for such broad age groups. Another household membership change which varied little with age was that of piecemeal departures from the parental household.[11] However, this only happened in a very small number of cases. It is somewhat surprising that the percentages of piecemeal departures were so low, since the moderately high unemployment of 1973-74 was particularly hard on young adults.[12]

Panel losses due to nonresponse were substantial. However, the greatest losses were among the younger ages, which also contained the greatest number of cases remaining in the panel. Of the original sample of 3,956 children aged 10-18 in 1968, 868 were lost either because they were members of nonrespondent families or because they became nonrespondent splitoffs; 3,088 of the original 3,956 were still part of the panel in 1974.[13]

IV. CHANGES IN HOUSEHOLD MEMBERSHIP AND HOUSEHOLD ECONOMIC STATUS OF YOUNG ADULTS

Changes in household membership had large and often adverse effects on economic status. This relationship is shown in Tables 4.2, 4.3, and 4.4. Tables 4.2 and 4.3 describe the simple bivariate relationship between household membership changes and change in economic status measured by the percentage change in both mean real family income and mean family income relative to a needs standard. Table 4.2 applies to the younger age group; Table 4.3 applies to the older age

---

[11]A piecemeal departure occurs when an individual who has become a splitoff returns to become a member of the parental household at least once.

[12]Of the splitoffs who returned to parental households during the seven years, however, only slightly over one-fifth of those in the older age cohort and less than one-seventh of those in the younger age cohort were classified as unemployed or looking for work when they returned. On the other hand, over half of all splitoffs who returned during the period 1968-1974 did so in 1973, a year of very high unemployment.

[13]A sex differential in nonresponse did exist, however. Of those lost due to nonresponse, over half of the younger age cohort and over two-thirds of the older age cohort were males.

TABLE 4.2

Seven-Year Change in Economic Status
by Seven-Year Change in Household Membership Status
(For Children Aged 10-18 in 1968)

Change in Household Membership Status	Number of Cases	Weighted Percent	Average 1967 Family Income	Percent Change in Average Real Income 1967-1973	Average 1967 Family Income/Needs	Percent Change in Average Real Family Income/Needs 1967-1973
Remained in Parental Household	2067	60.8%	$10,716	35.6%	2.126	42.7%
Returned to Parental Household	27	0.7	9,191	-66.4	1.668	-25.4
Became Single Head	295	9.9	10,713	-65.1	2.197	-25.4
Became Married Head or Wife	602	25.8	9,870	-18.9	1.999	29.5
Became Divorced, Separated, or Widowed Head	66	2.1	8,106	-53.1	1.651	-7.7
Became Other	31	0.7	5,894	72.5	1.198	98.7
All	3088	100.0%	$10,397	10.0	2.080	31.3
Panel Losses	868		$10,603		2.052	

TABLE 4.3

Seven-Year Change in Economic Status
by Seven-Year Change in Household Membership Status
(For Children Aged 19-29 In 1968)

Membership Status	Number of Cases	Weighted Percent	Average 1967 Family Income	Percent Change in Average Real Income 1967-1973	Average 1967 Family Income/Needs	Percent Change in Average Real Family Income/Needs 1967-1973
Remained in Paren- tal Household	147	16.8%	$10,526	23.7%	2.581	34.0%
Returned to Parental Household	0	0.0	--	--	--	--
Became Single Head	96	13.3	10,921	-50.1	2.705	-9.8
Became Married Head or Wife	321	62.5	12,254	-12.3	2.970	15.7
Became Divorced, Separated, or Widowed Head	46	7.2	10,973	-27.7	2.794	7.6
Became Other	2	0.3	6,160	90.7	0.859	133.1
All	612	100.0%	$11,679	-12.5	2.851	14.8
Panel Losses	296		$10,936		2.752	

TABLE 4.4

Unadjusted and Adjusted Mean Change in Real Income/Needs
by Change in Household Membership Status
(For Children Aged 10-29 in 1968)

Household Membership Change	Children Aged 10-18 in 1968				Children Aged 19-29 in 1968			
	Number of Cases	Weighted Percent	Unadjusted Mean	Adjusted Mean*	Number of Cases	Weighted Percent	Unadjusted Mean	Adjusted Mean*
Remained in Parental Household	2057	61.1%	55.2	64.8	147	17.0%	52.1	39.5
Returned to Parental Household	27	0.8	14.9	3.6	0	0.0	--	--
Became Single Head	290	9.8	4.1	-6.0	92	13.3	33.7	28.5
Became Married Head or Wife	583	25.6	78.4	62.7	303	62.2	56.0	60.7
Became Divorced, Separated, or Widowed Head	65	2.1	31.8	-1.3	45	7.2	41.7	40.3
Became Other	31	0.7	169.2	162.7	2	0.3	128.5	124.4
All		100.0%	56.2		589	100.0%	51.5	

Eta^2			.048				.007	
F			30.83				8.38	
$Beta^2$				.057				.015
Partial R^2				.053				.007
F				36.98				20.28

Note: Cases where the percentage change in income/needs was more than five standard deviations above the mean were excluded.

*Statistical adjustments were made for the individual's age, race, sex, completed education, and the region and city size of his residence.

group. Columns in these two tables show the initial (1967) levels of mean real family income and mean real family income/needs and the percentage change in these two measures for each household group. Initial levels are of particular interest since a percentage change is a function of the initial level.

Individuals who remained in the parental household averaged substantial gains in economic status. For the younger group of children, the mean increases amounted to 35.6 percent. Young adults who split to become single heads, on the other hand, did not fare very well economically; these individuals averaged losses rather than gains in economic status, and these losses were greater than those of any of the other household membership groups. Many who split and subsequently became divorced, separated, or widowed heads did not do as badly as the single heads, but they also did not tend to do as well as those who remained with parents. Individuals who became married heads or wives fared better economically than any other group of splitoffs.[14] A very small household membership group registering by far the greatest gains in economic status, however, was composed of individuals who entered households headed by their grandparents, aunts, brothers, and so on. This change appears large because, on average, these children came from families with very low incomes.

As mentioned earlier, a substantial number of cases was lost due to non-response. However, as Tables 4.2 and 4.3 show, the initial economic status of the parental families of young adults who were lost due to nonresponse was very similar to that of young adults who remained part of the panel. Assuming that the characteristics of nonresponse families and of response families were correlated in the same manner with their children's characteristics, then response biases were negligible.

Table 4.4 is concerned with the relation between change in household membership and change in economic status, net of several relevant demographic factors.[15]

---

[14] It has been pointed out to us that concentration on change in average economic status resulting from change in family composition obscures some interesting behavior. In particular, the *variance* of change in average economic status was approximately three times greater for those individuals who split from the parental unit than for those who remained. One interpretation of this fact is that those individuals who began in poor families became relatively better off (especially in terms of income/needs) when they split, while those from more affluent families experienced a relative decline in economic status. Whether this phenomenon represents intergenerational mobility, a simple regression effect, or a result of differential early investments in human capital is a subject ripe for investigation. Unfortunately, it is also a topic beyond the scope of the present paper.

[15] See Tables A4.1a and A4.1b for details concerning factors controlled for.

The figures presented in the "adjusted" columns of this table have been adjusted
by multiple regression. Two separate MCA's, one for the younger cohort and one
for the older cohort, were performed on the percentage change in family real
income/needs as the measure of change in economic status. Change in household
membership status was included as a predictor along with the following demographic
factors: age, city size, region, completed education, race, and sex.

From the regression analysis it can be seen that, for individuals who remained
with parents, change in economic status varied with age. Those from the younger
age group fared better economically than those from the older age group, although
both groups who remained with parents averaged substantial gains in economic status. The trend appeared in both the simple bivariate relation between change in
household membership and change in economic status and in the multivariate relationship with controls for other relevant demographic characteristics.

The relationship between change in household membership and change in economic status was not as clear-cut for individuals who became married heads or wives
as it was for those who remained with parents. Those who became married averaged
substantial increases in economic status when income relative to a needs standard
was the measure used; however, as indicated in Tables 4.2 and 4.3, this group registered a decline in mean income. Those who married tended to fare worse economically than those who remained with parents when the measure of change in economic
status was either percentage change in mean family income or percentage change
in mean family income/needs; however, this tendency was reversed when mean percentage change in income/needs was the measure of change in economic status.

As we said earlier, splitoffs who became single heads fared worse economically
than any other group analyzed, although single heads from the older age cohort
tended to do better than those from the younger age cohort. When change in economic status was measured as percentage change in mean income or percentage change in
mean income/needs, as in Tables 4.2 and 4.3, single heads registered substantial
losses in economic status.[16] When mean percent change in income/needs was used
as the measure of change in economic status, as in Table 4.4, single heads registered only small economic increases.[17] Introduction of controls for other demographic characteristics made these increases even smaller and, in fact, turned the

---

[16]That the decrease in status is substantially smaller when income/needs is used
as the measure indicates that children who became single heads experienced declines in both income and needs.

[17]Mean change measures are much more sensitive to extreme cases than are change
in means measures. The increases in status indicated here are undoubtedly due
to a few individuals who had very large increases in income/needs relative to
their former levels.

increase into a decline for the younger age cohort.

The economic well-being of individuals who married and then became divorced, separated, or widowed varied directly with age. In the younger age group, divorced, separated, or widowed heads registered declines in mean income and mean income/needs (Table 4.2). They also registered a mean increase in income/needs which changed to a decrease when other demographic factors were controlled for (Table 4.4). In the older age group, divorced, separated, or widowed heads, although averaging a decline in mean income, registered an increase in mean income/needs (Table 4.3) and a mean increase in income/needs (Table 4.4), the latter holding irrespective of controls for other demographic factors.

Individuals who entered the households of grandparents, aunts, brothers, and so on, registered the highest percentage increases in income and income/needs. The initial level of economic status (Table 4.2), on average, was quite low for these individuals, and they appeared to be moving out of the original households in order to improve their economic well-being.

The ability of change in household membership to explain variation in change in economic status is of importance in assessing the value of the results presented in this section. Since change in household composition was only one of the predictors used in the MCAs to explain variation in the change income/needs, its explanatory power can be compared with that of the other demographic factors included as predictors. Table 4.5 provides information concerning the relative importance[18] of change in household membership in explaining variation in change in economic status. For the younger group, change in household membership was more important than any of the other demographic variables used as predictors except age. For the older group, household membership change was surpassed in explanatory power by race, completed education, and age. Further information concerning the MCA results can be obtained from Tables A4.1 and A4.2 in the appendix.

Income Change

Disregarding the effects of other relevant demographic factors, some insight into the causes of the changes in economic status associated with changes in household membership may be gained by decomposing change in family income into the components of (1) change in the individual's own income and (2) change in the

---

[18]The importance of a predictor is its ability to explain variation in the dependent variable. Importance is measured by the Eta-squared and Beta-squared statistics. Each of these statistics measures the proportion of the total sum of squares explainable by the predictor. The Beta-squared statistic adjusts for the effects of all other predictors since it is based on the adjusted mean; Eta-squared statistics are based on raw means.

TABLE 4.5

Gross and Net Explanatory Power of Predictors
of Percentage Change in Real Income/Needs
(For Children Aged 10-18 in 1968 and Children Aged 19-29 in 1968)

Variable	Children Aged 10-18 in 1968			Children Aged 19-29 in 1968		
	Eta^2	$Beta^2$	Rank (by $Beta^2$)	Eta^2	$Beta^2$	Rank (by $Beta^2$)
Change in Household Membership	.048	.057	2	.007	.015	4
Age	.013	.093	1	.013	.018	3
City Size	.004	.005	5	.005	.002	7
Region	.006	.002	6	.020	.010	5
Completed Education	.010	.032	3	.029	.028	2
Race	.018	.017	4	.049	.047	1
Sex	.000	.000	7	.001	.004	6

income of other household members. The other household members in 1968 included all initial-year members of the parental family other than the given individual. The "other members" category in 1974, however, varied with household membership change. For those who remained at home, the "other members" category could have included father, mother, and any siblings still at home in 1974. For those who married, the "others" category would include a spouse. For those who entered households in which they were not a head or wife, "others" would include the head and other adults in that household. A decomposition of income change such as that described above was performed for younger and older children separately and the results are presented in Tables 4.6 and 4.7.

The major finding was that change in *family* real income primarily came from change in the income of household members *other* than the given individual. Almost all household and age groups experienced increases in *individual* real income. Only a few groups, however, averaged increases in the real income of other household members. Individuals who neither remained with parents nor entered a household headed by someone else (grandparent, etc.) tended to experience substantial declines in the real income of others in the household. This could be due to the loss of former household members and/or new household members having low income relative to former household members. Those who either remained in the parents' household or entered a household headed by someone else averaged both the greatest increases in other household members' real income and the smallest increases in individual real income. It appears that the principal financial benefit to an individual of continuing to live at home with his or her parents came at the expense of other earners in the household.

Summary

Most children split off from parental households between the ages of 18 and 25, daughters tending to split about one year earlier than sons. The majority of those who became splitoffs established married households. However, marriage seems to have been more closely related to splitting for females than for males. Only about one-tenth of all children became single heads of households by the end of the seventh year. The low frequency of splits to single households may well have been due to the economic hardships associated with such a move. Children who became single heads experienced, on average, greater declines in economic status than any other household membership group. Those who established married households fared much better. In fact, individuals establishing married households tended to do about as well as or better economically than those who remained with parents. Most of such change in economic well-being was due to changes in other household members associated with the particular change in household membership.

TABLE 4.6

Seven-Year Change in Family Real Income
by Source of Income and Change in Household Membership Status
(For Children Aged 10-18 in 1968)

Change in Household Membership Status	Number of Cases	Weighted Percent	Total Change in Family Real Income (1973-1967)	=	Change in Individual's Real Income (1973-1967)	+	Change in Others' Real Income* (1973-1967)
Remained in Parental Household	1969	59.9%	$3,862		$ 870		$2,992
Returned to Parental Household	27	0.7	4,151		2,187		1,964
Became Single Head	295	10.1	-6,974		2,639		-9,613
Became Married Head or Wife	602	26.4	-1,869		2,943		-4,812
Became Divorced, Separated, or Widowed Head	66	2.1	-4,301		2,035		-6,336
Became Other	28	0.6	5,683		1,506		4,177
All	2987	100.0%	$1,011		$1,638		$ -627

Note: Cases in which individual income was not ascertained are excluded.

*Some of the change in "others'" income resulted from change in household members, and some resulted from change in existing members' income.

TABLE 4.7

Seven-Year Change in Family Real Income
by Source of Income and Change in Household Membership Status
(For Children Aged 19-29 in 1968)

Change in Household Membership Status	Number of Cases	Weighted Percent	Total Change in Family Real Income (1073-1967) =	Change in Individual's Real Income (1973-1967) +	Change in Others' Real Income* (1973-1967)
Remained in Parental Household	127	15.6%	$2,640	$1,405	$1,235
Returned to Parental Household	0	0.0	--	--	--
Became Single Head	96	13.5	-5,470	3,647	-9,117
Became Married Head or Wife	321	63.4	-1,508	4,078	-5,586
Became Divorced, Separated, or Widowed Head	46	7.3	-3,037	4,428	-7,465
Became Other	2	0.3	5,590	629	4,961
All	592	100.0%	$-1,489	$3,620	$-5,109

Note: Cases in which individual income was not ascertained are excluded.

*
Some of the change in "others" income resulted from change in household members, and some resulted from change in existing members' income.

V. THE MODEL OF THE DECISION TO SPLIT OFF

Separation from the parental household is a normal part of the life cycle for most individuals. The first part of this chapter has shown, however, that there is considerable individual variation in the timing of this event. Since household composition has important effects on the economic well-being of the individuals involved, this variation warrants investigation.

The general view of the split decision is that both the child and the other members of the family (primarily the parents) want the child to form an independent household eventually. The timing of this departure, however, is affected by various factors. In particular, the chance that the child will remain in the household during any given period is a function of both his willingness to stay (the demand for current arrangement) and the willingness of other family members to have him stay (the supply of current arrangement). Each of these relationships would be affected, in opposite directions, by a "price" reflecting the extent to which the child carries his own weight financially and around the house. The position of the supply and demand relationship would be affected by various other factors which will need to be dealt with explicitly.[19]

The Price Variable

A key factor in the evaluation of the attractiveness of the current living arrangements relative to some alternative is the extent to which the child is subsidized by others in the household with respect to labor market and housework hours. This variable is simply the ratio of the child's total market and housework hours to the average housework and market hours of all family members.[20]

---

[19] Some admittedly important psychological and sociological variables were excluded from the analysis since measures of them were not available. This fact is regrettable but not necessarily disastrous. If we can assume that these omitted variables were either not systematically or strongly related to the variables *included* in the analysis, the estimated coefficients are valid.

[20] This variable was calculated according to the following formula:

$$\text{price} = \frac{\dfrac{\text{Child's Housework Hours + Child's Market Hours}}{\text{Family Housework Hours + Family Market Hours}}}{\text{Number of People in the Family}}$$

Several things should be noted about this specification of the price variable. First of all, the value of the price variable is directly proportioned to family size for any child who does some work. This reflects the assumption that in larger families the productive effort of a child is more important to the family

Because market hours are strongly correlated with age, in the analysis we standardized the price variable by age by measuring it for the year in which the child was 18 years of age.[21]

This net transfer variable is of particular importance in understanding the split decision because there are strong reasons to believe that its value (at least in part) is determined within the context of the model. For equity and financial reasons, the extent to which the child carries his own weight in the household (as measured by the net transfer variable) should affect the degree to which both the child and the other members of the family desire to maintain current living arrangements, though in opposite directions. These effects for the various parties involved should create incentives for adjusting the level of the net transfer variable toward the "equilibrium" level. For instance, if at some level of net transfer the child's desire to remain in the parental family is greater than the desire of other family members to have him do so, he should be able to rectify the situation by increasing his net transfer position by working more either in the home or in the marketplace. The desire of the other family members to maintain the current arrangements should be positively associated with the net transfer position, while that of the individual should be negatively associated with it. It is reasonable to believe that this condition would be met, and it is important to recognize and deal with the resulting simultaneity. To this end we have defined the "Demand Schedule for Current Arrangements" as the relationship between the child's desire to maintain the current living arrangements and the net transfer position variable. The position of this "demand schedule" would, of course, be affected by factors such as housing and employment conditions, and these have been included in estimating this relationship.

The "Supply Schedule for Current Arrangements" has been similarly defined as the relation between the desire of other family members to maintain the current living arrangments (quantity) and the net transfer position variable (price). It

---

and the child than in small families because the family's work "load" is larger. Second, no attempt is made to value the time inputs of the family members for the following reason: There is no theoretically sound way to evaluate housework hours. One would need to know the elasticity of substitution between each member's housework hours and those of all the wage earners in addition to elasticity of work hours to housework hours in order to evaluate this time.

[21]As many variables as possible were also measured during this year. Because of computer software limitations, however, some variables which probably should have been so measured were not. For this and other reasons mentioned below, age in 1968 (in dummy variable form) was included as a control in the estimation of all the relationships.

138

too should be affected by other factors.[22]

These other variables in the model of the split decision can be classified in one of three groups: those which affect both supply and demand, those whose effect is primarily on the level of demand, and those whose effect is primarily on supply.

Factors Affecting Both Supply and Demand

This group of variables includes age of child, whether or not the child has an income of his own, and race. Age should affect demand partly because it is closely related to the labor market opportunities available to the child. Employers are less willing to give jobs which involve substantial responsibilities (and, hence, good pay) to younger workers than they are to older, more settled workers. This would indicate that age should be related negatively to the demand for current living arrangements since older children are likely to face better employment opportunities which make alternative living arrangements more viable. Supply should also be negatively related to the child's age. Social mores are such that parents are discouraged from "kicking the kids out" at early ages, while at the same time they are encouraged to "cut the apronstrings" as the child ages.

Whether or not the child has an income of his own may also have an effect on both the supply and demand relationships. From the child's point of view, having some income whose allocation is at least partially discretionary makes it easier to finance a separate household and might also increase his confidence in his ability to survive independently of his parents. We therefore expected that having his own income would decrease the child's demand for current arrangements. On the supply side, if the child has some income of his own, he is less of a burden to the household than if he doesn't; hence, other family members should be more willing to maintain current arrangements.

The final variable which is seen to affect both supply and demand is race. While there are no clear *a priori* arguments which indicate the direction of racial effects on the relations involved in the split process, there are sufficient cultural differences between whites and nonwhites in this country to warrant inclusion of this variable in the analysis of supply and demand for current arrangements.

Factors Affecting Demand

The variables which are seen to affect the demand for current living arrange-

---

[22] It should be noted that these "other" variables affecting supply and demand are qualitatively different from the net transfer variable. Some of these variables may affect supply, some demand, and some even both, but none of these variables are determined within the model as is the net transfer variable.

ments relate to the child's evaluation of the merits of the potential household situation relative to the current one. There are at least two dimensions of merit which the child must consider. The first is the relative standard of living in the alternative households. Most children are probably willing to take some reduction in living standard in order to set up an independent household, but large reductions are likely to deter the child from leaving; and an improvement in living standard should act as a stimulus to splitting off. Since the change in living standard is likely to be negatively correlated with the initial (parental family) level, the standard of living in the parental household should be taken into account. Various measures of housing quality are included as proxies for the parental living standard. The variables measuring housing quality are (1) space (actual minus required number of rooms) (2) comfort (money value per room) and (3) privacy (whether the house is a single-family structure). Demand should be positively related to each of these measures since a child coming from a spacious luxurious house, *ceteris paribus*, can expect a larger decrease in living standard if he splits than a child whose family lives in a crowded apartment.

The second dimension which the child must consider is that of the employment opportunities available in the area of the parental household. Two aspects of this dimension are local unemployment and spatial concentration of jobs. The effect of local unemployment on the split decision is likely to be complex. On the one hand, the viability of establishing a new household is low when jobs are scarce, and children might do best by remaining with the parents and/or continuing their education. Some evidence of this effect was reported in Volume I of this series. On the other hand, high unemployment in one area might induce migration to less depressed areas. Children who seek employment might well be induced to split and migrate from depressed areas to less depressed areas. On *a priori* grounds, it is difficult to say which of these effects would dominate and, hence, it is difficult to predict how local unemployment would affect the demand for current living arrangements. Because of its policy relevance and potential importance, 1968 county unemployment was included as a predictor.

The concentration of jobs in the area of the parental home should have a less ambiguous effect on the child's demand for current living arrangements. If there are very few jobs within commuting distance of the parental home, the child, in order to find employment, is more likely to have to split off than if jobs are densely concentrated in the area of the parental home. As a proxy for the concentration of jobs, 1968 county population per square mile was included and was expected to have a positive effect on the demand for current arrangements.[23]

Factors Affecting Supply

The final group of variables included are those which primarily affect supply. It is difficult to pinpoint just what it is about children that makes parents want to have them around. One aspect of it undoubtedly is the extent to which the child satisfies the expectations of the parents in matters relating to education and career. If the child is satisfying these expectations, the parents should be more willing to supply the child's housing. To capture this effect, we have included a variable which is a measure of whether or not the child satisfies the parents' educational expectations.[24]

The economic well-being of the parental family may also affect its willingness to supply current arrangements. More affluent families can afford to keep children in the household even if they do not contribute much to the family. Hence, we would expect supply to be positively related to our measure of economic well-being, total family income relative to needs. One might argue that financial well-being should positively affect demand as well as supply. The view taken here, however, was that affluence *per se* is not the important factor which encourages the children to remain in the household, but rather it is the access to "consumption capital" (such as good housing and use of an automobile) which parental affluence provides. To the parents, on the other hand, family finances in themselves are very much a matter of concern.

Also related to family finances is the final supply factor—whether or not the child shares in family expenses. If the child does share in expenses, then not only would he be less of a financial burden to the family, but his apparent concern for the family well-being would be pleasing to the family. This should

---

[23] Population density is generally a very good proxy for the number of job "slots" within what people feel is commuting distance. In other words, except in areas with large numbers of retired persons, such as the Tampa-St. Petersburg area, or areas with chronic unemployment such as Appalachia, where there are people, there are jobs. Furthermore, if family size and labor force participation patterns do not vary greatly geographically, the ratio of persons per job slot would be fairly constant across geographic areas. Of course, it is the existence of job "openings" rather than job slots which is important to people seeking employment. The number of job openings in a given area, however, is highly correlated with the number of job slots.

[24] This variable was constructed by comparing responses to the question, "How much education do you expect your children to complete?" with the 1972 measure of the child's completed education. If the child was still in school throughout the panel period or if the child's education when he stopped was at least at the level expected by the parents, then the value of one was assigned for the variable; otherwise the value zero was assigned.

tend to increase the family's willingness to have the child remain in the household.

The Dependent Variable

There are several ways of measuring the timing of the split decision. One of the most obvious, using age at split as the dependent variable, has the serious drawback of not including those who did not split off during the time period measured. Another method, restricting the analysis to those individuals who did split during the period in question, would unfortunately discard an exorbitant amount of information, and the estimates thus obtained would require careful interpretation. For these reasons, the dependent variable used here was whether or not the individual remained in the household throughout the entire panel period.

The Sample

The sample that was used to estimate the model consisted of children who became 18 years old at some time during the years 1969 through 1972. Restriction of the sample to these individuals was necessary for three reasons. First, and most important, the relationships between the price variable and the dependent variable were felt to be so interrelated with age that normal application of the least squares regression technique would not adequately apportion the effects of the various independent variables on the dependent variable.[25] Therefore, the dependence of the price variable on the individual's age was purged by using measures for housework and market work hours for the year in which the individual was 18 years of age.

The second reason for restricting the sample in the above manner relates to technical and data limitations. Housework hours were not obtained for children in the first wave of interviewing and, hence, we could not include those children who were 18 years old in 1968. Furthermore, so few individuals split off between the ages of 18 and 19 that including those who became 18 in 1973 would add more "noise" than information to the 1974 analysis.

The fact that many fewer females than males became single heads of households suggests that the relationships between the split decision and the other variables

_____

[25]More technically, what was feared here was that age and the price variable were interactive in their effect of the willingness of the child to remain in the household. Not only was the demand curve of older children likely to be below that of younger, it was also likely to be steeper. The demand curve for older children was likely to be below that of younger children because as they grew older, children tended to become less willing to remain with the parents. Additionally, the demand curve for older children was likely to be steeper than the one for younger children because, with age, reductions in the amount of work expected relative to other family members became a less viable means of keeping the child in the parental home.

of the model were likely to differ considerably by sex. Indeed, since for so many women the split decision and the marriage decision were concurrent, it might have been argued that a marriage model would be more appropriate for female children. For this reason the model was estimated separately for males and females.

VI. ANALYSIS RESULTS FOR MALE CHILDREN

Table 4.8 shows the estimated effects of each of the variables on the probability of the child remaining in the household throughout the panel period. The third column of numbers in the table lists the estimated overall (or reduced form) effects and their standard errors. The first and second columns represent the effects of these variables on the demand and supply equations, respectively. These latter coefficients were estimated by using the two-stage least squares regression technique. (See Appendix B.) This technique was required in order to purge the estimated coefficients of biases resulting from the simultaneous nature of the two structural equations. In the following paragraphs these estimated effects are discussed in detail.

Price

Perhaps the most interesting finding of this analysis was that the coefficients on the price variable suggested that a market-type equilibrating mechanism was affecting the formation of new households by young male adults. Although the size of the price coefficient in the demand equation was less than twice its standard error, it was of the sign suggested by the model. For instance, the -1.245 coefficient on the price variable in the demand equation indicated that a child who did no market or housework would be approximately 60 percent more willing to remain in the home than a child whose work hours were half the value of the average family member's. Hence, it would appear that those children who received a net subsidy from their parental families had a stronger desire to remain with their parents than did other children.

On the supply side, the price coefficient was strong enough to achieve statistical significance and, as on the demand side, its effect was in the direction predicted; that is, parents who heavily subsidized their children were less willing to keep them in the household.

The +1.281 coefficient in the supply equation means that the willingness of the family to supply the nonworking child with housing was approximately 60 percentage points below that of the family whose child was working half as much as the average family member.

TABLE 4.8

Regression Results for Independent Variables Predicting
Whether Children Remain in Parental Home
(For Male Children 15-18 Years Old in 1969)

Endogenous	Two-Stage Least Squares Estimation of Demand Equation	Two-Stage Least Squares Estimation of Supply Equation	Ordinary Least Squares Estimation of Reduced Form Equation
Price	-1.245 (.756)	1.281** (.504)	
Exogenous			
Age:			
Whether 18 in 1969	-.195 (.129)	.025 (.135)	-.075 (.090)
Whether 17 in 1969	-.188 (.105)	-.291** (.107)	-.219** (.072)
Whether 16 in 1969	.108 (.152)	-.267* (.124)	-.072 (.067)
Race (Whether White)	.037 (.103)	-.049 (.112)	-.013 (.077)
Whether Has an Income	.403 (.332)	-.678** (.234)	-.133* (.059)
Whether Single-Family Dwelling	.189 (.121)		.156 (.087)
Actual-Required Number of Rooms	-.079* (.035)		-.035 (.018)
Value Per Room ($100)	.004 (.029)		.007 (.022)
1968 County Population per Square Mile (Thousands)	.021** (.007)		.011** (.004)
1968 County Unemployment	-.027 (.023)		-.016 (.015)
Family Income to Needs		.067 (.042)	.013 (.028)
Whether Shares in Expenses		.174 (.156)	.055 (.101)
Whether Satisfied Parental Education Expectations		.264** (.096)	.208** (.065)
R^2	.032	.007	.146
Number of Cases	309	309	309

* Significant at .05 level
** Significant at .01 level

NOTE: Standard errors are given in parentheses. The demand equation relates independent variables to the male child's demand for remaining in the parental home. The supply equation refers to the supply of current arrangements from the parents.

The Effects of Variables Common to Supply and Demand

The most surprising of the findings with respect to supply and demand variables was that the effects of having one's own income were *exactly* opposite to those expected for children in the sample. The coefficient on the supply side (-.678) indicated that the members of the parental household were strongly and significantly *less* willing to keep the child in the household if he had an income than if he didn't. Although the coefficient on this variable in the demand equation was not statistically significant, it too had a sign opposite to that expected. One possible explanation of these findings on the supply side is that the parents may have been willing to supply current arrangements when the child needed support, but when the child demonstrated his ability to support himself, the parents became much less willing to support him.

The *overall* effect of having his own income on the probability of the child remaining in the home during the panel period was negative and significant. The size of this coefficient, -.133, indicated the likelihood of splitting off during the panel period was 13.3 percent greater for those 18-year-old children who had some discretionary income than for those with no income.

The results for the age variable were somewhat mixed, but age, in general, affected the split decision in the predicted fashion. The demand coefficient of -.195 on whether the child was 18 years old in 1969 can be interpreted as meaning, for example, that those who were 18 years old in 1969 were 19.5 percent less willing to remain in the parental home throughout the panel period (to 1974) than were persons in the excluded age group (those who were only 15 years old in 1969). This negative relationship between age and remaining in the parental household also appeared in the reduced form estimates. Thus, it would seem that both the child and the parental family became less willing to maintain the current living arrangement as the child grew older.

Race appears to have had no significant effect on either the demand, the supply, or the reduced form equations.

The Effects of Demand Specific Variables

The most interesting policy-relevant relationship investigated in this chapter is between local labor market conditions and the demand for maintaining current living arrangements. Although it is not clear what public policy should be with respect to children remaining in the home, *per se*, it may well be that certain public programs which affect local market conditions also affect the formation of new households. The variables we used to measure local labor market conditions were the county unemployment rate and population density. As expected, county population density had significant positive effects on the male child's demand for current living arrangements. The probability of maintaining current arrangements was 1.1 percent greater for each added thousand people per square mile in the county of initial residence.

The county unemployment rate had a negative effect on the child's willingness to remain in the home, but the size of the effect was not sufficiently large to be statistically significant.

Of the housing-related variables, the only one to exhibit a significant effect on demand was the measure of space (actual/required number of rooms). Contrary to expectations, spaciousness of the home appears to have *decreased* the desire of sons to remain in it. This anomalous result may have appeared because spaciousness of the home is related to the position of the parents in the life cycle.

The Effects of Supply Specific Variables

Apparently the most important factor governing the willingness of parents to allow the male children to remain in the home was the degree to which the children satisfied the educational expectations of the parents. In both the supply and the reduced form equations, the coefficient on this variable was strongly positive and significant. The reduced form coefficient indicated a 20 percent higher likelihood of remaining in the parental family throughout the panel period for those children who completed the education expected of them by the parents than for those who did not. While both family financial well-being and whether the child shared in family expenses had the expected positive effect on supply, neither of their effects were statistically significant.

VII. ANALYSIS RESULTS FOR FEMALE CHILDREN

Table 4.9 lists the regression results for the supply, demand, and reduced form equations for female children. A quick comparison of these coefficients with those for the males shows that almost all the variable effects for the decision to split off were in the same directions for both sexes.

Price

For female children, as for males, the price variable had the predicted signs in both the supply and demand equations. For females, however, the size of the price effect was much smaller in each equation and, hence, failed to attain statistical significance. Thus, we can be much less confident that the equilibrating adjustments hypothesized were actually working in the case of female children.

The Effects of Variables Common to Supply and Demand

The age variables were stronger and more consistent predictors of the prob-

TABLE 4.9

Regression Results for Independent Variables Predicting
Whether Children Remain in Parental Home
(For Female Children 15-18 Years Old in 1969)

Endogenous	Two-Stage Least Squares Estimation of Demand Equation	Two-Stage Least Squares Estimation of Supply Equation	Ordinary Least Squares Estimation of Reduced Form Equation
Price	-.148 (.157)	.364 (.414)	
Exogenous			
Age:			
Whether 18 in 1969	-.402** (.097)	-.363** (.138)	-.442** (.107)
Whether 17 in 1969	-.259** (.077)	-.264** (.089)	-.278** (.078)
Whether 16 in 1969	-.319** (.075)	-.239* (.103)	-.290** (.073)
Race (Whether White)	-.153 (.091)	-.079 (.120)	-.173 (.087)
Whether Has an Income	-.049 (.089)	-.131 (.164)	-.019 (.061)
Whether Single-Family Dwelling	.220** (.082)		.214** (.079)
Actual-Required Number of Rooms	.008 (.027)		-.003 (.025)
Value Per Room ($100)	-.002 (.002)		-.002 (.002)
1968 County Population per Square Mile (Thousands)	.003 (.003)		.002 (.003)
1968 County Unemployment	-.031 (.018)		-.038** (.018)
Family Income to Needs		.095 (.056)	.062* (.027)
Whether Shares in Expenses		-.154 (.267)	.069 (.120)
Whether Satisfied Parental Education Expectations		.125 (.131)	.012 (.074)
R^2	.143	.036	.156
Number of Cases	270	270	270

*Significant at .05 level
**Significant at .01 level

Note: Standard errors are in parentheses. The demand equation relates independent variables to the daughter's demand for remaining in the parental home. The supply equation refers to the supply of current arrangements from the parents.

ability of maintaining current arrangements for females than they were for males. In fact, they were the most powerful predictors in all three equations for females.

Having had an independent income had only a weak and insignificant effect for females, which contrasted with that effect for males.

The race variable for females also had an insignificant effect in the structural and reduced form equations, although in both the demand and reduced form equations race came close to being significant. White female children were somewhat less likely to remain in the home throughout the panel period than were nonwhites.

It is not surprising that these demographic variables dominated the other variables in the analysis for females but did not do so for males when it is recalled that very few females, in contrast to males, split off to become single heads of households. During the panel period, most of the young women in the sample left home to marry. Age (and to some extent race) was a good predictor of marriage.

The Effects of Demand Specific Variables

The effects of the local labor market variables on the demand for female children to remain in the home had the same signs as for the males, but the relative importance of the two variables was reversed. For females, county unemployment was a much more important determinant of the split decision than was population density. The coefficient on the variable in the reduced form equation indicated in the cross section that every one percentage point increase in the unemployment rate reduced the probability that a female child would remain in the household by almost four percentage points. For young women, the model and data were deficient in the sense that it may well be the opportunities for jobs for potential spouses that mattered most, since there were still sex-based earning differentials and societal assumptions about main earners. The supply of potential husbands with jobs might have depended on local employment levels but not particularly on population density. Local unemployment might have led most of the single young men to leave the area in search of jobs and to find their wives elsewhere. It also seems probable that young women would have been less likely than young men to migrate to another area looking for jobs.

Except for value per room, which was insignificant in all equations, the housing-related variables affected demand for females to remain at home in the same direction as they did for males. Whether the house was a single-family dwelling was more important for females than for males, while actual/required number of rooms was less.

The Effects of Supply Specific Variables

One of the most interesting differences between the results for males and females was that whether or not the females satisfied the parents' educational expectations had no significant effect on the willingness of parents to supply housing. For males this was the most important variable in the supply equation.

It would seem that parents were not so concerned with their daughters' education as they were with their sons'. Traditionally, of course, education has not been as important to females as to males, since most women did not work outside the home. Perhaps many parents have not changed their attitudes in this regard despite the fact that most young women in the younger cohorts could expect to participate actively in the workforce sometime during their lives.

For females, the only significant variable of this group was family economic well-being. Female children from well-to-do families were more likely to remain in the home over the panel period than those from poorer families.

Summary

1. Most children in the sample split off from their parental households between the ages of 18 and 25 and established married households.

2. Females split off about one year earlier than did males, and they were more likely to marry immediately afterwards.

3. Most children experienced a considerable decline in economic well-being as a result of leaving the parental home, with those who became single heads of households faring the worst.

4. The decisions leading to the formation of new households by young adults were formulated into a supply and demand model and this model was estimated for male and female children separately.

5. Local labor market conditions had significant effects for both males and females. For females, local unemployment significantly decreased the probability of remaining in the parental household; while for males, population density increased that probability.

6. Of the other variables included, age was the most important for females, while whether the child had satisfied his parents' educational expectations was most important for males. Race was found to be of little importance for either males or females.

References

Morgan, James N. et al. Five Thousand American Families--Patterns of Economic
    Progress. Volume I. Ann Arbor: Institute for Social Research, 1974.

Shryock, Henry S. and Siegel, Jacob S. The Methods and Materials of Demography.
    Washington, DC: U.S. Government Printing Office, 1971.

Appendix 4.1

TABLE A4.1a (Sheet 1 of 2)

MCA of Seven-Year Percentage Change in Family Real Income/Needs
(For Children Aged 10-18 in 1968)

Variable	Number of Cases	Weighted Percent	Eta^2	Unadjusted Mean	Beta^2	Adjusted Mean
Age of Individual (1968)			.013		.093	
10	402	12.4		37.6		10.2
11	351	10.5		46.7		23.3
12	409	12.9		49.0		32.3
13	382	12.7		49.9		38.0
14	363	11.8		59.3		63.7
15	325	10.6		67.3		86.9
16	323	10.9		62.0		87.8
17	255	8.8		73.6		99.7
18	243	9.6		72.2		90.9
City Size (1974)			.004		.005	
500,000 or More	1289	35.1		51.3		52.1
100,000-499,999	656	23.3		52.6		52.8
50,000-99,999	355	13.5		65.5		67.8
25,000-49,999	155	6.5		46.4		42.9
10,000-24,999	209	9.4		65.9		64.9
Less than 10,000	389	12.2		64.5		61.2
Region (1974)			.006		.002	
Northeast	495	24.7		45.0		48.8
North Central	740	30.7		56.4		59.5
South	1381	27.3		67.1		57.8
West	437	17.3		54.5		57.9
Race			.018		.017	
White				49.9		49.9
Nonwhite				85.8		85.2
Completed Education (1972)			.010		.032	
0 Grades	9	0.1		80.8		72.4
1-5 Grades	5	0.1		0.4		4.3
6-8 Grades	468	13.9		44.8		75.1
9-11 Grades	1371	42.6		55.9		68.1
12 Grades	594	20.8		68.4		49.7
12+ Grades	48	2.0		80.3		47.3
College, No Degree	465	16.8		45.1		21.3
College, BA	65	2.5		78.6		54.3
Advanced Degree	1	0.1		-6.9		-40.7
Not Ascertained	27	1.0		60.5		37.7

TABLE A4.1a (Sheet 2 of 2)

Variable	Number of Cases	Weighted Percent	Eta^2	Unadjusted Mean	$Beta^2$	Adjusted Mean
Sex			.000		.000	
Male	1544	50.8		55.7		54.8
Female	1509	49.2		56.6		57.3
Household Membership Change			.048		.057	
Remained Child	2057	61.1		55.2		64.8
Returned to Parental Household	27	0.8		14.9		3.6
Became Single Head	290	9.8		4.1		-6.0
Became Married Head or Wife	583	25.6		78.4		62.7
Became Divorced, Separated, or Widowed Head	65	2.1		31.8		-1.3
Became Other	31	0.7		169.2		162.7

R^2 (adjusted) = .096

Mean of dependent variable = 56.2

Standard deviation = 102.9

N = 3053

TABLE A4.1b (Sheet 1 of 2)

MCA of Seven-Year Percentage Change in Family Real Income/Needs
(For Children Aged 19-29 in 1968)

Variable	Number of Cases	Weighted Percent	Eta^2	Unadjusted Mean	Beta^2	Adjusted Mean
Age of Individual (1968)			.013		.018	
19	177	30.6		53.6		53.4
20	122	20.9		48.4		48.0
21	113	20.1		65.9		67.8
22	66	11.5		41.7		46.7
23	32	5.5		48.4		49.9
24	19	2.9		74.5		74.5
25	14	1.9		21.7		13.0
26	19	3.1		38.5		25.3
27	8	0.7		38.8		24.5
28	12	1.8		12.2		-7.8
29	7	1.0		6.5		19.4
City Size (1974)			.005		.002	
500,000 or More	247	41.1		46.0		49.7
100,000-499,999	122	20.3		46.1		54.6
50,000-99,999	64	11.9		55.5		53.5
25,000-49,999	32	6.3		68.9		67.3
10,000-24,999	45	7.1		52.3		49.9
Less than 10,000	89	13.3		64.5		43.9
Region (1974)			.020		.010	
Northeast	118	29.5		40.7		43.8
North Central	148	30.4		56.9		57.8
South	246	24.8		72.1		63.5
West	77	15.3		28.1		34.3
Race			.019		.047	
White	352	87.8		42.6		42.8
Nonwhite	237	12.2		115.3		114.0
Completed Education (1972)			.029		.028	
0 Grades	29	3.9		58.8		63.4
1-5 Grades	5	0.3		103.6		102.2
6-8 Grades	26	2.9		82.2		83.4
9-11 Grades	90	9.5		48.0		42.0
12 Grades	173	25.9		75.6		74.7
12+ Grades	38	7.7		35.2		31.6
College, No Degree	101	22.3		35.4		36.0
College, BA	68	16.6		35.2		38.3
Advanced Degree	28	5.6		38.4		42.8
Not Ascertained	31	5.3		70.6		70.0

TABLE A4.1b (Sheet 2 of 2)

Variable	Number of Cases	Weighted Percent	Eta^2	Unadjusted Mean	$Beta^2$	Adjusted Mean
<u>Sex</u>			.001		.004	
Male	337	61.6		48.9		46.4
Female	252	38.4		55.7		59.7
<u>Household Membership Change</u>			.007		.015	
Remained Child	147	17.0		52.1		39.5
Returned to Parental Household	0	--		--		--
Became Single Head	92	13.3		33.7		28.5
Became Married Head or Wife	303	62.2		56.0		60.7
Became Divorced, Separated, or Widowed Head	45	7.2		41.7		40.3
Became Other	2	0.3		128.5		124.4

R^2 (adjusted) = .063

Mean of dependent variable = 51.5

Standard deviation = 107.5

N = 589

Chapter 5

YOUNG CHILDREN AND "OTHER" FAMILY MEMBERS

Greg J. Duncan and James N. Morgan

Introduction

In order to round out the picture of the experiences of all our original panel members, in this final chapter we look at sample members under 10 years old and at the remaining "other" family members.

The youngest individuals--the children, grandchildren, nieces, nephews, and others who were under 10 years of age when the panel period began--occupied a special place in the analysis of family composition change. The family changes they experienced were, for the most part, completely beyond their control. They were the victims, or beneficiaries, of the changes in economic well-being that accompanied the changes in family composition of their elders. A bivariate analysis of the changes in their economic status is given in Section I.

There were also 318 family members who were neither husbands, wives, unmarried male or female heads, nor children of any of these and who were 10 years of age or older. Of these, 133 were 30 years old or older, and they were mostly parents or parents-in-law of the household heads. Among those under 30, most of whom were grandchildren or siblings of the household heads or wives, there were 91 males and 94 females. In this analysis we looked separately at the males and females in this under-30 group since the impact of splitting and/or marrying seemed likely to be different for the two groups.

For a number of reasons, we did not attempt to estimate a sophisticated model explaining what happened to these "extra adults" in families. They were a heterogeneous group whose mutual obligations with the main family were unknown and variable. They were more likely to have income, and the absence of information about their contribution to the family (e.g., whether they paid room and board) made it difficult to know the distribution of benefits from doubling up. Their alternatives to the current arrangements included not only a separate household, but institutional living for the older or disabled ones, or a return to a parental home for younger ones staying with grandparents, or other relatives.

Analysis

I. CHILDREN UNDER 10 YEARS OF AGE

Most of these young people (over 95 percent) were children of the household heads. Of the entire group, only about one-third were in families in which *no* family composition change occurred over the seven panel years (see Table 5.1). An additional 46 percent were in families with changes that didn't involve either the head of the household or, if present, the wife. Most of these changes were rather typical life cycle changes such as additional children born into the family and/or older children splitting off. Of course, the latter type of change affected the splitoff much more than the family members left behind.

Over one-fifth of the young people, however, were in families where the head of the household, or wife, changed through marriage, divorce, separation, or death. The changes in economic well-being that accompanied these family composition changes were dramatic.[1] While the average seven-year change in family income was a 34 percent increase, children who remained with the mother after a divorce or separation experienced a 14 percent decrease in family income and an 11 percent decrease in

---

[1] As in past chapters, two different definitions of well-being were used--total family income and total family income relative to a needs standard. The initial (1967) levels of these incomes and the seven-year percentage change in each are given in the last four columns of Table 5.1.

TABLE 5.1

Seven-Year Change in Economic Status
by Change in Family Composition
(All Individuals Under 10 in 1968)

Change In Family Composition	Number of Cases	Weighted Percent	Average 1967 Family Income	Percent Change In Average Real Income 1967-1973	Average 1967 Family Income/Needs	Percent Change In Average Real Family Income/Needs 1967-1973
Children:						
No Change in Family Members	1016	32.9%	$9,517	38.4%	2.30	21.4%
Change in Family Members Other Than Head and Wife	1754	45.7	9,388	36.9	2.04	30.3
Divorce or Separation – No Remarriage						
Children Go With Husband	45	0.7	6,556	49.4	1.43	46.6
Children Go With Wife	302	6.8	8,079	-13.8	1.90	-10.7
Death of One Parent – No Remarriage	68	2.0	9,052	-11.6	1.99	-7.2
Single Parent* Remarried	199	5.3	6,157	117.2	1.60	70.0
Other	86	2.2	7,241	25.4	1.88	-1.5
Other Relation To Head (Grandchild, Nephew, Etc):						
No Change In Head Or Wife	131	1.3	5,628	18.0	1.17	18.7
Change In Head And/Or Wife	128	3.1	8,872	-14.0	1.64	18.3
All	3729	100.0%	$9,034	34.4%	2.06	24.3%

*Includes parents who were unmarried in 1968 and those who were married in 1968 and subsequently divorced or widowed.

MTR 7120

family income relative to a needs standard.[2] Perhaps even more dramatic was the statistic reported in Chapter 1--that nearly one-quarter of the children whose families experienced this change fell into poverty as a result of it.

A smaller number of children were members of families in which one parent died. If the surviving spouse did not remarry, the adverse effects of the change due to death were similar to those in divorced families: Real income fell by 12 percent, income/needs by 7 percent.

But some family composition changes could also be beneficial rather than detrimental: About 5 percent of the young people were in families where a remarriage occurred--that of a parent who was unmarried at the beginning of the period or a parent who was divorced during the initial panel years. For these children, family income more than doubled and family income/needs rose by 70 percent. Almost one-quarter of these children were in poverty in the initial year but were out of it by the seventh year.

A final interesting group that benefited from family composition change consisted of the children who remained with the father after a divorce or separation. This group was small (one-tenth the size of the group that stayed with the mother) but the economic well-being of these children, by both income and income/needs definitions, rose by about 50 percent. *None* of the children in this group fell into the bottom fifth of the income/needs distribution. Before jumping to the conclusion that children would be better off if they went with fathers rather than mothers after divorce, it should be noted that these fathers may have been a selected subset of those most responsible and best able to care for the children.

II. "OTHERS" 30 YEARS OF AGE AND OLDER

Most of the "other" family members included among the 30 and older group were really very old.[3] Only a minority of them worked in 1968, and only a fifth worked as much as 1,500 hours. Fifteen percent of them were disabled; yet two-thirds of them were reported to be doing some of the housework and 30 percent were doing more than 20 hours of housework a week. Nearly a third of them, as many as had

---

[2] These numbers change little when adjusted by regression for the effect of several household demographic characteristics. The details of multivariate results are given in Table A5.1.

[3] There were 199 "others" 30 or older (mostly older people who probably died), 62 young "other" men and 71 "other" young women who were lost from the panel during the six-year span. Appendix 5.2 provides some comparisons of the characteristics of panel members and panel losses in each of these groups.

earnings, had transfer income, which again reflected their advanced ages.

Forty-one percent of these older "others" stayed in their initial households; another 41 percent became heads of their own separate household units without marrying; 13 percent became married family heads; and nearly 5 percent became wives. Those few who became married heads or wives improved their situation substantially (Table 5.2). Those who left the shelter of their initial households without marrying ended up substantially worse off in real income terms and somewhat worse off even in terms of the relation of 1973 income to their new lower level of needs. There were no differences between the two main groups--those who remained and those who became unmarried heads--in their initial family incomes, but the latter came from families with a lower income/needs level. The implication is that those who split off came from families somewhat less able to continue to provide for them, or less attractive for them to stay in.

III. "OTHER" FEMALES UNDER 30

Most of the females who were among the "other" individuals under 30 were in school (70 percent). They were in families whose incomes were somewhat lower than average and whose income in relation to needs were substantially below average. Nearly half were in families in the bottom fifth of the income/needs range (see Appendix 5.2). Twenty-nine percent had some income, almost always from earnings, and more than half of these shared in the family expenses. Three-fourths of them helped with the housework.

Few of these young women stayed in these initial households. More than half became wives in a new household and nearly a third ended up as unmarried heads of their own households (Table 5.3). Those who became wives came from families in better economic circumstances than those who became heads of their own households, but those who married increased their family income so much that they had a higher percentage increase in income/needs than those who stayed single.

IV. "OTHER" MALES UNDER 30

The young males among the group of "other" individuals were less likely than females to be in school initially and were more likely to have income. More than a third had earnings and, again, a majority of these shared in the family expenses. Seventeen percent (as against 10 percent of the females) were working 1,500 hours or more in 1967. Young men were less likely to be helping with housework than were young women: Only a little over a third did any and most of these less than ten hours of housework a week, whereas nearly a third of the young females did more

TABLE 5.2

Seven-Year Change in Real Income and Real Income/Needs
by Family Composition Change
("Others" 30 Years of Age or Older in 1968)

Relation to Head in 1974	Unweighted Number of Observations	Weighted Percent	Average 1967 Family Income	Percent Change in Average Real Income 1967-1973	Average 1967 Family Income/ Needs	Percent Change in Average Real Family Income/Needs 1967-1973
Unmarried Head	60	40.7%	$9,533	-20.9	2.364	-8.8
Married Head	10	13.4	8,854	5.4	1.795	50.6
Wives	4	4.9	5,576	125.4	1.392	241.2
Children	1	--	13,290	-91.9	1.970	-77.9
Remained Other	58	40.9	9,240	6.7	3.182	11.3
All	133	100.0%	$9,126	1.6	2.574	13.6
Panel Losses	199		$8,685		2.42	

MTR 2075

TABLE 5.3

Seven-Year Change in Real Income and Real Income/Needs
by Family Composition Change
(All "Other" Females Younger Than 30 Years of Age in 1968)

Relation to Head in 1974	Unweighted Number of Observations	Weighted Percent	Average 1967 Family Income	Percent Change in Average Real Income 1967-1973	Average 1967 Family Income/ Needs	Percent Change in Average Real Family Income/Needs 1967-1973
Unmarried Head	45	32.0%	$6,484	-16.4	1.809	1.5
Married Head	2	2.4	10,191	-8.8	1.570	145.4
Wives	37	54.4	9,169	10.4	1.905	58.9
Children	5	8.9	6,501	27.1	0.829	139.0
Other	5	2.3	5,272	-2.4	0.696	77.6
All	94	100.0%	$8,009	3.9	1.743	45.3
Panel Losses	71		$6,290		1.44	

MTR 2075

than ten hours of housework. These young men were in families with still lower average income and lower average income/needs than the families with whom the females resided.

Most of the young men, too, started new households as unmarried heads or as husbands. The young men who got married came from families with substantially higher incomes and income/needs than those who became single heads of households, but since relative change in status depended on both initial and ending position, even for those splitoffs who got married and who ended up better off than the others, their *percentage increase* was negative for real income and relatively smaller than others' for income/needs (Table 5.4).

Both males and females seemed more likely to marry if they came from families with higher incomes. More importantly, after splitting off they were clearly better off married than single. That this difference was greater for the females than for the males was yet another indication of the differential incomes of men and women resulting from different rates of pay and the societal assumption that women should stay home and take care of the children.

There were minorities among both the young male and young female "other" family members living in the household of a parent. These individuals and one or both parents may have been living with grandparents at the start of the study, and they generally became better off after splitting off.

Each of these groups of "other" individuals consisted of only a small number of cases and the relative panel losses were greater for them than for the other groups of sample individuals. Losses among the older "other" individuals were particularly great, largely because of death; 60 percent of them were 75 years of age or older in 1968, and 75 percent were 65 or older. Tables 5.2, 5.3, and 5.4 give the number of cases lost to the panel and their initial family income and income/needs. As the tables show, the panel losses do not appear to have differed substantially from persons still in the panel. Appendix 5.2 gives a number of descriptive characteristics for the three groups of "others" and for the similar "others" who were lost from the panel.

With such small numbers, averages can be distorted by extreme cases, but our change estimates, which are ratios of averages rather than average ratios, have reduced that danger somewhat. We have also looked at the *distribution* of changes in economic status rather than mean changes, using change in decile position on family income or on family income/needs. Both of these methods automatically take account of inflation. A set of such tables appears in Appendix 5.3. It shows the same pattern of dominance of change in economic status by changes in marital status.

TABLE 5.4

Seven-Year Change in Real Income and Real Income/Needs
by Family Composition Change
("Other" Males Younger Than 30 Years of Age in 1968)

Relation To Head in 1974	Unweighted Number of Observations	Weighted Percent	Average 1967 Family Income	Percent Change in Average Real Income 1967-1973	Average 1967 Family Income/ Needs	Percent Change in Average Real Family Income/Needs 1967-1973
Unmarried Head	48	45.8%	$5,246	20.1	0.992	67.8
Married Head	23	35.1	10,637	-20.9	2.595	5.0
Wife	0	--	--	--	--	--
Children	11	15.1	6,134	14.8	1.026	51.6
Other	9	4.1	5,771	20.5	0.761	80.0
All	91	100.0%	$7,293	-1.5	1.551	28.9
Panel Losses	62		$8,302		1.91	

MTR 2075

V. MULTIVARIATE ANALYSIS FOR "OTHERS"

The question arises whether the change in status for these three groups was
the result of anything except their changes in living arrangements and marital
status and/or whether the apparent effects of changes in living arrangements were
really partly the effect of age, race, education, or something else. Consequently,
we ran multiple regressions with categorical predictors on the percentage change
in income/needs from 1967 to 1973 for each of the three groups—young males, young
females, and "others" 30 or older. In each case we ran the analysis with and without their "ending family status" so that the increase in the multiple correlation
squared would give an indication of the partial or marginal effect of changed family situation. The results are given in Tables 5.5 and 5.6.

Whether or not the older "others" became household heads or remained where
they were had no significant net effect on their change in economic status. That
change was affected by their own education level and to some extent by their age.
Those who were older and better-educated did better, though a small group with no
education also did well.

For the young women, the adjusted effect of change in family status was much
greater after adjustment for intercorrelations with other characteristics and accounted for more than a fourth of the remaining variance. All the other characteristics accounted for about a fourth of the total variance in the dependent variable.
Young women who were 15-19 years old (in 1968), who lived in the north central or
southern section of the country, or who dropped out of high school attained a more
improved situation than did others.

For the young men, change in family status also increased in importance after
adjustments by regression, though this was less important than for the women. Age,
education, region, and size of the largest city in the area were all important determinants of changes in economic status of "other" young men. Those who did better were well-educated 15-19 year olds in 1968 who lived in north central or
southern states in or near a very large metropolitan area.

Since our focus is not on demographic explanations but on the impact of decisions about marriage and living arrangements, changes in income/needs which
have been adjusted for demographic differences, as well as the actual unadjusted
figures, are given in Table 5.6. The economic advantages to young men in staying
unmarried were substantially increased when correlated differences in age, education, and area were accounted for. The advantages to young women in getting married showed substantial increases when we included these variables. The economic
status of the older "others" were not much affected by living arrangements, whether
or not their demographic characteristics were taken into account.

TABLE 5.5

Relative Importance (Beta^2) of Various Characteristics in Accounting
For Percent Change in Income/Needs, 1967-1973
(For Initially "Other" Family Members)

Variable	Young Males			Young Females			Older Others 30 or Older		
	Eta^2	Beta^2	Rank (By Beta^2)	Eta^2	Beta^2	Rank (By Beta^2)	Eta^2	Beta^2	Rank (By Beta^2)
Age	.081	.087	5	.064	.124	3	.090	.047	2
Size (Area) of Nearest City	.120	.154	4	.210	.061	5	.035	.018	5
Region	.079	.310	2	.046	.112	4	.125	.036	3
Education	.218	.348	1	.279	.162	2	.651	.516	1
Race	.004	.019	6	.069	.056	6	.000	.011	6
Ending Status	.050	.157	3	.118	.258	1	.212	.028	4
Sex							.000	.000	7
Number of Observations	91			92			133		
Average Change in Income/Needs	87%			185%			33%		
Multiple Correlation Squared	.294			.467			.676		

MTR 2090

166

TABLE 5.6

Raw and Adjusted Percentage Increases in Income/Needs
For Initially "Other" Family Members (Neither Head, Wife, Nor Children),
Adjusted by Regression (see Table 5.5) But Not For Inflation

	Young Males			Young Females			Older Others (30 or Older)		
	Number of Observations	Unadjusted Mean	Adjusted[a] Mean	Number of Observations	Unadjusted Mean	Adjusted[a] Mean	Number of Observations	Unadjusted Mean	Adjusted[a] Mean
Unmarried Head	48	112%	144%	44	53%	-11%	60	4%	17%
Married Head	23	43	10	2	--	--	10	46	62
Wife	--	--	--	36	246	275	4	--	--
Children	11	118	97	5	--	--	1	--	--
Other	9	--	--	5	--	--	58	35	35
Eta²	.050			.118			.212		
F-Test of Eta²	1.7			2.9*			8.7**		
Beta²		.157			.258			.028	
Partial R²		.034			.271			.000	
F-Test of Partial R²		1.9			14.3**			0.0	

NOTE: Results based on fewer than ten cases are not shown.

*Significant at p < .05 level
**Significant at p < .01 level

[a]The means are adjusted by regression for the effects of age, city size, region, education, race, and sex.

MTR #2090

Applying standard statistical tests, which are nonconservative because of the clustered nature of the sample and some heteroscedasticity, we found that 1974 family status for young male "others" was not significant in the multivariate context, although the estimated effect becomes larger. For young females, a significant and strong unadjusted effect became much stronger and more significant when adjusted for the effects of other predictors. For the older "others," an apparently strong and significant effect became small and nonsignificant when age, education, and the other background variables were considered.

Summary

1. The experiences of the young children in the sample reinforced the findings of previous chapters regarding the relationship between family composition changes and changes in economic status. For the children, most changes that involved their parents were detrimental, especially if they resulted in a single parent heading the household.

2. The extra people in households (who were neither heads, wives, nor children) were of two different types. The first type, those 30 or older, were mostly quite old and were living with their children; their economic status was not much affected by whether they stayed there or formed their own households. In any case, many of them died and disappeared from the panel.

3. Among the second type, those under 30, decisions about splitting and getting married had substantial effects on their economic status, particularly for the females. Young women who started their own households without marrying ended up much worse off than other young women, even when their smaller needs and their higher initial status were considered. Young men who became married heads of new households ended up with higher incomes and income/needs than those who became single household heads; on the other hand, this group became somewhat worse off relative to their own initial position, which was quite high. Thus, leaving a doubled-up household situation involved some potential sacrifice, which was offset if the individual also got married, particularly if that individual was a young woman.

Appendix 5.1

TABLE A5.1a (Sheet 1 of 3)

MCA Results for Regression Analysis of Percentage Change
in Real Family Income Relative to Needs
(All Sample Individuals Under Age 10 in 1968)

Variable	Number of Observations	Weighted Percent	Unadjusted Mean	Adjusted Mean
Family Composition Change			$\eta^2=.040$	$\beta^2=.037$
Children:				
No Change in Family Members	1011	32.8%	30.2%	31.7%
Change in Members Other than Head and Wife	1750	45.7	41.6	41.8
Divorce or Separation:				
Children go with Husband	45	0.7	54.3	48.7
Children go with Wife	302	6.8	6.7	8.6
Death of One Parent -- No Remarriage	64	2.0	11.5	7.9
Single Parent Remarried	197	5.3	100.0	102.6
Other	86	2.2	27.7	29.8
Other Relation to Head:				
No Change in Head or Wife	131	1.3	37.4	17.5
Change in Head and/or Wife	128	3.2	76.1	53.9
Marital Status of Head, 1968			$\eta^2=.007$	$\beta^2=.021$
Married	2835	88.5	37.2	42.7
Single	157	1.7	51.7	20.0
Widowed	139	2.4	36.4	-22.8
Divorced	149	2.8	50.0	10.2
Separated	402	3.5	60.5	20.7
Married, Spouse Absent	29	0.9	23.4	-10.1
NA	3	0.1	203.8	174.5

TABLE A5.1a (Sheet 2 of 3)

Variable	Number of Observations	Weighted Percent	Unadjusted Mean	Adjusted Mean
Sex of Head, 1968			$\eta^2=.003$	$\beta^2=.017$
Male	2849	89.0	37.0	34.1
Female	865	11.0	52.8	74.0
Age of Head, 1968			$\eta^2=.007$	$\beta^2=.008$
< 25	303	7.5	44.4	33.1
25-34	1515	41.8	34.3	34.3
35-44	1262	37.4	37.6	39.1
45-54	515	10.6	47.0	48.4
55-64	102	1.7	62.3	67.4
65-74	11	0.9	103.6	103.4
>75	6	0.3	55.8	77.2
Head's Education			$\eta^2=.011$	$\beta^2=.007$
0 Grades	152	2.0	52.0	29.2
1-5	205	3.6	65.6	42.0
6-8	695	13.1	53.8	45.3
9-11	1012	21.2	30.2	30.8
12	687	20.1	29.6	30.9
12 + Nonacademic Training	316	11.3	36.6	41.7
Some College	320	13.4	47.3	52.3
BA Degree	194	9.7	35.1	40.4
Advanced Degree	96	5.1	35.8	44.8
NA	37	0.6	52.6	31.0
Race			$\eta^2=.004$	$\beta^2=.005$
White	1734	82.5	36.6	36.6
Black	1852	14.5	45.1	43.1
Spanish American	75	2.2	69.1	78.8
Oriental	42	0.7	61.7	68.3
NA	11	0.1	75.3	64.4
Region, 1968			$\eta^2=.007$	$\beta^2=.005$
Northeast	643	28.0	28.9	33.7
North Central	881	29.0	39.6	41.1
South	1655	26.8	50.5	47.6
West	535	16.2	34.8	30.2

TABLE A5.1a (Sheet 3 of 3)

Variable	Number of Observations	Weighted Percent	Unadjusted Mean	Adjusted Mean
City Size, 1968		η^2=.004		β^2=.003
>500,000	1703	39.0	31.8	32.4
100,000-499,999	751	21.1	43.0	41.8
50,000-99,999	388	12.7	43.9	45.0
25,000-49,999	150	4.9	38.6	39.6
10,000-24,999	247	9.6	42.7	43.5
< 10,000	465	12.7	45.0	43.6

$\bar{R}^2$ = .061

$\bar{Y}$ = 38.8% σ_y = 94.8%

Number of Observations = 3714

NOTE: Three observations fell more than five standard deviations above the mean and were eliminated.

Appendix 5.2

Some Characteristics of the "Other" Individuals in the Panel
and Those Lost During the Six Years

The tables in this appendix serve two purposes: to describe the three groups
of "others" in terms of their initial distributions on several dimensions and to
compare the distributions of those who were lost from the panel in case they were
different (in which case, the remaining panel members might provide biased inferences). We have already pointed out that the older "others" were mostly very old
in 1968 so that the losses are bound to be predominantly from death.

In general, there were really very few differences between the panel individuals and the panel losses among these "other" family members. The initial family
income/needs decile distribution was much the same (Table A5.2a), and the weighted
proportion still in the sample only varied between 43 and 59 percent across the
ten decile groups. Both groups were somewhat more likely to have been in the
lowest decile in 1967.

The "other" family members were likely to be either grandchildren or parents
of the household heads, but the differences between the panel members and the
lost members was insignificant (Table A5.2b).

The younger panel members were mostly in school, and the only difference
between panel members and lost members was that the young females who were lost
were less likely to have been in school in 1968 (Table A5.2c).

The older "other" individuals were more likely to have transfer incomes
(pensions), particularly those who were lost from the panel, but the differences
in sources of income between panel individuals and losses were insignificant (Table A5.2d). The bulk of the younger individuals had no income.

There was some tendency for young males who were lost from the panel to be
working 1,500 hours or more in 1967 (33 versus 17 percent, data not shown on
tables). There were no differences between panel individuals and those who were
lost in whether they were reported in 1968 as being likely to move out.

Finally, the heads of households were asked in 1968 whether the "other" individuals in their families who had any income shared in the expenses. Most of the
younger ones had no income. Among the older "others" with income, the vast majority shared in the expenses and, as we have noted previously in this chapter, they
also did a lot of housework. The younger males and females with income tended to
help with the family expenses, particularly the young males who were lost, but that
was largely because they were more likely to have income to share (Table A5.2e).

TABLE A5.2a

"Other" Individuals Still in Panel and Lost To It,
By Initial Family Money Income/Needs Decile

Family Money Income/Needs Decile In 1967	Young Males		Young Females		Older Others		All		Percent Still In Panel (Weighted)
	Panel	Losses	Panel	Losses	Panel	Losses	Panel	Losses	
Lowest Tenth	32	21	42	39	3	9	19	16	53%
2	12	9	6	6	8	11	8	10	43
3	17	11	11	14	14	14	14	14	50
4	10	17	5	13	15	14	11	14	44
5	4	7	6	8	12	9	9	9	48
6	5	4	8	11	9	7	8	7	51
7	7	14	1	6	15	10	10	9	49
8	2	8	7	3	7	8	6	7	43
9	8	6	0	7	8	10	6	9	40
Highest Tenth	3	3	14	0	9	8	9	6	59
Number of Cases	91	62	94	71	133	199	318	332	48%

MTR 7512 and 8071

TABLE A5.2b

Relation to Household of Other Individuals Remaining
in Panel and Lost to It

Relation To Head	Young Males		Young Females		Others		All	
	Panel	Losses	Panel	Losses	Panel	Losses	Panel	Losses
Brother or Sister	18	13	19	18	21	13	20	14
Parent	0	0	0	0	29	28	15	19
Grandchild	43	32	48	33	0	0	22	11
Other Relative	35	41	31	49	46	49	40	47
Non-Relative	5	15	2	0	4	10	4	9
	101	101	100	100	100	100	100	100

MTR 7512 and 8071

TABLE A5.2c

Educational Position in 1968 of "Others" by Whether Lost to Panel

Education Position of "Others" in 1968	Young Males		Young Females		Others		All	
	Panel	Losses	Panel	Losses	Panel	Losses	Panel	Losses
In School	59	51	70	43	0	0	31	17
Not in School	35	42	30	57	97	98	66	81
Not Ascertained	6	7	0	0	3	2	3	2
	100	100	100	100	100	100	100	100

MTR 7512 and 8071

TABLE A5.2d

Sources of Income of "Other" Individuals by
Whether Lost to Panel

Source of Income	Young Males		Young Females		Others		All	
	Panel	Losses	Panel	Losses	Panel	Losses	Panel	Losses
None	63	47	71	77	26	34	45	43
Labor	35	45	28	22	29	20	31	25
Transfers	2	4	1	0	29	36	16	25
Assets	0	0	0	0	1	1	1	1
Combination	0	0	0	0	13	2	7	2
Other	0	3	0	1	3	6	0	0
	100	99	100	100	101	99	101	101
Number of Cases	91	62	94	71	133	199	318	332

MTR 7512 and 8071

TABLE A5.2e

Whether "Other" Individuals Shared Expenses
with the Family in 1967 by Whether Lost to Panel

Whether Shared Expenses	Young Males		Young Females		Others		All	
	Panel	Losses	Panel	Losses	Panel	Losses	Panel	Losses
No Income	63	49	74	74	30	37	48	45
Yes, Shared	20	36	13	12	43	36	30	32
Yes, Qualified	3	0	2	1	1	2	2	2
No, Did Not Share	12	9	11	10	10	6	11	7
Not Ascertained	3	7	0	4	16	20	9	15

MTR 7512 and 8071

Appendix 5.3

Distributions of Change in Decile Position
for "Others" Show the Same Pattern

Table A5.3a shows that most of the young people in the "other" category became married or single heads of households, or wives if female, while most of the older people either became single heads or stayed "other."

More interestingly, young men were likely to be better off six years later if they became single heads and to be worse off if they became married family heads. On the other hand, young women were much more likely to be better off if they became wives than if they became single heads. Similarly, the older "other" people were more likely to be worse off if they became single heads and to be better off if they stayed as "other" in some family. Indeed, there were some substantial declines in economic status among women and those 30 or older (mostly women) who became single heads of units.

A second table, A5.3b, using change in decile position of family money income ignoring need (family size and structure) shows similar results except that young men who became single heads did not seem so much better off when we looked at income alone, ignoring their smaller needs.

TABLE A5.3a

Distribution of Change in Decile Position on Family Income/Needs by Ending Family Status
(For "Other" Family Members)

Change In Decile Position On Family Income/Needs	Under 30						30 Or Older		
	Male			Female					
	Became Single Head	Became Married Head	Others	Became Single Head	Became Married Head	Others	Became Single Head	Remained "Other"	Became Married Head Or Wife (Child)
5 or More Deciles Higher	21	11	4	0	22	31	8	0	10
2-4 Deciles Higher	26	15	71	15	37	66	15	16	26
Higher by One Decile	11	0	3	12	17	3	6	29	34
Same Decile	22	11	21	30	8	0	17	18	11
One Decile Lower	11	26	0	2	6	0	10	9	9
2-3 Deciles Lower	5	29	1	26	5	0	26	14	0
4-6 Deciles Lower	5	8	0	16	6	0	12	15	9
7-9 Deciles Lower	0	0	0	0	0	0	7	0	0
Total	101	100	100	101	101	100	101	101	99
SUMMARY:									
Better Off	58	26	77	27	76	100	29	45	70
Worse Off	21	63	1	44	17	0	55	39	18
Number of Cases	48	23	20	45	27	10	60	58	15

MTR 2070

TABLE A5.3b

Distribution of Change in Decile Position on Family Income by Ending Family Status
(For Three Groups of "Other" Family Members)

Change In Decile Position On Family Income	Under 30				30 Or Older	
	Male		Female			
	Became Single Head	Became Married Head	Became Single Head	Became Wife	Became Single Head	Remained "Other"
5 or More Deciles Higher	7	6	0	8	0	0
2-4 Deciles Higher	19	6	13	41	10	25
Higher by One Decile	9	13	10	8	10	25
Same Decile	22	13	28	16	18	16
One Decile Lower	31	1	5	10	17	13
2-3 Deciles Lower	6	48	28	10	17	14
4-6 Deciles Lower	5	13	16	3	13	8
7-9 Deciles Lower	0	0	0	4	14	0
Total	99	100	100	100	99	101
SUMMARY:						
Better Off	35	25	23	57	20	50
Worse Off	42	62	49	27	51	35
Number of Cases	48	23	45	27	60	58

MTR 2070

PART II

OTHER ANALYSES

Chapter 6

THE RELATIVE BURDEN OF HIGHER GASOLINE PRICES

John Holmes

Introduction

The Arab oil embargo of the winter of 1973–74 rudely awakened the American public to the ever-increasing dependence being placed on foreign oil imports to bridge the gap between domestic production and energy consumption. The recent quantum increase in crude oil prices coupled with the continued decline in domestic oil production has been cited as the major determinant of the two-digit inflation which currently plagues the U.S. economy. Furthermore, the quadrupling of oil prices in 1973 has deteriorated an otherwise healthy U.S. balance of payments position. Since no measurable increases in domestic oil supplies are forseeable prior to the latter part of this decade, any short-term solution to the oil problems must focus on curbing demand. Thus far, only voluntary measures have been pressed by Congress in an attempt to discourage consumption and exert downward pressure on world oil prices. Although higher energy prices and initial consumer response to appeals for conservation have reduced the growth in energy consumption, it appears that any attempt to restore a reasonable balance between domestic production and total oil consumption in the near term that relies wholly on *voluntary* measures will be woefully inadequate.

Since gasoline consumption accounts for slightly more than 40 percent of U.S. oil needs, a variety of measures for reducing demand have been suggested. Most of these plans rely on higher energy prices as the method for curtailing consumption. Since recent studies have concluded that gasoline consumption is rather price inelastic--that is, a very large price increase might be necessary to produce a rather small cut in consumption, it is important to identify any segment of the population that would suffer disproportionately from higher gasoline prices.

Analysis

Included in the seventh wave of the Panel Study of Income Dynamics was the following question: "During the last year how many miles did you and your family drive in your car/all of your cars?" As shown in Table 6.1, nearly 25 percent of all respondents reported family driving of 20,000 miles or more in 1973. Included in this distribution on annual mileage were families who did not own a car (15.9 percent). When only families who owned one or more cars were considered, the mean annual mileage per family was 15,400 miles.[1] As would be expected, car ownership and annual miles driven increased with income (see Tables A6.1a and A6.1b). Car ownership increased from slightly over 40 percent in the lowest income decile to virtually 100 percent in the highest income deciles. Also, multiple car ownership increased with income. Similarly, among car owners, the mean annual miles driven by families in the highest income decile was triple that for those families in the lowest income decile.

Commuting behavior was also measured in the panel data. For the head of a family who traveled to work either by driving alone or by car pooling, an assignment of number of trips per week was made based on the response to the question "... and, on the average how many *hours a week* did you work on your main job last year?" Combining this result with distance to work and number of weeks worked in 1973, the distribution of annual commuting miles of the head of the family was calculated.[2] Car poolers were assumed to have driven 50 percent of the time. Thus, their derived annual commuting miles were calculated to be half of those for drivers who did not belong to car pools. Ideally, the commuting miles of other members of the family unit should have been included; however, no information was available on their mode of travel to work. As shown in Table 6.2, more than 40 percent of all family heads did not drive to work, because they used other modes of transportation or because they were not currently employed. For family heads who were employed and who commuted to work via car, the mean annual commuting distance was 3,900 miles.

In analyzing the burden of higher gasoline prices, an "ability-to-pay" criterion was utilized. Using the average miles per gallon for U.S. cars (approximately 13 m.p.g.) and an average price of 55 cents per gallon for regular gasoline, the proportion of total 1973 family money income allocated to gasoline ex-

---

[1]Lansing and Hendricks (1967) reported an average of 15,800 miles for owners of one or more autos.

[2]Excludes any time attributable to vacation, sickness, being unemployed or on strike. Note, average hours worked per week refers to *main* job only.

TABLE 6.1

Total Miles Driven in 1973
(All Families)

Annual Mileage	Unweighted Number of Cases	Weighted Percent
Zero, Don't own car	1367	15.9
1 - 5,000	740	12.2
5,000 - 10,000	690	14.6
10,000 - 15,000	868	18.6
15,000 - 20,000	527	11.6
20,000 - 25,000	441	9.1
25,000 - 30,000	222	5.1
30,000 - 35,000	200	4.1
> 35,000	286	6.3
NA or Don't Know	176	2.4
Total	5,517	100.0

TABLE 6.2

Annual Commuting Miles* of Heads of Households in 1973
(All Families)

Annual Mileage	Unweighted Number of Cases	Weighted Percent
0, Doesn't Work/Drive to Work	2,538	42.5%
1 - 2,500	1,062	22.0
2,500 - 5,000	711	13.8
5,000 - 7,500	358	7.5
7,500 - 10,000	219	4.5
10,000 - 15,000	201	3.9
> 15,000	122	2.1
Not Ascertained	306	3.8
Total	5,517	100.0%

*Commuting miles refers *only* to those heads of households who drive/car pool to work.

MTR #M008947

TABLE 6.3

Mean Gasoline Expenditures as a Percentage
of Total Family Money Income (1973)
(All Families*)

Family Money Income Decile	Unweighted Number of Cases	Average Fuel Cost/ Family Money Income
Lowest	672	5.0%
Second	674	5.3
Third	604	5.3
Fourth	611	5.2
Fifth	573	4.8
Sixth	523	5.0
Seventh	482	4.2
Eighth	433	4.0
Ninth	392	3.4
Highest	374	2.7
	5,338	4.5%

*179 cases were not included because response on total miles question was NA or Don't Know.

MTR #M009817

penditures was calculated for all panel families. As shown in Table 6.3, on average, 4.5 percent of family money income was allocated to gasoline expenditures,
with the actual percentages declining from slightly over 5 percent in the lower
income deciles to approximately 3 percent in the upper income deciles.[3] It should
be noted, however, that these estimates included families who did not own cars.
Since car ownership increased significantly with income, this tended to diminish
the spread between the mean proportion of income allocated to gasoline expenditures in each income class. As Figure 6.1 shows, the mean proportion of income
spent on gasoline outlays in the lowest income quintile nearly doubled when the
sample was restricted to car-owning families. Thus, among car owners, the average percentage of income allocated to gasoline expenditures by families in the
bottom fifth of the income distribution was triple that for those in the highest
quintile.[4]

As Table 6.4 shows, there was considerable variation in the distribution of
auto fuel costs to family money income within the income deciles. About two-
thirds of the families in the bottom half of the income distribution (including
those without cars) spent less than 5 percent of their income on gasoline, but
for the upper income groups, the proportion increased steadily to 90 percent in
the highest income quintile. Among families who allocated more than 10 percent
of their income for gasoline, the disproportionate burden on some of the poor is
striking--15 percent of all families in the lowest income quintile spent more
than one-tenth of their income on gasoline, while only 2 percent of those in the
highest quintile did so. Perhaps even more astonishing is the finding that nearly
10 percent of all families in the lowest income decile allocated more than one-
fifth of their income to gasoline expenditures. Since 58 percent of the families
in the lowest income decile did not even own cars, this implies that 25 percent
of all car owners in the lowest income decile spent more than one-fifth of their
total income on gasoline charges.

Since the period covered for total miles driven was 1973, the above estimates

---

[3]These estimates are quite similar to those reported by the Energy Policy Project
(1974), pp. 116-118. Using results from the Washington Center for Metropolitan
Studies Lifestyle and Energy Surveys 1972-73, this study reported gasoline expenditures as a proportion of total annual income declined from 4.0 percent for
poor households to slightly over 2 percent for the well-off group.

[4]This inverse relationship between the proportion of income spent on gasoline and
family income persisted when *all* forms of direct energy consumption were included. Preliminary data from the Survey of Consumer Expenditures indicate that
families in the lowest income decile allocate a substantially greater share of
their income to energy use than those in the upper half of the income distribution (see Figure A6.1a). Thus, the findings of this analysis would not be altered by including expenditures on gas, electricity, and other fuels.

FIGURE 6.1

Mean Gasoline Expenditure as a
Percentage of 1973 Family Income
(Car Owners)

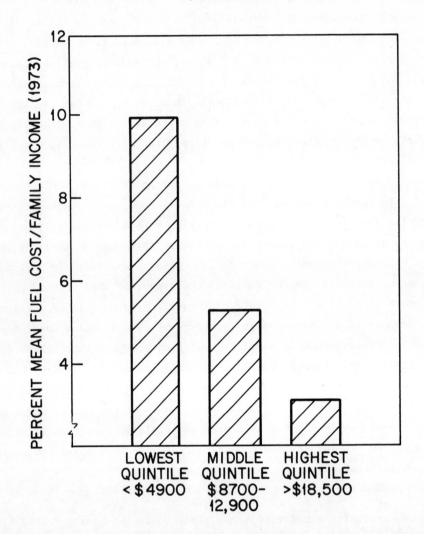

TABLE 6.4

Relative Burden of Higher Gasoline Prices
By Family Income Decile
(All Families)

Family Income Decile	Fuel Cost as Percentage of Income							
	No Car, Zero Percent	0–5 Percent	5–10 Percent	10–15 Percent	15–20 Percent	> 20 Percent	N/A	Total
Lowest	58.0%	16.7%	5.9%	4.3%	2.1%	9.3%	3.7%	100.0%
Second	36.9	29.8	14.0	6.2	3.4	5.4	4.3	100.0
Third	24.9	33.5	25.7	5.6	2.6	4.4	3.3	100.0
Fourth	13.5	49.2	20.3	10.1	1.0	2.5	3.4	100.0
Fifth	9.9	56.8	21.1	6.6	2.2	1.0	2.4	100.0
Sixth	5.9	59.0	23.8	6.3	0.9	1.8	2.3	100.0
Seventh	4.6	66.2	22.5	3.6	1.0	0.2	1.9	100.0
Eigth	1.9	75.1	19.6	1.2	0.6	0.0	1.6	100.0
Ninth	2.1	82.6	11.7	2.4	0.3	0.0	0.9	100.0
Highest	1.2	90.3	6.1	1.8	0.0	0.0	0.6	100.0

MTR #M008947

would *overstate* the actual burden of higher gasoline prices if consumers decreased their driving in response to the increased costs. Some preliminary evidence that higher gasoline prices alter the mode of travel to work is shown in Table 6.5. The proportion of heads of households who commuted to work via car pooling nearly

TABLE 6.5

Travel Mode Used by Heads of Households in Getting to Work

| | Spring | |
	1973	1974
Public Transportation	7.8%	7.2%
Car Pool	5.1	9.1
Drives Alone or with Members of Family Unit	80.4	77.1
Walk, Other	6.7	6.6
	100.0%	100.0%

doubled between 1974 and 1973. This apparent shift to car pooling may be only a reflection of the tightness of gasoline supplies in early 1974. Long queing lines at service stations, spot shortages in some areas, and restricted service hours probably forced some families to temporarily join car pools for commuting to work. Since gasoline supplies have become less scarce, the permanence of this increased use of car pooling is still uncertain. It should be noted, however, that the 1974 interviews were conducted *after* the increase in gasoline prices; thus, responses to the question on total miles driven may reflect *anticipated* mileage for that year.

Clearly, some proportion of the annual miles driven by a family is not essential to the functioning of the household. Frequent trips to stores, leisure driving, and so forth, are, in general, less essential to family well-being than is commuting to work. Some possible long-term responses to the increased cost of gasoline would be changing residence or job to be closer to work and buying fuel-economizing automobiles. Here we consider the short-term implications of the family's flexibility in adjusting its driving habits.

Focusing first on those families with low commuting/total miles ratios, we found that an average of about 40 percent of the families in each income decile spent less than one out of every ten total miles in commuting to work (see Table 6.6). Since car ownership was not nearly so widespread in the lower income

TABLE 6.6

Variation by Income Decile in Commuting*/Total Miles

(All Families)

Family Income Decile - 1973	No car	Commuting/Total Miles (Percent)								
		0-10	10-20	20-30	30-40	40-50	>50	Don't know	Total
Lowest	58.0%	30.9%	1.9%	.3%	.9%	1.1%	2.1%	4.8%	100.0%
Second	36.9	46.0	1.8	2.1	1.0	1.0	6.6	4.6	100.0
Third	24.9	43.6	6.5	6.0	1.8	2.8	9.8	4.6	100.0
Fourth	13.5	44.1	9.8	5.7	4.6	4.4	11.9	6.1	100.0
Fifth	9.9	40.4	10.6	7.9	6.3	4.5	16.0	4.5	100.0
Sixth	5.9	41.3	15.0	7.7	6.6	5.6	13.3	4.6	100.0
Seventh	4.6	35.5	17.3	7.8	7.7	6.9	17.0	3.1	100.0
Eighth	1.9	39.3	17.0	13.0	6.9	3.5	16.5	1.8	100.0
Ninth	2.1	40.5	15.5	12.3	9.2	5.5	12.4	2.4	100.0
Highest	1.2	39.6	20.6	13.3	7.6	3.9	12.1	1.8	100.0

Number of Cases: 5517

*Refers to annual commuting miles of head of household who drives to work.

strata, the proportion of car-owning families with low commuting/total miles ratios declined from 80 percent in the lowest income quintile to approximately 40 percent in the top half of the income distribution. This suggests that a substantial proportion of families had considerable flexibility in altering their driving in response to the increased cost of gasoline. Indeed, among car owners, commuting represented less than one-third of total miles driven for nearly 75 percent of all families in each income class. It should be noted, however, that a significant percentage of families may have been severely constrained in their short-term ability to decrease their driving. It appears that for one out of every seven car-owning families commuting represented more than half of their total driving. Although most of these families were in the upper half of the income distribution, a significant percentage of low-income families were also included in this group.

Thus far, we have discussed only one dimension--total family money income--in examining differences in proportion of income allocated to gasoline expenditures. Variables representing the region of residence, city size, and distance from the city center were also included to further delineate any subgroup which was particularly burdened by the higher price of gasoline. The influence of personal characteristics in determining the percentage of income spent on gasoline was investigated through the inclusion of data on the age, sex, race, education, and occupation of the head of household. A search algorithm, Automatic Interaction Detector (AID),[5] was employed to identify any subgroups for which the financial burden of higher gasoline prices widely differed. The AID technique assesses each predictor for the dichotomous division which explains the greatest amount of variance of the dependent variable. As Figure 6.2 shows, car-owning families in the three lowest income deciles whose heads were younger than age 55 allocated approximately 11 percent of their money income to gasoline outlays. This group represented nearly 10 percent of the entire population. A further subdivision of this group by income showed some families in the lowest income decile spending 15 percent of their total income on gasoline.

Ideally, only gasoline expenditures for *essential* driving would be of interest in estimating the burden of higher gasoline prices. Since the above analysis was based on total miles driven, it *overstates* the burden of increased gasoline outlays. Focusing on one of the heavily burdened subgroups--car-owning families in the three lowest money income deciles whose heads were younger than age 55 (see Figure 6.2)--we found that nearly 60 percent of these family heads traveled to work via car. The responses to the question, "...is there public transportation

---

[5]See Morgan, Baker and Sonquist (1973).

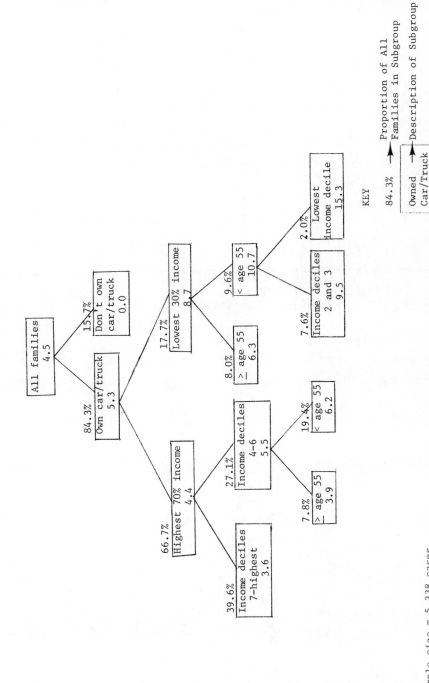

FIGURE 6.2

AID Analysis of the Relative Burden of Higher Gasoline Prices
(Average Fuel Cost/Family Income* -- Percent)

193

Sample size = 5,338 cases

* Any value greater than 48% (Ȳ + 5σᵧ) was assigned 48%

MTR #M009817

194

FIGURE 6.3

AID Analysis of the Relative Burden of Higher Gasoline Prices

(Average Fuel Cost/Family Income* -- Percent)

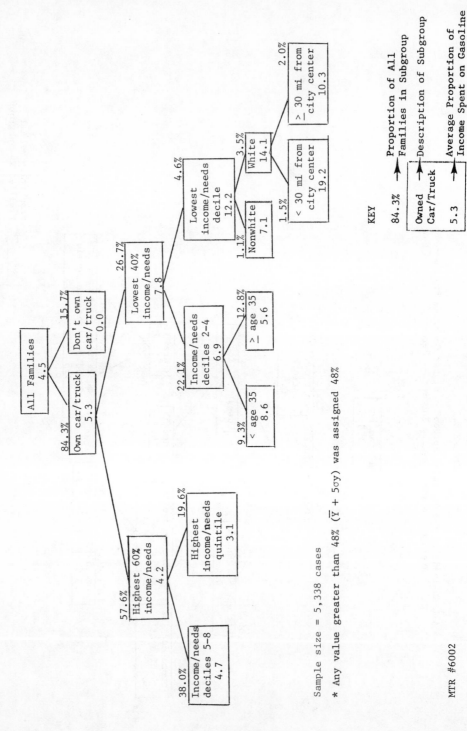

Sample size = 5,338 cases

* Any value greater than 48% ($\overline{Y} + 5\sigma y$) was assigned 48%

MTR #6002

KEY

84.3% ⟶ Proportion of All Families in Subgroup

Owned ⟶ Description of Subgroup
Car/Truck

5.3 ⟶ Average Proportion of Income Spent on Gasoline

within walking distance of (here) your house?" gave some indication of the availability of alternative transportation for these families. Nearly 55 percent of them reported that there was no public transportation within walking distance. When responses to the question "...is it (public transportation) good enough so that a person could use it to get to work?" were considered, the proportion saying that there was no alternate transportation available increased to over 70 percent.

Recognizing that families with the same total money income but with different family composition did not have the same ability to cope with the increased cost of gasoline, we measured the income of a family unit *deflated* by a minimum subsistence level.[6] This new indicator of economic well-being was substituted for money income and the same procedure described above was repeated. As shown in Figure 6.3, the income/needs variable dominated in isolating subgroups differing in proportion of income spent on gasoline. The basic difference between the results was the split on race when the other, more comprehensive, measure of economic status was employed. Among car owners in the lowest income/needs decile, the percentage of income allocated to gasoline expenditures by whites was double that for nonwhites. This division by race is somewhat puzzling. Further analysis has shown that these racial differences were only partially explained by differences in city size, distance from center of city, and adequacy of public transportation.

Summary

Although for all families gasoline expenditures as a proportion of income ranged from an average of 5 percent in the lower income deciles to slightly under 3 percent at the higher income deciles, there were subgroups in the lower income deciles for whom the proportion of income allocated to gasoline outlays were extraordinarily high. For the seven million car-owning families in the lowest third of the income distribution whose heads were younger than age 55, this amounted to slightly more than 10 percent of their total family money income. Over 70 percent of all families in this subgroup who drove to work reported having no viable public transportation alternative. Thus, unless it is possible for families such as these to join car pools, find alternative employment, or move

---

[6] A measure of minimum annual income needs for each family was constructed by using the "Low Cost Plan" for food expenditure requirements (adjusted for family size and composition) given in the Family Economic Review (1967).

closer to work, it appears that any public policy measure which attempts to discourage gasoline consumption through increased prices will result in a disproportionate burden for some families. It is hoped that prior to the enactment of measures such as increasing the federal gasoline tax, a temporary rebate system can be instituted to neutralize any detrimental impact on these groups.

References

Curtin, Richard T. "Consumer Adaptation to Energy Shortages," A Paper presented at the meetings of the American Psychological Association, Chicago, August 31, 1975. (mimeographed)

Duncan, Greg J. "Some Equity Aspects of Gasoline Price Inflation." In Five Thousand American Families--Patterns of Economic Progress, Volume III, edited by Greg J. Duncan and James N. Morgan. Ann Arbor: Institute for Social Research, 1975.

Energy Policy Project: The Ford Foundation. A Time to Choose--America's Energy Future. Cambridge: Ballinger Publishing Co., 1974.

Family Economic Review. Washington: U.S. Government Printing Office, June 1967.

Hill, Martha. "Modes of Travel to Work." In Five Thousand American Families--Patterns of Economic Progress, Volume II, edited by James N. Morgan. Ann Arbor: Institute for Social Research, 1974.

Lansing, John B. and Hendricks, Gary. Automobile Ownership and Residential Density. Ann Arbor: Institute for Social Research, 1967.

Sonquist, John A., Baker, Elizabeth Lauh, and Morgan, James N. Searching For Structure. Revised edition. Ann Arbor: Institute for Social Research, 1973.

Appendix 6.1

TABLE A6.1a

Variation by Income Decile in Total Miles Driven in 1973
(All Families)

Income Decile	No Car	Total Miles Driven in 1973 (Thousands)									Total
		0-5	5-10	10-15	15-20	20-25	25-30	30-35	35 +	NA/DK	
Lowest	58.0%	20.8%	7.0%	5.3%	2.5%	1.2%	0.4%	0.2%	1.0%	3.5%	100.0%
Second	36.9	24.6	15.9	8.6	2.8	3.2	1.1	1.0	1.5	4.3	100.0
Third	24.9	18.1	19.9	18.7	5.8	3.6	1.4	1.9	2.4	3.3	100.0
Fourth	13.5	16.0	23.9	19.4	8.2	7.9	2.1	2.8	2.8	3.4	100.0
Fifth	9.9	14.7	18.4	23.4	10.8	9.2	3.4	3.3	4.4	2.4	100.0
Sixth	5.9	7.9	13.3	28.2	14.6	10.2	5.9	4.8	6.9	2.3	100.0
Seventh	4.6	9.3	13.9	23.7	16.3	10.4	8.5	4.6	6.8	1.9	100.0
Eighth	1.9	4.2	10.1	23.1	22.4	13.9	7.5	6.4	9.0	1.6	100.0
Ninth	2.1	4.6	12.9	19.4	17.3	15.7	11.1	4.8	11.3	0.9	100.0
Highest	1.2	1.5	10.3	16.2	15.5	15.9	9.8	11.6	17.2	0.6	100.0

MTR #M008947

TABLE A6.1b

Mean Total Miles Driven in 1973 by Income
(Only Car Owners)

Family Income Decile	Upper Decile Limit	Unweighted N	Mean Annual Miles Driven
Lowest	$ 3,050	227	7,200
Second	4,900	337	9,000
Third	6,550	392	10,100
Fourth	8,700	466	12,000
Fifth	10,850	487	13,200
Sixth	12,900	475	16,000
Seventh	15,350	459	16,100
Eighth	18,500	419	18,200
Ninth	23,500	382	19,300
Highest	--	368	23,300
		4,012	15,400

MTR #M009635

FIGURE A6.1a

Mean Fuel Expenditures as a
Percentage of Total Family Money Income

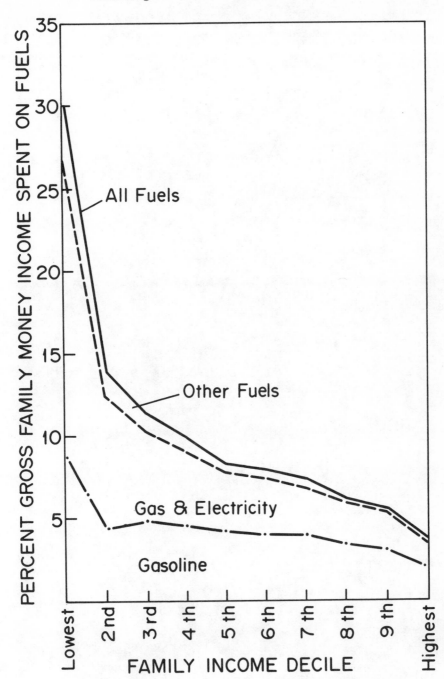

Source: Bureau of Labor Statistics, U. S. Department of Labor, Survey of
Consumer Expenditures - Diary: July 1972-June 1973.

Chapter 7

FOOD EXPENDITURE CHANGES BETWEEN
1972 AND 1974

Greg J. Duncan

Introduction

In the spring of 1974, after two years of rapidly rising food prices, panel families were making food expenditures at an average annual rate of about $2,130 per family. These expenditures represented an increase of some $427, or 25 percent, over the level of two years before.[1] This chapter presents some distributional data on the *composition* of these food expenditures, the *fraction* of family income they took up, and their change over the two-year period.

Analysis

Caveats

The data reported here come from the fifth and seventh panel waves. Food consumption questions relate to average family purchases in the spring of 1972 and of 1974. Income and food stamp information refer to the calendar years 1971 and 1973, thus creating the possibility that consumption and income flows may not be exactly matched. Additional analysis has shown, however, that the results reported for the fifth (1972) wave changed little when 1972 rather than 1971 income was used.

Further warning needs to be given concerning the comparability of the two expenditure figures. First, only the restaurant food and food stamp expenditure figures are exactly comparable between the two years. The home food expenditure information in 1972 had cigarette and alcohol expenditures edited out, but the 1974 interview did not contain questions relating to cigarette and alcohol consumption, and no such editing was possible. This was not as great a problem as it may seem, however, since less than one-tenth of the families that spent money

---

[1]The food component of the Consumer Price Index rose by about 28 percent between March 1972 and March 1974.

on cigarettes and alcohol in 1972 included these expenditures in their estimates
of home food expenditures. Second, a comparison of *total* food expenditures or
total value of food consumed by the family was not possible since questions relating to food purchased at work and school, food produced at home, or free food
were asked in 1972 but not in 1974. On the basis of 1972 information, these
omitted components of food expenditure and consumption made up about 12.3 percent
of the average total food consumption level of all panel families, and the relative importance of the sum of these components was reasonably constant across
income strata. We look first at out-of-pocket expenditures on food, that is,
expenditures excluding the value of food purchased from food stamp transfers
(bonus values), turning later to the impact of food stamps in allowing more food
consumption for the same expenditure.

Food Expenditure Levels and Changes

The average dollar expenditures on home and restaurant food by income and
income/need deciles are given in Tables 7.1 and 7.2, respectively.[2] Average annual amounts spent on home food rose from $1,463 to $1,800, a 23 percent increase.
Restaurant food purchase expenditures increased even more (38 percent) but since
the *level* of restaurant expenditures was less than one-fifth the level of home
food purchases, the weighted average increase in *total* expenditure (25 percent)
was close to that for the home food increase.

The *distribution* of expenditure increases across income (Table 7.1) and in-
come/needs (Table 7.2) deciles shows few consistent patterns. Expenditure increases were slightly higher for those in the lowest income decile than for those
in other parts of the income distribution. Families in the lowest income/needs
decile, on the other hand, had lower than average expenditure increases.

In addition to providing national sample comparisons at two points in time,
the panel data permit a look at changes in food expenditures for the same families. For families with no change in household heads during 1972-1974, total
food expenditures increased from $1,734 to $2,217, an increase of 27.9 percent.
When the expenditure changes were disaggregated by 1973 income/needs decile (in
Table 7.3), the picture was quite similar to that shown in Table 7.2.[3] Families
that ended up in the lowest income/needs decile had smaller than average food
expenditure increases, and there was no consistent pattern of change across the

---

[2]The breakpoints for the income and income/needs deciles are given in Table A7.1.
Home food expenditures include cash paid for food stamps but do *not* include the
"bonus value" of the stamps (i.e., the difference between cash paid for the
stamps and the amount of food that could be purchased with the stamps).

[3]Note that the families in the bottom income/needs decile in 1973 were not
necessarily in the lowest income/needs decile in 1971.

TABLE 7.1

Mean Annual Food Expenditures by
Income Decile for 1972 and 1974

Income Decile	Home Food*			Restaurant Food**			Total		
	1972	1974	% increase	1972	1974	% increase	1972	1974	% increase
Lowest	$ 630	$ 820	30.2%	$ 62	$ 97	56.4%	$ 692	$ 918	32.7%
Second	921	1118	21.4	121	163	34.7	1042	1281	22.9
Third	1103	1368	24.0	129	223	72.9	1232	1591	29.1
Fourth	1230	1491	21.2	195	220	12.8	1425	1711	20.1
Fifth	1380	1757	27.3	196	270	37.8	1576	2027	28.6
Sixth	1548	1873	21.0	217	361	66.4	1765	2235	26.6
Seventh	1650	2114	28.1	270	356	31.9	1920	2470	28.6
Eighth	1747	2065	18.2	292	437	49.7	2038	2502	22.8
Ninth	2048	2478	21.0	342	494	44.4	2390	2973	24.4
Highest	2374	2907	22.4	552	659	19.4	2926	3566	21.9
Average	$1463	$1800	23.0%	$238	$328	37.8%	$1701	$2128	25.1%

*From the questions: "How much do you (FAMILY) spend on the food that you use *at home* in an average week?" "Do you have any food delivered to the door which isn't included in that?" For food stamp users, the *cash paid* for stamps is included in these expenditure figures but the *bonus value* of the stamps is not.

**From the question: "About how much do you (FAMILY) spend in an *average week* eating out, *not counting* meals at work or at school?"

MTR 7101

TABLE 7.2

Mean Annual Food Expenditures by
Income/Needs Decile for 1972 and 1974

Income/Needs Decile	Home Food*			Restaurant Food**			Total		
	1972	1974	% increase	1972	1974	% increase	1972	1974	% increase
Lowest	$ 953	$1125	18.0%	$ 60	$110	83.3%	$1013	$1235	21.9%
Second	1172	1472	25.6	117	153	30.8	1289	1626	26.1
Third	1312	1634	24.5	130	173	33.0	1442	1807	25.3
Fourth	1418	1773	25.0	144	251	74.3	1562	2024	29.6
Fifth	1574	1877	19.3	194	247	27.3	1768	2125	20.2
Sixth	1549	1977	27.6	215	341	58.6	1764	2318	31.4
Seventh	1578	1947	23.4	288	374	29.9	1866	2321	24.4
Eighth	1714	1994	16.3	314	467	48.7	2028	2461	21.4
Ninth	1624	2013	24.0	359	476	32.6	1983	2489	25.5
Highest	1736	2181	25.6	557	689	23.7	2293	2870	25.2
Average	$1463	$1800	23.0%	$238	$328	37.8%	$1701	$2128	25.1%

*From the questions: "How much do you (FAMILY) spend on the food that you use *at home* in an average week?" "Do you have any food delivered to the door which isn't included in that?" For food stamp users, the *cash paid* for stamps is included in these expenditure figures but the *bonus value* of the stamps is not.

**From the question: "About how much do you (FAMILY) spend in an *average week* eating out, *not counting* meals at work or at school?"

MTR 7101

TABLE 7.3

1972 and 1974 Home, Restaurant and Total Food Expenditures, by 1973 Income/Needs Decile (For all Families with the Same Heads, 1972-1974)

1973 Income/ Needs Decile	Home Food*			Restaurant Food**			Total		
	1972	1974	% Change	1972	1974	% Change	1972	1974	% Change
Lowest	$ 967	$1183	22.3%	$ 64	$100	56.3	$1031	$1283	24.4%
Second	1209	1519	25.6	97	131	35.1	1306	1651	26.4
Third	1325	1711	29.1	125	154	23.2	1450	1865	28.6
Fourth	1435	1907	32.9	177	251	41.8	1612	2159	33.9
Fifth	1523	1958	28.6	172	241	40.1	1695	2199	29.7
Sixth	1594	2040	28.0	246	338	37.4	1840	2378	29.2
Seventh	1619	2009	24.1	282	368	30.5	1901	2376	25.0
Eighth	1666	2067	24.1	316	455	44.0	1982	2523	27.3
Ninth	1647	2085	26.6	355	467	31.5	2002	2561	27.9
Highest	1785	2218	24.3	515	683	32.6	2300	2900	26.1
All	$1492	$1887	26.5%	$243	$331	36.2%	$1734	$2217	27.9%

*From the questions: "How much do you (FAMILY) spend on food that you use *at home* in an average week?" "Do you have any food delivered to the door which isn't included in that?" For food stamp users, the *cash paid* for stamps is included in these expenditure figures but the *bonus value* of the stamps is not.

**From the question: "About how much do you (FAMILY) spend in an *average week* eating out, *not counting* meals at work or at school?"

MTR 7126

remaining income/needs deciles.

Further descriptive detail on changes in food expenditures for the same families was provided by an AID analysis conducted on the *absolute* change in food expenditure as the dependent variable. Independent variables included change in income and in food needs and demographic variables such as age, education, race, city size, and average income. As the "tree" diagram of Figure 7.1 shows, the change variables were most important in explaining changes in food expenditures. Families with falling incomes and needs, not surprisingly, had expenditure increases that were considerably smaller than those of other families. Among families with income increases, income level, family size, and age were important predictors.

Food Expenditures as a Fraction of Income

The burden of the food price inflation on families at various income levels is given in Table 7.4, which tabulates the fraction of total family money income allocated to food purchases by income decile. Overall, this fraction increased by 1.6 percentage points (from 18.1 percent to 19.7 percent) for home purchases and by 0.6 percent (from 2.6 to 3.2 percent) for restaurant expenditures. The change in the fraction of income allocated to food purchase was greatest for the poorest families. In 1974 the fraction of income allocated to home and restaurant food for families in the lowest income decile equaled 46.6 percent—up more than 5 percentage points from 1972. The absolute level of this expenditure may be slightly overstated because of the alcohol and cigarette component noted earlier, although the extent of overstatement is probably on the order of only 0.5 percent. Also, the restaurant expenditures were payments for service as well as for food. If only one-half of the restaurant expenditures were for food, then the fraction of income allocated to food purchase for the lowest decile would have increased from 38.0 to 44.6 percent over the period rather than from 40.1 to 46.6 percent. For the families at the highest end of the income scale, food expenditures took up a much smaller fraction of income; furthermore, the fraction increased only slightly between 1972 and 1974 (from 10.8 percent to 11.4 percent of income). A comparison of the burden of food expenditures for those at the top and bottom ends of the income distribution is given in Figure 7.2.

Restaurant Expenditures

One way in which families can avoid some of the burdens of food price inflation is to substitute less expensive food purchases for more expensive ones. While we had no data on the *composition* of home food purchases, we could look at the extent to which families cut back on the generally more expensive restaurant

FIGURE 7.1

AID on Absolute Dollar Change in Food Expenditures 1972-1974
(No Adjustment for Inflation)

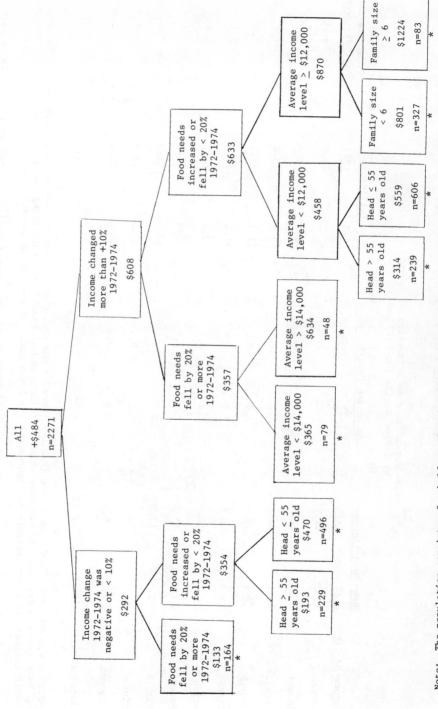

Note: The population consists of a half sample of families with the same head between 1972 and 1974. Expenditure figures include both at-home and restaurant expenditures. For food stamp users, the *cash paid* for stamps is included but the *bonus value* of the stamps is not. Food needs vary with number, age, and sex of family members and are based on the Department of Agriculture's low-cost food budget.

TABLE 7.4

Food Expenditure as a Fraction of Income
by Income Decile for 1972 and 1974

Income Decile	Home Food*/Income		Restaurant Food*/Income		Total/Income		1972 Cigarette and Alcohol/Income
	1972	1974	1972	1974	1972	1974	
Lowest	36.0%	42.7%	4.1%	3.9%	40.1%	46.6%	6.2%
Second	27.4	28.5	3.7	4.2	31.1	32.7	4.0
Third	22.4	24.0	2.7	4.0	25.1	28.0	3.3
Fourth	18.3	19.5	2.9	2.8	21.2	22.4	3.1
Fifth	16.7	18.1	2.4	2.8	19.1	20.8	2.7
Sixth	15.4	15.9	2.1	3.1	17.5	18.9	2.4
Seventh	13.6	15.0	2.2	2.5	15.8	17.6	2.1
Eighth	12.0	12.3	2.0	2.6	14.0	14.9	2.1
Ninth	11.2	12.0	1.9	2.4	13.1	14.3	1.4
Highest	8.9	9.4	1.9	2.0	10.8	11.4	1.2
Average	18.1%	19.7%	2.6%	3.2%	20.7%	22.8%	2.9%

*From the questions: "How much do you (FAMILY) spend on the food that you use *at home* in an average week?" "Do you
have any food delivered to the door which isn't included in that?" For food stamp users, the *cash paid* for stamps
is included in these expenditure figures but the *bonus value* of the stamps is not.

**From the question: "About how much do you (FAMILY) spend in an *average week* eating out, *not counting* meals at work
or at school?"

MTR #7101

FIGURE 7.2

Food Expenditures as a Fraction of Income,
by Income Group

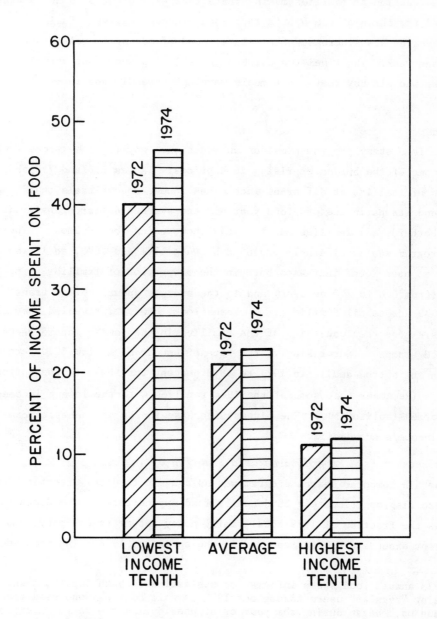

food in favor of home food. Results already presented in Tables 7.1-7.3 indicated that proportionate increases in restaurant expenditures were quite high for those in the lowest decile. Further evidence, presented in Table 7.5, shows that the fraction of families making restaurant expenditures in an "average" week increased for three of the bottom four income/needs deciles. Families in the higher deciles also increased their likelihood of eating in restaurants during an average week. The final two columns in Table 7.5 show, not surprisingly, that for those who did buy restaurant meals, average expenditures increased at all income levels.

Food Stamps

The food stamp program provides an additional way for low-income families to escape some of the burden of rising food prices. Tables 7.6 and 7.7 show the fraction of families at different income and income/needs levels that reported using food stamps in the previous year and the average dollar transfer (bonus value) both for all families and for only those using food stamps.[4] The food stamp program was considerably expanded between 1971 and 1973, so it was not surprising to have found increases both in the proportion of families using food stamps (from 6.6 to 7.0 percent) and in the average annual dollar transfer (from $32 to $39 across all families). A closer look, however, revealed some disturbing findings. Less than one-third of the families in the lowest income/needs decile used food stamps.[5] Surprisingly, the rate of use *dropped* from 32.0 percent for those in the bottom decile in 1971 to 30.2 percent for those in the bottom decile in 1973. (Remember that some of the 1974 families with the lowest incomes were newly formed (splitoffs).) The biggest increase in use and benefits came in the second income/needs decile.

AID Analysis on Food Expenditures as a Fraction of Income

The AID computer search program was used again to discover other subgroups that were disproportionately burdened by food expenditures. The dependent variable was the fraction of 1973 total family money income taken up by home food and restaurant expenditures, as reported in the spring of 1974. The independent var-

---

[4] The 1973 annual food stamp information was estimated both for those who reported being "regular" users throughout 1973 as well as those who used the stamps "off and on," began during the year or stopped during the year. Additional analysis has shown that data for the 56 percent who reported "regular" use were quite good, while the data for the 44 percent of food stamp recipients who were not regular users were less reliable.

[5] The Senate Select Committee on Nutrition and Human Needs has estimated that "only 38 percent of those eligible for food stamps are getting them." (<u>New York Times</u>, March 3, 1975, p. 1)

TABLE 7.5

Restaurant Food Purchase and Amount
by Income/Needs for 1972 and 1974

Income/Needs Decile	Proportion of Families with Restaurant Expenditures in "Average" Week		Annual Restaurant Expenditure for Families with Restaurant Expenditures	
	1972	1974	1972	1974
Lowest	30.3%	32.5%	$198	$338
Second	42.6	40.8	273	377
Third	53.3	56.1	245	308
Fourth	57.6	64.6	250	389
Fifth	67.1	63.2	289	392
Sixth	68.5	79.6	314	428
Seventh	79.6	83.2	362	450
Eighth	83.3	84.6	374	552
Ninth	86.1	87.8	417	542
Highest	89.9	88.7	619	777
Average	65.9%	68.1%	$361	$482

MTR 7101

TABLE 7.6

Food Stamp Usage and Benefits
by Income Decile for 1971 and 1973

Income Decile	Proportion of Families Using Food Stamps		Money Saved Using Food Stamps (Bonus Values) for Families Using Food Stamps		Money Saved Using Food Stamps— All Families	
	1971	1973	1971	1973	1971	1973
Lowest	19.9%	22.5%	$385	$499	$77	$101
Second	16.7	19.6	460	572	77	112
Third	10.5	10.2	600	667	63	70
Fourth	6.8	7.0	576	502	39	35
Fifth	5.6	3.8	655	563	36	21
Sixth	2.9	3.7	408	754	12	28
Seventh	2.2	1.7	*	*	12	9
Eighth	1.2	1.0	*	*	5	1
Ninth	0.7	1.0	*	*	1	13
Highest	0.0	0.0	*	*	0	0
Average	6.6%	7.0%	$485	$557	$32	$ 39

*Less than 25 observations

NOTE: Food stamp information comes from 1972 and 1974 reports of calendar years 1971 and 1973.

MTR #7101

TABLE 7.7

Food Stamp Usage and Benefits
by Income/Needs Decile for 1971 and 1973

Income/Needs Decile	Proportion of Families Using Food Stamps		Money Saved Using Food Stamps (Bonus Values) for Families Using Food Stamps		Money Saved Using Food Stamps- All Families	
	1971	1973	1971	1973	1971	1973
Lowest	32.0%	30.2%	$600	$672	$192	$203
Second	16.2	21.1	399	489	65	103
Third	9.0	10.1	372	488	33	49
Fourth	4.4	2.9	*	*	17	10
Fifth	2.3	2.1	*	*	7	6
Sixth	0.6	2.0	*	*	2	5
Seventh	1.9	1.0	*	*	5	9
Eighth	0.0	0.6	*	*	0	2
Ninth	0.0	0.4	*	*	0	2
Highest	0.0	0.0	*	*	0	0
Average	6.6%	7.0%	$485	$557	$ 32	$ 39

*Less than 25 observations

NOTE: Food stamp information comes from 1972 and 1974 reports of calendar years 1971 and 1973.

MTR 7101

iables included: family income decile, age and sex of head, family size, city
size, race, and region. The resulting "tree" is shown in Figure 7.3. In addition to the mean fraction of income allocated to food expenditures, calculations
of the proportion who received food stamps and the proportion who reported *no*
restaurant meal expenditures in an "average week" are shown for each subgroup.
For the entire population the mean fraction of income taken up by food and restaurant purchases was 22.3 percent; 33 percent of all families made no restaurant
expenditures in an average week, and 7 percent received food stamps.

Income and family size were the most important predictors of the fraction
of income allocated to food, with lower income levels and larger family sizes
associated with higher fractions. Among single-person families in the lowest income group, there was one split on race, with whites being burdened less than
blacks.

The subgroup found to be most burdened by food costs was comprised of 295
families in the lowest income decile with at least 2 family members. For this
group, the mean fraction of income allocated to food purchases was about 56 percent. About 30 percent of the families in this group ate in restaurants in an
average week and almost two-fifths were receiving food stamps. Although the food
stamp program limits cash expenditures for stamps to 30 percent of countable income, food stamp users may make additional food purchases beyond food stamp allot-
ment amounts. Future analysis will be directed toward these and related issues.

Summary

1. In the spring of 1974, panel families reported spending an average of
$35 a week for groceries and about $6 weekly in restaurants. These total food
costs were some 23 percent higher than they had been two years before,[6] an increase that was slightly less than that of the food component of the Cost of
Living Index. These increases showed little consistent variation across income
and income/needs categories.

2. Another way of looking at the burdens imposed by food price increases

---

[6]The change in expenditure figures may be overstated by a small amount. In
1972, when respondents were asked whether they had included expenditures for
alcohol and tobacco, less than one-tenth indicated they had done so, and the
data were revised accordingly. In 1974, questions about these inclusions were
not asked.

FIGURE 7.3

AID on 1974 Home and Restaurant Food Expenditure
as a Fraction of 1973 Income[a]

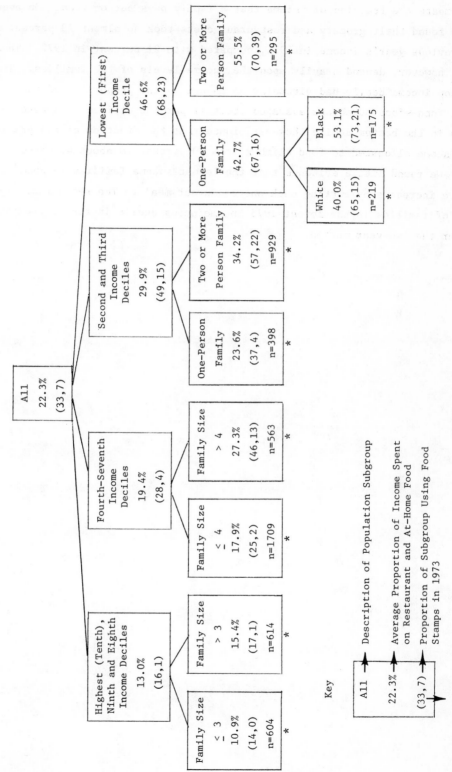

Key

All — Description of Population Subgroup

22.3% — Average Proportion of Income Spent on Restaurant and At-Home Food

(33,7) — Proportion of Subgroup Using Food Stamps in 1973

Proportion of Subgroup with no Restaurant Expenditure in "Average Week" in 1974

[a]Food Expenditure to Income ratios were truncated at 100%

is to compare the fraction of income that a family pays out on food. On average, families found their grocery and restaurant costs took up almost 23 percent of their previous year's income in 1974, compared with 21 percent in 1972. These figures, however, depend heavily upon the income levels of the families. Those in the top income decile had virtually no change in the proportion of income spent on food—food purchases averaged about 11 percent of income in both years. Families in the bottom decile, however, found that the fraction of the previous year's income allocated to food climbed from 40 percent to about 47 percent.

3. We found little evidence that the lowest income families responded to the price increases by cutting back on restaurant meals. The restaurant expenditures of families in the lowest 1973 income/needs decile increased from $60 to $110 over the two-year period.

Appendix 7.1

Table A7.1

Upper Limit Breakpoints for Income and
Income/Needs Decile for 1972 and 1974[*]

Decile	Income		Income/Needs[**]	
	1972	1974	1972	1974
Lowest	2,600	3,047	1.00	1.18
Second	4,169	4,899	1.45	1.74
Third	5,769	6,554	1.91	2.29
Fourth	7,519	8,714	2.39	2.82
Fifth	9,133	10,867	2.83	3.37
Sixth	11,249	12,899	3.36	3.94
Seventh	13,275	15,365	3.99	4.63
Eighth	16,009	18,499	4.76	5.47
Ninth	20,799	23,519	6.10	7.03
Highest	--	--	--	--

[*]"1974" is the 1974 report of income received during the calendar year 1973. Similarly, for 1972 report of the 1971 calendar year.

[**]The needs standard has been adjusted for inflation.

Chapter 8

CHANGES IN HOUSING COSTS 1968 TO 1974

James N. Morgan and Sandra J. Newman

Introduction

Housing costs have risen rapidly in recent years. While the Consumer Price Index rose by about 40 percent between 1968 and 1974, the housing component of the index rose by somewhat more than this amount, a combination of a 27 percent increase in rents and a 50 percent increase in home ownership costs.[1] In addition, the Census Bureau estimates that the price of new, constant-quality, one-family houses sold during the period rose by somewhat more than 50 percent.[2] What were the effects of these major cost increases for housing? Was the burden equitably distributed or were there differential impacts on particular groups of families? The purpose of this chapter is to explore the impacts on our panel families of housing cost increases between 1968 and 1974.

Overall, the 5,517 families who were in our panel in early 1974 had experienced an *average* increase in housing costs of 76 percent since 1968. (Information on housing quality was not included in the panel data until the 8th wave in 1975 and therefore could not be used in the present analysis.) At least four factors influenced the magnitude of this increase: (1) increases or decreases in income which the family has experienced during the seven-year period; (2) housing tenure--that is, whether one owns or rents; (3) mobility status--whether one has moved to a different house or apartment or has remained in the original residence; and (4) family composition--whether the family has been headed by the same individual for all seven years, whether a new family has been formed by an individual who has split off from the main family, or whether the household head has changed due to divorce or separation or death of the original head.[3]

---

[1] It should be remembered that the quality of items measured by the CPI (including housing) is ". . . kept essentially unchanged." See <u>Monthly Labor Review</u> (1975), p. 105.

[2] U. S. Bureau of the Census (1975).

[3] In conceptual terms, this overall change is made up of quite disparate elements, of course. Some 1974 families were newly formed, and we compare their housing

Clearly, these four factors are not mutually exclusive phenomena. Indeed, splitting off from an original panel family essentially means moving to a new residence, changing housing tenure, and, often, living on one's own income rather than relying on family income. What is suggested, however, is that differences in income, tenure, mobility, and family composition probably produce nonuniform impacts of housing costs. It is, of course, difficult to trace these impacts because of basic differences within some of the subgroups. We can look, for example, at movers and nonmovers. Movers are frequently securing better housing, so part of the increase in their costs reflects an increase in quality or quantity of housing. In contrast, the increase in rent for nonmoving renters is an increased current expenditure, while for nonmoving owners an increase in home value results partly in a nonmoney increase in both income (imputed rent) and consumption, and partly in visible increases in property taxes, utilities, and the like.

Another example concerns family composition. Obviously, the family is not a static entity over time. Older children split off from their immediate families and form households of their own; older families die. In view of these changes, the families in our sample can be thought of as a replacing panel, with newly-formed families replacing those families which die. In the present analysis these changes imply that the average increase in housing costs, based on the panel data, could be higher than the national average because the older families had higher costs as compared with the new, younger households with lower costs who replaced them.

It is also difficult to compare the housing costs of owners and renters. Here, the problem is to translate house values into annual housing costs. Since almost all of the economic costs of home ownership are proportional to house value (the main cost being the interest, paid or foregone, on the investment), we have taken 10 percent of the house value to represent its annual cost.[4]

---

costs with those of parental families in 1968. Some families moved and upgraded their housing quality, particularly those who bought their first house. Even among families who retained the same household head and the same residence, the increase in rents for renters increased costs out of pocket, while the owners were simply consuming a larger imputed rent on a house that had gone up in value.

[4] In one study in which owners were asked to identify rental value as well as market value of their homes, fitting a line through the pairs of values gave a relationship between annual rent and house value in each of the four regions that was about one-tenth for houses worth $10,000 or $1,000 in rents. The percentage was somewhat smaller for larger houses, but that was partly the result of fitting the line to predict rental costs rather than using rental costs to predict house value. See Morgan, David, Cohen, and Brazer (1962), p. 493.

In this chapter, we examine the differential impacts of housing costs within several of these major characteristics, but more importantly, across various combinations of these characteristics. In the next section, we present an overview of the percentage change in housing costs and income for subgroups of movers and nonmovers, owners and renters, and stable and changing families and compare these changes across the groups. We also discuss multiple regression analyses of percentage changes in housing costs between 1968 and 1974. Three separate equations are estimated: one for all 1974 families with the same household head as in 1968, a second for movers with the same household head all seven years, and a third for nonmovers with the same head. The second section is devoted to an examination of dollar changes in housing costs between 1968 and 1974, applying a method of analysis parallel to that used in examining percentage changes. This discussion is followed by a review of housing costs as a fraction of income. Particular emphasis is placed on the situation of renters who have not moved, since the impact of inflation is probably best observed within this group. In the final section the major findings are summarized and discussed. Since we compare changes in costs with changes in income, neither need be adjusted for inflation.

Analysis

I. OVERVIEW: PERCENTAGE CHANGE IN HOUSING COSTS AND INCOMES, 1968–1974, FOR MOVERS AND NONMOVERS, OWNERS AND RENTERS, AND STABLE AND CHANGING FAMILIES

Families with the Same Head

Of the 5,517 families who were part of the panel in early 1974, 65 percent had the same family head for all seven interviews. Taken as a whole, these families averaged an 85 percent increase in housing costs and a 79 percent increase in income. These percentages, as well as those for the other subgroups to be examined in this chapter, are listed in Table 8.1. There were, however, considerable differences in both income and housing cost increases when those families who had moved were compared with those who had remained in the same residence for the full period. Nearly half of all families with the same head (or 29 percent of *all* families) had moved at least once since early 1968, and these movers reported a 122 percent increase in housing costs and a 94 percent increase in income. Thus, among families with the same head, movers increased their housing costs substantially more than did nonmovers, even relative to their respective income increases. These percentages are consistent with the notion that many moves are motivated by a desire to upgrade the quality of residence. It is also

222

TABLE 8.1

Percentage Change in Housing Costs and Income and Their Relationship, 1967-1973
(For a Hierarchy of Subgroups)

	Group Averages			Correlations Within Groups			
	(1) Percentage Change in Housing Costs	(2) Percentage Change in Income	(3) Ratio (1)/(2)	% Δ HC = A + B (% Δ Inc) Correlation Coefficient	Regression Coefficient B	Number of Cases	Percent of Sample
All 1974 Families	76	67	1.13	.30	.31	5517	100
Same Head Only	85	79	1.08	.23	.27	3294	65
Did Not Move	55	67	.82	.09	.08	1628	36
Renter All Along	30	50	.60	.08	.06	321	5
Rest of Nonmovers	58	69	.84	.09	.07	1307	31
Moved	122	94	1.30	.27	.33	1666	29
Rented Before and After	74	99	.74	.36	.29	600	7
Became a Home Owner	210	141	1.49	.29	.33	448	7
Rest of Movers	101	67	1.50	.12	.18	618	14
Different Head	60	46	1.30	.35	.35	2223	35
Wife Became Widowed, Divorced, Separated	60	21	2.86	.15	.18	351	7
Single Female Married	167	245	.68	.46	.38	181	2
Splitoffs	51	34	1.50	.31	.33	1691	26

MTR 1139C

possible that those families which were nonmoving renters during the period were the beneficiaries of lags in their rent increases, or that nonmoving owners under-estimated the increased value of their homes.

Some additional clues to the most plausible interpretation were seen in the experiences of different groups of movers, namely, those who changed residences but remained in the same housing tenure class (owner to owner, renter to renter), and those who shifted from one class to another (renter to owner, owner to renter).

One-fourth of the *main* families with the same head shifted from renting to home owning.[5] The housing costs of these *new* home-owning families increased by 210 percent while their incomes increased by about two-thirds of that amount—141 percent. The rest of the movers included two main groups: those who moved from one rented home to another and those who sold one house and bought another.[6] Those who moved but remained renters fared better than the new home owners. They experienced an increase in rent of 74 percent and an average increase in income of 99 percent. The ratio of housing cost to income for those families who moved from one owned home to another was more comparable to those for new home owners. Therefore, moving owners had greater cost increases than those who moved from one rental property to another. In particular, the movers who remained owners had a 101 percent increase in housing costs and only a 67 percent increase in income. This reflects a more rapid nationwide increase in home prices than rents. It also suggests that owners who sold one home and bought another upgraded more than did renters who moved to another rented unit. More interestingly, it points to as much or more upgrading by owners who moved as by renters who became new home owners.

We can now turn our attention to those families who were most stable in family composition, income, housing tenure, and mobility. These families did not move during the period, had the same head for all seven years, and, because they were generally at later life-cycle stages, also had smaller relative income increases and fewer changes in family size than the families who moved. Overall, these nonmovers had an increase in housing costs of less than half of that of the movers: 55 percent compared with 122 percent. Again, this group was made up of both renters and owners, but in this case, neither group had moved or changed tenure class. The renters reported an average increase in rents of 30

---

[5] This constitutes 7 percent of all 1974 families.

[6] The average changes in housing cost and income for these two groups of movers were 92 percent and 78 percent, respectively.

percent and an average increase in income of 50 percent.[7] The nonmoving owners
experienced somewhat different changes--an increase in housing costs (or value)
of 58 percent and an income increase of 69 percent.[8] While some renters had certainly been faced with large rent increases, it seems apparent that the bulk of
the nonmoving renters benefited from considerable inertia in their rents. Nonmoving owners, in contrast, were somewhat less well-off, although it is important
to remember that the variable representing home owners' housing costs included
nonexpenditure items and was largely offset by increases in imputed rental income. Without current information on net equity in the house, imputed net rent
could not be estimated and added to money income.

In sum, when we looked at all families headed by the same individual between
1968 and 1974 and distributed changes in housing costs and income by mobility and
housing tenure status, we found that nonmoving renters were at one end of the
continuum, with relatively low average increases in rents, and increases in income which more than offset these rent increases. In contrast, families who
moved, either becoming home owners for the first time or moving from one owned
home to another, had relatively large housing cost increases; but their income
increases were not nearly great enough to offset the increased costs. It should
be noted, however, that the income increases for the latter owner group were
actually nearly double those of the nonmoving renters. The sizable income increases simply were accompanied by much more sizable cost increases.

Families with a Changed Head

Thus far, we have focused on the 65 percent of 1974 families who had the
same household head since 1968. We now turn our attention to the remaining 35
percent of the families whose 1974 head was not a sample-family head in 1968.
For the group as a whole, we found a 60 percent increase in housing costs and a
46 percent increase in income. It may be remembered that the corresponding figures for the families with the same head were 85 percent and 79 percent, respectively. One obvious explanation of the lower increases for these new families
is that, in most instances, we were comparing their new cost-income situation

---

[7]It should be noted that these nonmoving renters are a relatively small group
and represent only 4.5 percent of all 1974 panel families.

[8]In addition, the small number of families who neither owned nor rented was included with the groups of families who remained in the same owned home all
seven years. It seemed reasonable to include these families with the nonmoving owners because for both groups, the observed increase in housing cost
was not an actual outlay but rather an increase in an imputed income and an
imputed consumption.

with the income and housing costs of a parental family. Indeed, among the 35 percent who were new families, 26 percent were splitoffs, that is, children of original panel families who were starting households of their own. For this subgroup, we found even smaller increases in housing costs (51 percent) and in incomes (34 percent) as compared to the average figures for the group as a whole.

Of the remaining 9 percent, 7 percent were former wives who had become household heads through separation, divorce, or death of spouse. This group had, on average, a 60 percent increase in housing costs but only a 21 percent increase in income. In contrast, 2 percent of the families who experienced a change in household head were single females who married during the seven years. Overall, this group had an increase in housing costs of 167 percent, but they had a more than compensating increase in income of 245 percent--the largest income increase of all groups.

Because there were substantial changes in family composition for most of the new families, neither the change in housing costs nor the change in income, even within this group of new families, lends itself to easy interpretation. Probably a good deal of the explanation lies in differences in marital status, and more importantly, family size. Essentially, we would expect those with smaller families also to have small income and housing cost increases, while those who married and perhaps planned or began to raise a family had more need for greater income and larger living quarters. The last section of this chapter deals with these issues of change in housing cost burdens.

There is no simple relationship between the behavior of individuals and the behavior of averages or aggregates, and the ratio of average percentage change in housing costs to average percentage change in income for a group does not estimate the average family response to a change in family income. Hence, we used the data for individual families to estimate for each group the correlation between the family's change in housing costs and its change in income and to estimate the slope of the regression line (Table 8.1). Since we used percentage changes in both variables, that slope was an estimate of the percentage increase in housing costs associated with a 1 percent increase in income, that is, the income elasticity of the demand for housing. On the whole, it was apparent that there was a higher correlation between percentage changes in income and housing costs when substantial changes in income had taken place, and this was particularly strong when a move had been made. Again, we could speculate on the importance of family size as an additional, and perhaps basic, influence on this correlation. On the other hand, the correlation between changes in costs and income was quite low for nonmovers. This was not completely surprising, since nonmoving owners had very few, and relatively rarely used, options for adjusting their housing consumption (one of which would be to make additions to an owned home), while nonmoving renters had even fewer adjustment alternatives. The slopes for each regression, or the income elasticities of housing cost for each subgroup, were generally less steep than the one for all subgroups. Thus, it appeared that the percentage change in housing costs experienced by individuals or families was not nearly as high as the percentage change in income.

Housing, like food, is usually categorized as a necessity. Because every person must have some form of shelter, the demand for housing should take precedence over the demand for most other consumption. In addition, as income rises, the household is able to spend more for housing. The tendency we observed in our data, however, was that housing costs did not increase as much as income did, at least in percentage terms, as many have hypothesized in the past.[9] This might indicate that increases in housing costs were responding to inflation and/or to previous or expected income increases more than reflecting a conscious allocation of current income increases to housing consumption. At any rate, it is clear that even six years is not a long enough period in which to counteract or eliminate the effects of inertia, lags, and differential expectations of the future.[10]

Multivariate Analysis of Percentage Change in Housing Costs, 1968-1974

By simultaneously taking into account the effects of several potentially important variables, we could develop a more comprehensive, and realistic, model of the determinants of percentage changes in housing costs over the seven-year period.[11]

---

[9] Smith, Reid, Muth, and deLeeuw each derives estimates of about 1.0 for the income elasticity of housing.

[10] It is worth noting that the picture is further complicated by the differential increases in house prices relative to rents and the apparent lag of rent increases for nonmovers.

[11] An initial examination of the data revealed the existence of extreme cases. Therefore, 50 cases with percentage changes in housing costs which were more than 5 standard deviations from the mean were omitted from the analysis. These 50 cases included 9 nonmover and 41 mover records.

Because one difficulty with percentage increases is that extreme values are possible when the initial level is very low, we tried another method of handling extreme cases. We truncated increases of more than 1000 percent in either housing costs or income to equal 1000 percent. However, even after this adjustment, we found 147 cases with percentage increases in housing costs that were more than 4 standard deviations from the truncated average, and 59 of them were cases that had been truncated to 1000 percent. Both for this reason, and because of substantive interest in dollar changes, we turned next to an examina-

Although we found little evidence of nonadditivities in the searching analysis upon which Table 8.1 is based, we wanted to be able to make specific comparisons between movers and nonmovers across the range of predictors. Therefore, we actually estimated three separate equations: one for all 1974 families with the same head as in 1968, a second for movers only, and a third for nonmovers only.[12] In each case the same dependent variable and an almost identical set of categorical predictors was used. The dependent variable was defined as the percentage change in housing costs between the 1968 and 1974 data collections. The basic set of independent variables included:

- background variables--change in family size
  (1968-1974), age, sex-marital status, and race;

- environmental variables--region, size of largest
  city in the county, and distance to the center
  of the nearest city of 50,000 or more;

- one economic variable--change in income (1968-1974);

- measures of housing and mobility status--stayed a
  renter or became an owner; whether moved;

- one interaction term--increase in family size combined with an income that at least doubled.

Obviously, we deleted the "whether moved" variable from the predictors in the latter two regressions. We did, however, add one dichotomous interaction term to the regression for movers, which equalled one for those who had an increase in family size and an income that at least doubled, and zero otherwise.

In this group of regressions, 50 extreme cases were omitted and separate analyses were run for movers and nonmovers for all 1974 families with the same head as in 1968.

The results of the three regressions are shown in Table 8.2.[13] We again observe the marked difference in levels of mean housing cost increases for movers and nonmovers. This is not surprising because the nonmovers were affected mostly by inflation and had little interfamily variability to be explained, while the movers were making real decisions about housing costs.

For those who did not move, increases were smaller for renters as compared

---

tion of dollar increases in housing costs relative to dollar changes in income. This is presented in Section II.

[12]The analyses of movers and of nonmovers also focused only on same-head families.

[13]Details of the effects of each explanatory characteristic are given in Table A8.1a.

TABLE 8.2

Explanatory Power (Eta^2 and Beta^2) of Family and Environmental Characteristics
Accounting for Percentage Increase in Housing Costs 1968-1974
(For Families with the Same Household Head All Seven Years)

Characteristic	Number of Categories*	All With Same Head		Those Who Moved		Those Who Did Not Move	
		Eta^2	Beta^2	Eta^2	Beta^2	Eta^2	Beta^2
Percentage Change in Income	5	.041	.013	.059	.019	.016	.007
Change in Family Size	5	.050	.004	.057	.008	.006	.002
Age	7	.077	.011	.068	.017	.017	.008
Sex-Marital Status	3	.024	.006	.037	.004	.020	.007
Race	3	.001	.000	.003	.001	.000	.000
Region	4**	--	--	.012	.016	.011	.018
Size of Largest City	7	--	--	.011	.013	.006	.008
Distance to City Center	6	--	--	.016	.009	.007	.005
Housing Tenure/Mobility Status	3	.118	.052	.094	.048	.015	.011
Moved	2	.058	.009	--	--	--	--
Family Size Increased and Income Doubled or More	2	--	--	.032	.000	--	--
Number of Cases		3244		1625		1619	
Average		78		109		53	
Standard Deviation		114		140		72	
R^2 Adjusted		.172		.176		.052	

*The significance of the measure depends on the number of categories used. See Glossary and Appendix D.

**Plus two very small groups for noncontinental United States and the rest of the world.

MTR 1140

to owners or those who neither own nor rent, and smaller for residents of the
north central or western region, as compared to residents of the northeast or
south.

For movers, becoming an owner had the greatest effect on increased housing
costs, but change in income was also influential. It is interesting that although
change in family size, when considered alone, had a strong relationship to increased housing costs for movers regardless of their housing tenure status, the
combination of increased family size and increased income had no more effect than
the separate effects of each variable alone.[14] The effects of changes in income
and family size, after adjustment for the other factors in the regression, are
plotted in Figures 8.1 and 8.2. The first figure indicates the far more substantial increase in housing costs at higher incomes for movers as compared to nonmovers, while the second figure indicates that as one looks at mover families of
ever larger sizes, outlays for housing stabilize or even decline.

Another pattern which could be observed among movers was the substantially
greater set of increases among those who were young. The age pattern is shown in
Figure 8.3. This finding might suggest that residential mobility among younger
families was motivated primarily by the desire to upgrade and was not connected
simply with current changes in either income, family size, or becoming an owner
(each of which were included as separate predictors in the regression). A model
postulating lifetime accumulation of more consumer physical capital which is not
closely tied to current income, family needs, or the changes in each, would fit
these data.

Finally, increases in housing costs were larger for movers whose destination
was either the northeast or the south, and were also somewhat larger in areas
with small towns but no standard metropolitan area of 50,000 or more.[15]

II. DOLLAR CHANGE IN HOUSING COSTS, 1968-1974

Percentage change may be particularly useful in emphasizing the experiences
of individuals whose initial levels of housing cost or income are very low, but
for the same reason such percentage measures may be disadvantageous. In particular, extreme percentage changes may result specifically when initial levels are
very low. On the other hand, few extreme values result when absolute values are
used.[16] Thus it became useful to turn to an examination of dollar changes in

---

[14]The Eta-square of .032 drops to a Beta-square of .000.

[15]We can only speculate that these larger increases in small towns may reflect
the flight from the cities plus a spread of inflation from central areas outward.

[16]This is not to say absolute values are problem free. In particular, a major

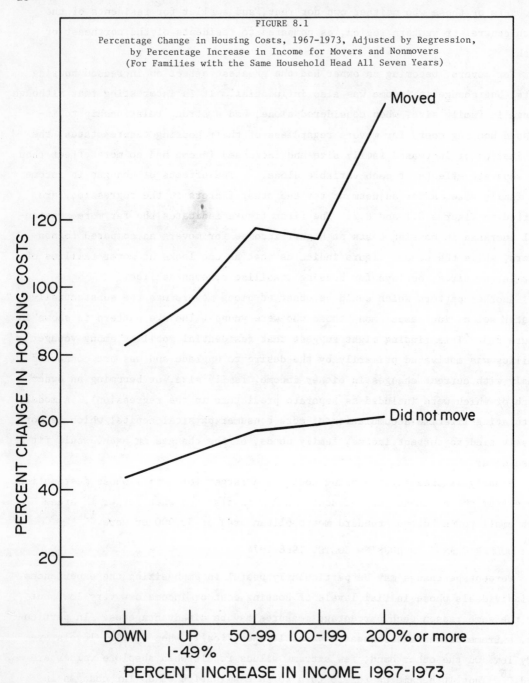

FIGURE 8.1

Percentage Change in Housing Costs, 1967-1973, Adjusted by Regression,
by Percentage Increase in Income for Movers and Nonmovers
(For Families with the Same Household Head All Seven Years)

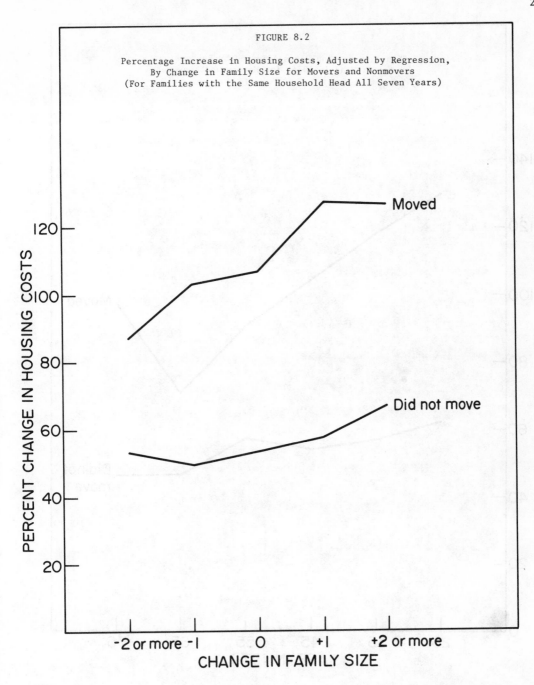

FIGURE 8.2

Percentage Increase in Housing Costs, Adjusted by Regression,
By Change in Family Size for Movers and Nonmovers
(For Families with the Same Household Head All Seven Years)

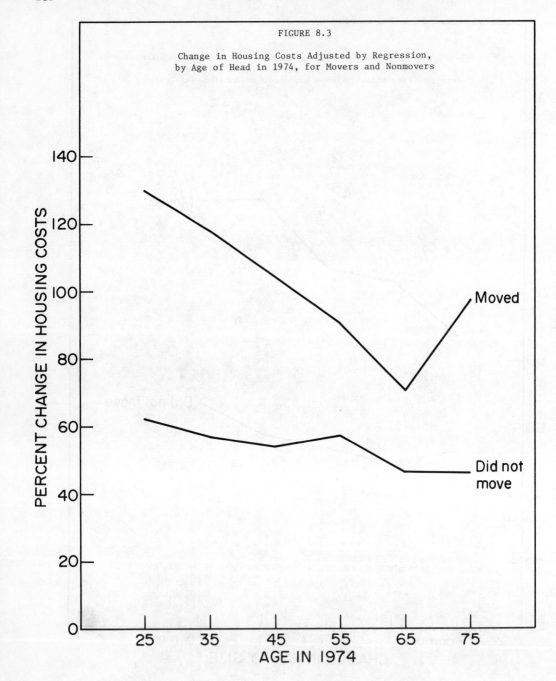

FIGURE 8.3

Change in Housing Costs Adjusted by Regression,
by Age of Head in 1974, for Movers and Nonmovers

housing costs relative to dollar changes in income. Just as the concept of elasticity was used earlier to summarize the relationship between percentage changes in housing costs and income, a parallel concept was used for dollar changes. This concept is known as the marginal propensity to consume housing: the dollar change in housing cost associated with a dollar change in income.

The sample population and the subgroups within the population were identical to those focused upon in the percentage change analysis. In order to moderate the influence of extremely large changes in costs and incomes, we rounded down increases in housing costs of more than $5,000 a year to $5,000, and increases in income of more than $50,000 to equal $50,000. This left only 12 cases beyond five standard deviations from the mean (and all represented substantial *decreases* in housing cost).

This analysis of dollar change in housing cost is similar to that presented earlier on percentage change in housing cost. The results are shown in Table 8.3. Again, it is clear that movers, and particularly those who became home owners, had much larger dollar increases in housing costs relative to dollar increases in incomes. The virtual lack of effect which changes in income had on changes in housing costs for the nonmovers, particularly the renters, could once more be observed in Figure 8.4. In this graph, we have plotted the relationship of dollar changes in housing costs to dollar changes in income for the nonmoving renters, nonmoving owners, movers who became home owners, movers who did not become home owners, and for people who get housing as part of their job, or for some other reason neither own nor rent.[17] It is not surprising to find that owners had larger absolute increases in housing costs due to inflation, because they tended to own larger, more expensive dwelling units than those leased by renters. Thus, an identical percentage figure for each group translated into a larger dollar amount for owners.[18] Movers who became home owners had larger increases in housing costs than did movers who did not become home owners, but these increases seemed to be unaffected by change in income during the period, as indicated by the parallelism of the upper two lines of the figure.

---

problem of measuring change in absolute terms is the close correlation between high initial values and large change.

[17]That is, movers who remained renters, movers who remained owners, and those who began and ended as neither owners nor renters, moved into this category, or moved out of it and became renters.

[18]Of course, if owners' costs are really less than 10 percent of house value, the dollar increase in their costs has been overstated.

TABLE 8.3

Dollar Change in Housing Costs and Income and Their Relationship, 1967-1973
(For a Hierarchy of Subgroups)

| | Group Averages | | | Correlations Within Groups | | |
| | (1) Dollar Change in Housing Costs | (2) Dollar Change in Income | (3) Ratio (1)/(2) | | $\$ \Delta HC = A + B (\$ \Delta Inc)$ | |
				Correlation Coefficient	Regression Coefficient B	Number of Cases
All 1974 Families	$3398					
	$575	$3398	.169	.39	.068	5417
Same Head Only	831	5177	.161	.32	.055	3194
Did Not Move	712	4904	.145	.23	.035	1628
Renter All Along	270	2198	.123	.10	.013	321
Rest of Nonmovers	777	5299	.147	.22	.033	1307
Moved	976	5513	.177	.40	.072	1566
Rented Before and After	509	3973	.128	.43	.057	600
Became a Home Owner	1613	7877	.205	.42	.063	448
Rest of Movers	887	5085	.174	.33	.070	618
Different Head	102	106	.962	.37	.069	2223
Wife Became Widowed, Divorced, Separated	319	-357	-.866	.05	.015	351
Single Female Married	113	9896	.011	.60	.008	181
Splitoffs	-49	-648	.076	.37	.068	1691

MTR 1139D

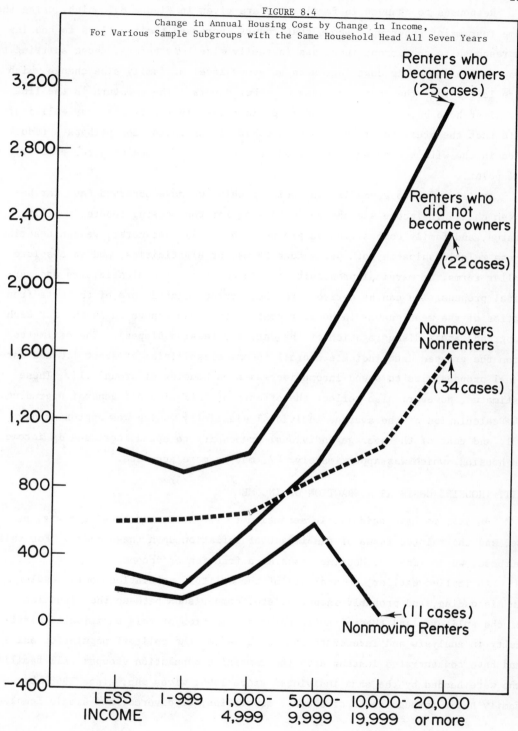

FIGURE 8.4

Change in Annual Housing Cost by Change in Income,
For Various Sample Subgroups with the Same Household Head All Seven Years

Responses to changes in family size are given in Figure 8.5 which, using the same four major subgroups, shows that movers increased their outlays to housing in response to concurrent increases in family size. As before, those shifting to ownership had housing cost increases at every level of family size change which were larger than the cost increases of other movers. The downturn in the line for first-home buyers who also had large increases in family size may well indicate that the pressure of increases in other living costs, and perhaps a reduction in the wife's earnings, inhibited the expansion of housing after some critical point.

It is useful to summarize the relationships we have observed thus far between change in income and change in housing for the housing tenure, mobility status, and family composition subgroups (Table 8.4). As noted, we can describe these relationships in both percentage terms, or elasticities, and in absolute dollar terms, or marginal propensities. In addition, the elasticities and marginal propensities can be derived from both an aggregated form of the data (the ratios of the mean change in housing cost to the mean change in income for each subgroup) and a disaggregation of the data (regression slopes). The estimates from the grouped data indicate overall income elasticities of about 1.0 and marginal propensities to spend income increases on housing of around .17. These estimates, however, also reflect the effects of inflation and general upgrading. The calculation of the average individual elasticity, which was approximately .31, and that of the average individual propensity to spend increases in income on housing, which was approximately .07, may be more accurate.[19]

III. HOUSING COSTS AS A FRACTION OF INCOME

As yet, we have paid little attention to the burden of housing costs, per se, and the related issue of the impact of inflation upon these costs. For this purpose, we now look at housing costs as a fraction of income.

As implied earlier, an analysis of the splitoff population would result in misleading, and probably inappropriate, comparisons between the situation of the splitoffs and that of their parents. In view of this anticipated difficulty in analysis and interpretation, we have set the splitoff population aside and have concentrated instead upon the remaining population groups: all families who were headed by the same individual since 1968; wives who, since 1968, became family heads through death of spouse, separation, or divorce; and single females

---

[19] The direction of the elasticity calculations was generally consistent with those recently discussed in Income Elasticity of Housing Demand. See Carliner (1973).

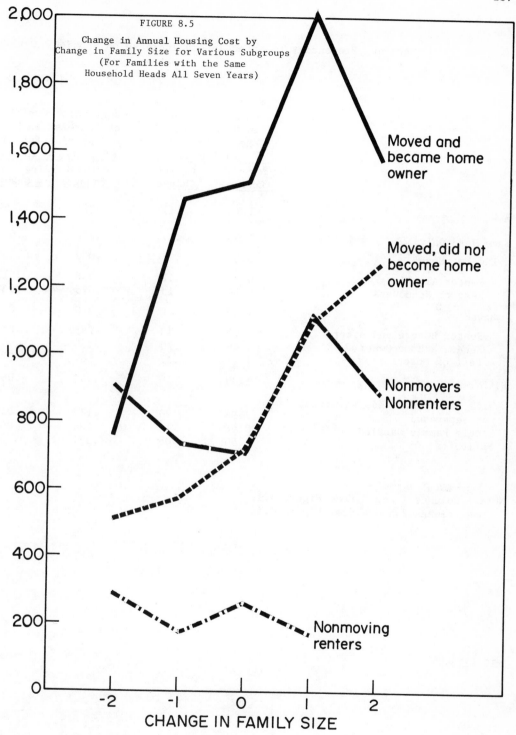

FIGURE 8.5

Change in Annual Housing Cost by
Change in Family Size for Various Subgroups
(For Families with the Same
Household Heads All Seven Years)

Moved and
became home
owner

Moved, did not
become home
owner

Nonmovers
Nonrenters

Nonmoving
renters

CHANGE IN FAMILY SIZE

TABLE 8.4

Marginal Propensity to Spend Income Increase on Housing

	Mean Increase in Housing Cost/ Mean Increase in Income		Regression Coefficient of Increase in Housing Cost as a Function of Increase in Income	
	Percent Change	Absolute Change	Percent Change	Absolute Change
ALL	1.13	.17	.315	.069
Same Head Only	1.08	.17	.268	.055
Did Not Move	0.82	.15	.080	.035
Renter All Along	0.60	.12	.058	.013
Rest of Nonmovers	0.84	.15	.075	.033
Moved	1.30	.18	.320	.072
Rented Before and After	.75	.13	.295	.057
Became a Home Owner	1.49	.20	.330	.063
Rest of Movers	1.51	.17	.184	.070
Different Head	1.30	.10	.362	.069
Wife Became Widowed, Divorced, or Separated	2.86	-.90	.178	.015
Single Female Married	0.68	.11	.384	.008
Splitoffs	1.50	.08	.331	.068

NOTE: Columns 1 and 3 from Figure 8.1.
Columns 2 and 4 from Figure 8.5.

MTR #11390

who married after 1968. Table 8.5 summarizes the behavior of housing costs relative to income for the major housing tenure and mobility status subgroups of
these three populations. The generally accepted standard of a 25 percent income
allocation for housing was used as the basis for evaluating changes in housing
costs relative to income. The table indicates that a relatively small proportion
of families in each housing tenure and mobility status group in 1968 reported
that their 1967 housing costs were less than 25 percent of their income but that
their 1973 housing costs were greater. (The proportion averaged somewhat less
than 15 percent.) The major exceptions to this trend were the owners who moved
and remained owners, the renters who moved and became owners, and the category of
"others"--those who moved into or out of the neither-own-nor-rent status, those
who were always in that status, or owners who became renters. For the owners who
moved but remained owners, most of the increase could be attributed to upgrading
through purchasing a higher quality "bundle" of housing combined with increased
imputed rent or value, which represented a capital gain in house value. Thus,
the increase did not entirely reflect an increased burden.

For renters who moved and became home owners for the first time, however,
the loss of interest on money used for down payment and interest payments on the
remaining balance represented real increases in cost. It is also true, though,
that this group of first-home buyers was more likely to sustain a lower housing
cost burden relative to income as compared with the mobile owners, probably because they tended to be young and to be experiencing relatively frequent and
large increases in their earnings and incomes.

The data on the subgroup of renters who moved but remained renters are perhaps the most interesting in the table. This group was most likely to report
housing costs constituting less than 25 percent of income in 1973 and constituting more than 25 percent of income in 1967. While this may indicate substantial
downgrading, it is more likely that these renters were young with rapidly rising
incomes. Thus, even if they consumed more costly housing, their growing incomes
more than compensated for these higher costs.

Renters who did not move displayed most clearly the burden of housing costs,
as changes in their housing costs relative to their incomes purely reflected
changes in income and/or in the price of housing. That their pattern of changes
did not differ much from the renters who moved might imply that nonmoving renters
faced substantial increases for the same facilities they had occupied for seven
years--perhaps the result of appreciation in value, but more likely stemming from
inflation. But there is also evidence that inflationary forces may operate er-
ratically or with substantial lags. Somewhat more than one-fifth of nonmoving

TABLE 8.5

Changes in Housing Costs Relative to Income
(For Those with Different Home Ownership Patterns)*

	Cost Was More Than 25% of Income in 1973		Cost Was Less Than 25% of Income in 1973 But More Than 25% in 1967	Percentage of All Families in 1974**	Number of Cases
	But Less Than 25% in 1967	And More Than 25% in 1967			
Owners Who Stayed Owners	15.1	17.1	10.1	44.1	1786
Owners Who Did Not Move	13.5	18.6	10.2	32.1	1310
Owners Who Moved	19.6	12.7	10.5	12.0	476
Renters Who Stayed Renters	10.8	10.5	13.1	14.4	1122
Renters Who Did Not Move	11.8	9.4	10.4	5.2	358
Renters Who Moved	10.3	11.0	14.6	9.3	764
Renters Who Became Owners	14.9	4.1	7.6	8.8	547
Others	19.6	12.0	14.5	7.2	398
All	14.6	13.7	11.0	74.5	3863

*For all families with the same head as in 1968, a 1968 wife who became head, or a single female who married.

**Data weighted for differential sampling and response rates; hence percentages differ from number of cases.

MTR 1136

renters had rent-to-income ratios of less than 10 percent in both 1967 and 1973, and two-fifths paid less than 15 percent of their incomes for rent in both years.[20]

We can perhaps most easily observe the pure effects of inflation on housing costs by looking only at changes in rents for nonmoving renters.[21] Because approximately 30 percent of renters moved each year, it seemed better to observe changes in rents over the three-year period from early 1971 to early 1974 rather than over the full seven years. In addition, we have focused only on 1974 families who had the same head in 1971. If we assume that those nonmoving-renter families having rent increases of less than 20 percent over the three-year period were benefiting from some lag in the adjustment of rent to inflation in housing costs and prices, then we find that about 71 percent of these families benefited from such lags.[22]

Table 8.6 shows the relationship between the 1973 measure of income relative to needs and the change in rent between 1971 and 1974 for the nonmoving renter families. The table indicates that those families with low income relative to needs in 1973 were somewhat more likely to report rent increases of *less* than 20 percent, but they were also somewhat more likely to report increases in rents by 30 percent or *more* over the three years. Approximately 82 percent of all of these nonmoving-renter families with 1973 income/needs of less than 1.13 (or 1 percent of all families) experienced increases in rents of less than 20 percent during the 1971-73 period, presumably because of delayed price increases. In contrast, the 16 percent of these families who were faced with rent increases of 30 percent or more (.2 percent of all families) were already suffering from inflation. Although each of these percentages admittedly represented small proportions of the total population, it should be remembered that both were also based upon a select segment of the population which did not include either movers or splitoffs starting new families. What may be even more important to note, however, is that if these proportions were applied to all 66 million fami-

---

[20] Tables A8.1b through A8.1g list the full detail of the transitions for the five primary housing tenure and mobility status subgroups as reported over the seven years from 1968 to 1974 for all 1974 families, for wives who became heads, and for females who were single in 1968 but married before 1974.

[21] We might not do equally well by looking at owners who did not move for at least two reasons. First, our self-report data on owners' housing costs probably provided rougher estimates than those of renters' costs; and, second, owners were much more likely than renters to upgrade their current residences through substantial alterations and modifications.

[22] Remember, however, that we were looking at only 8.7 percent of all 1974 families. Thus, 71 percent of them actually represented only 6 percent of all families.

242

TABLE 8.6

Change in Rent 1971 to 1974 for Renters
Who Did Not Move by Income/Needs in 1973
(For Families With the Same Household Head All Four Years)

Change in Rent--Early	1973 Income/Needs		
1971 to Early 1974	< 1.13*	1.13-2.24	2.25-
Down	24	11	6
0 - 4% Increase	43	44	31
5 - 9	6	6	10
10 - 19	9	16	19
20 - 29	2	11	22
30 - 49	10	6	5
50% or ore	6	6	8
	100	100	101
Number of Cases	193	212	248

_____

*Needs adjusted to the lower Census poverty levels, and Income
adjusted for inflation (combination is .94 if coded Income/Needs
unadjusted).

lies of the United States population, they would indicate that about 130,500 families in the country have had a low income to needs ratio while sustaining substantial rent increases, and that an additional 656,000 equally poor families have had such low rent increases to date that they will almost surely be faced with sizable ones soon.

Large rent increases were most frequent in the northeast and rarest in the north central part of the country. Little difference could be observed between the rent increase of whites and blacks. As shown in Table 8.7, in 1974 the largest relative rent increases among this group of families were most common among young, nonmoving renters as well as among those between the ages of 45 and 64. To some extent, we might expect both of these groups to be more able to afford these increases, the former because of increasing income and the latter because of decreasing needs. Finally, large percentage increases in rent were somewhat more frequent among those whose initial rents were very low (Table 8.8).

Summary

We have observed a wide diversity of changes in housing costs associated with differences in incomes, housing tenure, mobility status, and family composition. Whether we examined percentage or dollar change in housing costs, we found that among 1974 families who have been headed by the same individual since 1968, movers had substantially greater increases in their housing costs than did nonmovers, even relative to their respective income increases. This might mean that people have changed their residences primarily in an effort to upgrade their "bundle" of housing, while nonmoving renters have seemingly enjoyed some inertia or lag in their rents, at least for a while. Once both housing tenure and mobility were taken into account, we found that new home owners and owners who moved to another owned home experienced the greatest increases in housing costs, while renters who moved but remained renters had income increases which were, on average, more than 20 percentage points greater than their housing cost increases. For the nonmovers, both renters and owners had greater increases in their incomes than in their housing costs. Essentially, this seemed to indicate a lack of effect of changes in income on changes in housing costs. Overall it appeared that nonmoving renters were at one end of the range, having enjoyed relatively low average increases in rents along with increases in income which more than offset these costs. At the other end of the range were families who moved to self-owned homes. These families had large housing cost increases but relatively lower increases in income.

TABLE 8.7

Change in Rent, 1971 to 1974, for Renters
Who Did Not Move

(For Families With the Same Household Head All Four Years)

Change in Rent from Early 1971 to Early 1974	Age in 1974				
	18–34	35–44	45–54	55–64	65–
Down	8	12	14	10	7
0 – 4% Increase	37	33	39	29	41
5 – 9	7	5	10	11	8
10 – 19	13	21	5	22	19
20 – 29	18	18	15	12	17
30 – 49	5	2	6	11	5
50% or More	12	9	10	5	2
	100	100	99	100	99
Number of Cases	121	133	159	152	88

MTR 1134

TABLE 8.8

Change in Rent, 1971-1974, By Initial Rent Level
(For Renters Who Did Not Move)

Change in Rent From Early 1971 to Early 1974	Initial Rent (Annual)					
	< $500	$500- 999	$1000- 1499	$1500- 1999	$2000-	All
Down	5	13	8	9	10	10
0 - +4.9%	41	42	37	30	17	36
+5 - 9.9	1	8	10	13	9	8
10 - 19.9	9	13	22	23	21	17
20 - 29.9	15	15	10	17	32	16
30 - 49.9	10	3	7	5	11	6
50% or more	20	6	7	3	0	7
	100	100	101	100	100	100
Number of Cases	104	324	137	55	33	653

MTR 1134

Among those families who had a change in head during the seven-year period, increases in both housing costs and incomes were lower than those among families with the same head, but this difference was largely explained by the sizable proportion of new families which dominates this group. It was interesting to find that a much smaller segment of the group, namely, single females who married sometime during the seven years, had a considerable increase in housing costs on average (167 percent), but a more than compensating increase in income of 245 percent--the largest income increase of any group we studied.

Multiple regression analyses of housing cost increases for movers and for nonmovers added some additional insights into the determinants and impacts of these cost changes. Increases were greatest for residents of the northeast and the south, regardless of the individual's mobility status. For movers, becoming an owner was a primary stimulus to increasing housing costs, but change in income was also important, as was age: younger people experienced greater increases.

Our examination of housing costs as a fraction of income revealed that only a very small proportion of families in each housing tenure and mobility status group (less than 15 percent) which had reported their 1967 housing costs as less than 25 percent of their income later reported their 1973 housing costs as more than 25 percent. Two of these major groups were owners who moved but remained owners and renters who became owners. Because most of the increase for the former could be attributed to upgrading and increased imputed rent (which is a capital gain in house value), it did not really reflect an increased burden. For first home owners, however, the loss of interest on money used for down payment, in addition to interest payments on the remaining balance, represented real cost increases.

Perhaps the clearest case regarding the burden of housing costs could be found among the renters who did not move, as changes in their housing costs relative to their incomes purely reflected changes in income and/or in the price of housing. While about three-fifths of this group faced substantial increases in rents for the housing units they had occupied for all seven years, two-fifths paid less than 15 percent of their incomes for rent in both the first and last year. The erratic or lagged impact of inflation might explain at least part of this low rent to income ratio. In terms of changes in housing costs alone, nearly three out of four nonmoving renters had rent increases of less than 20 percent over a three-year period from 1971 to 1974. This inertia in rents is more common among those with low income to needs ratios--the very people for whom it would be most difficult to pay the increase in rent, which, though delayed up to now, is almost sure to follow.

References

Carliner, Geoffrey, "Income Elasticity of Housing Demand." The Review of Economics and Statistics, November, 1973, pp. 528-532.

"Current Labor Statistics." Monthly Labor Review (March, 1975).

deLeeuw, Frank. "The Demand for Housing: A Review of the Cross-section Evidence." The Review of Economics and Statistics, February, 1971, pp. 1-10.

Economic Report of the President, 1975. Washington, D. C.: U. S. Government Printing Office, 1975.

Morgan, James N., David, Martin H., Cohen, Wilbur J., and Brazer, Harvey E., Income and Welfare in the United States. New York: McGraw-Hill, 1962.

Morgan, James N. et al., Five Thousand American Families--Patterns of Economic Progress. Volume I. Ann Arbor: Institute for Social Research, 1974.

Morgan, James N., "Housing and Ability to Pay." Econometrica 33 (April 1965).

Muth, Richard. "The Demand for Nonfarm Housing" in A. Harberger (ed.), The Demand for Durable Goods. Chicago: University of Chicago Press, 1960.

Reid, Margaret. Housing and Income. Chicago: University of Chicago Press, 1962.

Smith, Wallace. Housing: The Social and Economic Elements. Berkeley: University of California Press, 1970.

Sonquist, John A., Baker, Elizabeth L., Morgan, James N., Searching for Structure, Second Edition. Ann Arbor: Institute for Social Research, 1973.

U. S. Department of Commerce, Bureau of the Census. Price Index of New One-Family Houses Sold: Second Quarter 1975. Washington, D. C., 1975.

248

Appendix 8.1

Table A8.1a gives the percentage change in housing costs, unadjusted and adjusted by regression, for mover and nonmover families with the same head.

Tables A8.1b through A8.1g show the relationship between the housing cost to
income ratio in 1967 to the housing cost to income ratio in 1973 for the following sample families:

> families headed by the same individual during the
> period;
>
> wives who became household heads during the period
> due to separation, divorce, or death of spouse; and,
>
> females who were single in the first year but married
> during the period.[23]

---

[23]It should be noted that these ratios actually relate housing costs as of early
1968 to 1967 income, and early housing costs to 1973 income.

TABLE A8.1a

Average Percent Increase in Housing Costs, 1968-1974, Unadjusted and Adjusted by Regression, and Explanatory Power (Eta^2 and Beta^2) of Family and Environmental Characteristics For Movers and Nonmovers by Categories of Independent Variables

Independent Variable	Those Who Moved			Those Who Did Not Move		
	Number of Cases	Unadjusted	Adjusted	Number of Cases	Unadjusted	Adjusted
Percentage Change in Income		η^2=.059	β^2=.019		η^2=.016	β^2=.007
Negative Change	260	53.18	82.41	277	38.02	42.80
0-49	383	91.47	95.75	469	49.50	50.66
50-99	380	119.70	117.51	426	59.16	57.63
100-199	357	124.98	114.15	312	63.92	59.87
200 or More	245	182.87	154.76	135	62.87	61.59
Change in Family Size		η^2=.057	β^2=.008		η^2=.006	β^2=.002
Smaller by Two or More	268	70.37	87.36	253	53.66	52.85
One Less	234	82.47	103.69	322	51.17	49.31
No Change	692	97.08	106.78	851	51.08	53.49
One Additional	263	164.15	127.62	138	67.99	57.66
Two or More Additional	168	167.62	126.89	55	73.14	67.60
Age		η^2=.068	β^2=.017		η^2=.017	β^2=.008
Under 25	3	-10.86	-23.70	2	-30.78	-10.38
25-34	430	157.86	129.93	83	70.64	61.08
35-44	407	127.67	118.84	309	63.47	57.71
45-54	382	86.56	104.05	456	56.95	55.22
55-64	245	75.22	90.62	373	54.73	58.46
65-74	115	48.24	70.16	263	41.79	45.50
75 or Older	43	63.16	97.68	133	40.70	44.07
Sex-Marital Status		η^2=.037	β^2=.004		η^2=.020	β^2=.007
Single Male Head	185	63.64	97.10	107	33.85	39.58
Single Female Head	430	64.36	92.79	398	38.21	44.77
Married Head	1010	126.27	114.45	1114	59.48	56.99
Race		η^2=.003	β^2=.001		η^2=.000	β^2=.000
White	936	110.67	110.59	1136	53.32	52.97
Black	625	90.98	97.95	441	55.38	57.14
Spanish American and Other	64	127.13	105.38	42	46.30	53.12

TABLE A8.1a (sheet 2 of 2)

Independent Variable	Those Who Moved			Those Who Did Not Move		
	Number of Cases	Unadjusted	Adjusted	Number of Cases	Unadjusted	Adjusted
Region*		η^2=-.012	β^2=.016		η^2=-.011	β^2=.013
Northeast	237	116.10	116.37	337	56.35	59.48
North Central	401	91.62	91.94	424	45.76	43.87
South	684	128.31	124.01	656	63.25	61.88
West	294	96.19	97.18	202	44.74	45.48
Size of Largest City		η^2=.011	β^2=.013		η^2=-.006	β^2=.008
500,000 or More	665	97.47	103.40	564	49.62	49.99
100,000-499,999	340	105.25	105.18	311	50.66	48.59
50,000-99,999	175	108.65	108.79	174	56.08	52.04
25,000-49,999	97	115.73	118.01	119	66.37	70.37
10,000-24,999	145	147.44	137.82	148	47.19	50.87
Less than 10,000	196	109.20	106.15	303	59.54	59.93
NA or Not in USA	7	58.62	-96.87			
Distance to City Center		η^2=.016	β^2=.009		η^2=-.007	β^2=.005
Less than 5 Miles	396	93.63	105.21	381	47.47	53.53
5-14.9 Miles	511	98.21	96.40	425	51.37	54.52
15-29.9 Miles	219	133.53	133.71	213	51.76	52.85
30-49.9 Miles	146	106.59	104.89	188	66.39	60.31
50 or More Miles	306	129.11	118.18	396	54.19	47.31
NA or Not in USA	47	59.74	78.10	16	78.60	83.65
Housing Tenure/Mobility Status		η^2=.094	β^2=.048		η^2=-.015	β^2=.011
Nonmoving Renter	1202	83.19	90.46	1299	56.67	56.26
Renter Who Became Owner				320	30.69	33.46
Nonmoving Owner; Renter Who Did Not Become Home Owner; Those Who Got Housing as Part of Their Job	423	186.37	164.19			
Family Size Increased and Income		η^2=.032	β^2=.000			
Doubled or More						
No	1409	99.61	108.89			
Yes	216	182.76	107.64			

*Plus two very small groups for noncontinental United States and the rest of the world.

MTR 1140A

TABLE A8.1b

Ratio of Housing Costs to Income in 1967
By Ratio of Housing Costs to Income in 1973
(For All Families With the Same Head)

1974 Annual Housing Cost	1968							
	Less Than 10%	10-14%	15-19%	20-24%	25-29%	30-49%	50% or More	All
<10%	8.3	6.0	2.7	1.2	0.4	0.8	0.4	19.8
10-14%	4.7	7.2	4.7	1.9	1.1	1.1	0.6	21.3
15-19%	2.5	4.7	4.2	2.8	1.4	1.4	0.7	17.7
20-24%	1.6	2.8	2.9	2.4	1.1	1.6	0.4	12.8
25-29%	0.9	1.3	2.1	1.2	1.1	1.2	0.6	8.5
30-49%	1.3	1.9	1.9	1.6	1.9	2.6	1.5	12.8
50% or More	0.4	0.6	0.6	0.8	0.4	1.6	2.8	7.2
All	19.7	24.6	19.1	12.0	7.3	10.3	7.1	100.0
Number of Cases								3853

TABLE A8.1c

Ratio of Housing Costs to Income in 1967
By Ratio of Housing Costs to Income in 1973
(For All Owners Who Stayed Owners)

1974 Annual Housing Cost	1968							
	Less Than 10%	10-14%	15-19%	20-24%	25-29%	30-49%	50% or More	All
< 10%	6.8	4.7	2.0	0.8	0.3	0.6	0.3	15.5
10-14%	4.0	7.5	5.2	1.9	1.0	0.6	0.6	20.9
15-19%	2.4	4.6	5.4	3.2	1.4	1.1	0.7	18.7
20-24%	1.1	2.5	2.8	2.7	1.1	2.0	0.4	12.6
25-29%	0.6	1.3	2.5	1.4	1.2	1.2	0.5	8.7
30-49%	1.2	1.8	2.0	1.7	2.6	3.1	2.1	14.5
50% or More	0.1	0.8	0.6	1.1	0.4	2.1	3.9	9.0
All	16.2	23.2	20.5	12.8	7.9	10.9	8.5	100.0
Number of Cases								1786

TABLE A8.1d

Ratio of Housing Costs to Income in 1967
By Ratio of Housing Costs to Income in 1973
(For Owners Who Did Not Move)

Housing Costs/Income in 1973	Housing Costs/Income in 1967							
	Less Than 10%	10-14%	15-19%	20-24%	25-29%	30-49%	50% or More	All
< 10%	7.1	5.2	1.9	0.8	0.3	0.4	0.3	15.9
10-14%	3.8	8.1	5.2	1.7	1.2	0.7	0.6	21.3
15-19%	1.5	4.4	5.6	3.4	1.5	0.7	0.5	17.5
20-24%	0.8	2.6	2.7	3.1	1.0	2.5	0.5	13.1
25-29%	0.4	1.2	2.4	1.6	1.1	1.1	0.5	8.3
30-49%	0.8	1.3	1.7	1.8	2.7	3.8	2.1	14.2
50% or More	0.1	0.5	0.5	1.2	0.3	2.5	4.5	9.6
All	14.5	23.3	19.9	13.5	8.0	11.8	9.0	100.0
Number of Cases								1310

TABLE A8.1e

Ratio of Housing Costs to Income in 1967
By Ratio of Housing Costs to Income in 1973
(For Renters Who Stayed Renters)

Housing Costs/Income in 1973	Housing Costs/Income in 1967							
	Less Than 10%	10-14%	15-19%	20-24%	25-29%	30-49%	50% or More	All
< 10%	12.7	7.3	3.5	1.8	0.8	0.8	0.2	27.2
10-14%	5.9	6.2	4.2	2.2	1.7	1.6	0.5	22.2
15-19%	1.4	4.3	2.7	2.9	1.8	2.0	0.4	15.6
20-24%	1.5	2.2	3.8	2.9	1.1	1.5	0.7	13.7
25-29%	0.7	1.2	0.8	0.6	1.4	1.3	1.0	7.0
30-49%	0.6	1.6	2.4	1.3	0.7	2.8	1.0	10.5
50% or More	0.8	0.1	0.5	0.2	0.1	0.6	1.6	3.8
All	23.6	22.9	18.0	12.0	7.7	10.5	5.4	100.0
Number of Cases								1122

TABLE A8.1f

Ratio of Housing Costs to Income in 1967
By Ratio of Housing Costs to Income in 1973
(For Renters Who Did Not Move)

Housing Costs/Income in 1973	Housing Costs/Income in 1967							
	Less Than 10%	10–14%	15–19%	20–24%	25–29%	30–49%	50% or More	All
< 10%	20.9	10.7	2.4	0.7	0.6	0.5	0.0	35.8
10–14%	4.3	5.1	2.0	2.1	1.6	1.2	0.3	16.7
15–19%	1.5	3.0	2.2	3.7	1.1	1.5	0.4	13.4
20–24%	0.6	2.0	4.3	2.9	1.5	1.0	0.7	12.8
25–29%	0.4	1.0	0.8	1.3	0.1	1.1	0.2	4.8
30–49%	0.6	1.2	3.0	1.4	0.4	3.2	1.0	10.9
50% or More	0.8	0.0	0.9	0.4	0.0	0.9	2.5	5.6
All	29.1	22.9	15.6	12.6	5.3	9.3	5.2	100.0
Number of Cases								358

TABLE A8.1g

Ratio of Housing Costs to Income in 1967
By Ratio of Housing Costs to Income in 1973
(For Renters Who Became Owners)

Housing Costs/Income in 1973	Housing Costs/Income in 1967							
	Less Than 10%	10-14%	15-19%	20-24%	25-29%	30-49%	50% or More	All
< 10%	9.0	4.8	4.1	1.4	0.2	0.9	0.1	20.6
10-14%	6.7	7.7	4.7	1.3	0.8	1.7	0.2	23.2
15-19%	5.4	7.5	3.7	2.0	0.5	0.9	1.4	21.3
20-24%	4.6	6.2	2.7	1.4	0.4	0.4	0.1	15.8
25-29%	1.7	1.7	2.6	0.3	0.4	0.6	0.0	7.3
30-49%	1.9	2.6	1.3	1.5	0.2	1.2	0.0	8.7
50% or More	0.2	0.7	0.0	0.4	0.4	0.6	0.7	3.0
All	29.5	31.3	19.0	8.3	3.1	6.2	2.5	100.0
Number of Cases								547

Chapter 9

LABOR MARKET DISCRIMINATION AGAINST WOMEN*

Michael Conte

Introduction

This analysis focuses on the difference in wages received by women and men in the American labor market. We found that there was a very large difference in the group mean wage and that this difference cannot be fully accounted for by adjusting women's wages for such productivity-related characteristics as education, experience, and so forth.

We proposed that the total inter-sex wage difference results from three factors: differences in productivity, differences in tastes (personal preferences), and discrimination. This is in contrast to the models of other economists who have divided the total inter-sex wage difference into only two parts: a *deserved* wage difference, stemming from differences in productivity, and a *discriminatory* wage difference, stemming from prejudice. We did not attempt to measure each part of the wage difference, but used the three-factor model to make an approximation of the part due to discrimination.

As part of our statistical procedure, we used two different measures of experience: a proxy variable (age minus education minus six) and a direct measure. The two measures are similar for men but quite different for women. We found that direct measurement of women's experience significantly affects the measurement of discrimination.

In addition to measuring these fractions of the total wage difference, we also attempted to associate fractions of the discriminatory part of the wage difference with women's respective personal characteristics. We found that a woman's marital status was the single most important indicator of the degree to which she would receive lower wages than an equally qualified man.

Finally, we proposed that women who receive "equal pay for equal work" may still be subject to discrimination in the form of different entry and promotional opportunities. Such occupational discrimination may account for part of the sex-

---

*The author wishes to thank Dr. Frank M. Andrews for his help in interpreting some of the intermediate results.

wage differential. Ignoring this may have led previous researchers to underestimate the amount of sex discrimination in the labor market.

Analysis

I. BACKGROUND

A growing body of empirical research has documented persistent divisions among American workers: divisions by race, sex, educational credentials, industry grouping and so forth . . .. These groups seem to operate in different *labor markets*, with different working conditions, different promotional opportunities, different wages, and different market institutions.[1]

Definition and Discussion of Discrimination

The average wage of the white working women in the sample in 1973 was 56 percent that of the white working men. The corresponding figure for 1949 was 67 percent.[2] We can see, therefore, that the sex-wage difference is persistent and has actually increased in 25 years.

The existence of such stable group differences in the labor market stands in defiance of early neoclassical arguments. These arguments suggested that a persistent wage differential could arise only on account of different group productivities, as measured by levels of education, experience and other personal characteristics.[3]

From Tables A9.3a and A9.3b, we see that men and women in the panel did not differ greatly on the majority of these characteristics.[4] Women, for example, had approximately the same amount of education as men. The main departures from

---

[1] Reich, Gordon and Edwards (1973), pp. 359-365.

[2] Calculated from Sanborn (1964), p. 534. These calculations are discussed below.

[3] Productivity is not directly measurable in most instances because of the inability to measure individual or group output in a large industrial or bureaucratic setting. With the rise of the human capital school of economics, however, it was argued that productivity could be measured as well on the input side as on the output. If the amount of education, work experience, and other characteristics of an individual determined his or her productivity, then one need only measure these personal characteristics.

[4] Columns 1 and 2 in each of these tables are measures of the mean values of the personal characteristics of men and women. The average wage is a geometric mean. The other averages are arithmetic. The two subsamples differ slightly because they correspond to regressions in which different variables were used with varying response rates on the differing variables.

equality were in the (direct) experience variable,[5] as shown in Table A9.3b, and in the proportions of women and men who worked part-time. (Women had only half the actual work experience of men and were more likely to work part-time.) As shown below, these differences in personal characteristics did not account for the full wage difference.

In response to this inability to explain the full wage difference on the basis of productivity differences, economists introduced the concept of labor market discrimination. In The Economics of Discrimination, Gary Becker presented perhaps the best known theoretical analysis of the labor market implications of what he called "tastes for discrimination," or prejudice. Any agent involved in or capable of affecting the labor market can have such tastes and act upon them. Discrimination, therefore, may be a result of the prejudices of capitalists, workers, consumers, or governmental bureaucrats. In general, "money, commonly used as a measuring rod, will...serve as a measure of discrimination. If an individual has a 'taste for discrimination,' he must act *as if* he were willing to pay something, either directly or in the form of a reduced income, to be associated with some persons instead of others."[6]

As Becker and others[7] have demonstrated, the nature of the expected labor market effects of discrimination depend, in good measure, upon the agent of the discrimination. For example, discrimination by employers is expected to result in lower wages for the victims of discrimination (and lower profits for the employer). Discrimination by other employees is expected to result in occupational segregation, but not necessarily in financial loss to anyone except the employer. Discrimination by consumers is generally found to result in occupational segregation, lower wages to the victims, and losses to the employer and consumer.

The major distinction to be made, from the point of view of the victim of discrimination, is between wage effects and employment effects. Employer discrimination affects wages directly. Employee, consumer, and "outsider" discrimination generally affects wages by limiting the job and/or promotion opportunities of the victim. This paper concentrates on wage discrimination, and on market segregation only insofar as it affects victims' (in this case, women's) wages.

Wage discrimination has generally been defined as the payment of wages in an amount determined by factors other than individual productivity. It is therefore

---

[5]The difference between the two experience variables is explained below.

[6]Becker (1957).

[7]In particular, Chiswick (1973) and Zellner (1972).

measured as a residual: i.e., the "unexplained" portion of the total wage difference. Before explaining the techniques one can use to measure this residual, let us first examine this concept of wage discrimination more closely.

The Wage Remnant

The problem with taking the residual of the wage difference--that is, subtracting from the wage difference the effects of productivity differences--and calling it the discriminatory difference in wage levels is that this residual need not be the result of discrimination (i.e., prejudice) alone. In fact, two persons with identical "personal characteristics" may receive different wages as a result of their own personal choices or preferences. That is, two persons who *can* perform at the same level *need not*. They may choose to exercise various fractions of their capabilities or simply have different subjective evaluations of the (marginal) trade-offs between labor and leisure. The actual choice of job can indicate the degree to which an individual chooses to exercise her or his productive capabilities.[8]

In theory, therefore, we can separate out *three* parts of the absolute wage difference: (1) a part due to differences in skills (leaving us with the "adjusted" wage difference), (2) a part due to differences in employee tastes, and (3) a part due to prejudice.[9] Hence, not all of what some economists have called "discrimination" is actually discrimination. For this reason, we call the residual after adjusting for differences in productivity the *wage remnant* rather than the "discriminatory difference." The wage remnant consists of a part due to different group preferences and a part due to discrimination. We can define the wage remnant as the difference between men's wages and what women's wages would be in the absence of productivity differences. The wage remnant plus all the adjustments for productivity differences equals the total absolute wage difference.

It would seem to follow that this confusion between what is discriminatory and what is not has led some economists to overestimate the amount of discrimination in the labor market by including in the discriminatory part of the wage difference a subject that is actually due to differences in preferences. It is interesting, therefore, to point out that this confusion may also have led some economists (as discussed below) to underestimate the amount of discrimination. To understand this, let us go back to the wage remnant. Suppose we wanted to adjust the wage remnant for differences in individual preferences. If we could do

---

[8] Difference in preferences may result from sex-role stereotyping in childhood and adolescence. That discussion, however, is beyond the scope of this paper.

[9] The theoretical separation of the parts due to taste and prejudice can be treated explicitly in a supply-demand framework. This is done for interested readers in Appendix 9.1.

this, we would be left with a residual equal to the actual discriminatory wage difference. How could we perform this adjustment? If, as mentioned above, we assume that personal preferences with regard to work "effort" are revealed in job selection, then all we need to do is to adjust for differences in group occupational distribution. As discussed below, Henry Sanborn did exactly this and concluded that there was very little of a (discriminatory) wage difference left. What this procedure assumes, however, is that men and women are equally free to exercise their occupational preferences, or, equally, that the difference in the occupational distributions of women and men is a function only of differences in preferences.

One can seriously question this assumption. In fact, one could equally well assume the opposite: that any inter-group difference in occupational distribution is due to coercion. Such coercion could be of a direct or indirect nature. Direct coercion could take the form of closed employment or promotion practices by employers or unions. Indirect coercion could be the result of sexual stereotyping, whereby wives "naturally" assume the bulk of household tasks and forfeit the labor market experience required to obtain a well-paying job or promotion. Most likely, the observed inter-group difference in occupational distribution results from some combination of different preferences and coercion. Surely, that part of the wage difference due to coercion in job assignment or job choice must be considered discriminatory.

We see, therefore, that adjusting for inter-group differences in occupational distribution, while intended to remove the effects of different preferences from the wage difference, can also remove the effects of occupational coercion. The question, then, is whether or not to adjust for occupation. The answer, of course, is that both adjustment for fine categories of occupation and no adjustment for occupation at all are probably incorrect. Figures arrived at using each of these two methods can serve only as brackets of the correct result. In the following section of this chapter, we discuss several methods of calculating these brackets. We then employ one of these methods and compare our results with those of previous investigators. We have made no attempt here to disentangle the effects of preferences and coercion.

Statistical Procedures

Statistical procedures of the analysis of discrimination are of two types: those employed to test the existence of labor market discrimination and those used to estimate the extent of discrimination. Barry Chiswick, for example, proposes that discrimination of the employee and consumer-based types may result in changes in the variance of intra-group wages.[10] Testing for discrimination against non-whites, he found that whites are willing to sustain higher degrees of inequality among themselves so as to avoid association with nonwhites. Chiswick's procedure cannot, however, be easily extended to the measurement of the effect of discrimination upon the recipients. It is also impossible, using his method, to distinguish between the effect of personal preferences in job selection and occupational coercion.

One inviting scheme for the measurement of the wage remnant might be to regress hourly earnings on a set of personal characteristics variables using a pooled sample of women and men. In addition to the regular independent variables, such as education and experience, one could enter a dichotomous dummy variable for sex. The significance of the coefficient on this variable, therefore, might serve as an indication of the presence of a wage remnant in the labor market.

It is tempting to interpret the size of the coefficient on the dummy variable for sex as an indication of the size of the remnant. If, for instance, the regression coefficients are significantly different for men and women, the coefficients in a pooled regression will represent an average of the two true estimates. Gerald Plato and J. Patrick Madden have shown that the men's and women's equations are, in fact, different.[11] Hence, the coefficient on the sex dummy variable in a pooled regression would represent a deviation from the *average* regression line and not from the "male" regression line. There would be, in other words, a downward bias in the estimate of the wage remnant.

A second possible method for estimating the size of the wage remnant is to adjust the difference in actual group mean wage levels by differences in personal characteristics. This can be done with sequential univariate adjustments or in a single multivariate procedure.

Henry Sanborn used the sequential univariate adjustment method to determine an "adjusted wage ratio." Beginning with a female-male *income* ratio of .58,[12] he first adjusted for hours worked, multiplying the income ratio by the ratio of men's hours worked to women's hours worked. In this way, he arrived at a *wage* ratio of .67. Similar adjustments were also made for education, age, "urbanness," and occupational distribution.

---

[10] See Chiswick (1973).

[11] Plato and Madden (1973).

[12] Sanborn used a combination of two sources for his occupation data: the Bureau of Census' Census of the Population 1950, and the Bureau of Labor Statistics' Occupational Wage Surveys from 1945-1955.

Sanborn found that adjusting for differences in education, age, urban-rural status and race raised the adjusted wage ratio to about .76. This means that women *with equal qualifications* (at least with respect to these four variables) receive an hourly wage that is .76 that of men.

After making these adjustments for personal characteristics, Sanborn also introduced adjustments for group differences in occupational distribution. Not only did he want to insure that he was comparing wage figures for women and men of equal qualifications, but he was also interested in comparing the wages of (equally qualified) women and men *who did equal work*. Using a very extensive and detailed list of occupational categories, he adjusted for 273 types of jobs, raising the adjusted wage ratio to .87. As an "explanation" of the effect of the occupation adjustment, Sanborn said:

> Part of the reason for the low sex-income ratio . . . is that men tend to be in higher paying occupations than women.[13]

Left unsettled in this explanation is the question of whether the inter-group occupational differences result fully, partially, or not at all from the exercise of individual preferences. Sanborn acknowledges this when he says:

> The only discrimination considered here is lower pay to women than to men for the same work. Another form of discrimination, not dealt with here, might be the refusal to give women equal opportunities for advancement.[14]

Thus far we have mentioned two types of statistics that can be used to measure the size of the wage remnant. The "shift coefficient" in the pooled regression method reflects the absolute wage difference, measured in dollars per hour, due to discrimination (subject to the qualifications we have introduced concerning preferences). The larger the shift coefficient, the greater the dollar per hour impact of discrimination.

The univariate, sequential adjustment measure uses a more informative statistic to measure the wage remnant, the ratio of the adjusted (average) women's wage to the actual (average) men's wage. The *higher* the estimate, the *lower* the wage remnant.

A third method to measure the wage remnant uses yet a different statistic, generally called the "discrimination coefficient." Rather than introduce new terminology, we will adopt this term with the, by now, obvious caveat on interpreta-

---

[13] Sanborn (1964), p. 534.

[14] Sanborn (1964), p. 534.

tion. This statistic measures the wage remnant as a fraction of the total wage difference. If we define $\overline{W}_f^o$ as the average women's adjusted wage or the wage that the average women would receive in a nondiscriminatory labor market, and $\overline{W}_m$ (men) and $\overline{W}_f$ (women) as the average actual men's and women's wages, then $\overline{W}_m - \overline{W}_f^o$ is equal to the wage remnant, and $\dfrac{\overline{W}_m - \overline{W}_f^o}{\overline{W}_m - \overline{W}_f}$ is equal to the wage remnant as a fraction of the total wage difference. Thus, we see that the total wage difference can be divided into two parts, one part representing a (partially) undeserved, or discriminatory, wage difference and the other part, $\dfrac{\overline{W}_f^o - \overline{W}_f}{\overline{W}_m - \overline{W}_f}$, representing a "deserved" part of the wage difference.

According to a procedure developed by Ronald Oaxaca,[15] these two parts of the wage difference can be estimated using two regression equations, one to estimate men's wages and the other to estimate women's. In each of these equations, the dependent variable is the log of the wage, and the independent variables are the personal characteristics. As shown in Appendix 9.2, the wage remnant, as a fraction of the total wage difference, is equal to the difference in the regression coefficients multiplied by average values of the respective personal characteristics (using the men's personal characteristics to estimate one bound and the women's to estimate the other). This is an intuitively plausible result because the difference in wage regression coefficients represents the difference in pecuniary returns to the personal characteristics of men and women. For example, a higher coefficient on education in the men's wage equation than in the women's would indicate that men are more highly rewarded for educational achievement than women. It is reasonable, therefore, that the amount of discrimination should be indicated by the size of this difference in coefficients, weighted by the average values of the respective personal characteristics. The remainder of the wage difference can be shown to equal the differences in personal characteristics multiplied by the regression coefficients. In sum, a deserved wage differential between groups results from differences in skills, while a discriminatory differential results from unequal returns to skills. Together, these two differentials add up to the full wage difference.

Note that the result of this procedure is a fraction representing the wage remnant divided by the total wage difference. This fraction does not indicate

---

[15] Oaxaca (1973). Oaxaca's derivation, along with several slight modifications, is given in Appendix 9.2 of this chapter.

the absolute level of the wage remnant or the wage difference. It tells us what percentage of the total wage difference results from discrimination and preference differences.

So far, we have outlined three approaches to the measurement of the wage remnant. The third method is statistically superior to the other two. In the next section, we analyze the data from the seventh wave of the panel study according to Oaxaca's technique and compare our results with his. While the technique is the same as Oaxaca's,[16] we expect different results because of the panel study's better data on women's experience and because of our generalization of the sample to include rural workers.

II. ANALYSIS RESULTS

In this section, we reproduce Oaxaca's study using a different sample.[17] Male and female wage regressions were run on a subsample of the 1973 panel data. The subsample consisting of 915 women and 1269 men eliminated the nonwhite and unemployed members of the sample. In contrast to Oaxaca's procedure, however, rural workers--those living in towns of less than 5,000--were *not* excluded (Oaxaca studied the urban labor market). There is good reason to exclude *farm* workers when care has not been taken to assure the homogeneity of the income concept across occupational categories. The panel data, however, was sufficiently well-articulated to make valid comparisons of farm and nonfarm incomes. In any case, farmers made up only 1.8 percent of the sample. We saw no reason to exclude the nonfarm workers who lived in municipalities of less than 5,000 (comprising about one-third of the sample) as long as some control was made for location.

The regressions included the same variables as in Oaxaca's study where possible. These were:

Education

Education^2

Experience

Experience^2

Whether part-time

Marital status

---

[16] Except for the minor modifications given in Appendix 9.2.

[17] In a recent publication, Blinder used the panel data from 1972 and a similar procedure to measure fractions of the total sex-wage difference. He excluded wives from the female subsample, however, because of the lack of information in that year's data on wives. Wives comprise about 90 percent of the female subsample.

Number of children

Size of the nearest SMSA

Region

Industry

Occupation

A description of each of these variables and the reason for including it in the model follows.

Education affects cognitive and/or manual skills at the job market entry point, as well as one's predisposition in choosing between labor and leisure. Education was entered as a continuous variable ranging from 2.5 through 18, reflecting years of formal education achievement.

The *experience* variable was intended to measure on-the-job training or other enhancement of skills received while working. Experience was measured in two different ways for both men and women, requiring each regression to be run twice. In the past, a proxy variable (age minus education minus six) has generally been used to measure experience because respondents were never asked the straightforward question: How many years have you worked? Such a question was asked in the seventh wave of the panel study, providing two separate experience variables.[18] A short discussion is in order to comment on the relationship between these two variables for men and women and to consider their possible effects on the measurement of discrimination.

We computed a simple correlation between the regular proxy variable for experience, called the indirect experience variable (age minus years of education minus six), and the answers to the experience question in the seventh wave of the panel study, the direct experience variable. This correlation for men was quite high, .92, while that for women was low, .50. It can be seen in Tables A9.3a and A9.3b that the proxy variable overstated the average woman's experience by almost 100 percent, while men's experience was measured about the same by both the proxy and direct measures. This is indicated also in the accompanying graph (Figure 9.1), which plots the direct experience variable against age for men and women. As the educational distributions were similar for men and women, this is close to a plot of the "direct" experience variable against the indirect experience variable. Women's actual experience was shown to be considerably lower than men's, especially at higher ages. As Table A9.3b shows, women have only half as much work experience as men and also only half as much work experience as would be indicated by

---

[18]The question was: "How many years have you (HEAD) worked since you were 18?" The same question was also asked about wives. If the response to the question was greater than the head's (wife's) age minus 18, then age minus 18 was used.

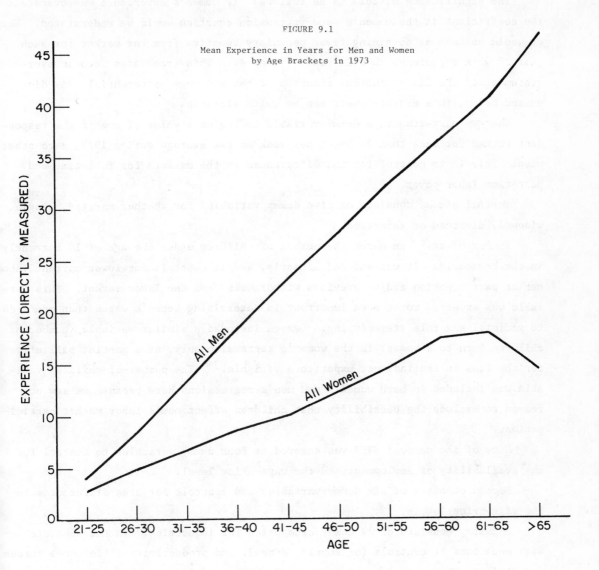

FIGURE 9.1

Mean Experience in Years for Men and Women
by Age Brackets in 1973

the proxy variable.

The significance of this is as follows: If women's experience was overstated the coefficient in the women's wage regression equation would be understated. Women would be seen as obtaining fewer pecuniary benefits from the market for each year of work experience than in reality they do. This translates into an overstatement of the discriminatory fraction of the sex-wage differential. As discussed below, this overstatement can be quite sizeable.

Whether part-time is a dummy variable taking on a value of one if the respondent worked for less than 35 hours per week on the average during 1973; zero otherwise. This is to control for the differences in the markets for full-time and part-time labor power.

Marital status consists of five dummy variables for whether married, single, widowed, divorced or separated.

Number of children means the number of children under the age of 18 currently in the household. It was entered linearly, and it controls for lower current labor market participation and/or previous withdrawals from the labor market. This variable was expected to be more important in determining women's wages than men's due to societal sex role stereotyping. Oaxaca included a similar variable (number of children born to a woman) in the women's regression only, as a partial palliative for the bias in the indirect experience variable. [19] The number-of-children variable was included in both women's and men's regressions here because we saw no reason to exclude the possibility that children affect men's labor market participation.

Size of the nearest SMSA was entered as four dummy variables to control for the availability of employment and the wage-price level.

Region consists of six dummy variables and controls for area differences in the wage-price levels.

Industry consists of 22 dummy categories for industries. In the separate wage equations it controls for supply, demand, and productivity differences across industries. When used to explain part of the wage difference between men and women, it controls for different distributions, by sex, across the 22 categories.

Occupation consists of eight occupational dummy categories and plays the same role as industry.

We employed Oaxaca's method with both the direct and indirect experience variables, both including and excluding occupation and industry in the wage regression

---

[19] Oaxaca's variable measures the experience loss to a woman better than ours because it is a measure of births specifically to the woman. The correlation between his variable and ours, however, is high.

equations. (The wage equations which include occupation and industry are called the "full scale" wage equations. Those excluding occupation and industry are called the "personal characteristics" wage regressions.) The regression results using the indirect (or "proxy") experience variable appear in Table A9.3a. These regressions were on the subsample whose independent and dependent variable appear alongside the coefficients. The regression results using the direct experience variable appear in Table A9.3b with the corresponding subsample means. The subsamples were slightly different because some individuals may have answered the question on age but not the question on work experience and vice versa. Cases where information on one or more variables was not ascertained were excluded.[20]

Let us first look at the differences in the results of the full scale regression analysis when the two alternative experience variables are used.

The results given in Table 9.1 indicate the proportion of the wage difference accounted for by differences in regression coefficients of the respective variables. We note first the differences between the effects of the experience variables themselves. Different coefficients as between the men's and women's regressions on the proxy experience variable accounted for 50.1 percent of the total wage differences, while different coefficients on the direct experience variable accounted for only 26.6 percent of the total wage difference. This confirmed our expectation that discrimination on the basis of different returns to experience is overstated when using the proxy experience variable.

Most interestingly, the better measurement of experience affected the measured impact of different returns to education and to marital status as well. According to the findings from the *proxy* experience regressions, women who are equal to men on the other personal characteristics receive *more favorable* returns to education than do men. As returns to education are generally realized in the first years of labor market participation, this conclusion, if accepted, would lead us to say that equally qualified women step into higher paying jobs than men at first, but advance much more slowly. The results from the direct experience variable, however, indicate that this is not the case. The discrimination and/or preference-induced difference in returns to education leaves women worse off than men at the beginning of their employment careers and dramatically so (differential returns to education, according to column (4), account for more than half of the total wage difference). Women fall further behind equally qualified men as they receive lesser promotions and/or raises, but not at the rate inferred from the regressions using the proxy experience variable.

---

[20]Low significance levels for some of the coefficients, particularly for women, result from small cell size. Therefore, the categories in which the coefficients were not significant were "weighted" less in the overall findings.

TABLE 9.1

Log of the Wage Remnant by Components
and Wage Remnant by Components as Fraction of the Total Wage Difference

	From Regressions Using the Proxy Experience Variable		From Regressions Using the Directly-Measured Experience Variable	
	$-\bar{Z}\Delta B$	$-\bar{Z}\Delta B \div \log \bar{W}$	$-\bar{Z} B$	$-\bar{Z}\Delta B \div \log \bar{W}$
	Log of Wage Difference Due to Difference in Coefficients	Log of Wage Difference Due to Difference in Coefficients as a Fraction of Log of Total Wage Difference *	Log of Wage Difference Due to Difference in Coefficients	Log of Wage Difference Due to Difference in Coefficients as a Fraction of Log of Total Wage Difference **
Constant	.0379	15.2	-.1315	-53.2
Education	-.0405	-16.2	.1389	56.2
Experience Indirectly Measured	.1253	50.1	--	--
Experience Directly Measured	--	--	.0658	26.6
Industry	-.0189	- 7.6	-.0206	- 8.3
Occupation	-.0242	- 9.7	-.0220	- 8.9
Whether Part Time	.0246	9.8	.0131	5.3
Marital Status	.2290	91.6	.1883	76.2
Number of Children in Family Unit	-.0023	- 0.1	-.0105	- 4.3
Size of Largest City in PSU	-.0313	-12.5	-.0356	-14.4
Region	-.0180	- 7.2	-.0199	- 8.1
Total	.2055	82.2	.1660	67.1

*The log of the total wage difference in the corresponding subsample equals .2500.

**The log of the total wage difference in the corresponding subsample equals .2472.

Finally, it is important to note that the single most important variable for explaining discrimination was neither experience nor education, but marital status. Variations on marital status itself accounted for a wage difference equal to three-fourths of the total wage difference between men and women. This result, in conjunction with the signs of the coefficients on all of the dummy variables for marital status in Tables A9.3a and A9.3b, indicates that married women and widows earn less per hour than equally qualified single women. This contrasts with the opposite result generally found for men. (Men earn significantly more if they are married.)

A variety of reasons can be suggested for the difference in wages between married women and single women. Married women may receive lower wages because they have less bargaining power in the labor market. Lower bargaining power may result from impediments to mobility (e.g., placing more importance on the husband's location than on the wife's) or a greater committment to household duties on the wife's part than on the husband's. On the other hand, career-oriented women may not marry *because* of these impediments to full participation. Other possible explanations have been suggested for the importance of marital status in the determination of wages, and, in particular, of women's wages. One is the notion that there is a societal tendency to pay people according to their needs as well as ability, and to assume that husbands, not wives, are supposed to support the family. The basic factor in each of these explanations is sex role stereotyping of some sort, which, in turn, is seen to have definite economic disadvantages for women.

The finding that differences in returns according to marital status account for three-fourths of the wage difference between men and women does not mean that marital status explains three-fourths of all discrimination. In fact, as shown in Table 9.1, education accounts for 56 percent of the wage difference, and experience for 27 percent. These proportions add to more than 100 percent. The 76.2 percent figure for marital status means that if there were no discrimination on the basis of marital status, women's wages would be higher by 76.2 percent of the total wage difference (i.e., by $1.74). No other single characteristic has such a large effect.

Our overall results and Oaxaca's are presented in Table 9.2. The first point to mention is the striking difference between Oaxaca's results and those obtained using the indirect experience variable. Recall that Oaxaca used the same proxy to measure men's and women's work experience. The results from the panel data were considerably higher than Oaxaca's. Our results may have been higher because of a difference in the sample, as noted above (implying that there is *much more* discrimination in small towns than in large ones), or because of a trend. Oaxaca worked with data from 1967, while the data here were for 1973.

TABLE 9.2

Estimates of the Wage Remnant as a Fraction of the Total Wage Difference

		Using Full-Scale Wage Regressions	Using Personal Characteristics Wage Regressions
(1)	Oaxaca	58.4%	77.7%
(2)	Panel data--using the indirect experience variable	82.2	86.7
(3)	Panel data--using the direct experience variable	67.1	75.3

NOTE: The wage regressions which include occupation and industry are called the *full-scale* wage regressions. Those excluding occupation and industry are called the *personal characteristics* wage regressions.

Either of these explanations could account for the 9 percent difference between rows (1) and (2) in column (2). The difference in column (1), however, is much larger (23.6 percent). This result indicates that jobs are much more sex-stereo-typed in rural areas than in urban areas. Unless we are prepared to admit that rural women are more different from urban women than rural men are from urban men in their labor market preferences, we can only conclude that women in rural communities suffer considerable discrimination in hiring and promotion.

Comparison of rows (2) and (3) indicates that using the direct experience variable makes a large difference. As noted above, we accept the results from the direct experience variable (row 3) as more valid. We can interpret the figures in row (3) as follows: At most, 75 percent of the wage difference between women and men results from discrimination. After standardizing for broad categories of occupation and industry, this figure was reduced to 67 percent. This reduction represents the possibility that women choose lower paying jobs because they prefer them. If we have adjusted for the total effects of differences in preferences be-tween the sexes, then this figure represents the discriminatory fraction of the wage difference. By adjusting for finer categories of occupation and industry, we could probably reduce our estimates further but may actually be adjusting for dis-crimination in hiring or promotion. (As shown above, this would most likely be the case in the rural labor market at least.)

The optimal, or correct, degree of adjustment by occupations is a subject for further research. For the present, we estimate that 67 percent of the wage dif-ference between men and women results from discrimination. In our sample, this

corresponds to an adjusted wage ration of .72.[21]   This implies that a woman's
wages are, on the average, about three-fourths those of an equally qualified man.

Summary

In this chapter we have discussed what is meant by labor market discrimination
against women, attempting to distinguish between the effect of personal preferences
and personal or societal prejudices. We then offered some criticisms of previous
studies which measured the amount of wage discrimination in the labor market.
These studies have generally tried to measure two parts of the inter-sex wage difference, one part due to a difference in group productivity and the other part due
to discrimination. We noted that a fraction of the latter is actually due to personal preferences and the remainder to discrimination. We then noted the para-
doxical result that this confusion may have led in the past to underestimation
of the amount of discrimination in the labor market.

We chose one from among three possible statistical techniques to use on the
data from the seventh wave of the panel study to estimate the percentage of the
inter-sex wage difference resulting from discrimination. We found, as a first
approximation, that 67 percent of the wage difference is caused by discrimination.
This figure is subject to the findings of any further research which would disentangle the effects of personal preferences and personal or societal prejudices.

We also concluded, on the basis of the importance of both education and experience on predicting the amount of wage discrimination that a woman is likely
to suffer, that discrimination occurs both upon entry into the labor market and
throughout her work career.

Finally, although discriminatory inter-sex differences in hiring and promotion are important explanatory factors, the most important factor in predicting

---

[21]In our sample, the average men's wage ($\bar{W}_m$) equals \$6.10, and the average woman's
wage ($\bar{W}_f$) equals \$3.60. So, a discrimination coefficient of .67 implies that:

$$\frac{\bar{W}_m - \bar{W}_f^o}{\bar{W}_m - \bar{W}_f} = .67,$$ where $\bar{W}_f^o$ equals the average wage that a woman would receive in a

labor market without discrimination or coercion. Substituting in the values
for $\bar{W}_m$ and $\bar{W}_f$ and rearranging, gives:

$$\frac{\bar{W}_f^o}{\bar{W}_m^o} = .72$$

274

the level of wage discrimination against women is marital status. Holding all else constant, marital status accounted for three-fourths of the total inter-sex wage difference.

References

Becker, Gary S. The Economics of Discrimination. Chicago: University of Chicago Press, 1957.

Blinder, Alan. "Wage Discrimination: Reduced Form and Structural Estimates." Journal of Human Resources, VIII, Fall 1973.

Chiswick, Barry. "Racial Discrimination in the Labor Market: A Test of Alternative Hypotheses." Journal of Political Economy, Vol. 81, No. 6, December 1973.

Oaxaca, Ronald. "Male-Female Wage Differentials in Urban Labor Markets." International Economic Review, Vol. 14, No. 3, October 1973.

Plato, Gerald E. and Madden, J. Patrick. "Low Wages and Long Hours." Working Paper No. 8. Pennsylvania State University: Department of Agricultural and Rural Sociology, December 1973.

Reich, Michael, Gordon, David, and Edwards, Richard. "A Theory of Labor Market Segmentation." The American Economic Review, Vol. LXII, No. 12, May 1973.

Sanborn, Henry. "Pay Differences Between Men and Women." Industrial and Labor Relations Review, July 1964.

Zellner, H. "Discrimination, Occupational Segregation and the Relative Wage." American Economic Review, May 1972.

Appendix 9.1

In terms of the supply of and demand for productive services, two groups of individuals can be assumed to face the same market demand curve (DD in Figure A9.1a). Two groups whose average skill levels are the same and which have similar preferences with respect to labor and leisure also exhibit identical labor supply curves (SS on Figure A9.1a).[22] Their wage, W_o, will be identical.

FIGURE A9.1a

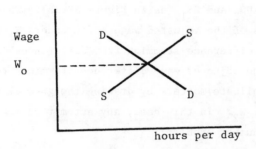

If either DD or SS is different for the two groups, we can expect them to receive different wages. Different market demand curves indicate that presence of discrimination against one or the other group. (Employers are willing to compensate individuals from one group at a lower rate than individuals from another group at the (specified) level of qualifications.) Different labor supply curves indicate different preferences as between groups. Consulting Figure A9.1b, therefore, we can see that even an adjusted wage difference--i.e., the difference between the wage levels of two equally qualified individuals--can be broken up into two parts. DD_1 in Figure A9.1b represents the demand for labor of the first type (men's labor, in our case). DD_2 represents demand for labor of the second type. Similar interpretations apply to the respective labor supply curves. Let us assume for the moment that the intersection of DD_1 and SS_2 occurs

---

[22] The abscissa in Figures A9.1a, A9.1b and A9.1c may represent either hours of work per working period (e.g., a day), as is the usual case, or effort per hour of work. Both of these are subject to individual preferences, and either could be used to demonstrate the point. The demand curve slopes downward in the first (usual) case and upward in the second. We use the first because the results are more readily apparent.

FIGURE A9.1b

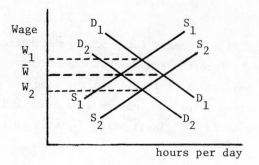

at the same height as that of DD_2 and SS_1 (as in Figure A9.1b). Then we can neatly point out the two parts of the adjusted wage difference: $W_1-\bar{W}$ represents the part of the adjusted wage difference stemming from differences in preferences. $\bar{W}-W_2$ represents the part of the adjusted wage difference stemming from discrimination. Of course, we can complicate matters by drawing the general case (Figure A9.1c) where $\bar{W}_1$ does not equal $\bar{W}_2$. In this case, any attempt to measure the two parts is subject to an index number problem.

FIGURE A9.1c

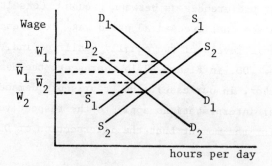

Appendix 9.2

The statistical derivation of the two parts of the wage difference has been worked out by Ronald Oaxaca.[23] Let

(1) $\quad G = \dfrac{\overline{W}_m - \overline{W}_f}{\overline{W}_f}$, so that

(2) $\quad \log (G + 1) = \log (\overline{W}_m) - \log (\overline{W}_f)$

where $\overline{W}_m$ and $\overline{W}_f$ are the average hourly wages for males and females, respectively. From the properties of ordinary least squares estimation, we have

(3) $\quad \log (\overline{W}_m) = Z'_m \hat{B}_m$

(4) $\quad \log (\overline{W}_f) = Z'_f \hat{B}_f$

where $\quad Z'_m$ and Z'_f = the vectors of mean values of the regressors for males and females, respectively, and

$\hat{B}_m$ and $\hat{B}_f$ = the corresponding vectors of estimated coefficients.

Upon substitution of (3) and (4) into (2), we obtain

(5) $\quad \log (G + 1) = Z'_m \hat{B}_m - Z'_f \hat{B}_f$

If we let

(6) $\quad \Delta Z' = Z'_m - Z'_f$

(7) $\quad \Delta \hat{B} = \hat{B}_f - \hat{B}_m,$

and substitute $\hat{B}_m = \hat{B}_f - \Delta \hat{B}$ into (5), then the male-female wage differential can be written as

(8) $\quad \log (G + 1) = \Delta Z' \hat{B}_f - Z'_m \Delta \hat{B}$

Essentially, a "deserved" wage differential between groups $(\Delta Z' \hat{B}_f)$ results from group differences in skills (inputs), while the discriminatory differential

---

[23]See Oaxaca (1973), pp. 696–697.

$(-Z_m' \Delta\hat{B})$ results from unequal returns to skills.

An alternative decomposition of the wage differential is obtained by substituting $\hat{B}_f = \Delta\hat{B} + \hat{B}_m$ into (5), giving

$$(9) \quad \log (G + 1) = \Delta Z' \ \hat{B}_m - Z_f' \ \Delta\hat{B}$$

In either case, $\Delta\hat{B}$ can be obtained by running parallel regressions on the log of men's and women's wages, and calculating

$$(10) \quad -Z_f' \ \Delta\hat{B} = \log (G + 1) - \Delta Z' \ \hat{B}_m$$

and

$$(11) \quad -Z_m' \ \Delta\hat{B} = \log (G + 1) - \Delta Z' \ \hat{B}_f$$

This establishes a range of possible values for the discriminatory portion of the wage difference. The results in Table 9.1 represent the average of these two extreme values.

We note one slight modification of Oaxaca's method. Equation (3) above is not exactly correct. It should be

$$(3') \quad \log (\overline{W}_m) = \overline{Z}' \ \hat{B} + \overline{e}$$

where $\overline{e}$ represents the average value of the error term. While ordinary least squares sets $\sum e^2$ equal to zero, this does not imply that $\overline{e}$ will equal zero. If $\overline{e}$ does not equal zero, then equation (8) will not hold exactly. To correct for this, we define

$$(8') \quad \log (G + 1) = \Delta Z' \ \hat{B}_f - Z_m' \ \Delta\hat{B} + \overline{e}$$

The wage remnant, therefore, can be taken as either $Z_m'\Delta\hat{B}$ or $Z_m'\Delta\hat{B} + \overline{e}$. There is not much difference between the values of these estimators. We used $Z_m'\Delta\hat{B}$. So the wage remnant, as a fraction of the total wage difference and using men's weights, is defined as:

$$\frac{\overline{Z}_m'\Delta\hat{B}}{\overline{Z}_m'\Delta\hat{B} + \Delta Z\hat{B}_f + \overline{e}}$$

TABLE A9.3a

Means of Personal Characteristics Variables and Regression Coefficients
For Men and Women in 1973 with Directly Measured Experience Variable and Corresponding Subsample

	$\bar{Z}_m$ Means of Men's Personal Characteristics (1)	$\bar{Z}_f$ Means of Women's Personal Characteristics (2)	From Men's Full Scale Wage Equation $\hat{B}_m$ (3)	From Men's Full Scale Wage Equation t-ratio (4)	From Women's Full Scale Wage Equation $\hat{B}_f$ (5)	From Women's Full Scale Wage Equation t-ratio (6)	From Men's Personal Characteristics Wage Equation $\hat{B}_m$ (7)	From Men's Personal Characteristics Wage Equation t-ratio (8)	From Women's Personal Characteristics Wage Equation $\hat{B}_f$ (9)	From Women's Personal Characteristics Wage Equation t-ratio (10)
Average Wage	$5.27	$2.97								
Log of Average Wage	.722	.472								
R^2			.412		.362		.296		.234	
Constant term			.2468		.3783		.2508		.4018	
Education	12.34	12.28	-.0079	0.8	-.0257	1.5	-.0037	0.4	-.0436	2.5
Education^2	162.90	157.85	.0012	2.9	.0017	2.2	.0013	3.1	.0033	4.6
Experience (proxy)	--	--	--	--	--	--	--	--	--	--
Experience^2 (proxy)	--	--	--	--	--	--	--	--	--	--
Experience (direct)	24.61	12.76	.0178	7.8	.0116	4.9	.0209	8.7	.0129	5.2
Experience^2 (direct)	729.09	271.77	-.0003	7.9	-.0002	3.5	-.0004	9.0	-.0002	3.7
Industry										
Agriculture	.0536	.0101	.0773	1.4	.0960	1.1	--	--	--	--
Mining	.0071	.0028	.2296	3.3	.0757	0.5	--	--	--	--
Construction	.0929	.0025	.1453	5.2	.3833	2.5	--	--	--	--
Manufacturing (durables)	.2230	.0911	.1611	6.7	.1223	3.5	--	--	--	--
Manufacturing (nondurables)	.0790	.1023	.1181	4.1	.0766	2.0	--	--	--	--
Transportation	.0551	.0062	.1614	5.2	.2271	2.3	--	--	--	--
Communications	.0141	.0177	.1018	2.0	.1269	2.1	--	--	--	--
Printing	.0211	.0136	.1600	3.7	.0621	0.9	--	--	--	--
Utilities	.0239	.0035	.1893	4.5	.4436	3.4	--	--	--	--

TABLE A9.3a (Sheet 2 of 3)

	$\bar{Z}_m$ Means of Men's Personal Characteristics	$\bar{Z}_f$ Means of Women's Personal Characteristics	From Men's Full Scale Wage Equation		From Women's Full Scale Wage Equation		From Men's Personal Characteristics Wage Equation		From Women's Personal Characteristics Wage Equation	
			$\hat{B}_m$	t-ratio	$\hat{B}_f$	t-ratio	$\hat{B}_m$	t-ratio	$\hat{B}_f$	t-ratio
	(1)	(2)	(3)	(4)	(5)	(6)	(7)	(8)	(9)	(10)
Trade, Wholesale	.0409	.0153	.0865	2.6	.2280	3.6	--	--	--	--
Trade, NA Kind	.0098	.0085	.1103	1.8	.2182	2.6	--	--	--	--
Trade, Retail	--	--	--	--	--	--	--	--	--	--
Finance	.0504	.0563	.0934	3.0	.1027	2.8	--	--	--	--
Business Service	.0120	.0153	.0721	1.3	.0535	0.8	--	--	--	--
Repair Service	.0299	.0023	-.0240	0.6	-.1225	0.8	--	--	--	--
Personal Service	.0096	.0915	-.1105	1.8	-.0291	0.9	--	--	--	--
Recreation	.0091	.0077	.0742	1.2	.1321	1.5	--	--	--	--
Medical Service	.0280	.1222	.1297	3.2	.0816	2.6	--	--	--	--
Education Service	.0611	.1702	.0662	2.0	.0960	3.2	--	--	--	--
Other Professional Service	.0315	.0356	-.0302	0.7	.0549	1.2	--	--	--	--
Government	.0445	.0417	.0897	2.7	.1892	4.5	--	--	--	--
Armed Services	.0059	.0022	.1834	2.4	.1460	0.8	--	--	--	--
Occupation										
Professional	.1888	.1878	.0437	1.7	.1561	5.5	--	--	--	--
Managers	.1343	.0394	.0907	3.8	.0734	1.8	--	--	--	--
Self-employed	.0937	.0114	-.0579	2.1	-.0704	0.9	--	--	--	--
Clerical and Sales Workers	--	--	--	--	--	--	--	--	--	--
Craftspersons	.2343	.0141	-.0234	1.0	-.0706	1.0	--	--	--	--
Operatives	.1373	.1425	-.0556	2.1	-.0141	0.4	--	--	--	--
Unskilled laborers and Service Workers	.0631	.2075	-.0997	3.2	-.0929	3.6	--	--	--	--
Farm Workers	.0410	.0022	-.2160	3.4	-.1206	0.7	--	--	--	--

TABLE A.9.3a (Sheet 3 of 3)

	$\bar{z}_m$ Means of Men's Personal Characteristics	$\bar{z}_f$ Means of Women's Personal Characteristics	From Men's Full Scale Wage Equation $\hat{B}_m$	t-ratio	From Women's Full Scale Wage Equation $\hat{B}_f$	t-ratio	From Men's Personal Characteristics Wage Equation $\hat{B}_m$	t-ratio	From Women's Personal Characteristics Wage Equation $\hat{B}_f$	t-ratio
	(1)	(2)	(3)	(4)	(5)	(6)	(7)	(8)	(9)	(10)
Whether Part Time										
Whether Part Time	.0333	.3328	.0869	2.6	.0155	0.8	.0879	2.5	-.0223	1.2
Marital Status										
Married	.9218	.7145	.1678	4.7	-.0415	1.2	.1843	4.8	-.0129	0.3
Widowed	.0128	.0920	.1389	2.3	-.0898	2.1	.1668	2.5	-.0707	1.6
Divorced	.0299	.1227	.0608	1.3	.0113	0.3	.0837	1.6	.0260	0.6
Single (never married)	--	--	--	--	--	--	--	--	--	--
Separated	.0081	.0143	.1329	1.8	.0174	0.2	.1111	1.4	.0358	0.5
Number of Children										
Number of Children	1.698	1.3003	-.0026	0.6	.0044	0.7	-.0032	0.8	0.0	0.0
Size of Urban Area										
Size of Largest City in PSU	2.856	2.8790	-.0275	8.1	-.0151	3.3	-.0334	9.5	-0.128	3.7
Region										
Northeast	.2586	.2416	-.0230	1.4	.0661	2.9	.0308	1.7	.0655	2.7
North Central	.3232	.2989	.0277	1.8	.0529	2.6	.0317	2.0	.0552	2.6
South	--	--	*	*	*	*	--	--	--	--
West	.1544	.1739	.0242	1.3	.0368	1.5	.0154	0.8	.0327	1.3
Alaska, Hawaii	.0009	--	.3575	1.8	--	--	.3404	1.6	--	--
Foreign Country	.0005	.0026	.3418	1.3	-.1193	0.8	.3965	1.4	-.1283	0.8

TABLE A9.3b

Means of Personal Characteristics Variables and Regression Coefficients
for Men and Women in 1973 with Proxy Experience Variable and Corresponding Subsample

	$\bar{Z}_m$ Means of Men's Personal Characteristics	$\bar{Z}_f$ Means of Women's Personal Characteristics	From Men's Full Scale Wage Equation		From Women's Full Scale Wage Equation		From Men's Personal Characteristics Wage Equation		From Women's Personal Characteristics Wage Equation	
			$\hat{B}_m$	t-ratio	$\hat{B}_f$	t-ratio	$\hat{B}_m$	t-ratio	$\hat{B}_f$	t-ratio
	(1)	(2)	(3)	(4)	(5)	(6)	(7)	(8)	(9)	(10)
Average Wage	$5.23	$2.95								
Log of Average Wage	.722	.470							.206	
R^2			.414		.339		.294			
Constant Term			.3386		.3765		.3514		.4194	
Education	12.338	12.242	-.0240	2.4	-.0142	0.8	-.0205	2.0	-.0339	1.9
Education^2	162.776	157.113	.0018	4.2	.0013	1.8	.0019	4.5	.0030	4.2
Experience (proxy)	26.441	26.285	.0167	8.0	.0023	0.9	.0187	8.5	.0036	1.3
Experience^2 (proxy)	844.392	851.579	-.0003	8.3	-.0000	0.3	-.0004	8.9	-.0000	0.9
Experience (direct)	--	--	--	--	--	--	--	--	--	--
Experience^2 (direct)	--	--	--	--	--	--	--	--	--	--
Industry										
Agriculture	.0534	.0109	.0542	1.0	.0959	1.1	--	--	--	--
Mining	.0070	.0027	.2515	3.6	.0697	0.5	--	--	--	--
Construction	.0935	.0025	.1441	5.2	.3670		--	--	--	--
Manufacturing (durables)	.2224	.0899	.1639	6.9	.1255	3.5	--	--	--	--
Manufacturing (non-durables)	.0788	.1047	.1269	4.4	.0813	2.1	--	--	--	--
Transportation	.0558	.0061	.1653	5.4	.2211	2.2	--	--	--	--
Communications	.0141	.0174	.1143	2.2	.1281	2.1	--	--	--	--
Printing	.0221	.01335	.1581	3.7	.0638	0.9	--	--	--	--
Utilities	.0238	.0035	.1951	4.7	.4157	3.2	--	--	--	--

TABLE A9.3b (Sheet 2 of 3)

	$\bar{Z}_m$ Means of Men's Personal Characteristics	$\bar{Z}_f$ Means of Women's Personal Characteristics	From Men's Full Scale Wage Equation		From Women's Full Scale Wage Equation		From Men's Personal Characteristics Wage Equation		From Women's Personal Characteristics Wage Equation	
			$\hat{B}_m$	t-ratio	$\hat{B}_f$	t-ratio	$\hat{B}_m$	t-ratio	$\hat{B}_f$	t-ratio
	(1)	(2)	(3)	(4)	(5)	(6)	(7)	(8)	(9)	(10)
Trade, Wholesale	.0408	.0151	.0854	2.5	.2361	3.6	--	--	--	--
Trade, NA Kind	.0097	.0084	.1145	1.9	.2333	2.7	--	--	--	--
Trade, Retail	--	--	--	--	--	--	--	--	--	--
Finance	.0503	.0569	.1006	3.2	.1022	2.7	--	--	--	--
Business Service	.0120	.0150	.0583	1.1	.0527	0.8	--	--	--	--
Repair Service	.0298	.0022	-.0273	0.7	-.0939	0.6	--	--	--	--
Personal Service	.0096	.0922	-.0998	1.7	-.0343	1.0	--	--	--	--
Recreation	.0090	.0076	.0861	1.4	.1291	1.4	--	--	--	--
Medical Service	.0279	.1227	.1251	3.2	.0803	2.6	--	--	--	--
Education Service	.0609	.1680	.0628	1.9	.1000	3.2	--	--	--	--
Other Professional Service	.0314	.0370	-.0285	0.7	.0293	0.7	--	--	--	--
Government	.0444	.0411	.0907	2.7	.1839	4.3	--	--	--	--
Armed Services	.0059	.0021	.1861	2.5	.1628	0.9	--	--	--	--
Occupation										
Professional	.1883	.1880	.0423	1.6	.1535	5.3	--	--	--	--
Managers	.1339	.0388	.0927	3.9	.0893	2.2	--	--	--	--
Self-employed	.0944	.0112	-.0563	2.1	-.0900	1.2	--	--	--	--
Clerical and Sales Workers	--	--	--	--	--	--	--	--	--	--
Craftspersons	.2348	.0139	-.0255	1.0	-.0591	0.8	--	--	--	--
Operatives	.1369	.1428	-.0580	2.2	-.0130	0.4	--	--	--	--
Unskilled laborers and Service Workers	.0637	.2088	-.1047	3.4	-.0985	3.8	--	--	--	--
Farm Workers	.0409	.0021	-.1921	3.1	-.0802	0.4	--	--	--	--

TABLE A9.3b (Sheet 3 of 3)

	$\bar{Z}_m$ Means of Men's Personal Characteristics	$\bar{Z}_f$ Means of Women's Personal Characteristics	From Men's Full Scale Wage Equation $\hat{B}_m$	t-ratio	From Women's Full Scale Wage Equation $\hat{B}_f$	t-ratio	From Men's Personal Characteristics Wage Equation $\hat{B}_m$	t-ratio	From Women's Personal Characteristics Wage Equation $\hat{B}_f$	t-ratio
	(1)	(2)	(3)	(4)	(5)	(6)	(7)	(8)	(9)	(10)
Whether Part Time										
Whether Part Time	.0333	.3329	.1141	3.4	-.0201	1.1	.1150	3.2	-.0619	3.4
Marital Status										
Married	.9220	.7134	.1785	5.0	-.0546	1.5	.1976	5.2	-.0259	0.7
Widowed	.1273	.0947	.1818	2.9	-.1051	2.4	.2140	3.2	-.0714	1.5
Divorced	.0299	.1209	.0785	1.6	.0120	0.3	.1040	2.0	.0259	0.6
Single (never married)	--	--	--	--	--	--	--	--	--	--
Separated	.0081	.0143	.1487	2.1	.0081	0.1	.1288	1.7	.0232	0.3
Number of Children										
Number of Children	1.7033	1.2956	-.0037	0.9	-.0028	0.4	-.0035	0.8	-.0103	1.5
Size of Urban Area										
Size of Largest City in PSU	2.8542	2.8846	-.0266	7.9	-.0157	3.4	-.0324	9.1	-.0133	
Region										
Northeast	.2598	.2422	.0243	1.4	.0630	2.7	.0325	1.8	.0664	2.7
North Central	.3223	.2972	.0307	2.0	.0521	2.5	.0354	2.2	.0563	2.6
South	--	--	--	--	--	--	*	*	*	*
West	.1540	.1740	.0232	1.2	.0388	1.6	.0133	0.7	.0365	1.4
Alaska, Hawaii	.0009	.0000	.3455	1.8	.0000	0.0	.3276	1.6	.0000	0.0
Foreign Country	.0005	.0026	.3498	1.3	-.1782	1.1	.4035	1.4	-.1814	1.1

Chapter 10

COMMUTING TIME AND SPEED

Jay Cherlow and James N. Morgan

Introduction

The time and money spent getting to work constitute an important tax on income. Public policy on highways and public transit, and such events as the recent dramatic increase in the price of gasoline and automobiles, help determine the commuter's burden. Individually, the traveler must make a set of decisions which determine the amount of time and money that will be devoted to commuting. These options include where to live and work and how fast and by what mode to commute to work.

We have analyzed commuting time and its relationship to the distance to work because the resulting costs affect people's decisions about job and residence. The relationship of cost to distance is not linear and is subject to change if the cost per mile becomes a more important part of the cost than the time cost. This may happen, for example, if gasoline prices rise relative to the imputed value of the person's time. The relationship may also shift, perhaps more dramatically, if people must switch to public transportation. Commuting costs may well affect labor supply and mobility and the way in which they vary from one area to another. Hence, though this chapter is largely descriptive, it does have policy implications.

Three possible variables can be studied: distance, time, and speed of travel--any one of which is determined as a combination of the other two. We have chosen to examine time and speed because, given their importance in choice of housing location, they are easier to interpret as decision variables. The time cost of travel can be thought of as comprising two parts, an overhead cost--the time spent parking and unparking a car or waiting to be picked up by a bus or car pool--and a marginal cost, measured in time per mile of travel (the inverse of the marginal travel speed). It is possible that people who commute substantial distances do so only if they can travel at least part of the way at high speeds, which implies that the marginal time cost per mile may be lower for the last added

mile of travel. The translation of distance into time cost should then be monotonic, but not proportional or even simply linear.

In the first section of this chapter we describe the searching procedures we
used to identify subgroups within the sample that exhibited considerable differences in commuting behavior, either in total time spent traveling or in marginal
speed of travel. Then we separately consider areas with different populations and
describe the regression analyses used to examine the most important predictors of
commuting time within each area. In the last section we look at factors that
account for changes over time in commuting behavior for the same individuals.

Analysis

I. COMMUTING TIME AND SPEED

The mode of travel and the impact of rising gasoline prices on the cost of
driving to work have been examined previously.[1] However, for most people the
major cost of commuting is likely to be the time spent. (This conclusion, of
course, depends on the price of gasoline and the valuation of travel time.) Commuting time is a function of both distance and speed of travel; since longer distance may be the price one pays for a better job or a more desirable place to
live, we consider both time and speed.

When asked in the spring of 1974 about their journeys to work, working household heads reported times and distances that resulted in averages of 9.8 miles
and 22 minutes per trip. These averages included trips made by all modes, as
long as there was a working head who made some journey to work. For people making
5 round trips per week for 50 weeks, 22 minutes per trip is equivalent to 183
hours per year, which is approximately a 9 percent addition to the standard working year of 2,000 hours.

Because people who traveled farther tended also to travel at a higher average
speed, we cannot assume from the above information that everyone averaged 27 miles
per hour (9.8 miles divided by 22/60 hours). If we fit a line to estimate a relationship between distance and time, we find that time is not proportional to
distance. The line implies that there is a 10 minute overhead cost plus a marginal cost of 1.3 minutes per additional mile; that is, the extra miles are
traveled at 47 miles per hour.

---

[1] Hill (1974), and Duncan (1975). See also John Holmes, "The Relative Burden of
Higher Gasoline Prices," in this volume.

Another way to see the same phenomenon is to look at those who traveled different distances:

Those Who Traveled to Work a Distance of:	Reported an Average of: (Distance)	And an Average Time of:	Which Means an Average Speed of:
Less than 6 miles	2.6 miles	12 minutes	13 mph
6-10 miles	8.1 miles	21 minutes	23 mph
11 miles or more	21.2 miles	37 minutes	34 mph

In addition, a fitted line relating time to distance for only those workers who traveled more than 10 miles to get to work implies that the time increases at .0182 hours for each added mile for a marginal speed of 55 miles per hour. These results make sense in that a person was not likely to drive a long distance to work unless at least part of the trip was made on high-speed highways.

People differed in their commuting times because they traveled unequal distances or at different speeds. We searched the data to see whether there were groups among which the whole relationship between time and distance differed.[2] Included among the possible categorizing (explanatory) variables was a bracket on the distance to work in order to allow for differences in marginal speeds of travel.

The results are given in Figure 10.1 in which each box shows:

$$\overline{H} = A + b (\overline{M})$$

$\overline{H}$ =	A	+	b	$(\overline{M})$
Average Hours Per Trip (One Way) =	Time at Zero Distance	+	Marginal Time/Mile	(Average Miles to Work One Way)

$$\text{Average Speed (approximate)} = \frac{\overline{M}}{\overline{H}}$$

$$\text{Marginal Speed} = \frac{1}{b}$$

and in which the average speed of travel is approximately $\overline{M}/\overline{H}$ and the marginal speed of the last mile is $1/b$.[3] The average commuting time in minutes is $60\ \overline{H}$.

The first split separated residents of areas with a central city of 500,000

---

[2] We used a computer program that searches for groups with different relationships of distance to time, a search procedure looking for significant covariances. See Sonquist, Morgan, and Baker (1973).

[3] The measure of average speed is only approximate because a ratio of averages is not precisely the same as the average ratio.

FIGURE 10.1

Covariance Search--For Groups Differing in Mean Commuting Time or in Relationship to Distance*
(Includes All Modes of Travel)

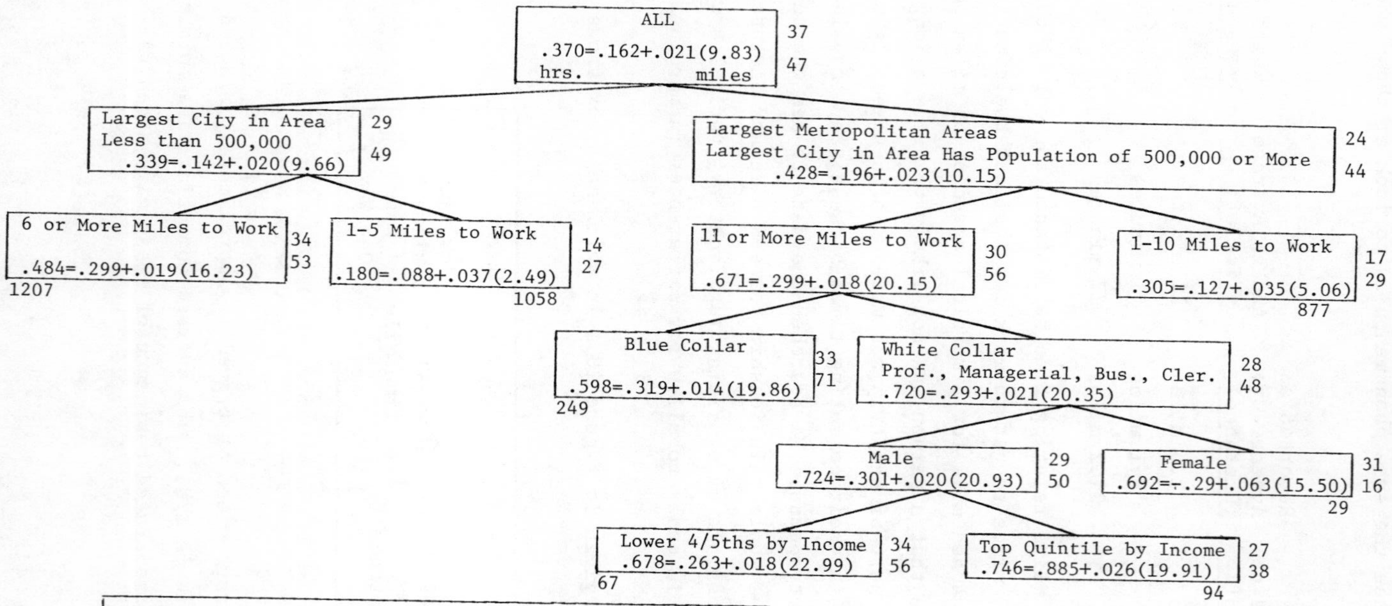

ALL	37
	47
$.370 = .162 + .021(9.83)$	
hrs.	miles

Largest Metropolitan Areas	24
Largest City in Area Has Population of 500,000 or More	44
$.428 = .196 + .023(10.15)$	

Largest City in Area Less than 500,000	29
	49
$.339 = .142 + .020(9.66)$	

1-10 Miles to Work	17
	29
$.305 = .127 + .035(5.06)$	877

11 or More Miles to Work	30
	56
$.671 = .299 + .018(20.15)$	

1-5 Miles to Work	14
	27
$.180 = .088 + .037(2.49)$	1058

6 or More Miles to Work	34
	53
$.484 = .299 + .019(16.23)$	1207

White Collar Prof., Managerial, Bus., Cler.	28
	48
$.720 = .293 + .021(20.35)$	

Blue Collar	33
	71
$.598 = .319 + .014(19.86)$	249

Female	31
	16
$.692 = -.29 + .063(15.50)$	29

Male	29
	50
$.724 = .301 + .020(20.93)$	

Top Quintile by Income	27
	38
$.746 = .885 + .026(19.91)$	94

Lower 4/5ths by Income	34
	56
$.678 = .263 + .018(22.99)$	67

*Results read:

$$\overline{H} = A + b \; (\overline{M})$$

| $\overline{H}$ | = | A | + | b | | $(\overline{M})$ |
| Average Hours per Trip (one way) | = | Time at Zero Distance | + | Marginal Time/Mile | (| Average Miles to Work One Way) |

Number of cases

Average Speed (approximate) $= \dfrac{\overline{M}}{\overline{H}}$

Marginal Speed $= \dfrac{1}{b}$

or more from the rest of the sample, as shown below:

	Minutes Per Trip	Miles Per Trip	Average Speed	Marginal Speed
Areas with a Central City of 500,000 or More*	26	10.15	24	44
All Other Areas	20	9.65	29	49
Entire Country**	22	9.83	27	47

---

*Of which the New York-New Jersey metro area averaged 31 minutes
at 24 mph, but the other large metro areas averaged 24 minutes
at the same 24 mph. New Yorkers commuted farther but no faster
than those in other big cities.

**Includes all modes of travel.

It took longer to get to work in the large metro areas because people were
traveling farther to work and at slower average speeds. Workers earned more in
these areas, but the commuting cost of earning was also higher.[4] The tendency
for added miles of commuting to be at higher and higher speeds caused the two
types of areas to split next by distance to work, but the split was differential.
The higher speeds applied only for travel beyond five miles in areas without a
very large city but only for travel beyond ten miles in areas with a central city
of 500,000 or more (Table 10.1).

We are in one sense explaining too much when we use distance to work to explain travel time, but we do learn about the situations faced by different subgroups. Among those in the largest metropolitan areas with long distances to work
(11 miles or more), blue-collar workers traveled faster, both on average and at
the margin, presumably because they were less likely to be commuting into the center of the city where travel was the slowest. The highest paid white-collar workers took the longest time at the slowest average speeds to get to work. They were
paying for good jobs in part with more commuting time, or, at least they were using
the benefits in ways which incurred such costs. This was a finding based on relatively few cases, however, and only appeared among those with long journeys to

---

[4]Workers in urban areas may have shorter work hours, offsetting the longer commuting times, but the relative commuting cost remained higher. See Dickinson
(1974).

TABLE 10.1

Commuting Time and Speed by Distance to Work
(For the Areas with Largest City 500,000
or More and the Rest of the Country)

Miles to Work	$\bar{Y}$ Hours/Trip	Average Speed Miles/Hour	Marginal Speed ΔMiles/ΔHours	Number of Cases
All Areas				
0 - 5 miles	.197	13	24	1580
6 - 10 miles	.359	23	34	843
11 or more miles	.622	34	56	1158
Largest City in the Area 500,000 or More				
0 - 5 miles	.236	12	21	522
6 - 10 miles	.402	20	21	355
11 or more miles	.671	30	56	439
All Other Areas				
0 - 5 miles	.180	14	27	1058
6 - 10 miles	.325	25	67	488
11 or more miles	.593	37	53	719

MTR 1131D

work in heavily-populated areas. Finally, there was some tendency for female white-collar workers who commuted moderate distances in large metropolitan areas to travel more slowly and, therefore, to take longer to get to work than similar men. (Remember that only household heads are studied here, not wives.)

Since the largest metropolitan areas and other city-size areas differed so greatly, it seemed useful to look separately at the explanatory ability of each of the characteristics used in analyzing each area. We used the square of the correlation ratio (Eta-squared), which is the fraction of the variance in commuting time accounted for by separate mean times for each subgroup of the characteristic in question. Ignoring distance to work itself, which automatically explains a great deal, we found that, beyond the usual impact of being in a large metro area, other city-size differences and residence specifically in the New York area also affected commuting time costs (Table 10.2). The details for six city-size areas are given in Table 10.3.

The distance of the respondent's residence from the center of the nearest city of 50,000 or more affected everyone's commuting time. This was especially significant outside the largest metropolitan areas, where people were more likely to go to the center of the nearest city to work. The one-center model of locational economics clearly fits better when there is a single large city in the county rather than a cluster of satellite cities around a metropolitan center. The detailed pattern of differences by distance from center of city is given in Table 10.3 and is shown for the largest metro areas and for other areas in Table 10.4. In both areas, commuting distances increased and average speeds increased with distance from center of town.

The only other important characteristic significantly associated with differences in commuting time and/or speed was economic status, defined by the earnings of the household head or family income. Upper-income people in the largest metro areas were likely to travel so much farther that even higher average speeds did not compensate, and their commuting time was greater than that of those whose time was presumably less valuable. The detailed relationships between the respondent's hourly earnings, commuting time, and speed are given in Table 10.3 and are presented separately for the two kinds of areas in Table 10.4. Interestingly enough, there was a much stronger tendency for high-wage people to have higher average speeds in the large urban areas. Marginal speeds did not vary systematically with earnings; they even seemed to be highest for those with the lowest hourly earnings.

Traditional urban models postulate that suppliers of residential housing are forced to accept lower prices for sites farther from the center of the city be-

TABLE 10.2

Strength of Association of Various Characteristics with Commuting Time
(Correlation Ratio Squared = Eta^2)***

Characteristics	All	Largest City 500,000 or More	Largest City Less than 500,000
Distance to Work	.416	.364	.453
Household Head's Hourly Earnings	.037	.048	.024
Size of Largest City in Area	.031	--	.015
Income Quintile**	.024	.036	.016
Distance to Center of Nearest City of 50,000 or More	.022	.015	.023
New York-New Jersey Area	.022	.023	--
Age of Head	.011	.007	.003
Occupation of Head	.010	.014	.021
Region	.009	.011	.002
Home Ownership	.008	.008	.008
Sex of Head	.007	.009	.008
Education of Head	.007	.005	.008
A Wife Who Works?*	.007	.014	.006
Race	.004	.006	.001
Number of Children	.002	.005	.001
Head Self-employed?	.000	.001	.000

*Distinguishes families with no wife, a working wife, or a nonworking wife; effect is largely the result of a wife's presence.

**See "Household Head's Hourly Earnings."

***For levels required for statistical significance, see Appendix D. But the fraction of variance accounted for is more important here.

MTR 1131D

TABLE 10.3

Commuting Time and Average and Marginal Speed
By Three Characteristics

	$\overline{Y}$ Hours/Trip	Average Speed Miles/Hour	Marginal Speed ΔMiles/ΔHrs	N
Size of Largest City in Area				
500,000 or more	.429	24	44	1316
100,000 - 499,999	.356	26	51	821
50,000 - 99,999	.344	28	47	416
25,000 - 49,999	.276	28	46	213
10,000 - 24,999	.293	30	49	317
Less than 10,000	.370	33	50	486
Distance from Center of Nearest City				
Less than 5 miles	.343	21	46	860
5 - 14.9	.397	24	43	1103
15 - 29.9	.414	30	46	499
30 - 49.9	.416	32	48	368
50 miles or more	.300	30	50	656
Head's Hourly Earnings				
Less than $2	.281	24	55	489
$2 - 2.99	.315	26	49	681
$3 - 3.99	.351	25	50	661
$4 - 4.99	.353	27	47	573
$5 - 5.99	.379	26	46	428
$6 - 7.99	.420	28	51	448
$8 or more	.472	28	42	301

MTR 1131D

TABLE 10.4

Commuting Time and Speed by Distance
from Center of City and by Head's Hourly Earnings
(For the Largest Metro Areas and for the Rest of the Country)

Distance From Center	12 Largest Metro Areas				All Other Areas			
	Hours/ Trip	Miles/ Hours	ΔMiles/ ΔHours	N	Hours/ Trip	Miles/ Hour	ΔMiles/ ΔHours	N
Less than 5 Miles	.400	20	42	412	.297	23	53	448
5-14.9 Miles	.438	23	44	581	.354	26	44	522
15-29.9 Miles	.434	27	41	214	.399	33	49	285
30-49.9 Miles	.529	29	45	58	.392	33	49	310
50 Miles or More	.649*	35*	53*	10	.302	30	50	646
Head's Hourly Earnings								
Less than $2	.334	20	51	142	.267	26	55	347
$2 - 2.99	.331	20	42	191	.309	28	50	490
$3 - 3.99	.420	20	46	226	.324	28	51	435
$4 - 4.99	.403	24	45	242	.327	29	48	331
$5 - 5.99	.395	22	45	172	.369	29	46	256
$6 - 7.99	.445	25	50	189	.401	30	51	259
$8 or More	.548	26	39	154	.387	30	48	147
Wife?								
None	.377	19	47	466	.302	27	48	576
Wife Works	.435	26	44	496	.351	29	49	1022
Wife Does Not Work	.471	25	42	354	.351	29	50	667

*Result based on ten observations.

MTR 1131D

cause workers will not incur heavy commuting costs unless they can simultaneously save on housing. Testing such models would require better measures of housing quality than we have available. The systematic association of longer commuting times with higher wages suggests a second model. Perhaps workers face a choice of jobs with a trade-off between higher wages and less commuting time. In other words, the higher paying jobs may be in places in which longer commuting times are likely. This issue is discussed more fully in Section III.

Having a wife was associated with longer commuting times, but whether she worked or not had no significant relationship to the husband's commuting time. Single heads, who did not need to consider family requirements or a wife's work location, reported the shortest commuting times in all areas (Table 10.4).

It is useful to note the factors that did *not* matter much, either overall or within the large metropolitan areas: home ownership, age, race, number of children, self-employment, education, and region. It is always possible, though, that the *lack* of a relationship is spurious, so a simultaneous multivariate assessment of the effects of various characteristics on commuting time appeared useful. There were such powerful differences between areas of different city size, however, that it seemed appropriate to ask whether the relative importance of certain characteristics vary in different areas. The following section describes such an analysis.

II. COMMUTING TIME IN THREE TYPES OF AREAS

Even though commuting time was not proportional to distance, nor even a simple linear function with a constant term, it was useful for us to take a more careful look at commuting time as such. Time is, after all, a good proxy for the cost of commuting, whether the commute is a long, high-speed trip or a shorter, lower-speed trip.

Much of the literature on traveling to work has focused on the trade-off between shorter journeys to work and cheaper unit costs of housing or land. The nature of that relationship is likely to depend on the size and population density of the area in question. A trade-off between higher wages and shorter journeys to work in job choice may also be more applicable in some kinds of areas than others. Several factors are involved. First, the *relative* concentration of employment opportunities in the center is lower in very large metropolitan areas with satellite centers than in smaller, single-centered areas. Second, in smaller ares in which journeys to work are typically shorter, a movement of one's residence from the center to the edge of the urbanized area is not likely to cause such a large increase in commuting time. Also, there might not be nearly so much difference in the unit cost of housing or land as in areas of larger population. Finally, the distribution of both job opportunities and residental locations available to workers of different incomes, races, and sexes may vary according to the population of the area in question. For these reasons we used multivariate analysis separately for three subgroups: those living in the largest metropolitan areas with central cities of 500,000 or more, those living in other areas with central cities of 50,000 or more, and those living in areas with no cities as large as 50,000.

The mode of travel to work may be thought of as part of a joint decision about where to live and work and how to commute, or as one of the independent variables explaining commuting time. Therefore, the regressions were made with and without mode as one of the explanatory characteristics. From one point of view, the mode forms part of the choice pattern (of the dependent variable), but from another point of view it partially accounts for travel time. When people select a job, a residential location, and a method of getting to work, either simultaneously or in some order, their choices determine daily cost in travel time as well as quality of residential environment, quality and speed of commuting, and wage rate.

In our analysis, we had to deal with three questions:

1. Were the same variables the principal correlates of commuting time in each of the three city-size areas?

2. Were some variables which seemed unimportant in the aggregate actually important in one city-size category?

3. Did the patterns of effect--the size and direction of the effects of other predictors--vary with city size?

An answer to the first question can be found in Tables 10.5 and 10.6 and in Figure 10.2. The distance from the worker's residence to the center of the nearest city of 50,000 or more was really important only in the middle-sized cities, where it was the most important predictor in the regression without using mode of travel and remained unchanged in importance when mode was considered (Table 10.6). Distance to center in the largest metro areas was insignificant, partly because so few people lived more than 30 miles from the center of a city 50,000 or more. But the main reason for the finding must be that the pattern of central-directed commuting (in which commuting time rose as distance from the center increased) applied best to middle-sized cities.

Hourly earnings were generally positively related to commuting time, and in two of the three area types they accounted for more variance than distance from the center (Table 10.5). However, they were more important in the small-town and rural areas than anywhere else. Figure 10.3 shows the pattern with some irregularities in small groups.

TABLE 10.5

Relative Importance (β^2) of Characteristics Other Than Travel Mode Associated with Commuting Time by City Size

Large Metro Areas	Eta^2	$Beta^2$	Other Metro Areas	Eta^2	$Beta^2$	Rural	Eta^2	$Beta^2$
Hourly Earnings	.045	.026	Distance from Center	.045	.040	Hourly Earnings	.030	.059
Sex and Race	.020	.021	Hourly Earnings	.019	.015	Income/Income Needs	.003	.018
Age	.020	.020	Income/Income Needs	.015	.006	Region	.013	.016
Recent Mobility*	.003	.017	Age	.007	.004	Sex and Race	.028	.013
Income/Income Needs	.023	.017	Recent Mobility	.020	.004	Distance from Center	.014	.010
Distance from Center	.015	.016	Region	.004	.004	Whether Working Wife	.011	.006
Whether Working Wife	.016	.008	Sex and Race	.008	.004	Whether School Age Children	.000	.005
Region	.009	.007	Whether School Age Children	.000	.003	Age	.004	.003
Whether School Age Children	.003	.000	Whether Working Wife	.007	.003	Recent Mobility	.004	.002
$R^2 =$	.096		$R^2 =$	.058		$R^2 =$	.057	
$N =$	1357		$N =$	1243		$N =$	1016	

R^2 is adjusted for degrees of freedom, but Eta^2 and $Beta^2$ are not. Below .020 either can be considered unimportant. See Appendix D for significance levels.

*This variable classifies households according to whether or not they have moved in the past four years and the direction of any move relative to the nearest city of 50,000 or more.

TABLE 10.6

Relative Importance (β^2) of Travel Mode and Other Predictors of Commuting Time by City Size

Large Metro Areas	Eta	Beta
Mode	.161	.173
Hourly Earnings	.045	.018
Distance from Center	.015	.018
Whether Working Wife	.016	.018
Age	.020	.014
Recent Mobility	.003	.013
Income/Income Needs	.023	.012
Sex and Race	.020	.007
Region	.009	.004
Whether School Age Children	.003	.000
R^2 =	.249	

Other Metro Areas	Eta	Beta
Mode	.082	.080
Distance from Center	.045	.040
Hourly Earnings	.019	.016
Income/Income Needs	.015	.005
Sex and Race	.008	.004
Recent Mobility	.020	.004
Region	.004	.004
Age	.007	.003
Whether School Age Children	.000	.002
Whether Working Wife	.007	.001
R^2 =	.133	

Rural	Eta	Beta
Mode	.093	.076
Hourly Earnings	.030	.042
Region	.013	.011
Sex and Race	.030	.011
Income/Income Needs	.003	.010
Distance from Center	.014	.006
Whether Working Wife	.011	.005
Whether School Age Children	.000	.004
Age	.004	.001
Recent Mobility	.004	.001
R^2 =	.126	

R^2 is adjusted for degrees of freedom, but Eta and Beta are not.

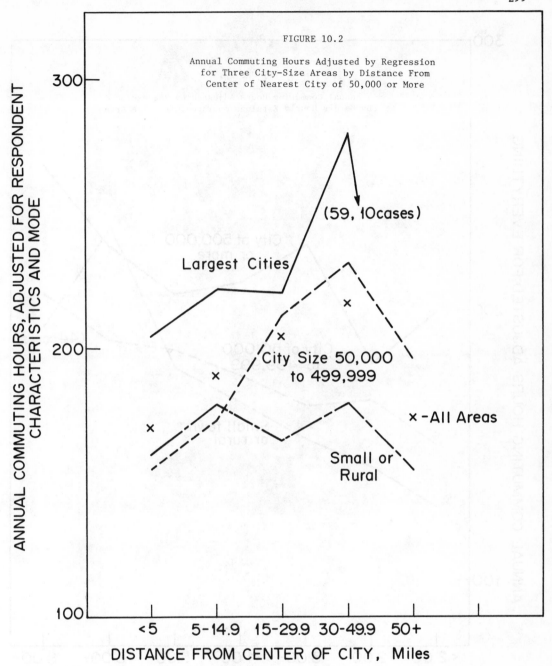

FIGURE 10.2

Annual Commuting Hours Adjusted by Regression
for Three City-Size Areas by Distance From
Center of Nearest City of 50,000 or More

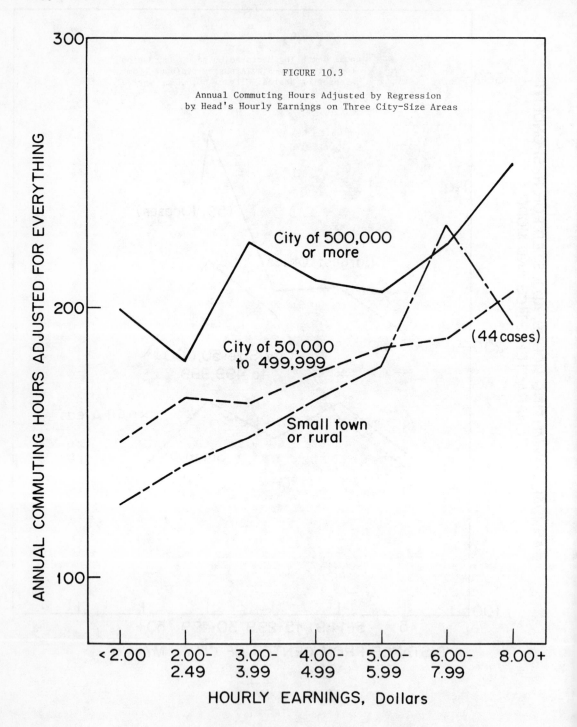

FIGURE 10.3

Annual Commuting Hours Adjusted by Regression
by Head's Hourly Earnings on Three City-Size Areas

Finally, the sex-race interaction and age variables appeared to matter only in the largest metropolitan areas. Even after an adjustment was made for mode of travel, sex and race remained insignificant, but this adjustment hid one serious racial difference; namely, blacks had longer commuting times largely because they were more likely to use public transportation. As Table 10.7 shows (for the largest metro areas only), it was race, not sex, that produced variation, and adjustment for mode reduced the difference. Clearly, black females in large cities commuted longer largely because they used public transportation. Again, no other factors accounted for much of the variance.[5]

The impact of mode as such was very important, particularly in the large metropolitan areas. This was because only there did more than a small fraction of the sample use public transportation. Elsewhere, more than 90 percent drove to work or commuted in car pools, but in the largest urban areas 17 percent used public transportation.

Our second question was whether some apparently unimportant variables in the overall picture were important in one of the city-size categories. The answer to this can be seen by comparing Tables 10.5 and 10.6 with Table 10.8, the latter applying the same regression analysis to the pooled data set. There were only two variables which appeared to have some small effect in one subarea type, but not overall: recent mobility, as defined in Table 10.5, and family income/needs. Both are variables that would appear to duplicate other variables. The mobility variable (which distinguishes moves toward the center of town or away from it) was used even though we also used distance of the residence from the center of city in hope of separating the effect of moving in a particular direction from the effect of living a particular distance from the center. We used the income/ needs classification, in addition to the head's hourly earnings, in the hope that we could sort out the effects of general well-being and the desire for a pleasant residential location (as measured by income/needs) from the opportunity cost of travel and the advantage of living near the job (as measured by the head's hourly earnings).

Income/needs did have the expected positive relationship with commuting time, but instead of becoming stronger when introduced simultaneously with hourly earnings, it lost most of its effect and became U-shaped or even negative (as in rural areas). The hourly earnings variable had a positive relationship with commuting

---

[5]Three variables were excluded because previous analysis indicated their total unimportance: home ownership, self-employment, and whether the household head had recently changed jobs without moving his residence.

TABLE 10.7

Adjusted Mean Annual Commuting Hours by Race and Sex
(Areas with Central City of More than 500,000 Only)

	Adjusted Hours*		Number
	Without Mode	With Mode	of Cases
White			
Male	209	216	566
Female	205	201	127
Black			
Male	258	233	499
Female	285	235	203

*Adjusted by regression for differences in seven other characteristics, or seven plus mode of travel.

TABLE 10.8

Relative Importance of Characteristics Associated with
Commuting Time, With and Without Mode of Travel
(For All City Sizes)

	Without Mode			With Mode	
	Eta^2	$Beta^2$		Eta^2	$Beta^2$
Hourly Earnings	.036	.030	Mode	.130	.124
Distance from Center	.023	.015	Hourly Earnings	.036	.022
Sex and Race	.012	.010	Distance from Center	.023	.012
Region	.009	.006	Region	.009	.004
Age	.009	.005	Whether Working Wife	.008	.003
Recent Mobility	.008	.004	Sex and Race	.012	.003
Whether Working Wife	.008	.002	Age	.009	.003
Whether School-Age Children	.000	.001	Recent Mobility	.003	.003
Income/Needs	.014	.000	Whether School-Age Children	.000	.001
			Income/Needs	.014	.001

$R^2 =$ .067   .179

N =   3616   3616

R^2 is adjusted for degrees of freedom, but Eta and Beta are not.

time and retained its sign and much of its strength in the multivariate analysis, even becoming stronger in the small-town and rural areas. Thus, our findings did indicate the importance of a trade-off between higher wages and shorter journeys to work more clearly than between better residential location (when affordable) and shorter commutes.

We have already answered part of the third question concerning different effects operating in different areas. We noted that the effects of distance from the center of the nearest city of 50,000 or more could be quite disparate, varying with the size of the largest city in the area. The influence of this predictor was greatest in the areas with a largest city of between 50,000 and 499,999. The effect of hourly earnings was largest where the largest city was less than 50,000.

Other differences in the effects of particular predictors showed up, particularly when we did not include mode choice as one of the explanatory characteristics. We have just seen, for example, that the adjusted effects of income/needs were positive in the large metropolitan areas but negative in the small-town and rural areas. Figure 10.4 shows the means adjusted for all factors except mode. (Care should be taken in making inferences from these data since the high correlation between hourly earnings of the head and the family money income/needs could lead to some erratic adjustments.)

Another city-size difference involved blacks. Among that group, females spent more time than males in metropolitan areas of both sizes, although in rural or small-town areas black males spent much more time commuting than did black female family heads. In the pooled regression, such offsetting distinctions were averaged out. The details of the adjusted effects for each of the three area types are given in Tables A10.1a and A10.1b.

As a final check on the importance of separate consideration of the three city-size areas, we ran a Chow test of the null hypothesis, which states that the parameters of the three regressions are really the same for each predictor class. Using three separate regressions rather than one on the pooled data reduced the residual (unexplained) sum of squares by another 5 percent, whether mode was included or not. Thus, among the three area types, there were clearly significant differences in the effects of variables on commuting time.

III. CHANGE IN COMMUTING TIME

Many previous studies of residential location decision-making in urban areas have investigated models in which people select a residential location that minimizes a combination of housing costs and commuting costs. But changes in residential location are often "upgrading" moves that involve using increased income to

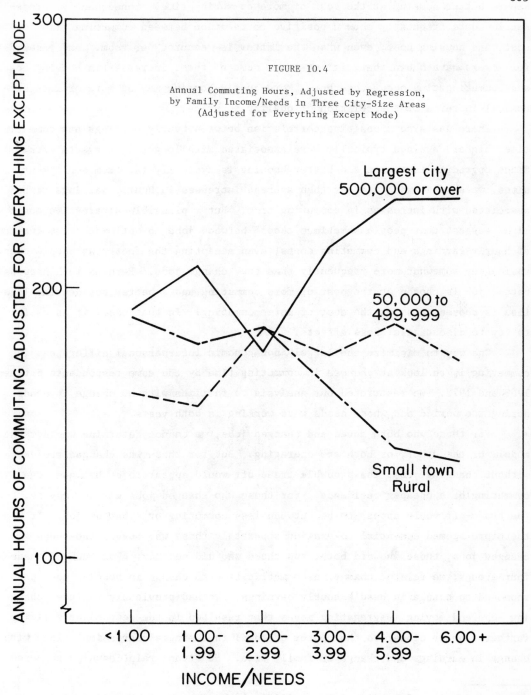

FIGURE 10.4

Annual Commuting Hours, Adjusted by Regression,
by Family Income/Needs in Three City-Size Areas
(Adjusted for Everything Except Mode)

Largest city
500,000 or over

50,000 to
499,999

Small town
Rural

ANNUAL HOURS OF COMMUTING ADJUSTED FOR EVERYTHING EXCEPT MODE

300

200

100

<1.00   1.00-   2.00-   3.00-   4.00-   6.00+
        1.99   2.99   3.99   5.99

INCOME/NEEDS

secure better housing at the cost of more commuting time. Consequently, cross-section data frequently show a positive correlation between commuting time, or cost, and housing cost, even when the latter is measured per room. And panel data for movers have shown that, for at least some of them, increases in housing costs and commuting time occur together. More costly housing may be more or less economical in terms of the relation of quality to price.[6]

There was also a positive correlation between hourly earnings and commuting time; higher earnings typically were associated with longer journeys to work. Since upgrading is common and better housing is typically far from employment sites, we should expect larger than average increases in hourly earnings to be associated with increases in commuting time. But a plausible alternative model might suggest that people sometimes choose between jobs to optimize a combination of hourly earnings and commuting costs, even accepting the fact that people change residences somewhat more frequently than they change jobs. Perhaps each happens—a better job is chosen at the cost of more commuting and a better residential location is chosen, also at the cost of more commuting. In that case, it is useful to try to disentangle these effects.

One way to minimize the largely noneconomic interpersonal differences in commuting is to look at *changes* in commuting time by the same respondents between 1969 and 1973. We restricted our analysis to families with no change in heads during the period and whose heads were working in both years.

For those who both moved and changed jobs, we cannot determine whether one model, or the other, or both are operating. But for those who changed residence without changing jobs, the probable trade-off would appear to be between less commuting or a cheaper residence. For those who changed jobs without moving, the trade-off would appear to be between less commuting or a better job. It therefore seemed essential to examine separately those who moved, those who changed jobs, those who did both, and those who did neither. For each of these four groups, we related change in commuting time to change in housing cost per room and to change in head's hourly earnings. We had previously included changing jobs and moving (segregating moves that resulted in the respondent's living farther from or closer to the center of town) in a single regression, along with change in earnings and change in family size. No strong relationships appeared

_____

[6]Measuring units of housing is very difficult because homes are so heterogeneous. More sophisticated models that separate supply and demand effects can detect the trade-off that households face with respect to lower unit costs of housing versus higher commuting costs. A study by Cherlow, which uses the residential location decisions of the panel members to infer values of commuting time, finds such a trade-off, at least for middle-sized cities.

except that of those moving farther from the center ending up with longer commuting times.

The most interesting analysis was that of the 549 families who moved between 1969 and 1973 and whose heads did not change jobs. Among these families, annual commuting time of the household heads increased by an average of 30 hours, and there was a barely discernible tendency for those with middle-range increases in housing costs or middle-range increases in hourly earnings to increase commuting times more than others. There was certainly no systematic negative relationship between the changes in housing costs and the changes in commuting costs--those who got a better housing value (in cost per room) did not do so at the expense of longer commuting times, either before or after taking account of changes in earnings.[7]

Those who changed jobs without moving did not appear to be getting higher hourly earnings at the expense of longer commuting times, either. Nor was there any systematic relationship for this group between change in housing cost per room and change in commuting.

Those who neither moved nor changed jobs would not be expected to report substantial changes in commuting time and, indeed, the average such household reported a small (2.5 hours per year) decrease in commuting time. This decrease can be attributed to improved roads and higher speeds.

Those who both moved and changed jobs spent an average of ten fewer hours a year commuting in 1973 than in 1969. It seems more likely that they moved in response to a change in jobs rather than the reverse, although there was no systematic negative relationship between change in housing costs (per room) and change in commuting time, nor any positive correlation between change in hourly earnings and change in commuting time. If there were economic trade-offs of either sort, they were being swamped by changing opportunities over time, upgrading or retrenching, errors in measuring change in commuting time, or other considerations that affect people's decisions.

Summary

1. A longer commuting time means a greater cost of travel, both because the person's time is valuable, and because each mode carries a per minute travel cost. It also means a wider range of residential location options for a given job location or a wider range of job options for a given residential location. We have found substantial time costs and substantial variation in those costs in areas of different types. The traditional models fit best where the central

---

[7] Better measures of housing quality might still reveal such a trade-off.

city has a population of 50,000-499,999.

2. The costs were generally positively related to both hourly earnings and family income/needs, but when both were introduced into a simultaneous regression, the relationship with income/needs became curved or even negative.

3. The relationship between time and distance indicated a kind of overhead cost in time, plus higher and higher speeds for the marginal miles; thus the average speed increased with distance. Average speed was also heavily influenced by population density and distance of the residence from the center of a city.

4. Mode of travel had a predominant influence on speed and time, particularly in the largest metropolitan areas where an appreciable fraction of the respondents were using public transportation.

5. An analysis of change in commuting times from 1969 to 1973 found little evidence of economic trade-offs of either type.

References

Cherlow, Jay R. "Urban Commuting Behavior and the Value of Travel Time." An unpublished PhD. dissertation at the University of Michigan, 1975.

Dickinson, Jonathan. "Labor Supply of Family Members." In Five Thousand American Families--Patterns of Economic Progress. Vol. I. James N. Morgan, et al. Ann Arbor: Institute for Social Research, 1974.

Duncan, Greg J. "Some Equity Aspects of Gasoline Price Inflation." In Five Thousand American Families--Patterns of Economic Progress. Vol. III. Edited by Greg J. Duncan and James N. Morgan. Ann Arbor: Institute for Social Research, 1975.

Hill, Martha. "Modes of Travel to Work." In Five Thousand American Families--Patterns of Economic Progress. Vol. II. Edited by James N. Morgan. Ann Arbor: Institute for Social Research, 1974.

Morgan, James N., Baker, Elizabeth Lauh, and Sonquist, John A. Searching for Structure. Revised edition. Ann Arbor: Institute for Social Research, 1973.

Appendix 10.1

TABLE A10.1a (Sheet 1 of 2)

Adjusted Means of Commuting Time by City Size

(Without Mode)

	Large Metro Areas		Other Metro Areas		Rural Areas	
	Adjusted Means	N	Adjusted Means	N	Adjusted Means	N
Age						
< 25	222	(224)	164	(266)	153	(189)
25–34	184	(405)	174	(371)	156	(306)
35–44	226	(279)	181	(232)	164	(179)
45–54	245	(277)	186	(231)	176	(199)
55 +	223	(172)	185	(143)	164	(143)
Hourly Earnings						
< $2.00	199	(152)	151	(161)	112	(191)
$2 – 2.99	182	(206)	162	(244)	142	(251)
$3 – 3.99	226	(236)	166	(227)	153	(203)
$4 – 4.99	203	(246)	176	(172)	163	(151)
$5 – 5.99	200	(174)	186	(168)	188	(87)
$6 – 7.99	223	(191)	191	(169)	237	(89)
$8 +	262	(152)	202	(102)	202	(44)
Whether Working Wife						
No wife in FU	206	(495)	181	(382)	150	(209)
Nonworking wife	236	(364)	177	(333)	156	(334)
Wife works < 20 hrs/wk	192	(73)	158	(91)	167	(60)
Wife works 21+ hrs/wk	219	(425)	179	(437)	175	(413)
Sex and Race						
White male	209	(566)	179	(708)	160	(645)
White female	205	(127)	166	(127)	153	(95)
Black male	258	(409)	180	(233)	219	(212)
Black female	285	(203)	198	(125)	113	(38)
Other male	262	(49)	177	(44)	180	(24)
Other female	---	(3)	---	(6)	---	(2)
Income/Needs						
< 1	192	(62)	161	(72)	189	(79)
1 – 2	209	(249)	156	(208)	(179	(208)
2 – 3	175	(274)	185	(252)	186	(239)
3 – 4	215	(264)	175	(258)	163	(193)
4 – 6	233	(305)	187	(274)	141	(205)
6 +	233	(203)	173	(179)	136	(92)

TABLE A10.1a (Sheet 2 of 2)

	Large Metro Areas		Other Metro Areas		Rural Areas	
	Adjusted Means	N	Adjusted Means	N	Adjusted Means	N
Recent Mobility						
Moved farther from center	223	(226)	190	(273)	148	(129)
Moved, no change	218	(388)	176	(354)	167	(407)
Moved closer to center	251	(316)	173	(253)	167	(128)
Didn't move	197	(386)	172	(337)	161	(326)
Distance from Center						
0 - 5 miles	202	(429)	153	(423)	160	(31)
5 - 15	225	(596)	175	(491)	176	(33)
15 - 30	220	(222)	217)	(174)	169	(111)
30 - 50	269	(59)	225	(82)	186	(225)
50 +	93	(10)	189	(50)	151	(596)
Grand Mean	218	(1357)	177	(1243)	163	(1016)

TABLE A10.1b (Sheet 1 of 2)

Adjusted Means of Commuting Time by City Size

(With Mode)

	Large Metro Areas		Other Metro Areas		Rural Areas	
	Adjusted Means	N	Adjusted Means	N	Adjusted Means	N
Age						
< 25	223	(224)	167	(266)	161	(189)
25–34	191	(405)	174	(371)	159	(306)
35–44	222	(279)	179	(232)	165	(179)
45–54	241	(277)	186	(231)	172	(199)
55 +	223	(172)	185	(143)	156	(143)
Hourly Earnings						
< $2.00	200	(152)	150	(161)	127	(191)
$2 – 2.99	181	(206)	166	(244)	142	(251)
$3 – 3.99	224	(236)	164	(227)	152	(203)
$4 – 4.99	210	(246)	176	(172)	166	(151)
$5 – 5.99	206	(174)	185	(168)	178	(87)
$6 – 7.99	223	(191)	188	(169)	231	(89)
$8 +	253	(152)	206	(102)	193	(44)
Whether Working Wife						
No wife in FU	191	(495)	179	(282)	150	(209)
Nonworking wife	242	(364)	177	(333)	159	(334)
Wife works < 20 hrs/wk	201	(73)	164	(91)	156	(60)
Wife works 21+ hrs/wk	225	(425)	179	(437)	175	(413)
Sex and Race						
White male	216	(566)	181	(708)	162	(645)
White female	201	(127)	167	(127)	151	(95)
Black male	233	(409)	169	(233)	207	(212)
Black female	235	(203)	172	(125)	95	(38)
Other male	270	(49)	174	(44)	169	(24)
Other female	---	(3)	---	(6)	---	(2)
Income/Needs						
< 1	222	(62)	178	(72)	177	(79)
1 – 2	212	(249)	159	(208)	177	(208)
2 – 3	177	(274)	184	(252)	180	(239)
3 – 4	222	(264)	175	(258)	159	(193)
4 – 6	230	(305)	186	(274)	146	(205)
6 +	225	(203)	172	(179)	148	(92)

TABLE A10.1b (Sheet 2 of 2)

	Large Metro Areas		Other Metro Areas		Rural Areas	
	Adjusted Means	N	Adjusted Means	N	Adjusted Means	N
Recent Mobility						
Moved farther from center	230	(226)	190	(273)	151	(129)
Moved, no change	222	(388)	176	(354)	163	(407)
Moved closer to center	242	(316)	175	(253)	165	(128)
Didn't move	197	(386)	171	(337)	166	(326)
Distance from Center						
0 – 5 miles	204	(429)	155	(423)	161	(31)
5 – 15	222	(596)	173	(491)	179	(33)
15 – 30	221	(222)	212	(174)	165	(111)
30 – 50	280	(59)	232	(82)	180	(225)
50 +	95	(10)	196	(50)	154	(596)
Mode						
Public transit	351	(303)	303	(81)	---	(5)
Car pool	226	(91)	239	(141)	250	(144)
Drive	194	(864)	169	(935)	157	(739)
Walk	88	(75)	90	(55)	70	(72)
Grand Mean	218	(1357)	177	(1243)	163	(1016)

Appendix 10.2

A Note on the Covariance Search Procedure

Regressing annual hours of commuting time on the number of miles the household head commutes to work (one way) gives a relationship that can be converted into a kind of marginal miles per hour, that is, a ratio of increased time to increased miles which can be inverted. We chose hours as the dependent variable because it is the least error-prone measure and the best total cost indicator since cost includes the value of the time as well as the pure travel costs. Statistically, of course, we should have used the variable with the least error as the explanatory variable and regressed miles on time, which would have given lower marginal miles per hour.

The covariance search procedure looks for groups with widely different relationships of hours to miles, which account by their two different levels and slopes for more of the variance in hours than any other pair of subgroup relations. In fact, two subgroup regressions explain more than a single pooled regression largely through differences in levels, that is, in average hours, rather than through differences in slopes (marginal speeds). In any case, the data we have are the average hours and average miles for each subgroup from which we can estimate the average miles per hour (imprecisely, since the ratio of two averages is not identical with the average ratio) and the regression slope. From the regression slope we can estimate the added distance covered by added hours (the marginal speed of travel) which is likely to be different from the average, since there are overhead costs at both ends and since people with longer trips usually travel faster than those with shorter trips. Stated simply, people will undertake longer commutes when they can travel faster.

As we pointed out, errors in estimating miles, which we would think would be likely, should lead to a spuriously steep relationship between speed and distance and, hence, to an exaggeration of the difference between average and marginal speeds. On the other hand, errors in estimating commuting time would lead to a spurious negative relationship between speed and time.

There is also a problem in using trip miles in conjunction with annual hours, since the latter variable was edited for those who worked less than a full year, or fewer than 5 days a week. To adjust for this, we used the edited annual hours divided by weeks worked and divided by 10 to estimate time per trip. The average commuting time per trip was 22 minutes and the standard deviation was

314

17 minutes.

There were 17 extreme cases in the annual variable (greater than the average by more than 5 standard deviations); however, they were all within the range from 111 to 206 minutes and, hence, were not likely to distort our estimates much in samples of this size.

Chapter 11

PATTERNS OF INCOME AND FERTILITY
AMONG AMERICAN HOUSEHOLDS, 1967-73*

Richard T. Curtin

Introduction

The most elementary and yet the least clearly understood economic determinant of fertility is income. Although people spontaneously mention the prominent role of income when questioned about their family planning, exactly how income affects fertility remains unclear. Some empirical results point toward a negative income-fertility relationship: Judged by historical standards, current income levels would suggest larger family sizes than now exist; international comparisons indicate that the more developed countries have lower fertility rates; and in recent cross-section studies of the American population, lower income groups have been shown to exhibit higher fertility rates than the more affluent. Other empirical studies have uncovered positive income effects on fertility. Long-term swings in economic conditions correspond with long-term fertility trends, and past studies have shown that short-term fluctuations in aggregate income and employment corres-pond with deviations from trends in fertility-related variables.[1] It should be noted, however, that during the decade of the 1960's no such positive income ef-fect appeared but rather its reverse was observed: vigorous economic expansion was coupled with steep declines in fertility.

A series of contributions to the economic theory of fertility has done much to help sort out these often complex, and at times counter-balancing, income-fertility relationships. The major thrust of these advances has been to (1) es-tablish an analytic framework in which the costs and benefits an added child brings to a family can be systematically evaluated; (2) differentiate between the quantity and quality aspects of fertility decisions; (3) expand the analytic frame-work to include the entire household's potential income and opportunity costs as

*The analysis reported here was performed at the Survey Research Center of The University of Michigan in accordance with NICHD contract N01-HD42856, under the direction of Burkhard Strumpel.

[1] Much of this empirical evidence has been gathered and summarized by Simon (1974).

well as intrahousehold resources allocation, particularly the use of time; and
(4) distinguish between short-term income effects and long-term effects, and at
the same time, between direct and indirect effects of income on fertility.[2] Short-
run analysis can assume that people's desired family size remains constant, the
role of income being thereby limited either to that of a barrier to or to a facilitator of fertility plans. This type of direct effect of income on fertility is
most prominent in the short run--but past effects do accumulate. In the long run,
income experiences can also be expected to affect fertility preferences, usually
through indirect, socioeconomic channels. It is because this indirect long-term
effect can differ, and even counteract, the direct effect of income on fertility
that the two must be carefully distinguished.

As a consequence of the multifaceted, and at times offsetting, effects of income on fertility, we cannot deduce on theoretical grounds alone whether income
increases will ultimately lead to increased or decreased fertility.[3] Empirical
observations and estimates of crucial parameters therefore need to play a larger
role in building our understanding of the income-fertility relationship.

Empirical analysis of the income-fertility relationship based on cross sectional data unfortunately cannot be unambiguously interpreted, because observed
income can take on different meanings in different analytic contexts. In one
instance, income can serve as a proxy for social status, usually a lasting, cul-
turally anchored family characteristic. In another, income expresses the present
economic condition of the individual family unit as compared to an earlier or expected condition. Since one-shot, cross-section studies usually fail to disentangle these two meanings of the income variable, this investigation utilizes the
panel data for isolating each of these income effects on fertility.

Analysis

I. FERTILITY BEHAVIOR

As measures of income position can take on distinctive meanings, so can
changes in fertility rates: observed changes in fertility can be alternately

---

[2] For a more detailed summary of these developments, see, for example, Easterlin
(1969), Leibenstein (1974), pp. 457-79, and the entire supplement to the Journal
of Political Economy (March/April 1973).

[3] For a further discussion that reveals the problems of interpreting and analyzing
the relationships of income to fertility, see Keeley (1975), pp. 461-468, and
Leibenstein (1975), pp. 469-472.

categorized as stemming from period effects or from cohort effects. A *period effect* refers to some specific time period and the effect of societal events at that time on overall fertility, whereas *cohort effect* refers to the individual's year of birth or marriage and the effect of conditions at these times on fertility. By definition, all members of the same cohort are subjected to the same period forces; for people of different ages, the two differ. This investigation of the effects of recent income experience on fertility was directed toward learning more about the forces behind the period effect--toward understanding the relationship between people's income experience and the fertility behavior of all cohorts, regardless of the stage they may be at in their reproductive life cycles. The longitudinal design of this data base is thus doubly advantageous in that it allows for greater specification of people's income change experiences and period fertility rates.

In the analysis which is described here, the number of children born to stably married couples during the seven-year panel period (1967-73) were examined in relation to the pattern of the husband's labor income over that same period. Only respondents whose wife was age 45 or under by 1973 were included in the analysis. In providing a more homogeneous sample, these restrictions helped to isolate from analysis the confounding effects of marital disruption on fertility.

The analysis also avoids the complexities encountered by the temporal interdependence on the wife's working and procreative life. How the wife's expected future income, if she planned to work, affected current fertility decisions and the effect of nonlabor income on fertility were left unaccounted; the sole focus was on the impact of the husband's income on fertility. Giving a more prominent position to the husband's income over these other sources was justified by this temporal interdependence of women's work and procreative roles, as well as by social norms. This investigation limited analysis to the effects of husband's labor income in an effort to simplify and systematize; other sources of income and the whole range of issues they raised are themselves important topics for research.

Since it was the number of children born during the panel period that was investigated, analysis was also limited to the effect of income on the *quantity* of children demanded, not *quality*. This distinction between quantity and quality can be easily grasped by an example: Other things being equal, an increase in income may prompt some couples to have another child, while for others it will signal that a college education for their existing children is now within their means. In the former instance, the effect of income on fertility is quantitative rather than qualitative and directly affects the size of the population; the latter tells more of intrafamily resource allocation and only indirectly affects population size. This is an important distinction, because the effect of income on child quantity could be expected to differ from the effect of income on child quality.[4] In particular, it can be expected that while the long-run income elasticity of child quantity demand approaches zero, the short-run income-child quantity elasticity is likely to be positive. The reverse, however, is apt to be true for the income elasticity of child quality demands: the long-run income elasticity for child quality is likely to be positive, while in the short run, with given *tastes*, it may approach zero.

II. HUSBAND'S INCOME EXPERIENCE, 1967-1973

Income profiles over the seven-year panel period can be characterized by their rate of change, trend stability, and average level.

Rate of income change. How much income change people have experienced over the panel period reflected the progress, stagnation, or deterioration of people's economic condition as compared to earlier times. Higher rates of income change were expected to facilitate births, for given family size preferences. And because these income effects may have cumulated over time, people's desired family size may even have enlarged or decreased with respect to previous intentions.

Income instability. People are assumed to become accustomed to some expected rate of change in real income over time; unexpected departures from this trend lead to uncertainty and worry. Income instability was therefore expected to give rise to postponement of births, and hence act as a barrier to the fulfillment of family size intentions. Coupled with the effect of real income change on fertility, a more detailed hypothesis would state that the higher the income trend and the less the variance in income about that trend over time, the greater the positive impact of income on fertility.

Average income levels. Using the husband's average seven-year income level minimized the impact of transitory income fluctuations on this measure of relative income position. Moreover, whereas the above two measures relfected solely the course of income change during the panel period, current average income levels also included the cumulative effects of past income experience. In addition, whereas rates of income change and its trend stability could be expected to affect birth spacing or timing decisions directly--a dimension of child *quantity* demand --relative socioeconomic position is more directly associated with issues of child *quality*. More specifically, since the long-run income elasticity of child

---

[4]On this topic see Willis (1973) and the accompanying "Comment" by Ryder (1973).

quantity demand was hypothesized to be zero, the effect of differences in average relative incomes on fertility was expected to be small (approaching zero) when estimated over the seven-year panel period. It was also hypothesized that the income elasticity of child quality demand was relatively higher than for quantity demand in the short run and positive in the long run (as opposed to zero long-run quantity elasticity). Thus, in so far as quantity and quality competed for the same limited household resources, and if child quality demand was more responsive to income change than the quantity of children, a near zero relative income level effect could be expected to dominate any positive, but temporary and indirect, short-term income effects on quantity.

Distinguishing between these several facets of people's income experience can be symbolized as follows: Let

$$Y_{it} = a_i + b_i(\text{Time}) + U_{it},$$

where Y_{it} is defined to include only the husband's annual labor income deflated by the Consumer Price Index, for the ith family in year t. The time variable was defined in yearly intervals and took on values from -3 to +3 corresponding to the sample years 1967 through 1973, respectively. The "error term" U_{it} represented income variability around a constant trend and was taken to represent income instability. When these coefficients were estimated for each individual respondent using ordinary least squares regression techniques, the estimated constant term equals the husband's mean income, and the time variable coefficient indicated the expected yearly increment in income under the assumption of a linear time trend. From these estimates, three measures of income change experience could be derived as follows:

1. Income change: $\hat{b}_i$ = expected yearly increase in real income.

2. Income instability: $\hat{\sigma}_{Ui}$ = root mean square deviation about expected real income trend.

3. Income level: $\hat{a}_i$ = average seven-year real income.

A more detailed specification would recognize nonlinear time trends and that people's expected income trends could be best specified as a constant *rate* of change in real income, not as a constant dollar *amount* of increase. To capture these effects, the following model is proposed:[5]

---

[5] For a detailed discussion of this commonly used data transformation to estimate nonlinear relationships, see Johnston (1963), pp. 44-7. For a rigorous empirically based investigation of different measures of income instability (including the measure used in this study), see Benus (1974).

$$Y_{it} = a_i (1 + b_i)^t U_{it}$$

In this version, b_i represents the rate of growth of the income base (a_i) over the panel period. Taking logs and transforming we find:

$$LnY_{it} = Lna_i + Lnb_i(Time) + LnU_{it}$$

$$= a_i^* + b_i^*(Time) + e_i^*$$

It should be noted that if the error term was assumed to be of the form e^U rather than simply U, the term LnU_{it} in the above equation would reduce to simply U_{it}. In addition, another plausible formulation of the income change profile over time could simply be that the log of income changes linearly over time, but with a (well-behaved) random disturbance. Chance variations in income would then be considered additive rather than multiplicative. As basic formulations differed so did the derived analytic results: in one case, estimation assumed that a* and e* were given in log units, while other interpretations would have one or both estimated in natural units. The estimates given below assumed the error term to be estimated in natural units and these values to be randomly distributed with a zero mean and constant variance (the usual regression assumptions.) The estimation procedure was invariant with regard to whether a* was assumed to be given in logs or not; the interpretation accorded analytic results, however, do differ.

When this revised equation was estimated for each individual respondent using ordinary least squares regression techniques, the operationalized measures of income change were then:

1. Level: $\hat{a}_i^*$ = average seven-year log real income.

2. Change: $\hat{b}_i^*$ = rate of real income change (Lnb_i = rate for small b).

3. Instability: $\hat{\sigma}_{ei}^*$ = root mean square deviation about expected real income trend.

It is of some interest to note the intercorrelations among these three measures of income experience:

	1	2	3
1. Level	1.00		
2. Change	.077	1.00	
3. Instability	−.553	−.061	1.00

As shown above, only a small positive correlation existed between a respondent's average seven-year income level and his estimated rate of change over that
period, and those respondents with higher rates of real income change were only
marginally less likely to have unstable incomes by these estimates. Although each
of these relationships was in the expected direction, less expected was their insignificant size. In contrast, the data demonstrated a strong negative relationship between the respondents' average seven-year income and income instability over
that period. When combined, these results indicated that higher average incomes
were subject to much less instability, but were only marginally more likely to grow
at a higher rate than incomes that were initially low.[6]

III. THE EFFECT OF INCOME ON FERTILITY

Table 11.1 reports regression analyses of the number of children born between
1967 and 1973 to stably married respondents, using as explanatory variables the
three constructed measures of income experience during the panel period, as well
as other commonly identified determinants of fertility behavior. The inclusion
of the wife's education was intended not only to reflect differences in fertility
preferences and contraceptive knowledge and its effective use, which are associated with differences in educational attainment, but can also be interpreted as
reflecting the wife's potential wage, and hence incorporates opportunity cost
effects into the model. Because our theoretical interest has been in how income
experience affects fertility decisions at the margin, and because the number of
children born during this period depended on how many children the respondents
already had, each equation controls for the number of children already present at
the start of the panel period (initial parity). As column (1) in Table 11.1 indicates, and as has often been documented, high-income people tended to have
fewer children, and, also as expected, relatively high rates of real income growth
were associated with more frequent births. Contrary to expectations was the lack
of associations between income instability and births.

A more complete inspection of columns (1) to (4) of Table 11.1 revealed,
however, that in large part this relationship was due to age, not income: The
younger respondents were more apt to have higher rates of income growth and have
children more frequently.[7] After controlling for differences in age (age at mar-

---

[6] These relationships are documented and discussed in greater detail by Benus (1974).

[7] This result is long-standing. Elderton, et al. (1913), in reviewing a prior empirical study on the relationship between income and fertility conducted at the
turn of the century in England, concluded that "...it is absolutely needful to

TABLE 11.1

Regression Analyses of the Number of Children Born Between 1967 and 1973
(For Stably Married Couples with Wife Under Age 45 in 1973)[a]

Independent Variables	Dependent Variable: Number of Children Born Between 1967 and 1973			
	(1)	(2)	(3)	(4)
Income Level	-.077* (.039)	-.026 (.036)	-.014 (.038)	
Income Change	.299* (.141)	.145 (.129)	.151 (.129)	
Income Instability	.009 (.057)	.001 (.052)	.007 (.053)	
Age of Wife at Marriage		-.045** (.008)	-.048** (.009)	-.048** (.008)
Marital Duration		-.066** (.005)	-.065** (.005)	-.066** (.005)
Race (1 = Nonwhite)			.150 (.082)	.156 (.081)
Religion (1 = Catholic)			.113* (.056)	.109 (.056)
Rural Background (1 = Farm)			-.028 (.054)	-.026 (.054)
Education of Wife (Years)			-.009 (.010)	-.010 (.010)
Initial Parity	-.140** (.015)	-.014 (.017)	-.028 (.017)	-.028 (.017)
Constant	1.64	2.46	2.50	2.40
SEE	.787	.717	.715	.715
RSQD-Adj.	.098	.251	.255	.256

---

[a]Table entries are partial regression coefficients with associated standard errors in parentheses. These coefficients are calculated based on weights which account for differential nonresponse, for sampling problems from families where a sample person married a nonsample person, and for original oversampling of lower income, younger families. The unweighted number of respondents was 951.

*Significant at the .05 level of probability.

**Significant at the .01 level of probability.

riage and marital duration), the net impact of the income variables became negligible (compare columns (1) and (2)). Also note that the net (direct) effect of initial parity on subsequent births was also greatly reduced by taking account of marital duration--in terms of a "path" analysis, a logically prior variable. Interestingly, demographic factors such as race, religion, rural background, and education were not significantly associated with fertility differentials over this period. A comparison of columns (3) and (4) yielded perhaps the best overall summary of the net impact of the husband's income experience on births: there was none.

IV. INTERPERSONAL INCOME EVALUATIONS

This analysis has assumed that income levels, rates of change, and stability have the same effect on fertility no matter what the respondents' age, education, work skills, or experience. The underlying income-fertility relationship, however, may be better specified if we assume that people compare themselves to "similar others," rather than to the prevailing societal average, when evaluating what income change they personally experience. Rates of real income change, for example, would then be hypothesized to affect fertility only to the extent that they differ from what rates of change the respondent expects, based on what people with similar education, skills, and work experiences receive. Only deviations from expected or reference standards would matter; having the same income change profile as people similar in age and education would provide no incentive for additional births. In addition, the income level people come to expect was also assumed to be based on differences in their productive inputs, such as skills, abilities, and experience. Positive deviations from expected levels were expected to be associated with higher fertility because people's average income levels were higher than incomes of those with similar characteristics, and this relative income advantage among peers was expected to be reflected in higher fertility, other things being equal. In this framework, relative *expected* income levels can be interpreted as a proxy for socioeconomic position and thus serve as a measure of differences in fertility norms (tastes and preferences).

The regression equations reported in Table 11.2 were used to estimate the expected values of each of the three measures of income experience, based on the husband's education, work experiences, and race. The work experience variable was defined as the husband's age minus the number of years in school. These variables represented the standard human capital approach to explaining differences

---

correct for age before the significance of the data can be determined." (p.1) And after having corrected for age differences, they report the observed positive correlation between husband's income and family size became negative.

in earnings in productive inputs.[8] The underlying model also accepted that differences in productive inputs--or "human capital"--justify differences in incomes. Consequently, people would come to expect and accept different income profiles over their working life cycle. These income expectations then would function as a standard by which people could evaluate themselves in comparison to others.

As shown in Table 11.2, differences in these input factors accounted for almost 25 percent of the variance in average income levels, but less than 6 percent of the variation in rates of income change or trend instability. Also notice that the signs of the coefficients predicting income instability indicate that nonwhite respondents and those with the least work experience had the most unstable incomes.

TABLE 11.2

Regression Analysis of Three Measures of Income Experience, 1967-1973
(For Stably Married Males with Wife under Age 45 in 1973)[a]

Independent Variables	Dependent Variables		
	Seven-Year Average Log Income $(\hat{a}_i{}^*)$	Rate of Growth In Real Income $(\hat{b}_i{}^*)$	Income Instability from Trend $(\hat{\sigma}_{ei}{}^*)$
Education	.116** (.019)	.018** (.005)	-.022 (.015)
Work Experience	.126** (.023)	.008 (.006)	-.044* (.018)
Work Experience Squared	-.003** (.001)	-.001 (.001)	.001* (.000)
Education (Times) Work Experience	-.001 (.001)	-.001** (.000)	.001 (.001)
Race (1 = Nonwhite)	-.203** (.077)	.007 (.020)	.147* (.059)
Constant	6.70	-.120	.780
SEE	.691	.178	.526
RSQD-Adj.	.242	.051	.018

---

[a]Table entries are partial regression coefficients with associated standard errors in parentheses. The education of the husband and his work experience are scaled in years. The unweighted number of respondents was 951.

*Significant at the .05 level of probability.
**Significant at the .01 level of probability.

---

[8]See, for example, Juster (1975), especially the included article by Mincer.

From the cross-section regressions listed in Table 11.2, an expected value, or reference standard, for each of the three income measures could be computed for each individual respondent. Operationally, this simply involved computing the predicted values for each respondent, using the coefficients listed in Table 11.2. The modified income experience measures would then take the form of deviations from these expected values. Symbolically expressed, these are:

Relative income level: $\qquad\qquad \hat{a}_i^* - \hat{\hat{a}}_i^*$

Relative income change: $\qquad\quad\; \hat{b}_i^* - \hat{\hat{b}}_i^*$

Relative income instability: $\;\; \hat{\sigma}_{ei}^* - \hat{\hat{\sigma}}_{ei}^*$

In each case the first term (those with one "hat") represents *intra*individual time trend estimates; the second term represents their estimated expected values based on cross-section *inter*individual regressions. The former represents income patterns as experienced over time; the latter forms the referent or standard of comparison.

As easily detected from Table 11.3, these modified measures of income experiences did not relate to births during the panel period. Indeed, because these deviation measures already excluded most of the (confounding) effects of age, even their unadjusted relations to fertility were all insignificant. (See column (1).) Moreover, whereas demographic correlates of fertility, aside from income, could account for one-fourth of the variance in births (see column (4), Table 11.1), the income variables made no net addition to "explained" variance. These data, even after differences in both intertemporal and interpersonal income reference standards have been taken into account, thus again refuted the hypothesized income effects on fertility.

This analysis incorporated two crucial assumptions about the nature of the income-fertility relationship. One involved the timing of income developments and fertility decisions, and implied that fertility plans were revised continuously based on income experience (past, current, and expected) throughout the period of marital fecundity. The second assumption involved the nature of the family size decision itself, holding that decisions to have one, two, three, or more children were influenced equally by income developments. Because most births occur relatively soon after marriage, it could be argued that the income-fertility relationship may be better specified if family planning decisions are assumed to be made early in marriage, and once made, tend to endure despite income developments that occur only late in married life. It is only during these early years of marriage that information on past and expected income develop-

TABLE 11.3

Regression Analyses of the Number of Children Born Between 1967 and 1973
(For Stably Married Couples with Wife Under Age 45 in 1973)[a]

Independent Variables	Dependent Variable: Number of Children Born Between 1967 and 1973		
	(1)	(2)	(3)
Relative Income Level[b]	.032	.036	.034
	(.046)	(.041)	(.042)
Relative Income Change[b]	-.016	.084	.090
	(.145)	(.132)	(.132)
Relative Income Instability[b]	.029	.021	.022
	(.060)	(.054)	(.054)
Age of Wife at Marriage		-.046**	-.047**
		(.008)	(.009)
Marital Duration		-.068**	-.066**
		(.005)	(.005)
Race (1 = Nonwhite)			.154
			(.081)
Religion (1 = Catholic)			.108*
			(.056)
Rural Background (1 = Farm)			-.022
			(.054)
Education of Wife (Years)			-.011
			(.010)
Initial Parity	-.145**	-.014	-.028
	(.015)	(.017)	(.017)
Constant	.980	2.26	2.41
SEE	.791	.718	.715
RSQD-Adj.	.089	.250	.255

---

[a]Table entries are partial regression coefficients with associated standard errors in parentheses. The unweighted number of respondents was 951.

[b]See text and Table 11.2 for a detailed description of these variables.

*Significant at the .05 level of probability.

**Significant at the .01 level of probability.

ments is most relevant for understanding fertility decision. Moreover, family size decisions are bounded by social norms. Few couples remain childless and few have large families. Within the intermediate range, however, differences in family sizes can be expected to be less subject to social norms and more responsive to individual preferences and economic circumstance.

A number of additional empirical tests were consequently performed to determine the sensitivity of the above results to these considerations. Strategies involved partitioning the sample by length of marriage, by family size at the start of the panel period, and by reformulating the dependent variable to more clearly focus on discretionary births. Thus, for example, separate estimates of the effects of income on fertility were derived for couples married ten years or less and who already had one child at the start of the panel period. Furthermore, within these various subgroups, as defined by length of marriage and initial family size, both individual and cumulative birth patterns were investigated. No significant income-fertility relationships, however, were uncovered.

V. BIRTH INTENTIONS AND ECONOMIC WELL-BEING

Table 11.4 reports on one further extension of the basic empirical model. These regressions reflected the inclusion of planned birth intentions and subjective evaluations of well-being. At the time of the initial interview, respondents were asked if they "expect to have any more children." As column (1) of Table 11.4 shows, people's birth expectations were highly correlated with their subsequent fertility during the panel period.[9] It should also be noted that this expectational measure alone accounted for as much variance in births as did all the demographic variables combined in previous regressions. (See column (4), Table 11.3.)

These attitudinal measures are best considered as intervening variables, positioned between their underlying determinants and subsequent fertility behavior. Consequently, for example, a comparison of the coefficients on the expected birth variable reported in columns (1) and (4) in Table 11.4, and of the increase in R^2 between Table 11.3, column (3) and Table 11.4, column (4), demonstrates that these fertility intentions exerted an independent, net direct effect on fertility, in addition to the contributions of the other included variables.

At the close of the interview administered in the fifth panel year, respondents were asked:

---

[9]On this issue, see Cramer (1974), pp. 279-317.

TABLE 11.4

Regression Analyses of the Number of Children Born Between 1967 and 1973
(For Stably Married Couples with Wife Under Age 45 in 1973)[a]

Independent Variables	Dependent Variable: Number of Children Born Between 1967 and 1973			
	(1)	(2)	(3)	(4)
Expect Another Child (1 = Yes)	.845** (.053)		.839** (.053)	.613** (.060)
Subjective Level Well-Being[b]		-.082** (.027)	-.062* (.024)	-.037 (.024)
Subjective Change Well-Being[b]		-.020 (.025)	-.027 (.023)	-.035 (.022)
Relative Income Level				.032 (.040)
Relative Income Change				.023 (.125)
Relative Income Instability				.008 (.051)
Age of Wife at Marriage				-.034** (.008)
Marital Duration				-.039** (.005)
Race (1 = Nonwhite)				.149 (.077)
Religion (1 = Catholic)				.040 (.054)
Rural Background (1 = Farm)				-.024 (.051)
Education of Wife (Years)				-.011 (.010)
Initial Parity	-.029 (.015)	-.151** (.015)	-.035* (.015)	.002 (.017)
Constant	.378	1.40	.744	1.86
SEE	.701	.787	.699	.678
RSQD-Adj.	.284	.099	.288	.332

[a] Table entries are partial regression coefficients with associated standard errors in partntheses. The unweighted number of respondents was 951.

[b] These variables are scored 1-5, with higher values indicating a more favorable evaluation.

* Significant at the .05 level of probability.

** Significant at the .01 level of probability.

> We have been visiting you and your family for five years now
> and asking a lot of questions, but we are also interested in
> your overall impression of this period. How would you say
> things have gone for you during the last five years?

Over three-quarters of the respondents gave codable responses relating to their
level of well-being, while just over half answered in terms of *change* in well-
being; some respondents gave answers indicating evaluations of both level and
change. The operationalized measure of subjective level evaluations was scaled
according to whether the respondent mentioned his level of well-being as being
"good" or "couldn't be better" ranging to those stating that during this period
things were "bad" or "couldn't have been worse." In a similar fashion the second
measure scaled respondents as to whether they mentioned change in well-being,
ranging from responses stating that things are now "better" or have "shown progress" to those responding that things have become "worse" or have "deteriorated."
For each measure scores ranged from 1 ("bad," "worse") to 5 ("good," "better");
those respondents who did not mention either a favorable or an unfavorable level/
change were assigned the midpoint score. As examination of columns (2) through
(4) of Table 11.4 reveals, a greater sense of subjective well-being, somewhat
surprisingly, was related with fewer births, not more: the greater the number of
children born to respondents during the panel period, the more likely these respondents were to evaluate unfavorably their level and trend in well-being over
this same time period. This negative correspondence between additions to family
size and subjective evaluations of well-being remained even after taking account
of other objective predictors of fertility behavior and the income conditions on
which these subjective measures of well-being themselves depended, although it
dropped to an insignificant level.

VI. DISCUSSION

The conceptual model underlying this investigation implicitly assumed a temporal sequence and the separation of intermediate from ultimate objectives. The
more general short-run model can be depicted as follows:

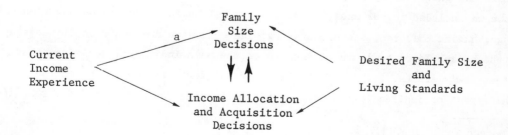

Achieving desired family living standards was taken as the ultimate goal; intermediate decisions with regard to how family incomes are spent, whether one or
both spouses entered the labor market, as well as decisions on when and how many
children to have are made in accordance with these ultimate objectives. This
analysis sought to investigate how the husband's current income experience acts
to affect fertility behavior (arrow a) so as to best serve desired family living
standards. It was expected that family size and timing decisions would be responsive to concurrent income experience so as to dampen the effect of any changes in
income on desired family well-being. Unfavorable income experience was hypothesized to lead to postponement of births, consequently lowering what would have
otherwise been an excessively large burden on household resources, and hence lowering the family living standard below what was desired. Positive income experience was hypothesized to promote more frequent births, other things being equal.

Contrary to expectations, births were not responsive to income experience,
in the service of desired family living standards. Rather, family size intentions were carried out even to the detriment of people's sense of material well-
being. The majority of couples who at the start of the panel period expected to
have another child did so regardless of the husband's income experiences during
this period. But after having had another child, they were more likely to judge
their pattern of economic progress unfavorably at the end of the fifth panel
year. This results in part because family life cycles and people's career or income life cycles often leave current needs unmet by current resources, immediate
material gratification being sacrificed for life-long goals.

Rather than acting as a barrier to or a facilitator of fertility plans,
income thus seemed to act as a barrier to or facilitator of desired material
living standards for a given, predetermined family size. In terms of the above
short-run model, family-size must be considered in large part exogenously determined, that is, not being dependent on concurrent income experience. But this
is not to say that family-size decisions do not in turn have direct and important
consequences on household well-being. Indeed, an extensive analysis of the observed patterns of economic progress among these same panel data has led to the
conclusion that "family composition change is the most important of all the variables we included in our analysis of changed well-being. Decisions about marriage, having children, and encouraging older children and other adults to stay
in the household or to leave it seem to be the main individual decisions that
affect one's status. . ."[10] Thus the effect of fertility decisions on the
achievement of desired levels of economic well-being was direct and far-reaching.

---

[10]Morgan (1974), p. 337.

Yet, as noted in the introductory paragraph, the role of current income experience in shaping short-term fertility decisions still remains unclear. Future analysis must systematically incorporate other sources of household income, notably that of the wife, together with data on preferred patterns of market and nonmarket time use, as well as aspirations for having more material goods as opposed to having more children before the role of income is fully clarified.

Summary

1. This investigation was directed toward building our empirical understanding of the relationship between income and fertility by observing people's income experiences and their fertility behavior over a seven-year period.

2. Analysis examined the relationship between the number of children born to stably married couples during the panel period and three aspects of the husband's concurrent income experience: rate of change, variability, and average level. It was hypothesized that the higher the rates of real income growth and the less the variability of income about this trend, the greater would be fertility.

3. Although the expected positive effect of high rates of income change on fertility was evidenced in these data, this correspondence proved spurious upon further examination. Younger families were both more likely to have favorable income trends and to have relatively more children than older families. After taking account of differences in age at marriage and marital duration, differences in the husband's income experience demonstrated no net effect on fertility.

4. Even when analysis was extended to take into account differences in income profiles among people similar in age, work experience, and education, no significant income effect on births was detected.

5. Two additional factors provided help in understanding this lack of association. First, most births that did occur were expected by respondents in the initial year of the panel period. Second, respondents who did have children during the panel period were also more likely to judge unfavorably their economic well-being toward the end of this period.

6. In sum, the data demonstrated both the widespread presence of family planning and the lack of effect husband's income had on altering these plans during the period investigated.

Benus, Jacob. "Income Instability: An Empirical Analysis." PhD Dissertation.
    Ann Arbor: The University of Michigan, 1974.

Cramer, James. "Births, Expected Family Size, and Poverty." In Five Thousand
    American Families--Patterns of Economic Progress, Volume I, edited by James
    N. Morgan. Ann Arbor: Institute for Social Research, 1974.

Easterlin, Richard A. "Towards A Socioeconomic Theory of Fertility: A Survey of
    Recent Research on Economic Factors in American Fertility." In Fertility
    and Family Planning: A World View, edited by S. J. Behrman, L. Corsa, and
    R. Freedman. Ann Arbor: University of Michigan Press, 1969.

Elderton, Ethel M. et al. On the Correlation of Fertility with Social Value. A
    Cooperative Study. Vol. III. London: DuLau and Co., 1913.

Johnston, J. Econometric Methods. New York: McGraw-Hill, 1963.

Journal of Political Economy. Supplement. 81(2) (March/April 1973).

Juster, F. Thomas, ed. Education, Income, and Human Behavior. New York: Nation-
    al Bureau of Economic Research, 1975.

Keeley, Michael C. A Comment on "An Interpretation of the Economic Theory of
    Fertility." Journal of Economic Literature 13 (June 1975).

Leibenstein, Harvey. "An Interpretation of the Economic Theory of Fertility:
    Promising Path or Blind Alley?" Journal of Economic Literature 12(2) (June
    1974).

Leibenstein, Harvey. "On the Economic Theory of Fertility: A Reply to Keeley."
    Journal of Economic Literature 13 (June 1975).

Mincer, Jacob. "Education, Experience and the Distribution of Earnings and Em-
    ployment." In Education, Income, and Human Behavior, edited by F. Thomas
    Juster. New York: National Bureau of Economic Research, 1975.

Morgan, James N. et al. Five Thousand American Families--Patterns of Economic
    Progress. Volume I. Ann Arbor: Institute for Social Research, 1974.

Ryder, Norman B. "Comment." Journal of Political Economy. Supplement. 81(2)
    (March/April 1973).

Simon, Julian L. The Effects of Income on Fertility. Carolina Population Center,
    Monograph 19. Chapel Hill, N.C.: Carolina Population Center, 1974.

Willis, Robert J. "A New Approach to the Economic Theory of Fertility Behavior."
    Journal of Political Economy. Supplement. 81(2) (March/April 1973).

Chapter 12

INCOME INEQUALITY

Saul Hoffman and Nripesh Podder

Introduction

Poverty standards and their definition have varied historically with increasing affluence and vary even now between countries. Poverty is clearly a relative condition, relative to current norms and standards of living, rather than a measure of the numbers of families living at or below a bare physical subsistence minimum. Christopher Jencks writes that the "cost of living is not the cost of buying some fixed set of goods or services. It is the cost of participation in the social system."[1] Martin Rein describes poverty and its relationship to inequality this way:

> Poverty cannot be understood by isolating the poor and treating them as a special group. Society is seen as a series of stratified income layers and poverty is concerned with how the bottom layers fare relative to the rest of society. Hence, the concept of poverty must be seen in the context of society as a whole. The study of the poor then depends on an understanding of the level of living of the rich, since it is these conditions relative to each other that are critical to the conception of inequality. To understand the poor we must study the affluent.[2]

The clear implication is that poverty cannot be understood in terms of some objective criterion, but rather that poverty is inherently a matter of relative deprivation. And the extent to which people feel deprived is determined largely by the amount of inequality that exists, relative to some equity norms that take account of the different contributions individuals make to society.[3]

In this chapter we focus on strict economic inequality and treat it as though it were made up of separable parts. We first segregate special groups whose dif-

---

[1] Jencks (1972), p. 5.

[2] Rein (1970, p. 71.

[3] For a discussion of equity interpretation of inequality, see Bronfenbrenner (1973) and Curtin (1975).

ference from the rest has a rather special explanation, leading to rather special policy issues. These groups include the very affluent, the aged, and the disabled. Then we examine other major subgroups of the population to see how much inequality exists between and within them.

This kind of analysis requires measures of inequality with appropriate properties, such as decomposibility, so we start with a discussion of alternative measures, and then present some empirical comparisons as they relate to different definitions of income or economic status.

Analysis

I. MEASURES OF INEQUALITY

The choice of an appropriate measure of inequality is, like the definition of poverty, an important one, with serious implications for empirical work. Two general kinds of inequality measures have been primarily used by other researchers. First are those measures which try to evaluate the extent of inequality in some *objective* sense, usually employing some statistical measure of income dispersion. The other kind of inequality measure attempts to evaluate inequality in terms of some *normative* criterion such as a social welfare function. Generally, measures of this kind assume that greater equality corresponds to a higher level of social welfare. Sen has argued that the objective measures are preferable in that they allow one to distinguish between "'seeing' more or less inequality and 'valuing' it more or less in ethical terms. In the normative approach, inequality ceases to be an objective notion and the problem of measurement is enmeshed with that of ethical evaluation."[4] In this study, we adopted the first approach and used objective measures of inequality. As our discussion below makes clear, however, the choice among them is not totally objective.

The measure of inequality most widely used in this study is based on the information theory concept of entropy.[5] While it might seem at first to be unrelated to the measurement of inequality, the information theory measure turns out to have a series of properties which make it extremely useful for that purpose. Here, we discuss the measure in a heuristic manner only and outline its properties; a complete derivation is presented in the appendix to this chapter.

---

[4]Sen (1973), p. 22.

[5]In thermodynamics, entropy refers to the disorder of a closed system. In information theory, it is used to express the amount of informational content in a message.

The information theory measure is given by

$$I(x:p) = \sum_{i=1}^{n} x_i \ \log \left(\frac{x_i}{p_i}\right)$$

where x_i is the income share,

p_i is the population share of the ith unit, and

n equals the population size.

In the case of perfect equality ($p_i = x_i$), the measure is equal to zero. Its maximum value is log n, and this occurs when the ith unit receives all the income.

Essentially, the usefulness of the information theory measure is two-fold. First, it has sensible properties for an inequality measure: it is invariant with respect to a proportional change in all incomes; its upper limit (maximum inequality) varies with the size of the population;[6] and a transfer of income from a richer person to a poorer person, without changing the ranking of the two individuals within the income distribution, decreases inequality. Second, it allows for an exhaustive decomposition of total inequality into two categories: the inequality *between* specified groups and the remaining inequality *within* these groups. The total inequality within all groups is itself a weighted average of the various within-group inequality measures where the weights are the population (or income) shares of each group. This means that if a group is a small fraction of the population or accounts for a small fraction of aggregate income, then even if there is a great deal of inequality among its members, its contribution to the *total* inequality within groups or between groups will be relatively small.

We use two information theory measures of inequality in our discussion, one based on the income shares of subgroups, the other on population subgroups. The population-based measure cannot be interpreted in terms of entropy. However, it can be explained as the expected information content of the indirect message which transforms the income shares as prior probabilities into population shares as posterior probabilities. Further information on the differences between these two measures is provided in the appendix to this chapter.

A third inequality measure which is emphasized in this analysis is the variance of the logarithm of income. One prominent feature of this measure is that it attaches a greater weight to inequality within the bottom tail of the distribution. It has been widely used in previous studies of income inequality.

We also consider the Gini coefficient and the coefficient of variation in

---

[6]This is not always a virtue, since it complicates the comparison of inequality between groups of unequal sizes.

somewhat less detail. The Gini coefficient is probably the most widely-used statistic in measuring the degree of inequality in the distribution of income and
in comparing distributions at different times or in different geographical units.
It is equal to the ratio of the area between the Lorenz curve (which relates
cumulative population shares to cumulative income shares) and the 45° line of
equal distribution to the total area under the 45° line. It ranges from 0 to 1
where 1 represents absolute inequality (one person has all the income) and 0 represents perfect equality. The coefficient of variation is simply equal to the
standard deviation divided by the mean.

II. ALTERNATIVE DEFINITIONS OF INCOME

The measurement of inequality may itself be sensitive not only to the choice
of the measure but also to the definition of income and the length of the accounting period over which income is measured. In a previous analysis which used the
first four years of data from the Panel Study of Income Dynamics, Benus and Morgan
found, for example, that the Gini coefficient was sensitive to the definition of
income used but not to the length of the period.[7] In this section we draw on
seven years of data to investigate the effects on a number of inequality measures
of two income measures--income and income relative to a needs standard--and two
accounting periods--one year and an average computed over seven years.

Using a single year's absolute income introduces two potential measurement
problems. First, families with similar incomes might differ widely in family
size and hence in the actual standard of living which their income provides them.
Second, in any single year, a great number of families might have earned incomes
which were, for any number of reasons, atypical. The first of these difficulties
was recognized by use of the income/needs measure which adjusts income for differing family needs; the extension of the accounting period to seven years did much
to correct the second problem. Combining a longer time period with the income/
needs measure probably would provide a more appropriate picture of the degree of
inequality than any of the other income measures. Further, we might expect the
seven-year measures to reflect a lesser degree of inequality because many of the
random income fluctuations of any single year would be "averaged out" over seven
years. The effects on measured inequality of using income/needs were more difficult to predict. Older and younger families with low incomes would show relative
increases in welfare while all large families would exhibit declines. The net
effects would be ambiguous.

---

[7] Benus and Morgan (1975). Of course, different policy questions point to different time periods as appropriate for measuring poverty or inequality. Emergency
aid programs are concerned with short-run deficits with a year, estimation of
payoffs to education or taining call for longer-term earnings.

Table 12.1 presents the cumulative income shares by population deciles for these four income measures (two income measures computed over two time periods). While the differences were not particularly large, the measures did vary in a systematic way. Replacing 1973 income by a seven-year average increased equality at every decile point. The distribution of seven-year income was, then, unambiguously more equal than the distribution of 1973 income. Comparison of either income measure with its corresponding income/needs measure yielded a less certain result. In both cases, the distribution of income/needs was more equal for the bottom eight deciles, but less equal for the top quintile.

Table 12.2 presents comparison among five inequality measures using the same four definitions of income. With only a few exceptions, the relationship suggested by the cumulative distribution was confirmed. Replacing income by income/needs for a single year (1973) reduced inequality according to every measure. Similarly, substituting seven-year income or income/needs for the corresponding 1973 measure also decreased measured inequality in every case. In particular, the Gini coefficient (row [1]), computed directly from the cumulative distribution, fell monotonically as income was replaced by income/needs and the corresponding seven-year measures.

However, the various measures were not all equally sensitive to changes in the way income is measured. By far the most sensitive was the variance of the logarithm of income, where measured inequality decreased 25 percent using income/needs and 20 percent using seven-year average income. Each of these revisions of the income measure primarily altered the relative income of some families at the bottom of the income distribution--for example, the old or the temporarily poor. Since logarithmic variances are based on percentage rather than absolute differences between individuals, the effect of these two income measures was to reduce the logarithmic variance. The Gini coefficient, based on absolute income differences, showed the least variation of all the income measures. Because the coefficient of variation uses squared differences, it was more sensitive to extreme cases and changed substantially as the accounting period was extended to seven years. Finally, the information theory measures were intermediate in their sensitivity to the income measure employed. One implication of these findings is that where the interest in assessing inequality is primarily motivated by concern for those living in poverty rather than for those at the very top of the income distribution, the logarithmic variance is a more sensitive measure of inequality and of changes in inequality than is the Gini coefficient.

III. DECOMPOSITION OF INEQUALITY

The real comparative advantage of the information theory measures of inequal-

TABLE 12.1

Distribution of Income for Selected Income Measures

Cumulative Percentage of Population	Cumulative Percentage of:			
	1973 Income	1973 Income/Needs	Seven-Year Average Income	Seven-Year Average Income/Needs
10	1.5	2.1	1.9	2.5
20	4.6	5.8	5.5	6.7
30	9.3	11.0	10.8	12.3
40	15.7	17.0	17.7	19.2
50	23.7	25.4	26.0	27.3
60	33.3	34.6	35.8	36.7
70	44.5	45.3	47.0	47.5
80	57.7	58.0	60.2	60.2
90	73.9	73.6	75.9	75.5
95	83.8	83.4	85.5	84.9

NOTE: Analysis is based on 3,294 families with the same head all seven years.

MTR #7502

TABLE 12.2

Inequality of Income For Selected Measures
of Inequality and Definitions of Income

Inequality Measure	1973 Income	1973 Income/Needs	Seven-Year Average Income	Seven-Year Average Income/Needs
Gini Coefficient	.379	.361	.345	.331
Coefficient of Variation	.766	.758	.669	.680
Variance of Logarithm of Income	.130	.097	.103	.080
Information Theory Measure (Income Based)	.107	.098	.087	.081
Information Theory Measure (Population Based)	.124	.103	.100	.086

NOTE: Analysis is based on 3294 families with the same head all seven years.

ity lies in their ability to decompose inequality exhaustively into between-group and within-group inequality. In this section, we illustrate this procedure as a means of answering two policy-relevant questions. First, what is the extent of remaining inequality after we separate out those groups most amenable to special-purpose income redistribution programs and least amenable to manpower and human capital-augmenting programs? And second, looking only at the remaining group, what is the relative extent of inequality within some major subgroups?

There are three groups which contribute to overall inequality in ways that leave them outside the realm of conventional government poverty programs. These are very high income families, the aged, and the disabled. Only the tax system directly affects the incomes of the most affluent families. Special identifiable circumstances are usually responsible for the relatively low incomes of the aged and the disabled. Specific categorical aid programs are provided to assist them, and there is little concern with increasing their employability in order to make them self-supporting. It is the rest of the population--those who are not very rich, not very old, and not disabled--which is the primary focus of most poverty-related programs, particularly those programs which attempt to make poor families independent and self-supporting and not just nonpoor.

In Table 12.3 we decompose the population successively into four groups-- those families in the top decile, those not in the top decile but headed by some-one aged 65 or older, those not in the top decile nor older than 65 but disabled, and all others. Since we are confining this analysis to inequality in the dis-tribution of 1973 income only, all families in our sample in early 1974 were in-cluded in the analysis.

Table 12.3 contrasts the relative contribution of each group to the total in-equality within groups with that same group's share of population (for the popula-tion-based information theory measure) or of income (for the income-based mea-sure).[8] It similarly contrasts each group's relative logarithmic variance with its population share and presents the absolute logarithmic variance for each group as well. If each group contributed to total inequality exactly in relation to its respective population or income share, then within-group inequality would be everywhere equal. On the other hand, a group whose percentage contribution to

_____

[8]It is important that the information theory measures be interpreted appropriate-ly. In particular, it is not legitimate simply to compare the raw inequality measures themselves. This is because the maximum amount of inequality is itself an increasing logarithmic function of the size of the relevant group. Thus, a smaller group with a lower inequality measure does not necessarily have less relative inequality than a larger group with a higher measure. Table 12.3 and the tables that follow do not, then, present the raw information theory measures.

TABLE 12.3

Inequality of Income for Selected Groups, 1973

Group	Number of Cases (1)	1973 Mean Income (2)	Information Measure (By Population)		Information Measure (By Income)		Logarithmic Variance	
			Weighted Percentage of Population (3)	Percentage Contribution to Total Within-Group Inequality (4)	Weighted Percentage of Income (5)	Percentage Contribution to Total Within-Group Inequality (6)	Within-Group Variance (7)	Percentage Contribution to Total Within-Group Variance (8)
Top Decile	382	$33,350	10.0%	2.5%	26.7%	13.9%	.018	2.1%
Not in (1) and Age 65 or Older	651	6,320	17.7	24.1	8.8	16.0	.105	21.1
Not in (1) or (2) and Disabled	292	6,590	3.6	6.3	1.9	4.0	.137	5.6
All Others	4192	11,500	68.7	67.1	62.6	66.1	.091	71.2
All Families	5517	$12,610	100.0%	100.0%	100.0%	100.0%	.133	100.0%
Within-Group Inequality as a Fraction of Total Inequality				61.7%		43.4%		66.1%

MTR 7512

total within-group inequality was larger than its population or income share would be characterized by a relatively high degree of inequality. Thus, it is the comparison of column (3) with columns (4) or (8), or column (5) with column (6) that is most revealing.

The sequential elimination of the three special groups clearly did lead to a reduction in measured inequality. This is most clearly seen by comparing the logarithmic variances for rows 4 and 5: the logarithmic variance fell by more than 30 percent as the sample was reduced and the Gini coefficient (not shown) fell more than 20 percent. While some portion of this reduction followed definitionally from the elimination of the top decile, the table shows that the other two groups—the nonrich aged and the nonrich, nonaged disabled—were characterized by a high degree of inequality in the distribution of income. According to all three inequality measures, both groups contributed a disproportionately large share to the total inequality within groups. Surprisingly, there seemed to be comparatively little inequality within the top decile.[9] This was true for all of the measures.

Any characteristic of individuals, such as race or education, which is used to divide people into groups contributes to total inequality in two ways. First, the mean income of each group may differ, even where the individuals within each group have the same income. In this case, all the inequality exists *between* groups. Alternatively, the group means may be identical, but the individuals within each group may receive widely differing incomes. Here, all the inequality exists *within* groups.

The distinction between the inequality between groups and the inequality within them has more than an accounting significance. Indeed, the concern of individuals might focus largely on one source of inequality or the other, depending on their own situation. For example, people aged 55-64 might not be too concerned with the fact that their average incomes are below those of younger people or above those of retired people, since, in many ways, this would be natural and expected and because their needs might also decline with age. They might, however, be very much concerned with inequality within their own age group. On the other hand, blacks might be more concerned with the low average income of blacks than with inequality within their own age group.[10]

---

[9] This may partly reflect the fact that incomes are truncated at $99,999, but the effect should be minor.

[10] The concern with lifetime incomes can go too far, however, as it did in the recent article by Paglin (1975). Paglin argued that because the income of most individuals varies systematically over the life-cycle, conventional measures of inequality such as the Gini coefficient exaggerate real differences in income by

In Tables 12.4 to 12.7, we present a series of decompositions of the nonaffluent, nonaged, nondisabled population according to various demographic and personal characteristics. The analysis focuses on the inequality within and between groups, as well as the relative inequality within the groups.

As shown in Table 12.4, whites earned on average nearly 30 percent more than blacks in 1973, but most of the inequality in income--between 92 percent and 96 percent--existed among individuals of the same race rather than between blacks and whites. Other studies have noted that there is a great deal more inequality in income among blacks than among whites.[11] All three of the inequality measures presented here confirmed this. A comparison of column (4) with column (3) or of column (6) with column (5) shows that the inequality within the black population accounted for a disproportionately large amount of the total inequality within all groups. Similarly, the variance of the logarithm of income was much greater for blacks than for whites.[12]

Throughout the 1960's education was widely regarded by economists as the most effective way of breaking the "poverty cycle." Education was to be the pathway to higher incomes, and a more equal distribution of educational opportunity and attainment would, it was hoped, be gradually translated into a more equal distribution of income. Now, in the light of the experience of the last decade, it is probably fair to say that economists are a good bit less certain about the nature--and the inevitability--of the relationship between income and educational attainment.

Table 12.5, which looks at inequality within groups defined by their educational attainment, bears on many of these issues. First, and most prominently,

---

looking at income only at a single point in time. He went on to construct a modified Gini coefficient which nets out the inequality due to age and concluded that "the overstatement of inequality has lent false urgency to the demand for rectification of our income distribution" (p. 608).

There are two basic problems with this approach. First, if the aged are really in bad shape economically, it is little comfort--and poor public policy--to tell them that all the aged are poor and that they had a higher income earlier. Second, income needs vary over the life-cycle as well, and public policy should be more concerned with the distribution of income relative to needs than the distribution of income. But differences in needs can best be dealt with directly by introducing a needs standard rather than indirectly as Paglin does. In that case, one can still think of various reference groups (age, race, education, work effect) with whom people might compare themselves when thinking about inequality.

[11] See Smith and Welch (1975).

[12] It should be remembered that this measure of inequality is especially sensitive to income differences at the low end of the income distribution.

TABLE 12.4

Inequality of Income by Race, 1973

Race of Head	Number of Cases (1)	1973 Mean Income (2)	Information Measure (By Population)		Information Measure (By Income)		Logarithmic Variance	
			Weighted Percentage of Population (3)	Percentage Contribution to Total Within-Group Inequality (4)	Weighted Percentage of Income (5)	Percentage Contribution to Total Within-Group Inequality (6)	Within-Group Variance (7)	Percentage Contribution to Total Within-Group Variance (8)
White	2427	$11,955	84.9%	76.6%	88.3%	83.6%	.080	72.0%
Black	1651	8,440	12.6	18.2	9.2	14.3	.150	21.4
Spanish-American	114	11,340	2.5	1.3	2.5	2.2	.056	1.0
All	4192	$11,500	100.0%	100.0%	100.0%	100.0%	.097	100.0%
Within-Group Inequality as a Fraction of Total Inequality				92.5%		96.1%		95.5%

NOTE: Analysis limited to those families who are not in the top income decile, in which the head of the family is under 65 and not disabled.

MTR 7502

as Christopher Jencks and many others have emphasized, inequality in educational attainment accounts for relatively little of the inequality in income.[13]   For example, a recent human capital analysis of income differences found that education explained only 7 percent of the total variance in individual incomes.[14]   The information theory measure confirmed this finding: depending on the measure, only 4 to 7 percent of total inequality lay between groups with different levels of education.

Also of interest was the pattern of inequality within the educational attainment groups. Economists had generally assumed that education increased an individual's income by increasing his or her productivity. Recently, however, some economists have argued that education increases income simply by acting as a credential which labels persons by their level of education, allowing employers to sort individuals into job slots conveniently and inexpensively. According to this view, the relationship between education and income, while statistically genuine, is unrelated to the effect of education on worker productivity and learning capacity.

One variant of this credentialist argument is the "sheepskin" theory which proposes that additional years of education are not equivalent in their impact on income, as the human capital theorists would argue. Rather, an additional year of schooling which resulted in a diploma would be more valuable than one which did not. One implication of this is that graduates of high school or college might be most clearly labeled and, hence, uniformly treated in the labor market. Nongraduates at any level would be less narrowly classified by their credentials, and hence various personal factors--luck, personality, connections--might have a relatively greater influence on income.

The pattern of within-group variances shown in columns (3) to (8) of Table 12.5 provided some tentative support for this view of the relationship between education and income. As the logarithmic variances clearly indicate, the degree of inequality was not monotonic, but rather alternated in a systematic fashion. Within-group inequality was much lower for high school graduates than for those who dropped out of high school. Inequality increased among individuals who attended college without receiving a degree, but then dropped sharply again for college graduates.

The information theory measure showed a similar pattern. High school and college graduates both contributed less than their share to the total inequality

---

[13]Jencks, op. cit.

[14]Mincer (1974), p. 92.

TABLE 12.5

Inequality of Income by Education, 1973

Level of Education	Number of Cases (1)	1973 Mean Income (2)	Information Measure (By Population)		Information Measure (By Income)		Logarithmic Variance	
			Weighted Percentage of Population (3)	Percentage Contribution to Total Within-Group Inequality (4)	Weighted Percentage of Income (5)	Percentage Contribution to Total Within-Group Inequality (6)	Within-Group Variance (7)	Percentage Contribution to Total Within-Group Variance (8)
0-8 Grades	794	$ 9,890	13.8%	16.2%	11.9%	14.5%	.093	14.2%
9-11 Grades	1048	9,960	20.0	25.7	17.3	21.8	.125	27.7
High School Graduate	1395	11,945	35.3	28.4	36.7	32.7	.070	27.3
College, But No Degree	610	11,900	18.7	18.9	19.3	18.1	.098	20.2
College Graduate	345	13,955	12.2	10.8	14.8	12.7	.078	10.5
All	4192	$11,500	100.0%	100.0%	100.0%	100.0%	.097	100.0%
Within-Group Inequality as a Fraction of Total Inequality				96.1%		93.2%		96.1%

NOTE: Analysis limited to those families who were not in the top income decile, in which the head of the household was under 65 and not disabled.

within groups, while those who dropped out of high school contributed more.

These results are obviously not conclusive evidence that the relationship between education and income is not based on increases in productivity. Further information concerning the age and employment experience of the individuals, would be necessary, at a minimum. It is also possible that there are significant differences in both personality traits and cognitive ability between individuals who complete high school or college and those that do not. These differences, and not the diploma, might generate the pattern of inequality we observed. In any case, the apparent alternative distribution of inequality across education groups does suggest that the relationship between education, productivity, and income may be an extraordinarily complex and subtle one.

Table 12.6 presents an identical decomposition by age of head of household. Column (2) shows a conventional cross sectional age-earnings profile with income rising rapidly at first, then leveling off, and finally decreasing in the last age group. While more of the inequality here was between the groups (about 15 percent), most of it still lay within the age groupings. Within-group inequality was greatest by all three measures for those under 25, then fell through age 45 before increasing again. This is consistent with the human capital model which predicts an initial decrease in the variance of individual incomes and a subsequent increase as a consequence of differences in individual investments in human capital.[15]

Chapter 2 of this volume notes the strong relationship between marital status and economic status, particularly as if affected women who were divorced or separated. Table 12.7 examines this relationship in a slightly different way, using the various measures of inequality. Again, differences in mean income were evident between female-headed families and those headed by married couples. The income differences among female-headed families by age of youngest child were relatively slight. In all, the four groups accounted for about 13 to 14 percent of total inequality. The three inequality measures did suggest that, in general, there was greater inequality among families with female heads than among those with male heads. The only exception to this was the group of female-headed families with children over five, and this relative equality may well have reflected the absence of both welfare and high salaries among women able to work.

---

[15] See Mincer, op. cit., pp. 32-33, 126.

TABLE 12.6

Inequality of Income by Age of Head, 1973

Age of Head	Number of Cases (1)	1973 Mean Income (2)	Information Measure (By Population)		Information Measure (By Income)		Logarithmic Variance	
			Weighted Percentage of Population (3)	Percentage Contribution to Total Within-Group Inequality (4)	Weighted Percentage of Income (5)	Percentage Contribution to Total Within-Group Inequality (6)	Within-Group Variance (7)	Percentage Contribution to Total Within-Group Variance (8)
<25 Years Old	905	$ 7,430	19.7%	31.8%	12.7%	20.5%	.143	35.0%
25-34	1251	11,835	29.0	21.2	29.8	25.0	.055	19.8
35-44	763	13,815	18.5	12.1	22.2	16.3	.053	12.2
45-54	748	13,435	19.2	16.6	22.4	20.3	.071	16.9
55-64	525	10,810	13.7	18.2	12.9	17.9	.094	16.0
All	4192	$11,500	100.0%	100.0%	100.0%	100.0%	.097	100.0%
Within-Group Inequality as a Fraction of Total Inequality			84.2%		85.7%		85.4%	

NOTE: Analysis limited to those families who are not in the otp income decile, in which the head of the family is under 65 and not disabled.

MTR 7502

TABLE 12.7

Inequality of Income by Marital Status, 1973

Marital Status of Family Head	Number of Cases (1)	1973 Mean Income (2)	Information Measure (By Population)		Information Measure (By Income)		Logarithmic Variance	
			Weighted Percentage of Population (3)	Percentage Contribution to Total Within-Group Inequality (4)	Weighted Percentage of Income (5)	Percentage Contribution to Total Within-Group Inequality (6)	Within-Group Variance (7)	Percentage Contribution to Total Within-Group Variance (8)
Female Head with Child < Age 5	313	$ 7,965	4.2%	6.3%	2.9%	5.1%	.109	5.7%
Female Head with Child > Age 5	384	8,760	6.0	5.6	4.6	5.3	.059	4.3
Female Head with No Children	415	6,830	11.8	18.7	7.0	12.1	.120	17.6
Married Male Head	3080	12,610	77.9	69.3	85.5	77.3	.075	72.4
All	4192	$11,500	100.0%	100.0%	100.0%	100.0%	.097	100.0%
Within-Group Inequality as a Fraction of Total Inequality			86.1%		87.0%		86.7%	

NOTE: Analysis limited to those families who are not in the top income decile, in which the head of the family is under 65 and not disabled.

350

Summary

1. Poverty can be defined and measured in many ways. We have argued that
poverty is best understood in the context of the entire distribution of income.
This emphasizes that poverty is a relative condition and implicitly defines it in
terms of inequality. The measures of inequality we used include the Gini coefficient, the logarithmic variance, and two measures derived from information
theory. These measures varied in important ways. Logarithmic variances, for example, were most sensitive to inequality in the lower end of the income distribution, while the Gini coefficient treated all income differences equivalently.

2. The definition of income and the time period over which income is measured also influenced the measured degree of inequality. The distribution of income for a single year was more unequal than the same year's distribution of income relative to a needs standard. When income or income/needs were measured
over a seven-year period, inequality was reduced even further. The pattern was
true for all five measures of inequality which were considered.

3. From a public policy perspective, it is useful to segregate special
groups whose difference from the rest seems to have a rather special explanation
and leads to rather special policy issues. The groups that we considered this
way were the very affluent, the aged, and the disabled, since they are not the
primary focus of poverty-related programs--particularly those programs which attempt to make poor families independent and self-supporting, and not just nonpoor.
When these three groups were eliminated, overall inequality fell more than 30 percent. One reason for this was that both the aged and the disabled exhibited a
great deal of income inequality.

4. The more homogenous population of the nonrich, nonaged, and nondisabled
was subjected to further analysis. The population was divided into subgroups according to race, education, age, and marital status in order to examine the pattern of inequality within groups and the relationship between the inequality
within groups to that between groups.

5. In most cases, the greatest part of total inequality was within groups.
While whites earned on average 30 percent more than blacks in 1973, 92 to 96 percent of total inequality was among individuals of the same race. Inequality
among blacks was significantly greater than among whites. Education also accounted for a small portion of total inequality--only about 6 percent. High school
and college graduates had the least income inequality of all the groups. Some
tentative support was drawn from this for the credentialist or screening hypothesis concerning the relationship between education and income.

Age accounted for about 15 percent of total inequality. The relative inequality within age groups was highest for individuals less than 25 years old and fell through middle age, before rising among persons 45 years or older. Finally, families headed by women not only had lower mean incomes than those headed by a married male head, but also were characterized by a greater degree of income inequality than were the families headed by married males.

References

Benus, Jacob and Morgan, James N. "Time Period, Unit of Analysis, and Income Concept in the Analysis of Income Distributions." In The Personal Distribution of Income and Wealth, edited by James P. Smith. New York: National Bureau of Economic Research, 1975.

Bronfenbrenner, Martin. "Equality and Equity." In Annals of the American Academy of Political and Social Science 409 (Sept. 1973), p. 9-23.

Curtin, Richard T. Perceptions of Distributional Equity, Their Economic Bases and Consequences. An unpublished PhD. dissertation at the University of Michigan, 1975.

Horowitz, Ann R. "Trends in the Distribution of Family Income Within and Between Racial Groups." In Patterns of Racial Discrimination, Volume II, edited by George von Furstenberg, Ann R. Horowitz, and Bennett Harrison. Lexington: Lexington Books, 1974.

Jencks, Christopher. Inequality. New York: Basic Books, 1972.

Mincer, Jacob. Schooling, Experience, and Earnings. New York: National Bureau of Economic Research, 1974.

Paglin, Michael. "The Measurement and Trend of Inequality: A Basic Revision." American Economic Review 65 (Sept., 1975), p. 598-609.

Rein, Martin. "Problems in the Definition and Measurement of Poverty." In The Concept of Poverty, edited by Peter Townsend. London: Hunemann Educational, 1970.

Seastrand, Frans and Diwan, Romesh. "Measurement and Comparison of Poverty and Inequality in the United States." Unpublished, 1975.

Sen, Amartya. On Economic Inequality. Oxford: Clarendon Press, 1973.

Smith, James P. and Welch, Finis R. Black/White Male Earnings and Employment: 1960-1970. Santa Monica: Rand Corporation, 1975.

Taubman, Paul and Wales, Terence. "Education as an Investment and a Screening Device." In Education, Income and Human Behavior, edited by F. Thomas Juster. New York: McGraw-Hill, 1975.

Theil, Henry. Economics and Information Theory. Amsterdam: North-Holland Publishing Co., 1967.

Appendix 12.1

I. Derivation of the Information Measure

If x is the probability of an event E, the information content of a
message that the event E has actually occurred should be a decreasing function
of the probability x. In other words, the more unlikely the event the larger
will be the information content (surprise) that the event has occurred. Let
h(x) denote the information content of the message. The choice of the function
h(x) could be made from the set of decreasing functions of x. The function
that is generally used is the logarithm of the reciprocal of probability x.
Thus,

$$(1) \qquad h(x) = \log (1/x)$$

The advantage of this function over other decreasing functions is that it becomes additive in the case of independent events. Thus, if x_1, x_2,...., x_n are
the probabilities of occurring of n independent events, E_1, E_2, ..., E_n respectively, the information content of the message that all of them have occurred
is then

$$(2) \qquad h(x_1,....,x_n) = \sum_{i=1}^{n} h(x_i)$$

If E_1, E_2, ..., E_n is a set of mutually exclusive and exhaustive events
in the sense that one of them is sure to occur, then their probabilities,
x_1, x_2 ...., x_n should add up to unity. Thus,

$$(3) \qquad \sum_{i=1}^{n} x_i = 1, \ x_i \geq 0 \ \text{for} \ i = 1, 2,...., n$$

Before a message comes in the expected information content that one of the events
has occurred is the weighted sum of information content of each event, where the

weights are the respective probabilities. Symbolically,

$$(4) \quad H(x) = \sum_{i=1}^{n} x_i \, h(x_i) = \sum_{i=1}^{n} x_i \, \log \, (1/x_i)$$

The expected information, $H(x)$, is called the entropy which is a measure of disorder in thermodynamics.[15]

Now consider a group of n income recipients each receiving a nonnegative fraction x_i, $i=1,\ldots,$ n of total income, such that condition (3) above is satisfied. $H(x)$ then could be treated as a measure of income equality. When every unit has the same income share $1/n$, $H(x)$ attains its maximum value which is log n. If we subtract $H(x)$ from its maximum value, we obtain a measure of income inequality which is

$$(5) \quad \log n - H(x) = \sum_{i=1}^{n} x_i \, \log \, nx_i$$

Obviously this measure of inequality varies from zero (the case of complete inequality) to log n (the case of complete inequality). The dependence of the upper limit of inequality on the number of income units is justified by the fact that when a community consists of two income units, inequality is greatest when one receives all income and the other receives nothing, in which case the value of (5) is log 2. When the community consists of two million units, inequality is at its peak when 1,999,999 units receive nothing, in which case the value of (5) becomes the logarithm of 2×10^5.

It can be seen that when all incomes change proportionately, the shares remain unchanged and hence the value of (5) would remain unaffected. It can also be shown that an order preserving transfer of income from a rich person to a poor person reduces inequality.

To decompose total inequality, let us rewrite (5) as

$$(6) \quad I(x:p) = \sum_{i=1}^{n} x_i \, \log \, (x_i/p_i)$$

to $1/n$. Suppose, the population is divided into G sets, S_1, S_2, $\ldots$, S_g, on the basis of some criterion. Each unit then belongs to exactly one such set.

354

Let n_g denote the number of units in S_g. Then $\sum_{i=1}^{G} n_g = n$ and we can write

$$(7) \quad I(x:p) = \sum_{g=1}^{G} \left[\sum_{i \varepsilon S_g} x_i \log (x_i/p_i) \right]$$

Consider the expression in brackets:

$$(8) \quad \sum_{i \varepsilon S_g} x_i \log (x_i/p_i) = X_g \sum_{i \varepsilon S_g} \frac{x_i}{X_g} \left[\log \left\{ \left(\frac{x_i}{X_g} \middle/ \frac{p_i}{P_g} \right) \left(\frac{X_g}{P_g} \right) \right\} \right]$$

$$= X_g \sum_{i \varepsilon S_g} \frac{x_i}{X_g} \left[\log \left(\frac{x_i}{X_g} \middle/ \frac{p_i}{P_g} \right) + \log (X_g/P_g) \right]$$

$$= X_g \cdot I_g (x:p) + X_g \log (X_g/P_g)$$

where

$$(9) \quad X_g = \sum_{i \varepsilon S_g} x_i, \quad P_g = \sum_{i \varepsilon S_g} p_i, \quad P_g = \sum_{i \varepsilon S_g} p_i, \quad \text{and}$$

$$I_g (x:p) = \sum_{i \varepsilon S_g} \frac{x_i}{X_g} \log \left(\frac{x_i}{X_g} \middle/ \frac{p_i}{P_g} \right), \quad g = 1, \ldots, G$$

On combining the results of (8) with (7) we obtain

$$(10) \quad I(x:p) = \sum_{g=1}^{G} X_g \log (X_g/P_g) + \sum_{g=1}^{G} X_g I_g (x:p)$$

The first term on the right hand side is the between sets inequality, X_g being the income share of S_g. The second term is the weighted sum of within-set inequalities, weights being the income shares of the respective sets.

I $(x:p)$ in (6) can be interpreted as the expected information content of the indirect message which transforms the population shares p_1, p_2, ..., p_n as prior probabilities into income shares x_1, x_2, ..., x_n as posterior probabilities.

Analogous to (6), Professor Theil proposed an alternative measure of inequality,

$$(11) \qquad I(p:x) = \sum_{i=1}^{n} p_i \log (p_i/x_i)$$

which can be interpreted as the expected information content of the indirect message which transforms the income shares as prior probabilities into population shares as posterior probabilities. (11) can be decomposed as

$$(12) \qquad I(p:x) = \sum_{g=1}^{G} P_g \cdot \log (P_g/X_g) + \sum_{g=1}^{G} P_g \cdot I_g(p:x)$$

which is similar to the decomposition (10). The important difference is that the within-group differences are now weighted by population shares instead of income shares.

II. Variance of the Logarithms of Incomes

Using the same notations as before and letting z_i be the income of the ith unit, we define the logs of the geometric means as

$$\log Z = \sum_{i=1}^{n} p_i \log z_i$$

$$(13)$$

$$\log Z_g = \sum_{i \varepsilon S_g} \frac{p_i}{P_g} \log z_i$$

the relationship between the two being

$$(14) \qquad \log Z = \sum_{g=1}^{G} P_g \log Z_g$$

The variance of the logarithms of incomes is then

$$(15) \qquad \sigma_i^2 = \sum p_i (\log z_i - \log Z)^2$$

This can be decomposed as

$$(16) \qquad \sigma_i^2 = \sum_{g=1}^{G} \sum_{i \varepsilon S_g} p_i [(\log z_i - \log Z_g) + (\log Z_g - \log Z)]^2$$

$$= \sum_{g=1}^{G} \sum_{i \varepsilon S_g} p_i (\log z_i - \log Z_g)^2 + \sum_{g=1}^{G} P_g (\log Z_g - \log Z)^2$$

$$+ 2\sum_{g=1}^{G} \sum_{i \varepsilon S_g} p_i (\log z_i - \log Z_g)(\log Z_g - \log Z)$$

which can be simplified as

$$(17) \quad \sigma_i^2 = \sum_{g=1}^{G} P_g (\log Z_g - \log Z)^2 + \sum_{g=1}^{G} P_g [\sum_{i \varepsilon S_g} \frac{P_i}{P_g} (\log Z_i - \log Z_g)]^2$$

The first term on the right hand side of (17) is the between-set logarithmic variance and the second term is the weighted average of the within-set variances, weights being the population shares of the respective sets.

III. Gini's Mean Difference

Gini's mean difference or the concentration ratio is defined as the arithmetic mean of the absolute values of the differences between all pairs of incomes. Thus,

$$(18) \quad CR = \frac{\Delta}{2\mu}$$

where $\mu = E(Z)$, the mean income, and

$$\Delta = \frac{1}{N^2} \sum_{i=1}^{n} \sum_{j=1}^{n} |Z_i - Z_j| \quad .$$

When the units are arranged in ascending order of their incomes, the concentration ratio could be written as

$$(19) \quad CR = \frac{2}{N-1} \sum_{i=1}^{n} i x_i - \frac{n+1}{n-1}$$

where x_i, the income share of the ith unit is defined previously. The concentration ratio can be shown to be equal to twice the area between the Lorenz curve and the egalitarian line.

Chapter 13

THE SENSITIVITY OF THE INCIDENCE OF POVERTY
TO DIFFERENT MEASURES OF INCOME:
SCHOOL-AGED CHILDREN AND FAMILIES*

Richard D. Coe

Introduction

The definition and measurement of poverty will affect the allocation of poverty funds to geographical areas, the eligibility rules for income maintenance or
other subsidized programs, and the assessment of trends in economic well-being
for subgroups or subareas. Even if it is impossible to use the most precise or
sophisticated definition in practice, it is useful to know how well the simpler
and more available measures relate to the more comprehensive measures one might
find more theoretically satisfying.

The congruence among various measures can be assessed in several ways.
First, one can look at the simple correlations between the measures for individuals and for families. These correlations will show how accurately one can predict
the level of economic well-being or poverty status of an individual or family for
one measure if one knows the level or status as indicated by some other measure.
A second way is to see whether the relationship between poverty and other variables, particularly those reflecting policy options or easily ascertainable demographic characteristics such as age, sex, and race, depends on how poverty is defined. Third, one can see to what extent families or individuals are differentially classified as poor under alternative definitions of poverty.

This chapter deals with the effect of incorporating some improvements in the
measures commonly used to determine the economic status and the incidence of poverty for both families and school-aged children. Certain nonmoney components of
income, such as the amount saved on food stamps and the imputed rent enjoyed by
home owners, were added to family money income, while one particular cost of

---

*This chapter is for the most part a reprint of a study done for the Office of
the Assistant Secretary for Education, Department of Health, Education, and
Welfare on the relationship between the incidence of poverty and different
measures of income, with particular attention focused on school-aged children.
The main part of that report is reproduced here in the hope that a wider audi-
ence will find the results of interest.

earning income, namely, the amount of federal individual income taxes, was subtracted. The measures were then calculated for a one-year period (1971), and also
for a five-year period (1967-1971) in order to discover what differences resulted
from lengthening the time horizon. These income measures were related to a needs
standard to ascertain the economic status of a family and to examine the extent
of poverty.

Analysis

I. THE SENSITIVITY OF THE INCIDENCE OF POVERTY AMONG SCHOOL-AGED
   CHILDREN TO DIFFERENT MEASURES OF INCOME

Introduction

The definition of poverty consists of two parts--a definition of income and
a definition of needs. In 1965 the Bureau of Census developed what has become
the officially recognized definition of poverty. The Bureau selected total annual
family money income as its measure of income, and it chose as its definition of
needs a standard based on the "Economy Food Plan" developed by the Department of
Agriculture. (At 1975 prices, for nonfarm families this standard equals $1,770
plus $820 per person, or $5,050 for a family of four.)[1] Total annual family money
income is the sum of all money income, including both public and private transfer
income, received by all members of the family unit in a given year. If the measure is less than the minimum needs standard of the family for that year, the family (and all individuals in the family) are officially designated as poor by the
Bureau of the Census.

Both the income measure and the needs standard employed by the Bureau have
been the subject of sharp criticism. The needs standard has been criticized for
being based on a diet which is not nutritionally adequate when followed regularly
(and which requires an unrealistic degree of expertise in food management in order
to meet minimum nutritional levels even if the requisite money is available) and
for not adequately accounting for the differential impact of inflation across different sectors of the economy. The income measure is deficient, it has been argued, because it fails to account for nonmoney income that certain families enjoy,
such as rent-free housing provided as part of a job. A family with low money income may be able to comfortably meet its minimum needs if it does not have to pay
for its housing but may still be classified as poor by the official definition of

[1]Community Services Administration (1975).

poverty. On the other hand, the official income definition is a gross, rather than a net, measure as it fails to account for certain costs that individuals incur in receiving their money income, such as taxes, child care costs, and commuting costs. A family may earn an adequate amount of income to cover basic needs, but if a portion of that income must go to pay federal, state, and local taxes, the family may not actually be able to meet those needs. The official definition, however, would not count the family as poor.

The annual measure of income used by the Bureau of Census has also been criticized as an inaccurate determinant of a family's "true" economic status. Over an individual's lifetime he can expect to average a particular level of income each year. However, in any given year, his actual income may deviate quite substantially from his normal level of income. Part of these deviations can be accounted for by life-cycle effects on income. Young people, for example, may experience a low level of annual income as they obtain their education or acquire experience on their jobs, but often can expect much higher income in the future. The reverse pattern in income levels is generally true for elderly people. In short, annual income is not sufficiently broad to differentiate among individuals situated at various stages of the life-cycle. Deviations in the normal level of income can also result from intermittent fluctuations in annual income because of temporary unemployment, illness, or extraordinary business losses or gains. In order to capture the life-cycle effects and the irregular fluctuations to arrive at an accurate determination of a family's normal economic status, the time horizon would have to be extended over a longer period than a single year.

While this is an interesting theoretical issue, its real importance arises in attempting to allocate funds for government programs aimed at helping the needy. Which geographical regions most require help? Which individuals should qualify? Clearly, the answer depends on what kind of problem the program is aimed at alleviating. In allocating emergency help enabling families to eat and pay rent, a short-run measure of income would be more appropriate. But if the program is directed toward offsetting the effects of persistent poverty, for example, by compensating for an inadequate home environment through extra help at school, a longer-run measure of income may be more suitable.

The first part of this study concentrates on the effect of incorporating some suggestions from these various criticisms of the official income measure in determining the incidence of poverty among school-aged children. Three different measures of income were calculated. Income I was total family money income—a measure equivalent to that used by the Bureau of Census. Income II was then formed by subtracting from family money income one particular cost of earning income (federal individual income taxes) and adding certain nonmoney components of income (the value of free housing received either as part of a job or from friends or relatives, the amount saved on food at work or school, and the net imputed rent enjoyed by home owners). Another nonmoney component of income (the amount saved on food stamps by the family) was then added to Income II to form Income III. These measures were all calculated for a one-year period, 1971. Then, in order to analyze the effects of extending the time span over which income is measured, both Incomes I and III were averaged over a five-year period, 1967-1971. To determine the economic status of the survey individuals, these five measures were related to a needs standard which was virtually equivalent to that used by the Bureau of Census. Those school-aged children in families with income less than needs for the different time periods were defined as in poverty according to the various measures. Finally, to focus on the persistence of poverty among school-aged children, the years in which income was less than needs were counted, for both Income I and Income III. (For a detailed description of the needs standard and the different measures of income as well as a description of the other variables used in the analysis, see Appendix 13.2.)

Correlations Between the Different Measures of Income

The first question, then, is what difference these various measures make in ascertaining the relative economic status of school-aged children. An overview is provided by the correlations between these different measures, as given in Table 13.1.[2] The correlations between the various measures of annual income were quite high—greater than .98 for all definitions of income, indicating that better than 96 percent of the variance in one measure could be explained by differences in another measure. The correlation between five-year average Income I and five-year average Income III was likewise in excess of .98. The relationship between annual income and the annual income/needs ratio was not as strong as that between the annual measures of income, with the correlation coefficients dropping to between .85 and .89. This means that it did matter whether different family compositions and, hence, different needs were taken into account. The importance of time in determining economic status was indicated by the further drop in the coefficients when annual income was compared with the five-year measures of income/needs. In general, however, the high values of the correlation coefficients for Income I, Income II, and Income III when measured alone, when related to needs, and when calculated for an annual or a five-year time period, indicated that few differences arose as a result of the different definitions of income in determining the relative economic status of the entire population of

---

[2] The tables are presented in systematic order at the end of this chapter in order to facilitate comparisons between tables.

school-aged children.

Income and Family Characteristics

Which demographic characteristics were most important in explaining the different levels of these measures for school-aged children? Because some important demographic characteristics are interrelated, it is important (and often difficult) to separate out the independent influence of each of the characteristics. For example, the age and the educational attainment of the household head may both be important determinants of a family's relative economic status. Families headed by poorly educated or elderly persons are both more likely to have a lower level of economic well-being. However, elderly heads tend to have less education and thus, lower economic status, and age itself may be of little independent importance. The independent power (as indicated by Beta^2) of a selected set of demographic variables in explaining differences in the levels of these various measures for families with school-aged children is shown in Table 13.4.

The educational level of the head was by far the dominant determinant of income, as might have been expected given the powerful influence of education in the labor market. The effect of education was even more pronounced in the longer-run measures than in the annual measures, indicating that even highly-educated people may have experienced temporary slumps, and that people with less education may have reached income peaks. The race variable is particularly interesting. Its effect on one-year money income was extremely low; it was slightly more powerful in explaining differences in five-year average money income, but still ranked low in importance compared to the other demographic variables. However, when family size was taken into account in determining income/needs, the relative (and absolute) importance of race increased, and the increase was especially marked when a five-year time perspective was taken. This was the result of two sets of factors. Black families in the panel had a higher number of school-aged children, on the average, than did white families. Black families comprised 10.4 percent of the panel families (Table 13.12), but 15.2 percent of all the school-aged children were in black families. White families, on the other hand, accounted for 86.9 percent of the families, but only 80.1 percent of the school-aged children. This higher average number of children would systematically give black families a higher needs standard than white families. Moreover, black families with school-aged children had consistently lower incomes than did white families. This showed up in the race variable's ability to explain the number of years in poverty (Table 13.8). Indeed, race was the most powerful predictor of the length of time in poverty, even outranking education. These two factors resulted in race being a more powerful predictor of income/needs than of income, and a more powerful predictor of long-run measures than of annual measures.

The Incidence of Poverty

The discussion so far has examined the relationship of the different measures of income to the determination of the economic status of all school-aged children. Although a large degree of uniformity was found when the different definitions of income were employed across the entire cross-section of school-aged children, it is possible that significant differences occurred at the lower end of the income distribution which were swamped by a great degree of similarity at the higher end of the income distribution. Because of this, it is important to analyze separately the effects of the different measures of income on the count and on the composition of the groups of school-aged children in poverty. And as shown by Table 13.5, the type of income measure used did make a difference in determining whether a school-aged child was in poverty. For some children one measure of income showed them to be in poverty while another measure did not, as was indicated by the correlation coefficients of less than 1.00 between the different measures of poverty.[3] This result is not surprising, especially when comparing the different *annual* measures of income. Adding the amount saved on food stamps to family income, for example, should lift some children above the poverty line. The lower correlations between the annual measures and the five-year measures suggest that the time horizon employed may have a more significant effect on determining the poverty status of school-aged children than any of the adjustments to the annual measures of income.

These tentative conclusions can be examined in greater detail with the help of Table 13.6, which gives the unadjusted and adjusted proportions of school-aged children in poverty for different demographic groups and for different measures of income. The unadjusted proportions are the percentages of children in the particular demographic group who were in poverty according to a particular definition of income. The adjusted proportions isolate the influence of a particular demographic characteristic in order to give a better idea of the pure effect of that characteristic, a process similar to that described in determining what demographic characteristics were most important in explaining differences in the relative economic status of school-aged children. An illustration of how this adjustment works may be helpful. Table 13.6 shows that 39.6 percent of children in black families were in poverty according to the Income I measure, and 46.8

---

[3] A correlation coefficient of 1.00 would mean that all children who were in poverty by one definition would be in poverty by another definition, and all children who were not in poverty by one definition would not be in poverty by another definition.

percent of children in families headed by persons with less than five grades of education were also in poverty. These two groups undoubtedly overlapped--many black families were also poorly educated. The adjusted proportions accounted for the interrelationship and isolated the pure effect of the race variable by assuming that the heads of black families had the same distribution of educational attainment as the heads of nonblack families. The estimate that 26.9 percent of black school-aged children would be in poverty *even if* the heads of black families had the same educational attainment as the heads of nonblack families indicated that the low education of the heads of black families was not the sole reason that black school-aged children suffered from a disproportionately high incidence of poverty. Other factors (such as racial discrimination in the labor market, lower quality of education for the same years of schooling, etc.) were exerting a strong influence.

Several points are illustrated by Table 13.6 concerning the incidence of poverty among school-aged children. Under the most basic income measure--total family money income (Income I), 12.7 percent of all school-aged children were in families who were in poverty in 1971, with the incidence disproportionately high for children in black families, in families with unmarried female heads, and in families headed by persons who were poorly educated or disabled. When federal income taxes were subtracted from money income and certain nonmoney income components were added (Income II), the proportion of children in poverty fell to 10.7 percent--a 16 percent reduction. Thus, for families with children in poverty, the amount of nonmoney income exceeded the amount of federal individual income taxes (on the average). For all families with school-aged children, however, the amount of taxes exceeded the amount of nonmoney income (on the average), as can be seen from the lower means for 1971 Income II/Needs than for 1971 Income I/Needs for the entire population (Table 13.3). These contrasting results could be the consequence of a high concentration of nonmoney income in the poverty families, but more likely reflect the progressive nature of the federal individual income tax. When another nonmoney component of income--the net value of food stamps--was added to Income II, the proportion of school-aged children in poverty fell by 15.7 percent to 9.0 percent of all children. This beneficial effect of food stamps appears to have been concentrated among those groups which had the highest incidence of poverty--black families and those families headed by the poorly educated, by the disabled, and by females.

Within a five-year time perspective, the overall incidence of poverty among school-aged children fell, according to both Income I and Income III. However, this decrease was not evenly distributed across the various demographic groups.

Two groups of children which were most heavily hit by poverty when measured on an annual basis, those in black families and those in families with a poorly educated head, were even harder hit when the time horizon was lengthened. Using Income I as the income measure, for families whose head had less than six grades of education, lengthening the time period from one to five years *increased* the proportion of children in poverty from 46.8 percent to 52.7 percent. On the other hand, among high school graduates, lengthening the time period *reduced* the proportion of children in poverty from 8.3 percent to 5.9 percent. The results were equally striking when the differences between the one-year and five-year figures for blacks and whites were compared. Using the Income I measure, the proportion of black children in poverty decreased somewhat less than that of white children in terms of absolute percentage points (1.7 compared to 2.9 for whites) and decreased much less in terms of percentage reduction (4.3 percent for blacks compared to 38.2 percent for whites). These results were dramatically reinforced by the distribution of school-aged children according to the number of years in poverty, shown in Table 13.7. Using the Income I measure, over one-fifth of the black children (21.9 percent) were in poverty all five years, compared to only 1.3 percent of the white children. Viewed in another light, only 38.4 percent of the black children were able to avoid poverty in each of the five years, while 85.4 percent of the white children were out of poverty in each of the five years.

While the economic position of blacks and the poorly educated seems worse when viewed over a longer period, the five-year perspective shows an improved position for one group of children who were disproportionately poor on an annual basis--children in families with unmarried female heads. The proportion of these children who were poor under Income I fell from 34.7 percent on an annual basis to 28.6 percent on a five-year basis. This drop was probably a result of some female heads who were unmarried in 1971 being married at some time during the previous five years and thus having higher income in those years. Those higher incomes would have been included in the five-year average income, thus improving the longer-run position of children in these families relative to their annual position.

Poverty and Family Characteristics

Isolating those family characteristics which were most important in explaining why school-aged children were in poverty further strengthened the results discussed above, as Table 13.8 shows. On an annual basis, race and sex-marital status of the head of the family stood out as the most powerful predictors of poverty for school-aged children, and the amount of education of the household head was also important. When a five-year measure of poverty was used, sex-marital status lost some of its relative and absolute predictive power, while both race and education increased in explanatory power. In other words, race and education were more powerful variables in determining the long-run poverty status of school-aged children than they were in determining the short-run status, a finding which follows from the discussion of the differential effects of lengthening the time period on the incidence of poverty among certain subgroups of the population. Primarily because of the increased power of these two variables, the overall power of all the variables was greater in explaining long-run poverty than short-run poverty, as seen by the higher R^2 for the long-run measures. Race and education were also the most powerful predictors of the number of years in poverty for school-aged children, and race once again was the single most important factor.

Two crucial findings emerged from the above analysis: (1) Few differences arose when different income measures were utilized to determine the relative economic status of the entire population of school-aged children. (2) Substantial differences occurred, however, when different definitions of income were used to examine the incidence of poverty among school-aged children. This latter finding can be seen clearly in Table 13.9, which shows the percentage of children in poverty according to one definition of income who were *not* in poverty according to a different definition of income. For example, illustrating a point made earlier, 15.7 percent of the children who were poor when Income II was used as the income measure were not in the poverty group when food stamps were added to form Income III. The results for annual income measures compared with five-year income measures are particularly interesting in that they showed a large amount of change in the poverty status of school-aged children. Of the 12.7 percent of all children who were in poverty by the most basic income measure--annual Income I, 47.5 percent were not in poverty by the most comprehensive measure of income--five-year average Income III. In other words, 6 percent of *all* school-aged children were differentially classified as in poverty or not, depending on the income measure chosen. But the change worked both ways. Of the 8.5 percent of all children who were in poverty according to the most comprehensive measure, 21.2 percent (or 1.8 percent of all school-aged children) were not in poverty according to the annual Income I measure. These classification differences illustrate the importance of selecting the appropriate definition of poverty in attempting to determine the incidence of poverty among school-aged children.

II. THE SENSITIVITY OF THE INCIDENCE OF POVERTY AMONG FAMILIES
TO DIFFERENT MEASURES OF INCOME

Introduction

Section I discussed the sensitivity of the relative economic status and the incidence of poverty among school-aged children to different measures of income. Families with no school-aged children were excluded from that analysis; the families not excluded were implicitly weighted by the number of school-aged children in the family. This section examines the sensitivity of the relative economic status and the incidence of poverty among *all* families, independent of the number of school-aged children in the family. In the discussion of the general findings for this group, special attention is given to significant similarities and differences with respect to the results found for school-aged children.

Correlations Between the Different Measures of Income

The first objective was to learn what differences would occur from using each of the different measures of income in determinng the relative economic status of all the panel families. The correlations between the different measures of annual income were extremely high, as shown in Table 13.10. The coefficients dropped somewhat but still remained quite high (averaging about .92) when the annual income measures were correlated with the five-year measures. The different five-year measures were all highly correlated (.99 or above). When annual income was compared to an annual income/needs ratio the correlations dropped noticeably to about .82. These lower coefficients indicated the importance of family size in determining the relative economic status of families: Families with the same money income often had widely differing income/needs ratios because of differences in family size. When annual income was related to five-year income/needs ratios, the correlations dropped even further. The relationship was stronger between annual income/needs and five-year income/needs, but the fact that the relative economic position of families can change greatly over time was still apparent. There appeared to be little difference in whether Incomes I, II, or III were used in forming either the annual income/needs measures or the five-year income/ needs measures, for the correlations between these measures for a given time period were all very high (.98 or greater). Thus, while it appeared that differences in family size and the income measurement period had substantial effects on the relative economic status of families, adjustments to money income for certain costs of earning income and for certain non-money components of income had little overall effect on the relative economic status of families.

As a comparison between Table 13.1 and Table 13.10 shows, there appeared to

be no significant differences in these correlations when families were weighted
by the number of school-aged children in the family. The one-year and five-year
income measures were somewhat more highly correlated with the one-year and five-
year income/needs measures in the analysis for children than in the family analysis. This was probably a result of the decreased variance in family size due to
the elimination of all families without school-aged children from the former
analysis. The correlations between the different income and income/needs measures and the number of years in poverty were also slightly higher for families
with school-aged children than for all families, indicating that the poverty
status of families with school-aged children may be more stable than that of all
families. Overall, however, the results were notably similar.

Income and Family Characteristics

In general, there was a large degree of uniformity in the relative strength
of association of certain demographic characteristics across the different measures of income and income/needs, as shown by Table 13.13. Education of the head
of the family was the dominant factor in explaining differences in all of the
measures, both short-run and long-run, with the explanatory power being somewhat
greater in the long run. The sex-marital status of the head was a crucial determinant of the level of family money income, illustrating the effect of having a
second income earner available in the family. But when income was adjusted for
family size, the relative importance of this variable decreased; the significance
of having a second income earner was probably neutralized somewhat as a result of
these families being larger, and thus having greater needs. As was found for
school-aged children, the relative power of this variable to explain longer-run
measures for all families was somewhat lower than its power to explain annual
measures. This was a result of many female heads who were unmarried in 1971
having been previously married and consequently enjoying higher family income in
earlier years. Age of the household head was a consistently powerful variable
in explaining differences in the level of income and income/needs, demonstrating
the life-cycle effects of both income and family size.

Comparing the results in Table 13.13 with those presented in Table 13.4
provides some interesting insights into the differences between determining the
economic status of school-aged children and determining the economic status of
all families. While education of the household head maintained its dominant position in explaining differences in all of the measures, race was a much more
important factor for families with school-aged children than for all families in
explaining differences in the level of income/needs, especially five-year average income/needs. What this says, in effect, is that while five-year income/needs

ratios were roughly equally distributed across *all* white and black families
(after taking account of other factors), when families without school-aged children were eliminated from the analysis and the remaining families were weighted
by the number of school-aged children in the family, the distribution of income/
needs ratios became much less evenly distributed across black and white families.
This was probably the result of two factors: (1) a proportionately larger number
of poor white families than poor black families were eliminated from the analysis
(for example, older families, who were disproportionately poor, were also disproportionately white); and (2) larger families, which were both disproportionately
poor and disproportionately black, were counted more heavily in the school-aged
children analysis. This result was also indicated by a comparison of the poverty
population within the two racial groups in the two analyses (from Tables 13.6 and
13.15). When five-year average Income I was used as the income measure, 24.9 percent of all black families were in poverty, while 37.9 percent of black school-
aged children were in poverty. Conversely, 5.0 percent of all white families,
but only 4.7 percent of white school-aged children, were in poverty.

Another difference between the results in Table 13.13 and those in Table
13.4 is in the importance of the age variable. In explaining differences in in-
come/needs ratios for all families, age was the second most powerful variable.
However, it was the least powerful variable in explaining differences in income/
needs ratios for families with school-aged children. This result is easily understandable. In the analysis of school-aged children, the life-cycle effects of
family size eliminated most elderly families, and along with them the life-cycle
effects of income.

The Incidence of Poverty

Thus far the discussion has focused on the determinants of the relative economic status of families across the entire range of values for the various measures. In general, a high degree of uniformity has been observed for the different measures of income and the different time periods. The next concern was
whether the use of these different concepts would show any significant differences in the incidence of poverty among the entire population and within different subgroups of the population. The results shown in Table 13.14 provided the
first clue. The generally low correlation coefficients between the different
measures of poverty indicated that substantial differences in the incidence of
poverty among families could arise from the use of different definitions of income. This appeared to be especially true when a longer time horizon was taken.
Table 13.15, showing the proportion of various subgroups of the population in
poverty for the different measures of income, provides detailed verification of

this conclusion. According to the most basic income measure--total annual family money income (Income I), 8.8 percent of the survey families were in poverty in 1971. Blacks, the elderly, unmarried females, the uneducated, and the disabled were particularly disadvantaged. When federal individual income taxes were subtracted from money income and nonmoney components of income added to form Income II, the proportion of families in poverty fell sharply--by 26 percent. Virtually all subgroups of the population shared in this reduction, with elderly families experiencing a marked decrease in poverty due primarily to their generally large amounts of imputed rent from their mostly mortgage-free homes. Adding the value of food stamps to income (Income III) further reduced the measured incidence of poverty, with an additional 7.5 percent of the families who were poor being lifted above the poverty line (see Table 13.16). (It is interesting to note that food stamps had a greater effect on school-aged children than on families, as illustrated by a comparison of Tables 13.9 and 13.16. Food stamps lifted 1.7 percent of the total population of school-aged children but only 0.7 percent of all families above the poverty line.) Overall, 5.9 percent of the panel families were in poverty after all the adjustments had been made to annual money income, reflecting a 33 percent decrease from the poverty group as defined by the annual money income measure.

Lengthening the time horizon also had a substantial effect on the incidence of poverty among families. When five-year average money income was used instead of annual income, the proportion of families in poverty decreased by 19.3 percent. The decrease was somewhat less (16.9 percent) when Income III was used, indicating the greater stability of imputed rent as a component of income. When the most basic income measure (annual Income I) was compared to the most comprehensive income measure (five-year average Income III), the results were dramatic --the overall incidence of poverty was reduced by 44 percent.

But, as was seen in the analysis of school-aged children, these aggregate figures hid even more substantial changes in the poverty status of families (Table 13.16). While averaging family money income over a five-year period reduced the overall incidence of poverty by 19.3 percent, this lengthening of the time horizon moved 36.1 percent of the families who were poor according to the annual money income measure out of the poverty classification. This improvement was offset, however, by the fact that 1.5 percent of the panel families--families who were not poor on an annual basis--were in poverty when a longer time perspective was taken. Comparing annual money income with five-year average Income III resulted in even larger changes--over one-half (53.8 percent) of the families who were poor under the official definition of poverty were not poor when average

Income III was used as the income measure. On the other hand, 17.7 percent of
the families who were poor according to this broader income measure were not poor
according to the more basic measure.

It was observed in the analysis of school-aged children that certain subgroups of the population (namely blacks and the poorly educated) who suffered a
high incidence of poverty when measured on an annual basis were actually in a
relatively worse position when the time period was lengthened. This result also
appears in Table 13.15. For example, using the Income III measure, when the time
horizon was extended the percentage of white families who were poor fell from 4.1
percent to 2.8 percent. For blacks, however, the percentage actually increased--
from 19.4 percent to 22.1 percent. Thus, whites were not only less likely than
blacks to be poor, but, if poor, were more likely to be so only temporarily.
Similar results occurred for families headed by individuals with less than five
grades of education. (This group overlapped to a degree with black families,
thus some similarity was to be expected.) While race and education were no doubt
important determinants of long-run poverty, it is possible that the increases in
the proportions of these groups in poverty when the time span was lengthened were
partially due to the recent expansion of the food stamp program. With the 1970
liberalization of the food stamp eligibility requirements, many poor families
must have received larger amounts of food stamp benefits in 1971 than in the first
three years of the five-year period measured. If the food stamp program had not
been expanded, it is possible that as many of the black and the poorly educated
families would have been poor in 1971 as were poor over the entire five-year period. The fact that the proportion of black families in poverty did not increase
in the long run when just money income was used lends some support to this explanation. However, when the time horizon was extended, the proportion of the poorly educated who were in poverty increased slightly even when food stamps were not
considered.

It is of interest to note that the incidence of poverty was higher among
school-aged children than among all families, as a comparison of Tables 13.15
and 13.6 reveals. For example, 8.8 percent of all families were in poverty in
1971 according to Income I, while 12.7 percent of all school-aged children were
in poverty according to the same measure. This was a result of two factors.
Families with more children were more likely to be poor as a consequence of their
higher need standard. Furthermore, large families were disproportionately black,
and black families were disproportionately poor.

Poverty and Family Characteristics

The demographic factors which were most important in explaining differences

across all levels of the various measures were not equally important in predicting whether a family would be in or out of poverty. (Compare Tables 13.13 and
13.18.) Education of the household head remained the most powerful variable in
predicting a family's poverty status on an annual basis, and was even more powerful in explaining long-run poverty. Sex-marital status, on the other hand, was a
better predictor of annual poverty than of longer-run poverty, indicating the importance of family composition change in determining the economic status of families over time. Age of head, which was relatively very powerful in explaining
differences in the level of the various income/needs measures, was the least powerful variable in predicting whether a family was in poverty. Once other factors
had been taken into account in the analysis, it appeared that the incidence of
poverty was evenly distributed across all age groups. This result was a bit puzzling, given the relatively high incidence of poverty among older families. A
probable explanation is that the disability variable captured much of the power
of the age variable in explaining why families were in poverty but not in explaining the level of the income/needs ratios. Once disabilities were taken into account, older people were more likely to have lower income/needs ratios than mid-
dle-aged people, but not so low as to fall into poverty. It was only when a disability was added to the age handicap that older families were likely to fall
into poverty. Thus, disability was a relatively powerful predictor of poverty but
not of the level of the income/needs, while the reverse was true for age. A check
of the age distribution of disabled heads of households added further support to
this possibility. Of the disabled heads, 44.7 percent were over the age of 64,
while 48.9 percent of the heads over the age of 64 were disabled.

The results for the race variable are of interest. As was seen in Table
13.13, race was the least powerful variable in explaining differences in the
levels of various measures. Race remained a relatively (and surprisingly) low
predictor of annual poverty, except when Income II was used as the income measure. This was probably the result of black families having lower imputed rent
than white families, since blacks are less likely to own homes. However, the
relative and absolute power of the race variable increased when the five-year
average income measure was used and when the number of years in poverty was
counted. This was especially true under the broader Income III measure, again
indicating the effect of imputed rent. In short, race was more strongly associated with the persistence of poverty than with short-term poverty.

When these results for families were compared to the results obtained for
school-aged children, the race variable again provided the most significant difference, as shown by a comparison of Tables 13.8 and 13.18. Race alone was rel-

372

atively unimportant in predicting the one-year poverty status of families, but it was of crucial importance in determining one-year poverty status of school-aged children. And while race was an important explanatory variable of whether families were in poverty in the long run, its relative and absolute importance was even greater in explaining whether school-aged children were in poverty. The results support earlier conclusions--black families, which were disproportionately poor to begin with, had more school-aged children on the average than white families, thus resulting in an even disproportionately larger percentage of black children in poverty than of white children.

The other point to note in comparing the results for school-aged children and the results for families is that the disability of head, an important explantory variable for families, was not as powerful in predicting the poverty status of school-aged children. This was due partially to the fact that households headed by disabled persons had fewer school-aged children on the average. And if it is true that in the family analysis the disability variable was to a large degree capturing the effect of old age in predicting poverty, the difference in the explanatory power of the disability variable in the two analyses is even more understandable. There was little explanatory power of the age variable to be captured by the disability variable in the school-aged children analysis, since few school-aged children were in elderly families.

Summary

1. On an annual basis, there was an extremely high correlation between the different definitions of income across the entire population of families and of school-aged children. Selected demographic characteristics exhibited the same degree of association with the different annual measures.

2. However, adjustments to annual income had a substantial effect on the incidence of poverty. Many fewer families and children were in poverty after the adjustments were made.

3. Extending the time horizon over which income was measured had an even greater effect on the incidence of poverty. A large number of children and families who were poor on an annual basis were *not* poor when a five-year measurement period was used. On the other hand, some children and families who were poor on a five-year basis were not poor when an annual measure of income was used.

4. Viewing poverty over a longer time period worsened the position of black

families and families with poorly-educated heads, while improving the position
of white families, families with better-educated heads, and female-headed families.
Both race and education of the head were more powerful determinants of five-year
poverty than of annual poverty.

   5. The effect of race was more crucial in evaluating the poverty status of
school-aged children than of families. While race was a surprisingly low predictor of annual poverty among families, it was the most powerful predictor for
most measures of annual poverty for school-aged children. This was a result of
black families being disproportionately poor and having a disproportionately
large number of children.

   6. Food stamps had a substantial effect on the incidence of poverty among
school-aged children, enabling 15.7 percent of the children who were poor after
other adjustments were made to annual family money to move above the poverty
line. The effect of food stamps was less substantial when families were analyzed,
as 10 percent of families who were in poverty were moved above the poverty line
as a result of food stamps.

   7. Adding asset income in the form of imputed rental income to home owners
significantly improved the economic position of the elderly. However, some care
must be taken in interpreting this result. Many of the elderly were overhoused,
and the large imputed rental income did not help buy food or medical care which
may be needed immediately.

References

Community Services Administration. CSA Instruction 6004-LG. "CSA Income Poverty
    Guidelines." Revised Edition. Washington, D.C.: Community Services Admin-
    istration, March 26, 1975.

LIST OF TABLES

TABLE 13.1

Correlation Coefficients of Various Measures of Income and Poverty
(For All School-Aged Children)

Measure of Income and Poverty	1971 Income I	1971 Income II	1971 Income III	5-Year Average Income I	5-Year Average Income III	1971 Income I/Needs	1971 Income II/Needs	1971 Income III/Needs	5-Year Average Income I/Needs	5-Year Average Income III/Needs	Number of Years Income I Less than Needs	Number of Years Income III Less than Needs
1971 Income I	--	.983	.983	.908	.902	.892	.866	.866	.796	.777	-.412	-.384
1971 Income II		--	.999	.889	.910	.855	.858	.856	.764	.765	-.443	-.415
1971 Income III			--	.888	.909	.852	.853	.853	.760	.760	-.424	-.398
5-Year Average Income I				--	.986	.823	.801	.800	.889	.864	-.445	-.419
5-Year Average Income III					--	.797	.796	.794	.857	.854	-.464	-.440
1971 Income I/Needs						--	.985	.986	.911	.902	-.439	-.413
1971 Income II/Needs							--	1.000	.904	.916	-.481	-.456
1971 Income III/Needs								--	.904	.915	-.470	-.446
5-Year Average Income I/Needs									--	.990	-.482	-.456
5-Year Average Income III/Needs										--	-.514	-.490
Number of Years Income I Less than Needs											--	.958
Number of Years Income III Less than Needs												--

TABLE 13.2 (Sheet 1 of 2)

Unadjusted and Adjusted Mean Income Levels for 1971 Income I
and Five-Year Average Income I,
by Selected Demographic Groups (For All School-Aged Children)

Demographic Group	Percent of All School-Aged Children	Unadjusted Mean	Adjusted Mean*
TOTAL POPULATION	100.0%		
1971 Income I		$13,677	$ --
Average Income I		12,911	--
Race of Head			
White	80.1		
1971 Income I		14,708	13,941
Average Income I		13,994	13,314
Black	15.2		
1971 Income I		8,455	12,005
Average Income I		7,731	10,854
Other	4.7		
1971 Income I		13,083	14,335
Average Income I		11,298	12,439
Age of Head			
Under 25	2.0		
1971 Income I		5,723	7,720
Average Income I		8,441	10,185
25-44	64.8		
1971 Income I		13,174	12,920
Average Income I		12,512	12,279
45-64	31.7		
1971 Income I		15,451	15,593
Average Income I		14,261	14,382
65 or More	1.4		
1971 Income I		8,381	13,227
Average Income I		7,392	12,125
Education of Head			
5 Grades or Less	5.8		
1971 Income I		7,706	8,459
Average Income I		6,821	8,015
6-11 Grades	35.2		
1971 Income I		10,631	11,230
Average Income I		9,995	10,529
12 Grades	20.3		
1971 Income I		12,731	13,077
Average Income I		12,092	12,322
12 Grades Plus Additional Training	22.6		
1971 Income I		15,541	15,063
Average Income I		14,788	14,261
College Degree or More	14.4		
1971 Income I		22,432	20,663
Average Income I		21,180	19,679
Not Ascertained	1.6		
1981 Income I		9,587	12,163
Average Income I		8,981	11,179

TABLE 13.2 (Sheet 2 of 2)

Demographic Groups	Percent of All School-Aged Children	Unadjusted Mean	Adjusted Mean*
Sex-Marital Status			
Married Couple	83.0		
1971 Income I		14,977	14,593
Average Income I		13,953	13,586
Unmarried Female	15.5		
1971 Income I		7,181	9,072
Average Income I		7,635	9,445
Unmarried Male	1.5		
1971 Income I		8,886	10,581
Average Income I		9,820	11,345
Region			
Northeast	27.3		
1971 Income I		15,198	--
Average Income I		14,351	--
North Central	29.4		
1971 Income I		14,660	--
Average Income I		13,835	--
South	26.5		
1971 Income I		11,359	--
Average Income I		10,626	--
West	16.8		
1971 Income I		13,142	--
Average Income I		12,563	--
Disability of Head			
No Disability	85.2		
1971 Income I		14,347	--
Average Income I		13,522	--
Disability	14.8		
1971 Income I		9,821	--
Average Income I		9,399	--

*Adjusted by Regression Using Categorical Predictors

TABLE 13.3 (Sheet 1 of 3)

Unadjusted and Adjusted Mean Income/Needs Ratios
for Different Definitions of Income and by Selected Demographic Groups
(For All School-Aged Children)

Demographic Group	Percent of All School-Aged Children	1971 Income/Needs Ratios		Five-Year Average Income/Needs Ratios	
		Unadjusted Mean	Adjusted* Mean	Unadjusted Mean	Adjusted* Mean
TOTAL POPULATION	100.0%				
Income I		2.86	--	2.76	--
Income II		2.70	--	--	--
Income III		2.72	--	2.61	--
Race of Head					
White	80.1				
Income I		3.12	2.98	3.03	2.90
Income II		2.95	2.83	--	--
Income III		2.96	2.84	2.86	2.74
Black	15.2				
Income I		1.63	2.29	1.53	2.16
Income II		1.58	2.14	--	--
Income III		1.63	2.18	1.51	2.04
Other	4.7				
Income I		2.41	2.65	2.12	2.32
Income II		2.11	2.33	--	--
Income III		2.13	2.34	1.93	2.11
Age of Head					
Under 25	2.0				
Income I		1.81	2.16	2.00	2.32
Income II		1.74	2.04	--	--
Income III		1.76	2.06	1.93	2.21
25-44	64.8				
Income I		2.81	2.75	2.78	2.72
Income II		2.65	2.59	--	--
Income III		2.67	2.61	2.61	2.56
45-64	31.7				
Income I		3.08	3.13	2.82	2.87
Income II		2.90	2.95	--	--
Income III		2.92	2.96	2.68	2.72
65 or More	1.4				
Income I		1.76	2.94	1.57	2.70
Income II		1.81	2.87	--	--
Income III		1.84	2.87	1.63	2.64
Education of Head					
5 Grades or Less	5.8				
Income I		1.37	1.66	1.22	1.63
Income II		1.37	1.67	--	--
Income III		1.41	1.71	1.25	1.63
6-11 Grades	35.2				
Income I		2.14	2.26	2.03	2.16
Income II		2.07	2.19	--	--
Income III		2.09	2.21	1.97	2.09

TABLE 13.3 (Sheet 2 of 3)

Demographic Group	Percent of All School-Aged Children	1971 Income/Needs Ratios		Five-Year Average Income/Needs Ratios	
		Unadjusted Mean	Adjusted* Mean	Unadjusted Mean	Adjusted* Mean
Education of Head (Continued)					
12 Grades	20.3				
Income I		2.77	2.81	2.71	2.73
Income II		2.66	2.69	--	--
Income III		2.67	2.71	2.59	2.60
12 Grades Plus Additional Training	22.6				
Income I		3.32	3.18	3.27	3.10
Income II		3.14	3.00	--	--
Income III		3.14	3.01	3.06	2.91
College Degree or More	14.4				
Income I		4.76	4.43	4.56	4.28
Income II		4.28	3.98	--	--
Income III		4.28	3.99	4.11	3.86
Not Ascertained	1.6				
Income I		1.97	2.43	1.90	2.31
Income II		1.89	2.30	--	--
Income III		1.93	2.33	1.84	2.21
Sex-Marital Status					
Married Couple	83.0				
Income I		3.09	2.99	2.95	2.86
Income II		2.90	2.81	--	--
Income III		2.91	2.82	2.77	2.69
Unmarried Female	15.5				
Income I		1.73	2.19	1.78	2.21
Income II		1.72	2.13	--	--
Income III		1.77	2.17	1.77	2.15
Unmarried Male	1.5				
Income I		2.20	2.62	2.38	2.83
Income II		2.20	2.54	--	--
Income III		2.23	2.56	2.31	2.67
Region					
Northeast	27.3				
Income I		3.09	--	2.99	--
Income II		2.93	--	--	--
Income III		2.94	--	2.83	--
North Central	29.4				
Income I		3.01	--	2.89	--
Income II		2.83	--	--	--
Income III		2.85	--	2.73	--
South	26.5				
Income I		2.47	--	2.36	--
Income II		2.34	--	--	--
Income III		2.36	--	2.23	--
West	16.8				
Income I		2.85	--	2.80	--
Income II		2.69	--	--	--
Income III		2.71	--	2.63	--

TABLE 13.3 (Sheet 3 of 3)

Demographic Group	Percent of All School-Aged Children	1971 Income/Needs Ratios		Five-Year Average Income/Needs Ratios	
		Unadjusted Mean	Adjusted* Mean	Unadjusted Mean	Adjusted* Mean
Disability of Head					
No Disability	85.2				
Income I		3.02	--	2.91	--
Income II		2.84	--	--	--
Income III		2.85	--	2.74	--
Disability	14.8				
Income I		1.96	--	1.89	--
Income II		1.93	--	--	--
Income III		1.97	--	1.87	--
Number of Years Head Had Disability					
Zero	68.9				
Income I		--	--	3.06	--
Income III		--	--	2.86	--
One	11.4				
Income I		--	--	2.42	--
Income III		--	--	2.31	--
Two	6.5				
Income I		--	--	2.06	--
Income III		--	--	2.01	--
Three	4.3				
Income I		--	--	2.09	--
Income III		--	--	2.03	--
Four	4.3				
Income I		--	--	2.14	--
Income III		--	--	2.09	--
Five	4.6				
Income I		--	--	1.31	--
Income III		--	--	1.39	--

*Adjusted by Regression Using Categorical Predictors

TABLE 13.4

Unadjusted and Adjusted Explanatory Power (Eta² and Beta²) of Selected Demographic Variables
for Different Measures of Income and Income/Needs (For All School-Aged Children)

Demographic Variables	1971 Income I			Five-Year Average Income I			1971 Income I/Needs			1971 Income II/Needs			1971 Income III/Needs			Five-Year Average Income I/Needs			Five-Year Average Income III/Needs		
	Eta^2	$Beta^2$	Rank of $Beta^2$	Eta^2	$Beta^2$	Rank of $Beta^2$	Eta^2	$Beta^2$	Rank of $Beta^2$	Eta^2	$Beta^2$	Rank of $Beta^2$	Eta^2	$Beta^2$	Rank of $Beta^2$	Eta^2	$Beta^2$	Rank of $Beta^2$	Eta^2	$Beta^2$	Rank of $Beta^2$
Education of Head	.225	.144	(1)	.267	.174	(1)	.224	.148	(1)	.243	.153	(1)	.241	.153	(1)	.274	.178	(1)	.294	.186	(1)
Race	.064	.006	(6)	.085	.013	(5)	.074	.015	(4)	.096	.025	(3)	.092	.023	(3)	.098	.025	(2)	.118	.035	(2)
Sex-Marital Status of Head	.106	.053	(2)	.089	.038	(2)	.062	.021	(3)	.068	.023	(4)	.065	.021	(4)	.058	.017	(4)	.062	.018	(4)
Region-City Size	.061	.033	(3)	.066	.034	(3)	.040	.023	(2)	.046	.027	(2)	.046	.027	(2)	.044	.023	(3)	.053	.028	(3)
Family Disabilities	.040	.011	(5)	.041	.010	(6)	.047	.014	(5)	.051	.016	(5)	.049	.015	(5)	.052	.013	(5)	.055	.014	(5)
Age of Head	.036	.029	(4)	.025	.018	(4)	.014	.010	(6)	.017	.014	(6)	.017	.013	(6)	.010	.003	(6)	.011	.004	(6)
	R^2=.362			R^2=.384			R^2=.308			R^2=.345			R^2=.340			R^2=.351			R^2=.388		

TABLE 13.5

Correlation Coefficients of Different Standards of Poverty
(For All School-Aged Children)

	1971 Income I Less Than Needs	1971 Income II Less Than Needs	1971 Income III Less Than Needs	Five-Year Average Income I Less Than Needs	Five-Year Average Income III Less Than Needs	Number of Years Income I Less Than Needs	Number of Years Income III Less Than Needs
1971 Income I Less Than Needs	--	.906	.824	.687	.604	.782	.718
1971 Income II Less Than Needs		--	.910	.642	.617	.736	.741
1971 Income III Less Than Needs			--	.583	.572	.673	.718
Five-Year Average Income I Less Than Needs				--	.876	.879	.854
Five-Year Average Income III Less Than Needs					--	.821	.853
Number of Years Income I Less Than Needs						--	.958
Number of Years Income III Less Than Needs							--

TABLE 13.6 (Sheet 1 of 3)

Unadjusted and Adjusted Proportions of School-Aged Children in Poverty by Selected
Demographic Categories for Different Definitions of Income

(Adjusted by Regression Using Categorical Predictors)

Demographic Category	Percent Of All School-Aged Children	1971 Income I Less Than Needs		1971 Income II Less Than Needs		1971 Income III Less Than Needs		Five-Year Average Income I Less Than Five-Year Average Needs		Five-Year Average Income III Less Than Five-Year Average Needs	
		Unadjusted	Adjusted	Unadjusted	Adjusted	Unadjusted	Adjusted	Unadjusted	Adjusted	Unadjusted	Adjusted
TOTAL	100.0%	.127	--	.107	--	.090	--	.105	--	.085	--
Race											
White	80.1	.076	.097	.053	.073	.044	.060	.047	.069	.030	.048
Black	15.2	.396	.269	.355	.262	.302	.226	.379	.285	.347	.269
Other	4.7	.218	.174	.218	.181	.183	.161	.197	.134	.168	.118
Age of Head											
Under 25	2.0	.191	.157	.174	.140	.167	.138	.130	.107	.108	.090
25-44	64.8	.116	.132	.098	.113	.078	.090	.079	.097	.064	.079
45-64	31.7	.131	.110	.108	.090	.099	.086	.142	.119	.113	.095
65 or More	1.4	.448	.224	.375	.151	.311	.127	.406	.127	.354	.101
Education of Head											
5 Grades or Less	5.8	.468	.364	.427	.319	.341	.242	.527	.400	.471	.354
6-11 Grades	35.2	.190	.155	.162	.127	.144	.113	.148	.110	.115	.081
12 Grades	20.3	.083	.087	.072	.079	.057	.066	.059	.069	.040	.048
12 Grades Plus Additional Training	22.6	.052	.091	.030	.069	.030	.065	.027	.073	.024	.067
College Degree, or More	14.4	.006	.081	.000	.072	.000	.060	.000	.071	.000	.063
Not Ascertained	1.6	.205	.098	.194	.093	.056	-.027	.235	.126	.197	.101

TABLE 13.6 (Sheet 2 of 3)

Demographic Category	Percent Of All School-Aged Children	1971 Income I Less Than Needs		1971 Income II Less Than Needs		1971 Income III Less Than Needs		Five-Year Average Income I Less Than Five-Year Average Needs		Five-Year Average Income III Less Than Five-Year Average Needs	
		Un-adjusted	Adjusted	Un-adjusted	Adjusted	Un-adjusted	Adjusted	Un-adjusted	Adjusted	Un-adjusted	Adjusted
Sex-Marital Status											
Married Couple	83.0	.081	.092	.065	.076	.054	.063	.069	.080	.055	.065
Unmarried Female	15.5	.347	.296	.316	.263	.263	.221	.286	.232	.244	.196
Unmarried Male	1.5	.374	.302	.277	.218	.277	.234	.241	.163	.109	.047
Family Disabilities											
School-Age Child Requiring Extra Care	1.4	.037	.070	.037	.069	.035	.061	.019	.057	.014	.051
Head Disabled	11.5	.342	.279	.290	.235	.214	.165	.292	.223	.225	.167
Other Family Member Disabled	9.2	.228	.161	.208	.140	.195	.140	.229	.155	.172	.100
No Disabilities	78.0	.085	.101	.069	.084	.060	.073	.064	.082	.055	.071
Region-City Size											
Northeast, 500,000 or More	16.4	.074	.085	.057	.070	.054	.065	.045	.061	.025	.040
North Central, 500,000 or More	10.6	.076	.083	.050	.057	.036	.039	.063	.068	.055	.058
South, 500,000 or More	4.4	.181	.109	.175	.100	.145	.087	.147	.075	.126	.057
West, 500,000 or More	6.9	.134	.117	.134	.112	.091	.072	.094	.077	.043	.025
Northeast, 100,000-499,999	4.9	.087	.104	.087	.102	.087	.100	.173	.179	.159	.166
North Central, 100,000-499,999	7.4	.083	.108	.062	.085	.054	.071	.042	.066	.039	.061
South, 100,000-499,999	6.2	.130	.095	.116	.084	.111	.083	.121	.085	.106	.070

TABLE 13.6 (Sheet 3 of 3)

Demographic Category	Percent Of All School-Aged Children	1971 Income I Less Than Needs		1971 Income II Less Than Needs		1971 Income III Less Than Needs		Five-Year Average Income I Less Than Five-Year Average Needs		Five-Year Average Income III Less Than Five-Year Average Needs	
		Un-adjusted	Adjusted	Un-adjusted	Adjusted	Un-adjusted	Adjusted	Un-adjusted	Adjusted	Un-adjusted	Adjusted
Region-City Size (con't)											
West, 100,000-499,999	4.0	.123	.096	.078	.048	.078	.052	.130	.103	.108	.085
Northeast, 25,000-99,999	4.5	.115	.158	.115	.160	.083	.117	.023	.078	.000	.056
North Central, 25,000-99,999	4.0	.044	.113	.044	.110	.044	.096	.020	.086	.020	.081
South, 25,000-99,999	5.4	.204	.159	.188	.140	.163	.126	.234	.178	.211	.159
West, 25,000-99,999	3.0	.059	.093	.059	.095	.059	.087	.000	.031	.000	.031
Northeast, 24,999 or Less	1.6	.079	.120	.079	.118	.079	.113	.000	.039	.000	.035
North Central, 24,999 or Less	7.4	.162	.233	.074	.143	.061	.122	.084	.162	.034	.104
South, 24,999 or Less	10.5	.253	.194	.245	.193	.206	.164	.253	.187	.234	.176
West, 24,999 or Less	2.9	.232	.205	.161	.137	.099	.089	.219	.208	.190	.187

TABLE 13.7 (Sheet 1 of 3)

Distribution of School-Aged Children by the Number of Years Income Was Less Than Needs
(For Incomes I and III) by Demographic Groups

Demographic Group	Percent of All School-Age Children	Average Number of Years in Poverty		Number of Years Income Less than Needs						TOTAL
		Unadjusted	Adjusted	Five	Four	Three	Two	One	None	
TOTAL POPULATION	100.0%									
Income I		.63	--	4.6	3.4	3.5	4.5	7.5	76.5	100.0%
Income III		.53	--	3.1	2.6	3.5	4.7	7.0	79.1	100.0
Race of Head										
White	80.1									
Income I		.33	.44	1.3	2.2	1.8	3.0	6.3	85.4	100.0
Income III		.25	.35	0.7	1.1	1.7	3.2	5.5	87.8	100.0
Black	15.2									
Income I		2.06	1.54	21.9	9.4	8.7	11.1	10.6	38.4	100.0
Income III		1.84	1.39	16.4	9.7	10.4	10.1	11.0	42.4	100.0
Other	4.7									
Income I		1.20	.93	4.6	4.2	15.1	7.6	19.3	49.3	100.0
Income III		1.08	.87	1.2	5.9	11.2	12.7	19.4	49.7	100.0
Age of Head										
Under 25	2.0									
Income I		1.07	.90	3.6	6.1	7.2	6.6	29.9	46.5	100.0
Income III		.95	.79	3.2	6.6	6.0	5.1	24.2	54.9	100.0
25-44	64.8									
Income I		.52	.60	3.2	2.4	3.0	4.4	8.1	78.8	100.0
Income III		.43	.50	1.9	1.9	3.3	4.2	7.0	81.6	100.0
45-64	31.7									
Income I		.77	.67	6.4	5.1	4.0	4.1	4.7	75.7	100.0
Income III		.65	.57	4.6	3.5	3.9	5.3	5.6	77.2	100.0
65 or More	1.4									
Income I		2.27	.95	30.5	4.9	5.2	13.6	12.4	33.4	100.0
Income III		1.98	.76	24.1	11.3	0.0	9.1	12.8	42.7	100.0

TABLE 13.7 (Sheet 2 of 3)

Demographic Group	Percent of All School-Age Children	Average Number of Years in Poverty		Number of Years Income Less than Needs						TOTAL
		Unadjusted	Adjusted	Five	Four	Three	Two	One	None	
Education of Head										
5 Grades or Less	5.8									
Income I		2.66	2.00	30.1	9.3	15.4	10.1	11.9	23.2	100.0%
Income III		2.31	1.69	19.2	15.6	9.0	15.9	11.0	29.2	100.0
6-11 Grades	35.2									
Income I		.92	.72	6.2	4.8	4.9	7.9	11.5	64.9	100.0
Income III		.79	.61	4.7	3.7	5.0	7.3	11.5	67.8	100.0
12 Grades	20.3									
Income I		.39	.44	2.3	2.7	1.8	2.4	6.3	84.5	100.0
Income III		.29	.34	1.6	0.7	2.5	3.0	4.6	87.6	100.0
12 Grades Plus Additional Training	22.6									
Income I		.22	.45	0.9	1.3	1.5	1.2	5.5	89.6	100.0
Income III		.17	.38	0.1	0.6	2.1	1.5	4.5	91.2	100.0
College Degree, or More	14.4									
Income I		.04	.40	0.0	0.0	0.6	0.4	1.0	97.9	100.0
Income III		.02	.34	0.0	0.0	0.0	0.4	0.6	99.0	100.0
Not Ascertained	1.6									
Income I		1.42	.86	2.3	18.1	4.6	18.1	8.0	48.9	100.0
Income III		1.12	.65	0.7	7.4	15.0	8.0	17.9	51.0	100.0
Sex-Marital Status										
Married Couple	83.0									
Income I		.43	.49	2.2	2.5	3.0	2.7	7.0	82.6	100.0
Income III		.35	.41	1.5	1.8	2.4	3.5	5.7	85.0	100.0
Unmarried Female	15.5									
Income I		1.68	1.38	16.7	7.2	6.2	13.3	10.1	46.5	100.0
Income III		1.43	1.17	10.8	7.5	8.1	10.9	12.9	49.8	100.0
Unmarried Male	1.5									
Income I		1.42	1.05	10.2	13.1	1.4	12.7	8.7	53.9	100.0
Income III		1.19	.88	10.2	0.1	14.5	3.0	18.3	54.0	100.0

TABLE 13.7 (Sheet 3 of 3)

Demographic Group	Percent of All School-Age Children	Average Number of Years in Poverty		Number of Years Income Less than Needs						
		Unadjusted	Adjusted	Five	Four	Three	Two	One	None	TOTAL
Region										
Northeast	27.3									
Income I		.37	--	0.6	3.5	1.4	3.2	9.7	81.7	100.0
Income III		.31	--	0.4	0.8	3.3	4.0	8.4	83.1	100.0
North Central	29.4									
Income I		.38	--	1.8	2.0	2.9	3.2	6.8	83.4	100.0
Income III		.29	--	0.7	1.3	2.4	4.0	5.0	86.6	100.0
South	26.5									
Income I		1.15	--	12.5	4.5	4.5	6.6	7.7	64.1	100.0
Income III		1.03	--	9.6	6.1	3.7	5.7	8.6	66.4	100.0
West	16.8									
Income I		.68	--	3.5	3.9	6.2	5.4	5.1	75.8	100.0
Income III		.52	--	1.6	2.5	5.5	5.2	5.6	79.5	100.0
Number of Years Head Had Disability										
Zero	68.9									
Income I		.33	--	2.1	1.3	2.1	2.2	6.6	85.7	100.0
Income III		.28	--	1.4	1.0	2.2	2.2	5.5	87.6	100.0
One	11.4									
Income I		.80	--	5.4	4.7	4.5	8.1	4.5	72.7	100.0
Income III		.71	--	4.5	3.9	2.6	10.1	3.4	75.6	100.0
Two	6.5									
Income I		1.14	--	4.6	9.3	8.0	10.0	9.9	58.2	100.0
Income III		.84	--	4.2	1.7	8.7	9.7	11.0	64.7	100.0
Three	4.3									
Income I		1.61	--	18.3	4.7	4.7	12.0	12.3	48.0	100.0
Income III		1.40	--	10.0	10.6	5.9	8.2	12.9	52.3	100.0
Four	4.3									
Income I		1.50	--	7.9	16.0	6.7	7.7	10.9	50.9	100.0
Income III		1.33	--	6.8	9.0	11.9	7.2	12.8	52.3	100.0
Five	4.6									
Income I		2.31	--	23.9	9.6	10.7	11.3	18.2	26.3	100.0
Income III		1.89	--	13.7	11.2	8.1	15.1	21.0	30.9	100.0

390

TABLE 13.8

Unadjusted and Adjusted Explanatory Power (Eta^2 and Beta^2) of Selected Demographic Variables for Whether School-Aged Children are in Poverty, According to Different Measures of Poverty

Demographic Variables	1971 Income I Less Than Needs			1971 Income II Less Than Needs			1971 Income III Less Than Needs			Five-Year Average Income I Less Than Five-Year Average Needs			Five-Year Average Income III Less Than Five-Year Average Needs			Number of Years Income I Less Than Needs			Number of Years Income III Less Than Needs		
	Eta^2	Beta^2	Rank of Beta^2	Eta^2	Beta^2	Rank of Beta^2	Eta^2	Beta^2	Rank of Beta^2	Eta^2	Beta^2	Rank of Beta^2	Eta^2	Beta^2	Rank of Beta^2	Eta^2	Beta^2	Rank of Beta^2	Eta^2	Beta^2	Rank of Beta^2
Education of Head	.108	.040	(2)	.109	.036	(3)	.085	.026	(3)	.156	.061	(2)	.147	.060	(2)	.204	.072	(2)	.196	.066	(2)
Race	.103	.035	(3)	.129	.051	(1)	.109	.046	(1)	.155	.064	(1)	.170	.082	(1)	.214	.085	(1)	.225	.097	(1)
Sex-Marital Status	.092	.053	(1)	.091	.050	(2)	.076	.044	(2)	.069	.033	(3)	.061	.029	(4)	.115	.058	(3)	.106	.052	(3)
Region-City Size	.035	.021	(5)	.042	.019	(5)	.032	.015	(4)	.065	.030	(4)	.076	.035	(3)	.083	.033	(4)	.087	.035	(4)
Family Disabilities	.070	.030	(4)	.063	.025	(4)	.043	.014	(5)	.073	.024	(5)	.048	.012	(5)	.086	.025	(5)	.074	.019	(5)
Age of Head	.015	.002	(6)	.012	.002	(6)	.011	.001	(6)	.023	.001	(6)	.020	.001	(6)	.031	.002	(6)	.030	.002	(6)
	R^2=.259			R^2=.267			R^2=.212			R^2=.319			R^2=.315			R^2=.428			R^2=.419		

391

TABLE 13.9

Comparative Classifications of School-Aged Children in Poverty
for Different Definitions of Income

Income Definition	(1) Percent of All School-Aged Children Who Were In Poverty By Row Definition of Income	Percent of Column (1) NOT Poor by Different Column Definitions of Income (Figures in Parentheses Are Percents Computed on the TOTAL Population of School-Age Children)				
		(2) 1971 Income I	(3) 1971 Income II	(4) 1971 Income III	(5) Five-Year Average Income I	(6) Five-Year Average Income III
1971 Income I	12.7%	--	16.0 (2.0)	29.2 (3.7)	34.4 (4.4)	47.5 (6.0)
1971 Income II	10.7	0.0 (0.0)	--	15.7 (1.7)	32.7 (3.5)	41.8 (4.5)
1971 Income III	9.0	0.0 (0.0)	0.0 (0.0)	--	32.7 (2.9)	40.9 (3.7)
Five-Year Average Income I	10.5	20.4 (2.1)	31.4 (3.3)	42.2 (4.4)	--	20.2 (2.1)
Five-Year Average Income III	8.5	21.2 (1.8)	26.7 (2.3)	37.2 (3.2)	1.3 (0.1)	--

TABLE 13.10

Correlation Coefficients of Various Measures of Income and Poverty
(For All Families)

Measure of Income and Poverty	1971 Income I	1971 Income II	1971 Income III	5-Year Average Income I	5-Year Average Income III	1971 Income I/ Needs	1971 Income II/ Needs	1971 Income III/ Needs	5-Year Average Income I/ Needs	5-Year Average Income III/ Needs	Number of Years Income I Less Than Needs	Number of Years Income III Less Than Needs
1971 Income I	--	.986	.986	.924	.914	.854	.820	.820	.761	.729	-.354	-.304
1971 Income II		--	1.000	.917	.931	.824	.817	.817	.742	.730	-.380	-.331
1971 Income III			--	.917	.931	.823	.815	.815	.740	.727	-.372	-.323
5-Year Average Income I				--	.990	.802	.780	.779	.847	.816	-.388	-.339
5 Year Average Income III					--	.777	.775	.774	.820	.809	-.406	-.360
1971 Income I/Needs						--	.983	.983	.912	.896	-.365	-.322
1971 Income II/Needs							--	1.000	.910	.920	-.394	-.357
1971 Income III/Needs								--	.910	.920	-.389	-.352
5-Year Average Income I/Needs									--	.987	-.400	-.358
5-Year Average Income III/Needs										--	-.422	-.387
Number of Years Income I Less Than Needs											--	-.909
Number of Years Income III Less Than Needs												--

TABLE 13.11 (Sheet 1 of 2)

Unadjusted and Adjusted Mean Income Levels for 1971 Income I
and Five-Year Average Income I by Selected
Demographic Groups (For All Families)

Demographic Group	Percent of All Families	Unadjusted Mean	Adjusted Mean*
TOTAL POPULATION	100.0%		
1971 Income I		$11,521	$ --
Average Income I		11,173	--
Race of Head			
White	86.9		
1971 Income I		12,001	11,666
Average Income I		11,672	11,367
Black	10.4		
1971 Income I		7,393	10,029
Average Income I		7,087	9,460
Other	2.7		
1971 Income I		12,100	12,069
Average Income I		10,937	11,039
Age of Head			
Under 25	2.0		
1971 Income I		7,718	7,650
Average Income I		6,501	6,289
25-44	39.1		
1971 Income I		12,941	11,213
Average Income I		12,243	10,663
45-64	38.0		
1971 Income I		13,225	13,344
Average Income I		12,879	12,997
65 or More	20.8		
1971 Income I		6,114	9,144
Education of Head			
Average Income I		6,503	9,272
5 Grades or Less	6.7		
1971 Income I		5,518	7,529
Average Income I		5,474	7,343
6-11 Grades	36.8		
1971 Income I		8,375	9,168
Average Income I		8,295	8,966
12 Grades	17.9		
1971 Income I		12,078	11,623
Average Income I		11,749	11,408
12 Grades Plus Additional Training	23.9		
1971 Income I		13,269	12,543
Average Income I		12,788	12,142
College Degree or More	13.5		
1971 Income I		19,123	17,940
Average Income I		18,172	17,080
Not Ascertained	1.2		
1971 Income I		12,852	12,348
Average Income I		11,704	11,295

TABLE 13.11 (Sheet 2 of 2)

Demographic Group	Percent of All Families	Unadjusted Mean	Adjusted Mean*
Sex-Marital Status			
Married Couple	67.9		
1971 Income I		13,771	13,279
Average Income I		13,111	12,660
Unmarried Female	23.8		
1971 Income I		6,176	7,174
Average Income I		6,554	7,451
Unmarried Male	8.3		
1971 Income I		8,477	9,597
Average Income I		8,583	9,666
Region			
Northeast	23.9		
1971 Income I		12,799	--
Average Income I		12,386	--
North Central	29.1		
1971 Income I		12,032	--
Average Income I		11,658	--
South	29.9		
1971 Income I		9,932	--
Average Income I		9,614	--
West	17.1		
1971 Income I		11,679	--
Average Income I		11,410	--
Disability of Head			
No Disability	77.2		
1971 Income I		12,859	12,068
Average Income I		12,391	11,700
Disability	22.8		
1971 Income I		6,984	9,661
Average Income I		7,039	9,378

TABLE 13.12 (Sheet 1 of 3)

Unadjusted and Adjusted Mean Income/Needs Ratios
For Different Definitions of Income and by Selected Demographic Groups
(For All Families)

Demographic Group	Percent of All Families	1971 Income/Needs Ratios		Five-Year Average Income/Needs Ratios	
		Unadjusted Mean	Adjusted* Mean	Unadjusted Mean	Adjusted* Mean
TOTAL POPULATION	100.0%				
Income I		3.57	--	3.45	--
Income II		3.40	--	--	--
Income III		3.41	--	3.27	--
Race of Head					
White	86.9				
Income I		3.77	3.67	3.64	3.55
Income II		3.59	3.50	--	--
Income III		3.60	3.50	3.45	3.37
Black	10.4				
Income I		2.08	2.82	2.01	2.70
Income II		2.01	2.67	--	--
Income III		2.04	2.70	1.94	2.56
Other	2.7				
Income I		3.03	3.31	2.77	3.07
Income II		2.76	3.11	--	--
Income III		2.77	3.11	2.55	2.89
Age of Head					
Under 25	2.0				
Income I		2.82	2.49	2.33	2.01
Income II		2.63	2.33	--	--
Income III		2.65	2.35	2.17	1.89
25-44	39.1				
Income I		3.56	3.06	3.42	2.95
Income II		3.27	2.83	--	--
Income III		3.28	2.84	3.14	2.73
45-64	38.0				
Income I		4.13	4.21	3.90	3.97
Income II		3.87	3.94	--	--
Income III		3.88	3.95	3.65	3.71
65 Or More	20.8				
Income I		2.66	3.49	2.79	3.57
Income II		2.87	3.61	--	--
Income III		2.88	3.60	2.95	3.63
Education of Head					
5 Grades or Less	6.7				
Income I		1.74	2.08	1.69	2.00
Income II		1.77	2.00	--	--
Income III		1.80	2.03	1.73	1.93
6-11 Grades	36.8				
Income I		2.60	2.70	2.58	2.66
Income II		2.61	2.66	--	--
Income III		2.62	2.67	2.56	2.59

TABLE 13.12 (Sheet 2 of 3)

Demographic Group	Percent of All Families	1971 Income/Needs Ratios		Five-Year Average Income/Needs Ratios	
		Unadjusted Mean	Adjusted* Mean	Unadjusted Mean	Adjusted* Mean
Education of Head (Cont.)					
12 Grades	17.9				
Income I		3.69	3.69	3.55	3.57
Income II		3.49	3.53	--	--
Income III		3.49	3.53	3.35	3.41
12 Grades Plus Additional Training	23.9				
Income I		4.19	4.06	4.02	3.91
Income II		3.96	3.87	--	--
Income III		3.96	3.87	3.77	3.70
College Degree or More	13.5				
Income I		5.83	5.63	5.54	5.35
Income II		5.26	5.12	--	--
Income III		5.26	5.12	4.99	4.86
Not Ascertained	1.2				
Income I		4.12	4.04	3.60	3.57
Income II		3.78	3.75	--	--
Income III		3.79	3.76	3.34	3.35
Sex-Marital Status					
Married Couple	67.9				
Income I		3.91	3.78	3.75	3.65
Income II		3.67	3.58	--	--
Income III		3.68	3.59	3.52	3.44
Unmarried Female	23.8				
Income I		2.59	2.83	2.60	2.81
Income II		2.62	2.79	--	--
Income III		2.63	2.80	2.61	2.74
Unmarried Male	8.3				
Income I		3.69	3.99	3.39	3.66
Income II		3.46	3.70	--	--
Income III		3.46	3.70	3.19	3.40
Region					
Northeast	23.9				
Income I		3.85	--	3.70	--
Income II		3.66	--	--	--
Income III		3.67	--	3.50	--
North Central	29.1				
Income I		3.67	--	3.53	--
Income II		3.50	--	--	--
Income III		3.51	--	3.36	--
South	29.9				
Income I		3.19	--	3.07	--
Income II		3.05	--	--	--
Income III		3.06	--	2.92	--
West	17.1				
Income I		3.71	--	3.63	--
Income II		3.50	--	--	--
Income III		3.51	--	3.42	--

TABLE 13.12 (Sheet 3 of 3)

Demographic Group	Percent of All Families	1971 Income/Needs Ratios		Five-Year Average Income/Needs Ratios	
		Unadjusted Mean	Adjusted* Mean	Unadjusted Mean	Adjusted* Mean
Disability of Head					
No Disability	77.2				
Income I		3.91	3.77	3.76	3.63
Income II		3.69	3.58	--	--
Income III		3.69	3.58	3.52	3.43
Disability	22.8				
Income I		2.40	2.92	2.40	2.83
Income II		2.45	2.80	--	--
Income III		2.47	2.82	2.43	2.72

TABLE 13.13

Unadjusted and Adjusted Explanatory Power (Eta² and Beta²) of Selected Demographic Variables
for Different Measures of Income and Income/Needs
(For All Families)

Demographic Variables	1971 Income I			Five-Year Average Income I			1971 Income I/Needs			1971 Income II/Needs			1971 Income III/Needs			Five-Year Average Income I/Needs			Five-Year Average Income III/Needs		
	Eta²	Beta²	Rank of Beta²	Eta²	Beta²	Rank of Beta²	Eta²	Beta²	Rank of Beta²	Eta²	Beta²	Rank of Beta²	Eta²	Beta²	Rank of Beta²	Eta²	Beta²	Rank of Beta²	Eta²	Beta²	Rank of Beta²
Education of Head	.192	.117	(1)	.209	.129	(1)	.188	.147	(1)	.195	.162	(1)	.194	.161	(1)	.204	.162	(1)	.209	.176	(1)
Race	.026	.003	(6)	.033	.006	(6)	.038	.010	(6)	.050	.013	(6)	.049	.013	(6)	.046	.013	(6)	.059	.017	(6)
Sex-Marital Status of Head	.144	.090	(2)	.137	.083	(2)	.043	.024	(3)	.040	.025	(4)	.040	.024	(4)	.041	.023	(4)	.038	.022	(5)
Region-City Size	.050	.032	(4)	.058	.037	(4)	.036	.022	(4)	.038	.025	(3)	.038	.025	(3)	.040	.026	(3)	.042	.028	(3)
Disability of Head	.079	.013	(5)	.084	.016	(5)	.056	.017	(5)	.055	.022	(5)	.054	.021	(5)	.058	.020	(5)	.054	.023	(4)
Age of Head	.108	.036	(3)	.109	.043	(3)	.042	.039	(2)	.033	.056	(2)	.033	.055	(2)	.034	.044	(2)	.028	.066	(2)
	$R^2=.391$			$R^2=.415$			$R^2=.291$			$R^2=.317$			$R^2=.314$			$R^2=.314$			$R^2=.340$		

TABLE 13.14

Correlation Coefficients of Different Standards of Poverty
(For All Families)

	1971 Income I Less Than Needs	1971 Income II Less Than Needs	1971 Income III Less Than Needs	Five-Year Average Income I Less Than Needs	Five-Year Average Income III Less Than Needs	Number of Years Income I Less Than Needs	Number of Years Income III Less Than Needs
1971 Income I Less Than Needs	--	.852	.806	.684	.591	.783	.701
1971 Income II Less Than Needs		--	.945	.638	.643	.702	.753
1971 Income III Less Than Needs			--	.615	.621	.674	.749
Five-Year Average Income I Less Than Needs				--	.811	.868	.816
Five-Year Average Income III Less Than Needs					--	.754	.841
Number of Years Income I Less Than Needs						--	.909
Number of Years Income III Less Than Needs							--

TABLE 13.15 (Sheet 1 of 3)

Unadjusted and Adjusted Proportions of Families in Poverty
By Selected Demographic Categories, For Different Definitions of Income
(Adjusted by Regression Using Categorical Predictors)

Demographic Category	Percent of All Families	1971 Income I Less Than Needs		1971 Income II Less Than Needs		1971 Income III Less Than Needs		Five-Year Average Income I Less Than Five-Year Average Needs		Five-Year Average Income III Less Than Five-Year Average Needs	
		Un-adjusted	Adjusted	Un-adjusted	Adjusted	Un-adjusted	Adjusted	Un-adjusted	Adjusted	Un-adjusted	Adjusted
TOTAL	100.0%	.088	—	.065	—	.059	—	.071	—	.049	—
Race											
White	86.9	.067	.075	.044	.051	.041	.047	.050	.058	.028	.034
Black	10.4	.256	.190	.227	.173	.194	.147	.249	.183	.221	.170
Other	2.7	.123	.105	.123	.104	.113	.101	.090	.070	.084	.065
Age of Head											
Under 25	2.0	.045	.084	.012	.048	.012	.042	.054	.089	.028	.057
25-44	39.1	.065	.107	.055	.090	.045	.076	.037	.077	.029	.057
45-64	38.0	.074	.070	.055	.051	.051	.049	.067	.064	.050	.048
65 or More	20.8	.160	.083	.110	.047	.104	.048	.145	.074	.088	.037
Education of Head											
5 Grades or Less	6.7	.365	.293	.291	.229	.256	.199	.368	.287	.294	.226
6-11 Grades	36.8	.125	.104	.095	.079	.088	.073	.096	.075	.064	.049
12 Grades	17.9	.049	.058	.032	.039	.027	.034	.034	.046	.014	.022
12 Grades + Additional Training	23.9	.026	.051	.013	.035	.013	.033	.016	.042	.012	.033
College Degree or More	13.5	.009	.044	.005	.033	.005	.030	.003	.039	.001	.028
Not Ascertained	1.2	.106	.106	.102	.098	.061	.058	.100	.099	.061	.055

TABLE 13.15 (Sheet 2 of 3)

Demographic Category	Percent of All Families	1971 Income I Less Than Needs		1971 Income II Less Than Needs		1971 Income III Less Than Needs		Five-Year Average Income I Less Than Five-Year Average Needs		Five-Year Average Income III Less Than Five-Year Average Needs	
		Un-adjusted	Adjusted	Un-adjusted	Adjusted	Un-adjusted	Adjusted	Un-adjusted	Adjusted	Un-adjusted	Adjusted
Sex-Marital Status											
Married Couple	67.9	.053	.063	.037	.045	.032	.039	.038	.049	.027	.035
Unmarried Female	23.8	.183	.164	.144	.129	.131	.118	.157	.137	.108	.094
Unmarried Male	8.3	.098	.071	.073	.052	.073	.054	.099	.070	.065	.043
Disability of Head											
No Disability	77.2	.048	.061	.033	.043	.030	.039	.032	.046	.021	.031
Disabled	22.8	.224	.180	.174	.142	.156	.125	.204	.157	.145	.113
Region-City Size											
Northeast, 500,000 or more	13.8	.037	.048	.023	.031	.022	.029	.020	.032	.015	.023
North Cent. 500,000 or more	9.2	.057	.047	.045	.034	.034	.026	.046	.035	.040	.029
South 500,000 or more	4.2	.095	.061	.074	.040	.061	.033	.075	.041	.056	.021
West 500,000 or more	6.8	.066	.071	.054	.055	.040	.039	.045	.049	.018	.018
Northeast 100,000-499,999	4.0	.068	.071	.058	.064	.058	.062	.075	.076	.046	.049
North Cent. 100,000-499,999	6.7	.044	.066	.021	.039	.020	.036	.020	.040	.010	.025
South 100,000-499,999	7.3	.102	.093	.077	.068	.070	.062	.080	.072	.056	.046

TABLE 13.15 (Sheet 3 of 3)

Demographic Category	Percent of all Families	1971 Income I Less Than Needs		1971 Income II Less Than Needs		1971 Income III Less Than Needs		Five-Year Average Income I Less Than Five-Year Average Needs		Five-Year Average Income III Less Than Five-Year Average Needs	
		Un-adjusted	Adjusted	Un-adjusted	Adjusted	Un-adjusted	Adjusted	Un-adjusted	Adjusted	Un-adjusted	Adjusted
Region-City Size (Cont.)											
West, 100,000-499,999	3.7	.048	.074	.038	.057	.038	.054	.061	.086	.044	.061
Northeast, 25,000-99,999	4.5	.068	.082	.068	.082	.060	.071	.037	.053	.016	.034
North Cent., 25,000-99,999	4.3	.042	.084	.042	.079	.042	.074	.029	.069	.022	.056
South, 25,000-99,999	6.3	.110	.087	.091	.070	.087	.070	.133	.107	.114	.089
West, 25,000-99,999	3.5	.043	.061	.021	.039	.021	.036	.045	.063	.011	.027
Northeast, 24,999 or less	1.6	.080	.090	.057	.070	.057	.068	.000	.009	.000	.010
North Cent., 24,999 or less	8.9	.128	.145	.078	.097	.074	.090	.079	.098	.036	.058
South, 24,999 or less	12.1	.205	.165	.162	.130	.145	.118	.194	.154	.144	.114
West, 24,999 or less	3.0	.110	.111	.066	.070	.053	.055	.081	.085	.066	.075

TABLE 13.16

Comparative Classifications of Families in Poverty
for Different Definitions of Income

Income Definition	(1) Percent of All Families Who Were In Poverty By Row Definition of Income	Percent of Column (1) NOT Poor by Different Column Definitions of Income. (Figures in Parentheses Are Percents Computed on the TOTAL Population of Families)				
		(2) 1971 Income I	(3) 1971 Income II	(4) 1971 Income III	(5) Five-Year Average Income I	(6) Five-Year Average Income III
1971 Income I	8.8%	--	25.5 (2.2)	33.0 (2.9)	36.1 (3.2)	53.8 (4.7)
1971 Income II	6.5	0.1 (0.0)	--	10.0 (0.7)	30.8 (2.0)	42.5 (2.8)
1971 Income III	5.9	0.1 (0.0)	0.0 (0.0)	--	29.5 (1.7)	41.3 (2.4)
Five-Year Average Income I	7.1	21.5 (1.5)	36.6 (2.6)	41.9 (3.0)	--	31.7 (2.3)
Five-Year Average Income III	4.9	17.7 (0.9)	23.6 (1.2)	29.9 (1.5)	1.0 (0.1)	--

TABLE 13.17 (Sheet 1 of 2)

Distribution of Selected Demographic Groups
by Number of Years Income Was Less Than Needs
for Incomes I and V* (For All Families)

Demographic Group	Percent of Total Population	Number of Years Income Less Than Needs						Total
		5	4	3	2	1	0	
TOTAL POPULATION	100.0%							
Income I		3.5	1.9	2.5	3.3	6.8	82.1	100.0%
Income V		2.2	1.3	2.3	3.2	5.9	85.1	100.0
Race of Head								
White	86.9							
Income I		2.3	1.2	1.8	2.8	6.0	85.8	100.0
Income V		1.3	0.7	1.5	2.6	4.9	89.0	100.0
Black	10.4							
Income I		13.2	7.3	6.7	7.4	11.8	53.5	100.0
Income V		10.1	6.8	7.2	7.4	13.0	55.7	100.0
Other	2.7							
Income I		2.9	1.8	7.3	3.9	13.3	70.8	100.0
Income V		2.6	0.9	8.8	4.9	10.2	72.7	100.0
Age of Head								
Under 25	2.0							
Income I		0.0	3.1	4.4	13.6	21.8	57.0	100.0
Income V		0.0	2.8	4.4	11.1	22.5	59.1	100.0
25-44	39.1							
Income I		1.5	1.0	1.9	2.5	6.3	86.9	100.0
Income V		1.0	0.8	2.3	2.3	5.5	88.1	100.0
45-64	38.0							
Income I		2.9	1.9	2.6	2.5	5.4	84.8	100.0
Income V		2.3	1.4	2.1	2.7	5.1	86.5	100.0
65 or more	20.8							
Income I		8.6	3.4	3.3	5.5	8.8	70.3	100.0
Income V		4.8	2.1	2.4	5.0	6.4	79.3	100.0
Sex-Marital Status of Head								
Married Couple	67.9							
Income I		1.6	1.2	1.7	1.8	5.0	88.6	100.0
Income V		1.1	0.6	1.5	2.1	4.6	90.1	100.0
Unmarried Female	23.8							
Income I		8.3	3.6	4.6	6.8	10.4	66.3	100.0
Income V		5.1	3.3	4.0	6.0	8.5	73.1	100.0
Unmarried Male	8.3							
Income I		4.9	2.4	2.7	5.5	10.6	73.8	100.0
Income V		3.1	1.6	3.6	4.2	8.6	78.8	100.0

*Income V equals Income II minus Social Security taxes.

TABLE 13.17 (Sheet 2 of 2)

Demographic Group	Percent of Total Population	Number of Years Income Less Than Needs						Total
		5	4	3	2	1	0	
Education of Head								
5 Grades or Less	6.7							
Income I		20.4	7.5	9.4	8.3	12.4	41.9	100.0
Income V		15.1	7.5	8.0	8.6	11.9	48.9	100.0
6-11 Grades	36.8							
Income I		4.4	2.7	3.6	5.3	9.8	74.1	100.0
Income V		2.8	1.7	3.3	5.0	8.7	78.5	100.0
12 Grades	17.9							
Income I		1.8	1.1	1.1	2.0	4.8	89.3	100.0
Income V		0.9	0.4	0.9	2.4	3.5	92.1	100.0
12 Grades Plus Additional Training	23.9							
Income I		0.6	0.4	1.1	1.5	4.7	91.7	100.0
Income V		0.2	0.4	1.3	1.0	4.1	93.0	100.0
College Degree of More	13.5							
Income I		0.0	0.1	0.6	0.3	2.2	96.9	100.0
Income V		0.0	0.1	0.1	0.3	1.6	97.9	100.0
Not Ascertained	1.2							
Income I		2.2	7.0	0.7	3.8	5.6	80.6	100.0
Income V		0.1	2.4	4.4	7.0	2.7	83.8	100.0
Number of Years of Disability of Head								
None	59.5							
Income I		0.9	0.7	1.0	1.7	4.9	90.8	100.0
Income V		0.6	0.6	1.0	1.4	4.4	92.0	100.0
One	11.9							
Income I		1.9	1.5	2.2	3.6	7.7	83.1	100.0
Income V		1.4	0.7	2.8	3.1	5.9	86.1	100.0
Two	6.8							
Income I		2.9	3.0	3.8	3.5	11.2	75.5	100.0
Income V		1.7	1.6	3.6	3.7	8.8	80.5	100.0
Three	5.6							
Income I		7.1	2.9	3.9	6.6	11.5	67.9	100.0
Income V		3.9	2.3	2.7	6.1	7.9	77.0	100.0
Four	7.6							
Income I		8.3	6.0	5.2	7.6	9.4	63.4	100.0
Income V		6.4	1.8	5.1	8.6	9.9	68.3	100.0
Five	8.5							
Income I		17.2	5.6	8.6	8.2	9.4	51.1	100.0
Income V		10.1	6.1	6.9	8.6	8.6	59.7	100.0

TABLE 13.18

Unadjusted and Adjusted Explanatory Power (Eta² and Beta²) of Selected Demographic Variables
for Whether Families are in Poverty, According to Different Measures of Poverty

Demographic Variables	1971 Income I Less Than Needs			1971 Income II Less Than Needs			1971 Income III Less Than Needs			Five-Year Average Income I Less Than Five-Year Average Needs			Five-Year Average Income III Less Than Five-Year Average Needs			Number of Years Income I Less Than Needs			Number of Years Income III Less Than Needs		
	Eta^2	$Beta^2$	Rank of $Beta^2$	Eta^2	$Beta^2$	Rank of $Beta^2$	Eta^2	$Beta^2$	Rank of $Beta^2$	Eta^2	$Beta^2$	Rank of $Beta^2$	Eta^2	$Beta^2$	Rank of $Beta^2$	Eta^2	$Beta^2$	Rank of $Beta^2$	Eta^2	$Beta^2$	Rank of $Beta^2$
Education of Head	.096	.045	(1)	.083	.038	(1)	.071	.031	(1)	.116	.054	(1)	.105	.050	(1)	.147	.062	(1)	.134	.061	(1)
Race	.042	.016	(5)	.052	.023	(3)	.041	.018	(4)	.056	.022	(4)	.075	.037	(2)	.080	.033	(4)	.096	.045	(2)
Sex-Marital Status	.037	.023	(3)	.033	.021	(4)	.031	.020	(3)	.038	.021	(5)	.025	.013	(5)	.059	.031	(5)	.046	.024	(5)
Region-City Size	.034	.019	(4)	.028	.016	(5)	.026	.015	(5)	.045	.023	(3)	.041	.021	(4)	.062	.034	(3)	.052	.028	(4)
Disability of Head	.068	.031	(2)	.057	.028	(2)	.050	.023	(2)	.078	.033	(2)	.058	.025	(3)	.097	.037	(2)	.076	.032	(3)
Age of Head	.018	.003	(6)	.009	.006	(6)	.010	.003	(6)	.024	.001	(6)	.010	.001	(6)	.036	.005	(6)	.017	.008	(6)
	$R^2=.181$			$R^2=.167$			$R^2=.141$			$R^2=.216$			$R^2=.197$			$R^2=.291$			$R^2=.266$		

Appendix 13.1

Data Base and Sample Size

For the school-aged children analysis, all children in the panel between the ages of 5-18 (inclusive) in the spring 1972 were counted, resulting in a sample of 5,834 individuals. This definition of school-aged children differs somewhat from that employed by the Bureau of Census, which defines a school-aged child as between the ages of 5-17 (inclusive).

For the family analysis, only those families in 1972 which included a male head from 1968, a female head from 1968, or a wife married to a male head in 1968 were counted. In effect, splitoff families formed by children leaving the original family were excluded from the analysis. This resulted in a sample size of 4,010 families. Because of this selective filtering, the sample for the family analysis was not a representative cross section of the entire population, as it undercounted families with young heads.

Appendix 13.2

Definition of Terms

DISABILITIES:

A. *DISABILITY OF HOUSEHOLD HEAD:* whether the household head reported a physical or nervous condition which limited the kind or amount of work which he or
she could do. This was in response to a direct question asked the respondents.
In addition, in 1968 and 1972 the respondents were asked the question, "How much
does it (the disability) limit your work?" Respondents who replied that they had
a disability but whose answer to the second question indicated that it put no
limitation on their work were not considered to have a disability. These individuals comprised 1.4 percent of the total sample in 1968 and 1.2 percent in
1972. Such a screening procedure was not available for 1969-1971.

In the school-aged children analysis, different figures were shown for the
percentage of school-aged children in a family with a disabled head. In Table
13.2, 14.8 percent of the children were shown to be in families with a disabled
head. In Table 13.6 the figure was 11.5 percent. This resulted from a coding
priority in the computer set-up which placed children who were in a family in
which both the head and another (nonschool-aged child) family member were disabled in the category "Other Family Member Disabled." The difference in the
figures indicates that 3.3 percent of the children were in families which had
both a disabled head and a disabled other member of the family.

B. *DISABILITY OF OTHER FAMILY MEMBERS:* whether a nonschool-aged child member of
the family other than head could not work or attend school or required extra care.
This is in response to a direct question asked the head in 1972.

C. *SCHOOL-AGED CHILD REQUIRING EXTRA CARE BECAUSE OF DISABILITY:* whether a
school-aged child required a lot of extra care because of poor health, but still
was able to attend school. This was in response to a direct question asked the
head in 1972.

INCOME I: total family money income. Essentially, this was the sum of labor
money income, asset money income, and transfer money income, both public and private, for all family members. This is virtually equivalent to the Census Bureau's
definition of income.

INCOME II: total family money income (Income I) minus federal individual income taxes plus (1) imputed rent to home owners, (2) rent value of free housing, and (3) amount saved on food at work/school.

INCOME III: Income II plus the amount saved on food stamps.

INCOME/NEEDS RATIO: the relevant income measure divided by the needs standard. For the five-year measures, five-year average income was divided by five-year average needs.

NEEDS STANDARD: an estimate of the amount of income needed in order for a family to escape poverty, as defined by the Census Bureau. It was based on the economy food budget developed by the Department of Agriculture. (This is equal to .8 of the low-cost food budget, which was used as the basis for creating the SRC needs standard variable.) In effect, it takes into account differences in family size and the age-sex composition of the family unit. It has been adjusted upward annually to take account of inflation. In addition, the needs standard for farmers was set at 85 percent of the standard for nonfarmers, the equivalence figure used by the Census Bureau. With these adjustments, the needs standard used in this study, and the resultant poverty threshhold levels, should be a very close approximation to the poverty threshhold levels employed by the Census Bureau.

REGIONAL-URBAN AREA: a variable which combined the four regions of the nation (Northeast, North Central, South, and West) with four ranges of the size of the largest city in the county where the family resided (500,000 or more, 100,000-499,999, 25,000-99,999, and 24,999 or less). The result was 16 geographical subareas in which families and children reside.

SCHOOL-AGED CHILDREN: a school-aged child in 1971 was defined as between the ages of 5 and 18 in the spring of 1972. This differs slightly from the Bureau of Census' definition of school-aged child for a particular year, which is a child between the ages of 5 and 17 in the spring of the following year.

SEX-MARITAL STATUS OF HEAD: the composite variable created in an attempt to isolate some of the interdependent effects of the "Sex of Head" variable and the "Marital Status of Head" variable. The "Unmarried Female" category included female heads who were single, widowed, divorced, or separated in 1972. The "Unmarried Male" category included male heads who were single, widowed, divorced, or separated in 1972. The remaining families composed the "Married Couple" category.

Chapter 14

SUMMARY OF OTHER RESEARCH

In this chapter we summarize some recent analysis of the Panel data being conducted here at the University of Michigan and elsewhere. A similar summary appeared in Volumes II and III, and here we attempt to bring that list of research completed and in progress up to date.

These analyses are in various stages of completion. Some have already been published in professional journals, some are currently at the "working paper" stage, and the remainder are just getting started.

Our list of analysis is certainly not complete. The task of contacting everyone working with the Panel data is impossible, but our hope is that the following summaries will help to coordinate future research.

RACE AND HOME OWNERSHIP: IS DISCRIMINATION DISAPPEARING?

Elizabeth A. Roistacher
Queens College

and

John L. Goodman, Jr.
The Urban Institute

(To appear in <u>Economic Inquiry</u>)

Racial differentials in home ownership rates are examined using data on households in the 24 largest metropolitan areas. Considerable recent reduction in racial discrimination is indicated, in contrast to the findings of a previous analysis of the St. Louis housing market. The results are maintained under a number of modifications of the model and estimation technique.

THE SINGLE-PARENT FAMILY: A COMPARATIVE STUDY

Michael J. Smith
Community Service Society
New York

Cross-sectional and longitudinal analyses are being conducted on subsamples of single and two-parent families with children. Within a structural-functional theoretical framework, a number of family conditions have been hypothesized as the effects of family status. A number of component variables and indices will be constructed from Panel data to investigate differences in social, economic and intra-familial functions between two-parent and single-parent families and among different groups of single-parent families.

Results will provide data on family need and will be used for the investigation of competing public policy rationales, i.e., whether the single-parent family should be considered as a distinct entity or as a loose conglomerate of family types.

PERMANENT-INCOME HYPOTHESIS OF HOUSING CONSUMPTION

T. H. Lee and C. M. Kong
Department of Economics
The University of Wisconsin-Milwaukee

According to the permanent-income hypothesis, the consumer reacts to his evaluation of long-term prospects, as summarized in his estimated permanent income. Since housing expenditures are usually made on the basis of the long-term needs of a consumer unit, the "horizon" of the consumer unit for evaluating long-term income prospects applicable to housing would be quite long, e.g., longer than that applicable to total consumption. Although most housing studies have accepted the permanent-income hypothesis, there are virtually no estimates of the horizon. Furthermore, when these studies used rough measures of the permanent income, their estimates of the permanent-income elasticity of housing varied widely, ranging from .5 to 2.1.

This study offers new evidence by using more powerful statistical methods and also by using five-year panel data from the Panel Study of Income Dynamics. The methods employed are an extended version of Livitan's instrumental variable method and the two-stage least squares method, based on micro household units. Our results yield an estimate of the horizon for the permanent income concept in housing and also provide robust estimates of the permanent-income elasticity. One important finding among others is that the magnitude of the permanent-income elasticity of housing is less than unity, thus differing from most other studies.

THE EFFECT OF FAMILY STATUS AND FAMILY LIFE-CYCLE STAGES ON HOUSING STANDARD, PERSONAL EFFICACY AND PLANNING, ECONOMIZING AND RISK AVOIDANCE OF FAMILIES WITH LOW INCOMES -- AN ECOLOGICAL APPROACH

Lula Tassin King, PhD

Michigan State University, 1975

The purpose of this investigation was to analyze the relationships between family status and stage of the life cycle and the variety in mode of housing, the level of personal efficacy and planning and the propensities to economize and to avoid risk among families with low incomes. The theoretical perspective used was the ecological approach. Specifically, the ecological framework forming the unit of inquiry was the ecosystem of the family. Herein, the family was defined as organism (O) in an organism to environment (E) relationship.

The ecosystem model used was a mixed model consisting of both "O" and "E" components as dependent and independent variables. The dependent measures of concern were housing standard, an "E" component and personal efficacy and planning, economizing and risk avoidance were "O" components. The independent variables were family status and family life cycle stages; these represented the "O" components. Also serving as independent variables were race, an "O" component, and degree of urbanization, an "E" component. These latter two variables are defined as third variables but treated as independent variables because the need to control for their effect was deemed necessary.

The results of the hypotheses tests revealed that the mode of housing and the level of efficacy and planning were significantly higher for two-parent families but that single-parent families did significantly more economizing than two-parent families. Significant differences were also located between families in their mode of housing, their propensity to economize and to avoid risk across the stages of the life cycle. Except for the contracting stage, the means for families in the middle years indicated that this stage was significantly better off on the variables tested than the other stages.

Black and white families differed significantly in the variety of their mode of housing and on risk avoidance as a function of stage in the family life cycle. White families tended to have significantly more variety in their mode of housing and to take significantly less risk than black families. Also significant was the main effect associated with degree of urbanization. Families tend to differ significantly in their mode of housing and personal efficacy and planning as a result of the degree of urbanization.

URBAN HOUSING MARKET STUDIES

W. Z. Hirsch, S. Margolis, J. Hirsch,
D. Atwater and J. Nelson
University of California at Los Angeles

While a substantial literature exists on landlord-tenant relations, little work has been done to examine economic implications of liability laws on landlords and tenants. This study provides a model which has been implemented empirically to evaluate the costs and benefits of various habitability laws. Historically, landlords have had no obligation to repair and maintain residential premises leased to tenants. Recently, major modifications of this landlord-tenant relationship have occurred—this study specifically looks at remedies available to the tenant in the form of repair and deduct laws, withholding and rent abatement laws, receivership laws, and laws to combat retaliatory eviction by the landlord. While these laws are designed to reduce the risk borne by tenants, this model determines the costs imposed by these laws and their distribution between landlord and tenants, as well as the resulting net costs or benefits.

A demand and supply framework is presented and implemented—specifically, demand by low-income urban renters and supply of urban low-cost rental housing in the 25 states in the sample. Finally, the shifts in these demand and supply curves as a result of the passage of habitability laws is analyzed and the distribution of costs and benefits is estimated.

Data from the Panel Study of Income Dynamics, 1968-1972, provided the data concerning rents and incomes of tenants as well as specific housing characteristics used to determine quantities of housing services consumed. These data were supplemented by legal and other data. A paper published in the California Law Review, October, 1975, reported a multiple regression analysis of the rents paid by low-income tenants that revealed significantly higher rents in states which had habitability laws than in those which did not. The results indicated that in 1972 indigents paid statistically higher rents--approximately $135 per year higher--in states which had receivership laws than in states which did not have such laws.

In a paper given at the National Bureau of Economic Research in May, 1975, on "Economics of Residential Location and Urban Housing Markets," Werner Hirsch and Steven Margolis reported that a multiple regression analysis of the rents paid by indigent tenants in the United States revealed not only significantly higher rents in states with such habitability laws as receivership, but also the increased costs outweighed the benefits. The latter conclusion was derived from the estimation of rental housing demand and supply functions, which used the Panel data to estimate expected average rents.

THE IMPACT OF INCOME CHANGES ON HOUSING DEMAND
Elizabeth A. Roistacher
Queens College

This research involves the estimation of the impact of income changes on residential mobility and housing expenditure. The analysis will employ the Panel data for households living in the 24 largest Standard Metropolitan Statistical Areas over the period 1968-73. These estimates of responses over time to changes in income will be useful for simulating the impact of such proposed policies as the negative income tax and the housing allowance program.

INCOME TRANSFERS AND FAMILY STRUCTURE

Isabell Sawhill, Jerry Peabody,
Carol Jones, and Steve Caldwell

The Urban Institute

A major cause of the high growth rate of female-headed families relative to two-parent families over the past decade is the rapid rise in divorce and separation rates which has far outstripped the increase in remarriage rates. These developments provide the context for the Urban Institute's analysis of divorce and remarriage using Panel data.

The analysis of separation and divorce is based on a sample of intact husband-wife families where the head was less than 55 in 1968.

One very interesting finding is that the stability of income, rather than the level of income per se is a critical factor in predicting divorce or separation; in addition, the analysis does not confirm the widely-accepted hypothesis that the current welfare system encourages family instability due to its restrictive eligibility requirements. On the other hand, the wife's earned income is associated with higher separation rates. Dissolution also occurs more frequently among couples who have few assets, married young, have been married only a short time, do not attend church frequently, and who live in the West and/or in the central city of a large metropolitan area. There are no significant racial differences in separation rates after controlling for all of the above variables (although there are some strong interactions between race and region).

The analysis of remarriage was carried out with a sample of female heads (single, divorced, separated, or widowed) where the head was less than 55 and there were dependent children present in the household. This analysis indicated that welfare recipiency is associated with a lower remarriage rate, holding all other factors constant. The probability of remarriage is directly related to income and inversely related to age, asset holdings and duration in nonmarried state. Nonwhites remarry less frequently than whites, having controlled for the above factors.

A publication written by Isabel Sawhill and Heather Ross summarizing the results of this work is scheduled to appear during the winter of 1975/1976, and a detailed research report entitled Income Transfers and Family Structure by Isabel Sawhill, Jerry Peabody, Carol Jones, and Steve Caldwell is currently available through the Urban Institute.

WORK IN PROGRESS
Christopher Jencks and Lee Rainwater
Harvard University

The Panel Study of Income Dynamics, along with ten other samples, is being used in an analysis of the determinants of social and economic success.

Among the general objectives is to determine the extent to which differences in survey techniques and samples influence conclusions. Multiple regression was used to examine the effects of background characteristics (e.g., father's education and occupation, number of siblings) on an individual's education, occupational status and earnings. To account for possible nonlinearities and interactions, squared and multiplicative interaction terms were constructed from background variables and were included in regressions. Regressions were also run using the logarithm of earnings as the dependent variable, estimating a model which implies multiplicative advantages.

In addition to analyses which seek to compare the Panel Study with other samples, Jencks and Rainwater are pursuing analyses of certain problems which can only be dealt with using the Panel Study of Income Dynamics. They are using questions on attitudes, as well as the Panel Study's measure of achievement motivation, to study the effect of adult personality and attitudes on earnings. They are attempting to determine the causal importance of such factors by using individual attitudes and earnings in the early years of the survey to predict earnings in the sixth and seventh years.

Jencks and Rainwater also use the Panel Study to investigate the determinants of family income. They are examining the interrelationship of family income components, and the extent to which each of these is determined by characteristics of family members. The earnings of a wife, for example, may not only be affected by her own personal characteristics, but also by her husband's characteristics and earnings. This sort of analysis will allow the study of the mechanisms by which family decisions influence family income.

HOUSING CONSUMPTION DISEQUILIBRIUM AND LOCAL RESIDENTIAL MOBILITY
John L. Goodman, Jr.
The Urban Institute

An economic theory of local residential mobility is developed and empirically examined. The theory predicts that local mobility is most likely to occur among households whose actual housing consumption deviates the most from their utility-maximizing levels and whose monetary and psychic costs of moving are least. Two separate models are used in applying the theory to data from a national household survey, and the empirical results offer partial support for this theory. But not all local moves are motivated primarily by housing considerations. Nearly a third of all local moves are associated with new household formation, marriage, or divorce.

PERFORMANCE REWARDS FOR SERVICES TO THE EMPLOYABLE POOR: A PROPOSED INCENTIVE PAY SYSTEM FOR CALIFORNIA JOB AGENTS

F. W. Blackwell, D. H. Greenberg, A. J. Lipson,
B. D. Rostker, and S. T. Wolfberg

The Rand Corporation

(This report was prepared for the Department of Human
Resources Development, State of California)

In designing an incentive pay system for California job agents, the Panel data were used to set norms for length of unemployment and post-employment earnings, using a subsample meeting the qualifying definition of "disadvantaged" and with some unemployment in 1968.

RESEARCH IN PROGRESS

Jonathan Dickinson

Institute for Research on Poverty
The University of Wisconsin

Data from the Panel Study of Income Dynamics is being used for ongoing research on the labor supply behavior of prime aged married males.

This analysis differs from previous labor supply research in several potentially important dimensions. The empirical model employed is of a general form which allows direct inference about the approximate structure of average income-leisure preferences in the population. Unique data available in the Panel Study make it possible to restrict the analysis to individuals who are free to reveal their work-leisure preferences. For this sample the estimated preferences structure is well-behaved and consistent with theoretical expectations. Contrasting estimates for a sample of workers with constrained work hours show much smaller behavioral responses which would imply counter-theoretical preference structures if they were presumed to represent optimal work leisure choices.

The time series dimension of the Panel Study allows identification of differential preferences among workers facing the same earnings opportunities. These results suggest that there is a ten to 20 percent bias in cross-sectional estimates of the substitution effect due to aggregation over diverse preferences. Additional results indicate that workers who generally work substantial amounts of overtime are notably more responsive to changes in economic variables than are those whose usual work hours are close to the standard work week.

INCOME ELASTICITY OF HOUSING DEMAND

Geoffrey Carliner

Institute for Research on Poverty
The University of Wisconsin

(Institute for Research on Poverty Discussion Paper #144-72)

This paper estimates a housing demand function from four years of the Panel Study of Income Dynamics. The findings indicate that the income elasticity of housing demand is around .6 or .7 for owners and around .5 for renters. This means that the percentage of income spent on housing declines as income rises and that the property tax falls more heavily on the poor than on the rich. This finding differs from earlier studies, which were based on city averages rather than panel studies, and is therefore more reliable. The study also found that, other things equal, the old demand more housing than the young, whites more than nonwhites, and female-headed households more than male-headed households.

SOCIAL SECURITY AND RETIREMENT DECISIONS

Michael J. Boskin

Stanford University and
National Bureau of Economic Research

The primary objective of Social Security is to replace income during retirement (or disability); in so doing, Social Security benefits supplement--and potentially substitute for--prior savings (including private pensions, equity in a home, savings accounts, stocks and bonds, etc.), intrafamily transfers of income and, perhaps most importantly, continued earnings. The purpose of the present paper is to focus on the potential inducement to retire earlier in the presence of Social Security than in its absence, and the corresponding substitution of Social Security benefits for potential earnings.

The results are based on a conditional logit analysis of the probability of retirement using a very small homogeneous subsample from the Panel consisting of 131 households headed all of the first five years by the same white married male, aged 61-65 in 1968. They are robust with respect to different definitions of retirement. They suggest that the huge increase in Social Security benefits, coverage, and earnings test are significant contributors to the rapid decline of the labor force participation of the elderly in the United States. At a time when the Social Security system is under a severe financial strain, it is inducing (or enabling) a substantial fraction of the elderly population to retire earlier than they would have in the absence of the system.[1]

---

[1] If present birth trends continue, Social Security taxes will have to double at the turn of the century to maintain the ratio of benefits to wages.

Appendix A

A SEVEN-YEAR CHECK ON THE POSSIBLE EFFECTS OF ATTITUDES, MOTIVES, AND BEHAVIOR PATTERNS ON CHANGE IN ECONOMIC STATUS

There has been very little evidence in previous reports that people's attitudes or behavior patterns had much influence on changes in their economic status. Even within subgroups such as the "target population" who were in the bottom quintile of the income/needs distribution at least one year, little systematic relation could be found that held up when checked on a fresh half-sample. It was always possible, however, that there was not enough time for the effects to show above the noise of random events and measurement error. Now, with seven years of data it is possible to average the measures of attitudes and behavior from the first five interviews and relate them to changes in income between the two subsequent years and the five previous years. This should reduce the errors in measuring attitudes and behavior, measure the outcomes clearly *after* the measurement of the attitudes and behavior, and stabilize the measure of change in status by using five-year average as the base.

We have reanalyzed the data using seven waves in this way, searching for possible effects of the following:

  1. The five-year average levels of:

     a. Three attitudinal indexes entitled Sense of Efficacy-Planning, Trust-Hostility, and Aspiration-Ambition.

     b. Five behavioral indexes--Real Earning Acts, Avoidance of Undue Risk, Planning Acts, Connectedness to Sources of Information or Help, and Money Earning Acts.

  2. The change from the first to the fifth years for the above eight indexes.

  3. The Index of Achievement Motivation for the fifth year.

These variables were included in regression simultaneously with education, age, race, sex-marital status, distance to center of city, and size of largest city in the area. This was done for three criterion (dependent) variables: change in the household head's hourly earnings, change in the head's annual earnings (to allow for differences in work hours or unemployment), and change in family income/needs (to allow for everything that could be done to change economic status).

We included families with no change in head in all seven years whose heads worked at least 1,500 hours each year, but we excluded families which were in the upper quintile on income/needs in every one of the seven years. The results were again overwhelmingly negative. Where a particular index seemed to matter in terms of explanatory power of subgroups on that index (or its change), the patterns were irregular. Only age had clearly significant effects on the changes in economic status experienced by these families, and the occupational patterns were ambiguous. Nothing else accounted for more than 1 percent of the variance in any of the dependent variables, with a few exceptions such as size of the largest city in the area. City size affected changes in hourly earnings, with larger increases in cities of 50,000 to 100,000 and smaller than average increases in cities of 10,000 to 25,000 outside the large metropolitan areas. Given the higher sampling errors for area data with clustered samples, it seemed wise to dismiss these differences.

Table A.1 gives the gross and net explanatory power of the various predictors for each of the three different criterion measures.

Table A.2 shows a rerun of the analysis for the "target population"--those who were in the lowest quintile on family income/needs for at least one year of the seven. The smaller sample and greater variance of the dependent variables gave larger measures of power, but they were not adjusted for degrees of freedom, and an examination of the patterns of effects revealed no systematic relationship. For example, the change in the index of Ambition-Aspiration was associated with higher than average increases at both extremes and in the middle for the "not always affluent."[1] (See Figure A.1)

A final analysis dropped measures of the changes in the indexes but added four other explanatory variables to eliminate their possible noise effect: a verbal text score, an index of achievement motivation, occupation the first year, and distance to center of the nearest city. Table A.3 shows that the attitudinal and behavioral indexes remained ineffective, and of the new variables only occupation seemed to matter. A small group of farmers had larger than average increases in earnings, and professionals had smaller than average increases, relative to the average of 1967-1971.

The age pattern in this final run was strikingly different for changes in income/needs as compared with changes in head's hourly or annual earnings.

---

[1] The Ambition-Aspiration Index is a combination of: "might make a purposive move of residence," "wanted more work and/or worked more than 2,500 hours," "might quit a job because not challenging," "prefer a job with chances for making more money even if dislike job," "dissatisfied with self," and "spend time figuring out how to get more money."

TABLE A.1

Explanatory Power (Eta^2 and Beta^2) of Various Characteristics
Related to Three Measures of Change in Economic Status*

Independent Variables	Head's Hourly Earnings		Head's Annual Earnings		Family Income/Needs	
	Eta^2	Beta^2	Eta^2	Beta^2	Eta^2	Beta^2
Education	.010	.005	.005	.004	.008	.005
Age	.031	.025	.034	.028	.023	.029
Race	.001	.001	.003	.003	.000	.000
Sex-marital status	.000	.001	.000	.002	.003	.003
Size of largest city	.011	.010	.018	.014	.016	.017
Changes in Indexes						
Increase in Efficacy	.003	.005	.008	.007	.001	.002
Increase in Trust	.001	.002	.005	.004	.006	.004
Increase in Ambition	.011	.011	.015	.013	.008	.008
Increase in Earning Acts	.004	.006	.002	.002	.007	.008
Increase in Risk Avoidance	.004	.003	.004	.003	.004	.006
Increase in Planning Acts	.003	.002	.005	.002	.005	.003
Increase in Connectedness	.001	.001	.002	.002	.002	.002
Increase in Dollar Earning Acts	.009	.010	.005	.004	.002	.002
Averages of Indexes						
Average Efficacy	.003	.005	.000	.001	.008	.006
Average Trust	.001	.000	.002	.001	.002	.000
Average Ambition	.009	.003	.008	.003	.002	.003
Average Real Earning	.006	.002	.007	.004	.002	.005
Average Risk Avoidance	.007	.004	.002	.001	.002	.001
Average Planning Acts	.001	.003	.001	.002	.000	.002
Average Connectedness	.003	.004	.001	.002	.004	.003
Average Dollar Earning Acts	.010	.007	.007	.005	.002	.002

$$R^2 = .048 \qquad R^2 = .046 \qquad R^2 = .037$$
$$\bar{Y} = 9.6 \qquad \bar{Y} = 9.3 \qquad \bar{Y} = 10.9$$
$$\sigma_y = 9.6 \qquad \sigma_y = 9.2 \qquad \sigma_y = 11.1$$

N = 1400

*For families with no change in head all seven years, whose heads worked at least 1,500 hours each year. Excludes those who were in the top quintile of income/needs in all seven years. Omits seven outliers.

MTR 1138B

TABLE A.2

Explanatory Power (Eta^2 and Beta^2) of Various Characteristics
Related to Three Measures of Change in Economic Status*

Independent Variables	Head's Hourly Earnings		Head's Annual Earnings		Family Income/Needs	
	Eta^2	Beta^2	Eta^2	Beta^2	Eta^2	Beta^2
Education	.095	.064	.056	.063	.018	.016
Age	.016	.004	.041	.019	.023	.027
Race	.002	.001	.001	.002	.007	.000
Sex-marital status	.026	.005	.004	.001	.009	.007
Size of largest city	.042	.009	.035	.011	.023	.025
Changes in Indexes						
Increase in Efficacy	.015	.020	.011	.017	.008	.014
Increase in Trust	.009	.010	.016	.011	.030	.019
Increase in Ambition	.108	.086	.068	.074	.040	.059
Increase in Earning Acts	.014	.008	.005	.013	.016	.006
Increase in Risk Avoidance	.008	.010	.004	.006	.006	.012
Increase in Planning Acts	.011	.009	.008	.010	.015	.008
Increase in Connectedness	.015	.004	.004	.004	.005	.007
Increase in Dollar Earning Acts	.012	.025	.012	.028	.009	.010
Averages of Indexes						
Average Efficacy	.008	.012	.004	.012	.007	.011
Average Trust	.008	.004	.016	.006	.009	.002
Average Ambition	.025	.004	.007	.013	.008	.004
Average Real Earning	.010	.005	.001	.000	.018	.017
Average Risk Avoidance	.024	.015	.006	.006	.016	.017
Average Planning Acts	.018	.014	.009	.011	.005	.003
Average Connectedness	.013	.005	.011	.007	.008	.001
Average Dollar Earning Acts	.050	.051	.035	.045	.016	.007

$R^2 = .242$ $R^2 = .164$ $R^2 = .106$

$\bar{Y} = 11.3$ $\bar{Y} = 10.6$ $\bar{Y} = 13.9$

$\sigma_y = 15.4$ $\sigma_y = 12.4$ $\sigma_y = 17.3$

N = 587

*For families with the same head all seven years and who worked at least 1500 hours each year and who were in the "target population" having been in the lowest quintile of income/needs in at least one year.

MTR 1138A

FIGURE A.1

Annual Percent Change in Head's Hourly Earnings
By Prior Changes in Index of "Ambition-Aspiration"
For the Target Population and the Not-Always Affluent
(Net Effects, Adjusted by Regression)

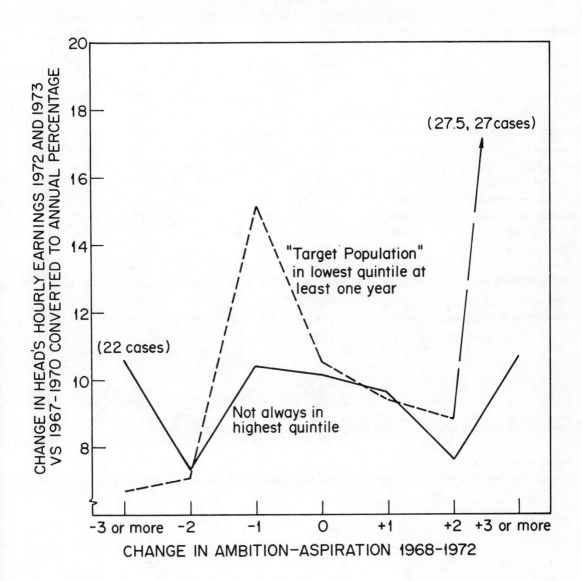

TABLE A.3

Explanatory Power (Eta^2 and Beta^2) of Various Characteristics
Related to Three Measures of Change in Economic Status*

Independent Variables	Head's Hourly Earnings		Head's Annual Earnings		Family Income/Needs	
	Eta^2	Beta^2	Eta^2	Beta^2	Eta^2	Beta^2
Education	.010	.004	.005	.005	.008	.004
Age	.031	.031	.034	.039	.023	.023
Race	.001	.001	.003	.003	.000	.000
Sex-marital status	.000	.000	.000	.000	.003	.005
Size of largest city	.013	.023	.007	.007	.011	.010
Distance to center of city	.002	.005	.002	.003	.000	.001
Occupation	.027	.027	.027	.036	.025	.025
Efficacy-Planning	.003	.004	.000	.001	.008	.006
Trust-Hostility	.001	.001	.002	.001	.002	.002
Ambition-Aspiration	.009	.002	.008	.003	.002	.003
Real Earning Acts	.006	.002	.007	.004	.002	.004
Risk Avoidance	.007	.004	.002	.002	.002	.002
Planning Acts	.001	.003	.001	.004	.000	.001
Connectedness	.003	.004	.001	.002	.004	.003
Dollar Earning Acts	.010	.003	.007	.001	.002	.001
Test Score	.008	.004	.004	.003	.009	.010
Achievement Motivation	.007	.006	.005	.003	.004	.003

$$R^2 = .062 \qquad R = . \qquad R^2 = .049 \qquad\qquad R^2 = .043$$
$$\bar{Y} = 9.6 \qquad\qquad\qquad \bar{Y} = 9.3 \qquad\qquad \bar{Y} = 10.9$$
$$\sigma_y = 9.6 \qquad\qquad\qquad \sigma_y = 9.2 \qquad\qquad \sigma_y = 11.1$$
$$n = 1400 \qquad\qquad\qquad n = 1100 \qquad\qquad n = 1399$$

*For families with the same head all seven years who worked at least 1500 hours each year,
 but excluding those who were in the top quintile of income/needs in all seven years.

Eta^2 is correlation ratio--gross effect.
Beta^2 is net effect in regression.

Changes are last two years as percent of first five converted to an annual percentage.

MTR 1138C

Figure A.2 shows the patterns. The differences were meaningful, since the arriv-
al of children increased the needs denominator and reduced the wife's earnings
in the numerator, but the situation was reversed as the children matured, went
to school, and left home. Whether the upturn in head's annual earnings around
age 50 and in hourly earnings around age 60 reflected real age and cohort effects
was uncertain, but it was a credible result of the fact that these cohorts benefited from the period when they entered the labor force. Perhaps those who got
in first (now 60) got the highest wage increases, while the next cohort got the
most responsibility.

It remained true that neither for the "target population" nor for the working population excluding the very top, could we find evidence that attitudes or
behavior systematically effected changes in economic status. If any of the components of the indexes mattered importantly, the index itself should have appeared to have *some* effect. It is possible that we did not measure the right
attitudes and behavior, did not measure them well enough, or failed to isolate
the subgroups for whom they mattered. In a different, more expansionary period
of history, individuals may have had more control over their fates. In particular it seems important to examine the increasing subset of *new* family heads, excluded from this analysis, who may have more options.

FIGURE A.2

Change in Economic Status, 1967–1973, by Age in 1968

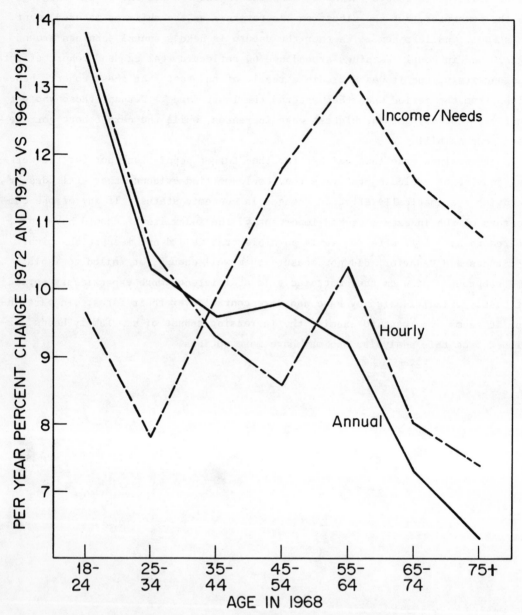

Appendix B

SIMULTANEOUS EQUATIONS ESTIMATION

The family composition change models presented in Chapters 2, 3 and 4 were formulated as systems of simultaneous equations. For proper statistical esti- mation of these models, a two-stage least squares procedures was employed. This technique is described in this appendix.

Consider a competitive market where the price (P) and quantity demanded and supplied (Q_D and Q_S) are determined by the following model:

(1) Demand: $Q_D = \alpha_1 + \beta_1 P + \gamma_1 X_1 + \varepsilon_1$

(2) Supply: $Q_S = \alpha_2 + \beta_2 P + \gamma_2 X_2 + \varepsilon_2$

The price variable acts as the equilibrating mechanism for adjusting the quantity supplied and demanded. Its value is determined simultaneously by the above equation system. We classify the price variable and the dependent variables-- Q_D and Q_S--as *endogenous* variables. That is, variables whose levels are *jointly* determined within the simultaneous framework described by equations (1) and (2). By contrast, the values of the other explanatory variables, X_1 and X_2, are deter- mined outside the system. Thus these *exogenous* (predetermined) factors are in- dependent of the disturbance (error) terms ε_1 and ε_2. In the models of family composition change presented in Chapters 2-4, the endogenous price variable is the net transfer position and the "quantity" variable is whether the initial living arrangements were maintained for the duration of the Panel Study. The exogenous variables in these chapters are variables such as educational attain- ment, the presence of children and local labor market conditions.

For equilibrium, the quantity supplied must equal the quantity demanded. Equating equations (1) and (2) and solving for the price variable gives

(3) $\alpha_1 + \beta_1 P + \gamma_1 X_1 + \varepsilon_1 = \alpha_2 + \beta_2 P + \gamma_2 X_2 + \varepsilon_2$

(4) $P = \dfrac{\alpha_2 - \alpha_1}{\beta_1 - \beta_2} - \dfrac{\gamma_1}{\beta_1 - \beta_2} X_1 + \dfrac{\gamma_2}{\beta_1 - \beta_2} X_2 + \dfrac{1}{\beta_1 - \beta_2} (\varepsilon_2 - \varepsilon_1)$

This represents the *reduced form* equation for the equilibrium price. The param- eters of the exogenous variables in equation (4) represent the net effect of a change in an exogenous variable on price. All endogenous variables in the system can be described in terms of the exogenous variables and the disturbances. Hence, a reduced form equation for the equilibrium quantity can also be derived:

$$(5) \quad Q = \alpha_1 + \frac{\beta_1(Q - \alpha_2 - \gamma_2 X_2 - \varepsilon_2)}{\beta_2} + \gamma_1 X_1 + \varepsilon_1$$

$$(6) \quad Q = \frac{\beta_2\alpha_1 - \beta_1\alpha_2}{\beta_2 - \beta_1} + \frac{\beta_2\gamma_1}{\beta_2 - \beta_1} X_1 - \frac{\beta_1\gamma_2}{\beta_2 - \beta_1} X_2 + \frac{\beta_2\varepsilon_1 - \beta_1\varepsilon_2}{\beta_2 - \beta_1} \quad .$$

Because our primary interest was in the net effect of the exogenous variables on the likelihood of maintaining the current living arrangement, only the reduced form equation for the equilibrium quantity is presented in Chapters 2-4.

Suppose we applied ordinary least squares (OLS) to the demand equation,[1] hoping to derive estimates of the parameters α_1, β_1 and γ_1. For simplicity, assume that the disturbance terms ε_1 and ε_2 are independent with zero means and constant variances.[2] Since the regressors X_1 and X_2 are considered exogenous and hence independent of the error terms, the valid application of OLS depends only on demonstrating that the endogenous price variable (P) is independent of the disturbance term ε_1. However, from the reduced form equation of the equilibrium price (see equation (4)) we see that, in general, the price is influenced by the disturbance term ε_1. Hence, the direct application of OLS to the demand equation will *not* yield unbiased estimates of α_1, β_1 and γ_1. Indeed, the bias will persist even for very large samples.

The fundamental problem in deriving consistent estimates of the structural parameters α_1, β_1 and γ_1 is the dependence between the included endogenous variable, P, and the error term ε_1. Prior to estimating the demand equation, we must first *purge* the price variable of any dependence with ε_1. This is the first phase of the estimating procedure called *two-stage least squares*[3] (2SLS).

---

[1]Prior to estimation, the researcher should check if the system is *identified*. In general, the number of excluded exogenous variables from the structural equation under consideration should *equal or exceed* the number of included endogenous variables in that equation. See Theil (1971), Chapter 9, for a further discussion. All of the systems we estimate in chapters 2-4 are identified.

[2]The covariance matrices of the error terms are assumed to be a scalar times the identity matrix ($\sigma_1^2 I$ and $\sigma_2^2 I$, respectively).

[3]The dependent variable in the analysis of family composition changes is the probability of maintaining the current living arrangement. Since this is a dichotomous variable coded 1 if no change occurs and zero otherwise, the esti-

First Stage

The objective of the first step is to find a modified regressor which resembles the price variable but is independent of the error terms. Since the set of exogenous variables, X_1 and X_2, are independent of the disturbances, this may be accomplished by regressing P on *all* the predetermined variables in the system.

$$(7) \quad P = a_1 + a_2X_1 + a_3X_2 + \varepsilon_3$$

where ε_3 is the error term.

The substitute price regressor, $\hat{P}$, is the estimated value from this reduced form:

$$(8) \quad \hat{P} = \hat{a}_1 + \hat{a}_2X_1 + \hat{a}_3X_2$$

where $\hat{a}_1$, $\hat{a}_2$, and $\hat{a}_3$ are the estimated coefficients from equation (7).

Second Stage

This estimated value of the price variable can now be substituted for P in the demand equation and OLS applied to estimate the structural parameters.

$$(9) \quad Q_D = \alpha_1 + \beta_1\hat{P} + \gamma_1X_1 + \varepsilon_1^*$$

Since this modified regressor, $\hat{P}$, is a linear combination of exogenous variables, it will be uncorrelated with the adjusted error term ε_1^*. Both the supply and demand equations of chapters 2-4 are estimated with the two-stage least squares procedure.

References

Kmenta, Jan, Elements of Econometrics, New York: Macmillan Company, 1971.

Theil, Henri, Principles of Econometrics, New York: John Wiley & Sons, Inc., 1971.

Wonnacott, Ronald J. and Wonnacott, Thomas H., Econometrics, New York: John Wiley & Sons, Inc., 1970.

---

mated probabilities are not constrained to the 0-1 range. A solution to this problem is the logit transformation. However, we are not aware of the extension of this procedure to simultaneous equations estimation. For a further discussion of this method, see Volume I, Appendix E.

A more *efficient* estimating procedure, *three-stage least squares*, is sometimes employed in simultaneous equations estimation. For details on this procedure, see Theil, 1971.

Appendix C

RESPONSE RATES AND DATA QUALITY

In Volume III of this series we investigated the possibility that the change from personal to predominately telephone interviews in 1973 might have had some adverse effect on the quality of the data, or the response rate, or both. Here we continue the investigation, adding 1974 information.

The proportion of interviews conducted by telephone continued to increase (Table C.1).

TABLE C.1

Proportion of Interviews by Telephone

Year	Sample Size	Number of Telephone Interviews	Unweighted Percent of Sample
1968	4802	--	--
1969	4460	--	--
1970	4655	67	1.4
1971	4840	108	2.2
1972	5060	134	2.6
1973	5285	4047	76.6
1974	5517	4554	82.5

We found no evidence, however, that response rates or data quality has suffered. From 1970 on, the response rate remained at 97 percent (see Table C.2). If telephone interviewing, with its abbreviated questionnaire, had increased the probability of nonheads being respondents, the quality of our data might eventually have been affected. Table C.3 shows that since 1972 there had been a reduction of 3.5 percent in the number of interviews taken with the family head-- a situation which bears watching in future panel waves. As seen in Table C.4, however, for the whole sample the accuracy of the panel data improved from year to year, and the need for assignments decreased--so as yet there seems to be no reason to worry.

TABLE C.2

Annual and Cumulative Panel Response Rates

	Percent	
Year	Annual	Cumulative
1968	76	76
1969	89	68
1970	97	66
1971	97	64
1972	97	62
1973	97	61
1974	97	59

TABLE C.3

Proportion of Family Heads Interviewed

Year	Total Sample	Proportion of Interviews by Head
1968	4802	92.6
1969	4460	93.1
1970	4655	93.2
1971	4840	93.3
1972	5060	93.5
1973	5285	91.1
1974	5517	90.0

TABLE C.4

Head and Wife Income Variables

Year of Interview	Sum of Accuracy Codes for Three Variables					
	0	1	2	3	4 or More	Total
1968	94.0	2.5	2.6	0.2	0.8	100.0
1969	95.6	1.6	1.9	0.1	0.8	100.0
1970	96.9	1.3	1.3	0.1	0.5	100.0
1971	97.7	0.9	0.9	0.1	0.4	100.0
1972	97.8	0.8	1.1	0.0	0.3	100.0
1973	97.9	1.1	0.7	0.1	0.2	100.0
1974	98.2	0.9	0.7	0.0	0.2	100.0

Table C.4 is based on three variables: Accuracy of Head's Labor Income, Accuracy of Wife's Labor Income, and Accuracy of Asset Income of Head and Wife.

Accuracy here is determined by the number of assignments made by the editors in order to recreate data missing from an interview. The more assignments, the less reliable the data. The accuracy code values and their meanings are:

0. Adequate response: No assignments made.

1. Minor assignment: Response was inadequate, but estimates could be made within a probable error of under $300 or 10 percent of the assignment by using previous years' data or other data in the interview.

2. Major assignment: Response was inadequate and estimates had a probable error of at least $300 and at least 10 percent of the value of the assignment, using any information available in previous interviews or in the current one. Usually these values were made from an assignment table.

Table C.4 shows the sum of the accuracy codes for the three different income measures. The maximum number possible here would be six for married couples, and four for single heads.

Appendix D

REGRESSION WITH CATEGORICAL PREDICTORS

A major goal of the social scientist is the explanation of individual variations in socioeconomic conditions. Statistically, the explanation takes the form
of estimating the portion of the original variation in a dependent variable which
can be attributed to the variation of an explanatory or predictor variable. For
example, if we are interested in the variation of wages, we might suppose that
part of this variation is associated with variation in the job experience of the
wage earner. If, for a particular sample, the original variance in wages was 10,
and the variance remaining after taking account of the variation in experience
(by least-squares regression) was 8, the proportion of the variation explained by
experience would be 20 percent (10-8)/10 x 100.

The particular name applied to this fraction depends on the nature of the
predictor variable and on the complexity of the analysis. In the example above,
the 20 percent would be termed "R-squared" because the explanatory variable was
continuous and the analysis was simple. If we had used race, a categorical variable, instead of job experience and found (via analysis of variance) that the
variance of wage was reduced from 10 to 7, the Eta-squared of race in explaining
wage would be 30 percent. The major reason for distinguishing between R-squared
and Eta-squared is not that their interpretations differ but rather that the
statistical techniques used to estimate them differ.[1]

When more complex analysis is performed, the need for additional measures
of explanatory power arises. Suppose in the above analysis that we wished to use
not only race as an explanatory variable of wage but also the variable of whether
or not the wage earner finished high school. If we computed the Eta-squared for
each of these variables, we might find that the race variable accounted for 30

---

[1] By using the subgroup averages to predict, instead of the overall average, one
reduces the error variance from the variance around the grand mean to the
smaller sum of variances around subgroup means. The reduction can be calculated
more simply as the weighted sum of the squares of the subgroup averages minus
$N\bar{y}^2$.

percent of the variation in wages, and high school completion accounted for 20
percent. The total portion of the variance explained by our multivariate analysis, however, would *not* be 50 percent but something less, perhaps only 40 percent.
The reason for this is that race and the completion of high school are interrelated. Proportionately fewer blacks finish school than whites. Hence, the variance explained by race and high school education overlap, and the whole is less
than the sum of the parts. The Eta-squared for race incorporates both the explanatory power of race and some of the power of education. In order to determine the unique power of race in explaining the variation in wages, we need a
statistic which adjusts for the interrelation of race and education. Beta-squared
is such a statistic. It measures the explanatory power of a predictor after the
effects of all the other included predictors which are related with it are taken
into account. If a predictor were not related to any other predictor included in
the analysis, then its Beta-squared would equal its Eta-squared.

The analogue to Beta-squared when continuous variables are employed is the
"normalized regression coefficient," or

$$\frac{b\sigma_x}{\sigma_y}$$

the number of standard units that y changes when x is changed by one standard
deviation. Both Beta measures are approximations of what is generally regarded
as the true marginal effect of a predictor, namely its partial R-squared with the
dependent variable. The two will be identical when the correlation of the dependent variable with the *other* predictors is as high as the correlation of the predictor in question with the other predictors. If the latter is large, Beta will
exaggerate the marginal power of the predictor.

For interpreting the results of categorical-predictor multiple regression
(sometimes called dummy-variable regression), all the reader needs to remember is
that Eta-squared measures the explanatory power of a single classification set of
subclasses, while Beta-squared measures the net power of that set in a multivariate context.

For those concerned with the loss of explanatory power in using a few categories or classes instead of a numerical predictor, it should be pointed out that
even if the relationship were truly linear, the fraction of explanatory power
still available using k classes instead of an infinite set of numbers is only
$(1-\frac{1}{k^2})$. With five subgroups of roughly equal size, one still has 96 percent as
much potential explanatory power and with seven groups, 98 percent. In addition,
if the relationship is nonlinear, one usually explains and learns *more* with cat-

egorical predictors.*

When levels of statistical significance are of concern, it must be kept in mind that the required size for significance of both Eta and Beta depends on the number of subclasses on which they are based as well as the number of cases. If intercorrelation among predictors is not serious, Beta-squared approximates the partial correlation squared, and we can use this to go from the F-ratio required for significance to the required Beta-squared, given the number of cases and the number of categories in the predictor classification. If we use the .01 probability level, but think of it as something higher than this because of the (nonrandom) design effects in the sample, we have the following approximation table:

TABLE D.1

Beta Squared or Eta Squared Required
To Be Significantly Different From Zero

Number of Categories of Predictors	Number of Cases						
	200	400	1000	2000	3000	4000	5000
Two	.033	.017	.007	.0033	.0022	.0017	.0013
Three	.045	.023	.009	.0046	.0031	.0023	.0018
Four	.057	.028	.011	.0057	.0038	.0029	.0023
Five	.065	.033	.013	.0067	.0045	.0033	.0027
Six	.074	.037	.015	.0076	.0051	.0038	.0030
Seven	.083	.041	.017	.0085	.0057	.0042	.0034
Eight	.092	.047	.019	.0093	.0062	.0047	.0037
Nine	.098	.050	.020	.0102	.0068	.0051	.0041
Ten	.106	.054	.022	.0110	.0073	.0055	.0044
Twenty	.174	.089	.036	.0180	.0121	.0091	.0073

---

*See D. J. Aigner, A. S. Goldberger, and G. Kalton, "On the Explanatory Power of Dummy Variable Regressions," International Economic Review 16 (June 1975), 503-510.

Appendix E

1969 AND 1974 QUESTIONNAIRES

Although the questionnaires, codes, and study procedures are described each year in a separate documentation volume, we reproduce two of the questionnaires in this appendix for readers without access to these volumes.

The questionnaire changed somewhat between 1968 and 1969 and then remained virtually unchanged until 1973, when we changed from personal to telephone interviewing. Since much of the analysis in Part I of this volume uses 1969 and 1974 information, we include the 1969 questionnaire. The analysis in Part II is largely based on the seventh (1974) wave.

STUDY OF FAMILY ECONOMICS
Project 768

BB # 116-R0135
Approv. Exp. 2-69

(INTERVIEW NUMBER)	

SRC SURVEY RESEARCH CENTER
INSTITUTE FOR SOCIAL RESEARCH
THE UNIVERSITY OF MICHIGAN

(Do not write in above spaces.)

1. Interviewer's Label

2. P.S.U. _____
3. Your Interview No. _____
4. Date _____
5. Length of Interview _____

A1. Are you the head of this household?

☐ YES ☐ NO - (ASK FOR HEAD)

A2. When did you move into this (house/apartment)? _____
(DATE, OR YEARS AGO)

A3. How many rooms do you have here for your family (not counting bathrooms)? _____

A4. Do you own this (home/apartment), pay rent, or what?

☐ OWNS OR
IS BUYING

☐ PAYS RENT -
(TURN TO A11)

☐ NEITHER OWNS NOR RENTS -
(TURN TO A14)

(IF OWNS OR IS BUYING)

A5. How much did all your utilities like heat and electricity cost you last year
-- was it less than $100, $100-200, $200-300, $300-400, or more than $400?

☐ LESS THAN $100 ☐ $100-200 ☐ $200-300
☐ $300-400 ☐ MORE THAN $400

A6. Could you tell me what the present value of this house (farm) is -- I mean about
what would it bring if you sold it today? $ _____

A7. Do you have a mortgage on this property?

☐ YES ☐ NO - (TURN TO PAGE 3, A19)

	1st Mortgage	2nd Mortgage
A8. How much are your monthly payments?	$ _____	$ _____
A9. About how much is the remaining principal on this mortgage?	$ _____	$ _____
(IF A9a. About how many more DON'T payments do you have KNOW) left to make?	$ _____	$ _____

A10. Do you also have a second mortgage?

☐ YES - (ASK A8-A9, FOR
SECOND MORTGAGE)

☐ NO - TURN TO PAGE 3, A19

(TURN TO A19)

2

A11. About how much rent do you pay a month? $_____

A12. Do you pay for any of the utilities yourself?

☐ YES   ☐ NO - (TURN TO A19)

A13. (IF YES) How much did they cost you altogether last year --
was it less than $100, $100-200, $200-300,
$300-400, or more than $400?

☐ LESS THAN $100   ☐ $100-200   ☐ $200-300

☐ $300-400   ☐ MORE THAN $400

(TURN TO A19)

(IF <u>NEITHER OWNS NOR RENTS</u>)

A14. How is that?_____

A15. Do you do some work in return for your housing? (What?)

_____

A16. How much would it rent for if it were rented? $_____ per _____
                                                                    (MONTH,
                                                                     YEAR)

A17. Do you pay for any of the utilities yourself?

☐ YES   ☐ NO - (TURN TO A19)

A18. (IF YES) How much did they cost you altogether last year -- was
it less than $100, $100-200, $200-300, $300-400,
or more than $400?

☐ LESS THAN $100   ☐ $100-200   ☐ $200-300

☐ $300-400   ☐ MORE THAN $400

(TURN TO A19)

(ASK EVERYONE)

A19. Did you have any work done on the (house/apartment) during the last year,
      or do any work on it yourselves?

☐ YES   ☐ NO (GO TO A28)

(IF YES)

A20. What was done? _____

A21. Did you (or your family) do any of it?

☐ YES   ☐ NO (GO TO A25)

(IF YES)

A22. What did you do? _____

A23. Did you save more than $50 by doing it yourself?

☐ YES   ☐ NO (GO TO A25)

A24. (IF YES) About how much money do you think you saved
              by doing it yourself?

$ _____

A25. Do you still owe anything on it?

☐ YES   ☐ NO (GO TO A28)

A26. (IF YES) Is what you owe for it included in your mortgage payments
              you told me about?

☐ YES (GO   ☐ NO
    TO A28)

A27. How much are your monthly payments?

$_____ per _____

A28. Do you think you might move in the next couple of years?

_____   ☐ NO - (TURN TO B1)

(IF MIGHT MOVE   A29. Why might you move? _____
 OR WILL MOVE)

_____

SECTION B

B1. How many people live here altogether? _____

(LIST ALL PERSONS, INCLUDING CHILDREN, LIVING IN THE DU, BY THEIR RELATION TO HEAD)			(ASK B3 FOR THOSE AGED 5-25 (EXCEPT HEAD AND WIFE)	(ASK B4 IF ANSWER TO B3 IS "NO")
B2. How old are they and how are they related to you?	Age	Sex	B3. Is (he/she) in school?	B4. How many years of school did (he/she) finish?
1. HEAD OF DWELLING UNIT			/////////	/////////
2.			☐ YES ☐ NO ——→	
3.			☐ YES ☐ NO ——→	
4.			☐ YES ☐ NO ——→	
5.			☐ YES ☐ NO ——→	
6.			☐ YES ☐ NO ——→	
7.			☐ YES ☐ NO ——→	
8.			☐ YES ☐ NO ——→	
9.			☐ YES ☐ NO ——→	
10.			☐ YES ☐ NO ——→	

B5. Anyone else? (LIST ABOVE)

B6. Do you (HEAD) have any children under 25 who don't live here with you?

☐ YES   ☐ NO - (GO TO B11)

B7. Are they sons or daughters?	B8. How old is (he/she)?	B9. Is (he/she) in school, working, in the army, or what?	B10. (IF NOT IN SCHOOL) How many years of school did (he/she) finish?
1.			
2.			
3.			

B11. Has anyone moved into your household in the last year?

☐ YES   ☐ NO - (GO TO B13)

B12. (IF YES) Who moved in? (CIRCLE LISTING NUMBERS OF MOVERS ABOVE)

B13. Has anyone moved out in the last year?

☐ YES ————→ B14. Who moved out?
                    (ENTER AGE AND ——→
☐ NO - (TURN TO B15)   RELATION TO HEAD)

RELATION TO HEAD	AGE

B15. INTERVIEWER: SEE B3 AND B9, AND CHECK ONE:

☐ CHILDREN IN SCHOOL   ☐ NO CHILDREN IN SCHOOL - (GO TO B20)

B16. Have you (or your wife) ever attended any meetings of a parent-teacher's organization?

☐ YES   ☐ NO - (GO TO B18)

B17. (IF YES) When was the last time? _____

B18. How much education do you think your children will have when they stop going to school?

_____

_____

(IF <u>UNCERTAIN</u>   B19. What do you really think will happen?
OR EXPRESSES
<u>HOPES</u> ONLY)   _____

_____

(GO TO B21)

B20. (ASK ONLY IF NOT CLEAR) Have you (HEAD) ever had any children?

☐ YES   ☐ NO (GO TO C1)

B21. When was your (HEAD'S) first child born? _____
(YEAR OR AGE)

SECTION C: CARS

(ASK EVERYONE)
C1. Altogether, how many people are there in your family here who can drive?

_____   ☐ NONE (GO TO C3)

C2. Do you or anyone else in the family here own a car?

☐ YES   ☐ NO
(TURN TO C6)

C3. Does not having a car cause you (FAMILY) any difficulties?

☐ YES   ☐ NO (GO TO C5)

C4. What are they? _____

_____

C5. Is there public transportation within walking distance of here that is adequate for you?

☐ YES   ☐ NO

(TURN TO PAGE 7, D1)

6

C6. How many cars do you and your family living here own?_____

(ASK FOR EACH CAR OWNED)

	CAR #1	CAR #2	CAR #3
C7. What year model is it?			
C8. What make of car is it?			
C9. Is it in good, fair, or poor condition?			
C10. Do you owe any money on it?	☐ YES (GO TO C13) ☐ NO	☐ YES (GO TO C13) ☐ NO	☐ YES (GO TO C13) ☐ NO

(IF <u>NO</u> <u>MONEY</u> <u>OWED</u> ON CAR)

	CAR #1	CAR #2	CAR #3
C11. Is that car insured?	☐ YES ☐ NO - (GO TO A)	☐ YES ☐ NO - (GO TO A)	☐ YES ☐ NO - (GO TO A)
C12. (IF YES) How much do you pay for your car insurance?	$_____ per_____	$_____ per_____	$_____ per_____

A GO TO C7 FOR NEXT CAR, OR TO C17.

(IF <u>MONEY</u> <u>OWED</u> ON CAR)

	CAR #1	CAR #2	CAR #3
C13. How much are your payments?	$_____ per_____	$_____ per_____	$_____ per_____
C14. How many payments do you have left?	_____	_____	_____
C15. Do they include insurance?	☐ YES - (GO TO B) ☐ NO	☐ YES - (GO TO B) ☐ NO	☐ YES - (GO TO B) ☐ NO
C16. (IF NO) How much is the insurance cost per year?	$_____	$_____	$_____

B GO TO C7 FOR NEXT CAR, OR TO C17.

C17. Does the car you (HEAD) drive most of the time have seat belts?

☐ YES   ☐ NO (TURN TO C19)   ☐ DOES NOT DRIVE (TURN TO C19)

C18. (IF YES) Do you have them fastened all the time while you are driving, part of the time, or practically none of the time?

☐ ALL THE TIME   ☐ PART OF THE TIME   ☐ PRACTICALLY NONE OF THE TIME

C19. Do you (or your family) do any of your own repair work on your car(s)?

☐ YES   ☐ NO (GO TO D1)

(IF YES)

C20. What kinds of things have you done on your car(s) in the last year?

_____

_____

C21. In the last year do you think you saved more than $50 that way?

☐ YES   ☐ NO (GO TO D1)

C22. (IF YES) About how much do you think you saved? $_____

C23. About how much time did that take you altogether? _____

(HOURS)

SECTION D

D1. We have talked about homes and cars. Do you (FAMILY) make any regular payments for other things you have bought?

☐ YES   ☐ NO (GO TO D3)

D2. (IF YES) About how much do you have to pay each month? $_____

D3. Are you (HEAD) covered by some hospital or medical insurance like Blue Cross?

☐ YES   ☐ NO

D4. (ASK ONLY IF 2 OR MORE PEOPLE IN FAMILY)

Does this insurance cover the entire family?

☐ YES   ☐ NO

(TURN. TO D6)

D5. Can you get free medical care in any way such as from medicare, medicaid, or as a veteran?

_____

_____

D6. Do you (FAMILY) have any savings, such as checking or savings accounts, or government bonds?

☐ YES   ☐ NO

    D7. (IF YES) Would they
            amount to as much as two
            months' income or more?

         ☐ YES -   ☐ NO ———

D8. Was there a time in the last five years when you had as much as two months' income saved up?

           ☐ YES   ☐ NO

          (GO TO E1)

SECTION E

(ASK EVERYONE)

E1. Now I have a few questions about food and clothing. About how many times a week do you (FAMILY) eat out at restaurants or drive-ins?

_____

E2. About how much do you (FAMILY) spend in a week eating out, including lunches at work (or at school)?

                                                      $_____

E3. Do you have any of your milk delivered to the door?

☐ YES   ☐ NO - (GO TO E5)

    E4. About how much do you (FAMILY) spend on that milk in a week or month?

                                $_____ per _____

E5. About how much do you spend a week on all the (other) food you use at home?

                                                         $_____

E6. How about alcoholic beverages -- how much do you (FAMILY) spend on that in an average week?

                           $_____   ☐ NONE - (TURN TO E8)

    E7. Is that included in the food bill?

         ☐ YES   ☐ NO

E8.   Do any of you smoke?

☐ YES   ☐ NO (GO TO E11)

> E9.   (IF YES)   About how many cigarettes do you (FAMILY) smoke in a day or week?
>
> _____   per   _____
> (CIGARETTES, PACKS, OR CARTONS)   (DAY, WEEK)
>
> E10.   Is that included in the food bill?   ☐ YES   ☐ NO

E11.   Are there any special ways that you try to keep the food bill down?

☐ YES   ☐ NO (GO TO E14)

E12.   (IF YES)   What special ways do you have for keeping the food bill down?

_____

_____

E13.   Anything else?   _____

E14.   (ASK IF 2 OR MORE PEOPLE IN FAMILY)   How much of the time does the family sit down and eat the main meal of the day together?   _____

E15.   Do you have any special ways of saving on clothing costs?

☐ YES   ☐ NO (TURN TO F1)

> E16.   (IF YES)   What are they?   _____
>
> _____
>
> E17.   Did you (FAMILY) save more than $50 on your clothing bill this way last year?
>
> ☐ YES   ☐ NO (TURN TO F1)
>
> E18.   (IF YES)   About how much did you save this way in the last year?
>
> $_____

SECTION F

(ASK EVERYONE)

F1. Now we would like to know about your present job, are you working now, unemployed, retired or what?

WORKING NOW OR LAID OFF ONLY TEMPORARILY	UNEMPLOYED (TURN TO G1 PAGE 14)	RETIRED, HOUSEWIFE, OR STUDENT (TURN TO H1, PAGE 17)	OTHER _____
			(GO TO F2 IF HAS JOB, TURN TO H1 OTHERWISE)

(IF WORKING)

F2. What is your main occupation? (What sort of work do you do?)

_____

(IF NOT   F3. Tell me a little more about what you do? _____
CLEAR)

_____

F4. Do you work for someone else, yourself, or what?

☐ SOMEONE ELSE   ☐ BOTH SOMEONE ELSE AND SELF   ☐ SELF ONLY (TURN TO F11)

F5. How important is it for you to make your own decisions on a job?

_____

F6. How long have you been working for your present employer?

_____ (IF 10 YEARS OR MORE TURN TO F11)

(IF LESS THAN 10 YEARS)

F7. What happened to the job you had before -- did the company fold, were you laid off, or what?

_____

F8. Would you say your present job is a better job than the one you had before?

_____

(IF NOT   F9. Does it pay more than the previous job? _____
CLEAR)

F10. How many different employers have you had in the last ten years?

_____

F11. Have you ever moved out of a community where you were living in order to take a job somewhere else?

☐ YES
(GO TO
F13)

☐ NO ──────▶

> F12. Have you ever turned down a job because you did not want to move?
>
> ☐ YES   ☐ NO

F13. How good would a job have to be before you would be willing to move somewhere else in order to get it?

_____

_____

_____

F14. Do you plan to try for a new job or line of work or will you keep the job you have now?

☐ TRY FOR NEW JOB,   ☐ KEEP JOB HAVE NOW (GO TO F20)
OR LINE OF WORK

> F15. What kind of job do you have in mind? _____
>
> F16. How much might you earn? $_____ per _____
>
> F17. Would you have to get additional training to qualify? _____
>
> _____
>
> F18. Have you been doing anything in particular about it?
>
> ☐ YES   ☐ NO (GO TO F20)
>
> F19. (IF YES) What have you done? _____
>
> _____

F20. How much do you like a job where you are told exactly what to do?

_____

_____

F21. Would you have any trouble getting another job if you wanted one?

☐ YES   ☐ NO (GO TO F23)

    F22. (IF YES) Why is that? _____

F23. Have you ever had an illness or accident that laid you up for a month or more?

☐ YES   ☐ NO (GO TO F25)

    F24. (IF YES) When was that? _____ (YEAR)

F25. Do you have a physical or nervous condition that limits the type of work or the amount of work you can do?

☐ YES   ☐ NO (GO TO F27)

    F26. (IF YES) How much does it limit your work? _____

_____

F27. Are there times when you are late getting to work?

☐ YES   ☐ NO GO TO F29)

    F28. (IF YES) About how often does that happen? _____

F29. Are there times when you don't go to work at all, even though you are not sick?

☐ YES   ☐ NO (GO TO F31)

    F30. (IF YES) How often does that happen? _____

F31. Have you ever been out of a job or on strike for two months or more at one time?

☐ YES   ☐ NO (GO TO F33)

    F32. (IF YES) When was the last time that happened? _____ (YEAR)

F33. In the last year, how many days were you unemployed, laid off, or without work?

_____

F34. How many days of work did you miss on your main job in the last year because you were sick or otherwise unable to work?

_____

F35. And how many weeks of vacation did you take last year? _____

F36. Then how many weeks did you actually work on your main job in 1967? _____

F37. Did you have a standard workweek on your main job?

☐ YES   ☐ NO

```
┌─────────────────────────────────────────┐   ┌──────────────────────────────────┐
│ F38.   How many hours a week is that?     │   │ F41.   On the average, how many  │
│                                           │   │        hours a week did you work │
│        _____  │   │        on your main job last year?│
│                                           │   │                                  │
│ F39.   Did you have any overtime or       │   │        _____ │
│        extra work on your main job?       │   │                                  │
│                                           │   │              (GO TO F42)         │
│        ☐ YES        ☐ NO (GO TO F42)      │   │                                  │
│          │                                │   └──────────────────────────────────┘
│          ↓                                │
│        F40.   How many hours did that     │
│               amount to last year?        │
│                                           │
│        _____  │
│                                           │
│                (GO TO F42)                │
└─────────────────────────────────────────┘
```

F42. Did you have any other jobs, or any other ways of making money in addition to your
     main job?

☐ YES   ☐ NO   (TURN TO F47)

(IF YES)

```
┌───────────────────────────────────────────────────────────────────────────────┐
│ F43.   What did you do? _____  │
│                                                                                  │
│        _____  │
│                                                                                  │
│ F44.   Anything else? _____  │
│                                                                                  │
│ F45.   About how many hours in all did that amount to in the last year?          │
│                                                                                  │
│        _____  │
│                                                                                  │
│ F46.   About how much did you make per hour for this?  $_____  │
│                                                            (PER HOUR)            │
└───────────────────────────────────────────────────────────────────────────────┘
```

F47. Could you have worked <u>more</u> if you had wanted to in 1967?

☐ YES (GO TO F49)   ☐ NO

F48. Would you have liked to work more?

☐ YES (TURN TO PAGE 18, I1)

☐ NO (GO TO F49)

F49. Could you have worked <u>less</u> if you had wanted to?

☐ YES (TURN TO
PAGE 18, I1)   ☐ NO

F50. Would you have preferred less work even
if you had earned less money?

☐ YES   ☐ NO

(TURN TO PAGE 18, I1)

SECTION G: IF UNEMPLOYED

G1. What do you do when you work? (What is your occupation?) _____

_____

_____

G2. Did you work at all last year?

☐ YES   ☐ NO (TURN TO G5)

(IF YES)

G3. How many weeks did you work last year? _____

G4. About how many hours a week did you work (when you worked)? _____

G5. Did the company you worked for fold, were you laid off, or what? _____

_____

G6. How many different employers have you had in the last ten years? _____

G7. Have you ever moved out of a community where you were living in order to take a job somewhere else?

☐ YES (GO TO G9)   ☐ NO

(IF NO)

> G8. Have you ever turned down a job because you did not want to move?
>
>   ☐ YES   ☐ NO

G9. Do you think you will be able to find steady work around here, or will you have to move?

_____

G10. How good would a job have to be, for you to be willing to move somewhere else in order to get it?

_____

G11. Is there anything in particular that might make it difficult for you to get another job?

☐ YES   ☐ NO (GO TO G13)

G12. (IF YES) What is that?_____

G13. How many places do you have your name in for a job? _____

G14. Have you applied for a job anywhere in the last 2 weeks?

☐ YES   ☐ NO (GO TO G16)

G15. (IF YES) How many places did you apply? _____

G16. How much do you like a job where you are told exactly what to do? _____

_____

G17. Have you ever had an illness or accident that laid you up for a month or more?

☐ YES   ☐ NO (GO TO G19)

    G18. (IF YES) When was that? _____
                                             (YEAR)

G19. Do you have a physical or nervous condition that limits the type of work, or the amount of work you can do?

☐ YES   ☐ NO (GO TO G21)

    G20. (IF YES) How much does it limit your work? _____

G21. When you were working, were there times when you were late getting to work?

☐ YES   ☐ NO (GO TO G23)

    G22. (IF YES) About how often did that happen? _____

G23. Were there times when you didn't get to work at all, even though you were not sick?

☐ YES   ☐ NO (GO TO G25)

    G24. (IF YES) How often did that happen? _____

G25. Have you ever been out of a job, or on strike for two months or more at one time?

☐ YES   ☐ NO (GO TO G27)

    G26. (IF YES) When was the last time that happened? _____
                                                                     (YEAR)

G27. Are there jobs available around here that just aren't worth taking?

_____

(IF JOBS NOT
WORTH TAKING)   G28. How much do they pay? $_____ per _____
                                                                            (HOUR, WEEK)

G29. How important is it for you to make your own decisions on a job?

_____

SECTION H: IF RETIRED, HOUSEWIFE, OR STUDENT

H1. During the last year (1967) did you do any work for money?

☐ YES   ☐ NO (GO TO H5)

(IF YES)

> H2. What kind of work did you do when you worked? (What was your occupation?)
>
> _____
>
> H3. How many weeks did you work last year? _____
>
> H4. About how many hours a week did you work (when you worked)? _____
>
> (GO TO H11)

H5. Are you thinking about going to work?

☐ YES   ☐ NO (GO TO H11)

(IF YES)

> H6. How many places do you have your name in for a job? _____
>
> H7. Have you applied for a job anywhere in the last two weeks?
>
> ☐ YES   ☐ NO (GO TO H9)
>
> H8. (IF YES) How many places did you apply? _____
>
> H9. Are there jobs around here that just aren't worth taking? _____
>
> _____
>
> (IF JOBS NOT
> WORTH TAKING)   H10. How much do they pay? $_____ per _____
> (HOUR, WEEK)

H11. Do you have a physical condition, or nervous condition that limits the type of work
or the amount of work you can do?

☐ YES   ☐ NO (TURN TO I 1)

H12. (IF YES) How much does it limit your work? _____

(TURN TO I 1)

SECTION I

(ASK EVERYONE)

I 1. Are you married, single, widowed, divorced, or separated?

☐ MARRIED

☐ SINGLE ⟶ | I 2. Have you ever been married? ☐ YES ☐ NO (GO TO I 6)

I 3. When were you first married? _____
                                          (SPECIFY DATE OR AGE)
                                                          GO TO I 6

☐ WIDOWED ⎫
☐ DIVORCED ⎬ ⟶ | I 4. For how long? _____ (YEARS)
☐ SEPARATED ⎭

I 5. When were you first married? _____
                                          (SPECIFY DATE OR AGE)
                                                          GO TO I 6

I 6. INTERVIEWER: CHECK BOX

☐ CHILDREN UNDER 12   ☐ NO CHILDREN UNDER 12 OR HEAD
   AND HEAD WORKS   IS NOT WORKING (TURN TO PAGE 20, J1)

I 7. How were the children taken care of while you were working?

_____

I 8   About how much did that cost you last year? $ _____
                                                          (TURN TO PAGE 20, J1)

(IF MARRIED)

I 9. Did your wife do any work for money last year?

☐ YES   ☐ NO (TURN TO I 16)

I 10. What kind of work did she do? _____

I 11. About how many weeks did she work last year? _____

I 12. And about how many hours a week did she work? _____

I 13. INTERVIEWER: CHECK BOX

☐ CHILDREN UNDER 12   ☐ NO CHILDREN UNDER 12 (TURN TO I 16)

I 14. How were your children taken care of while your wife was working?

_____

I 15. About how much did that cost you last year? $ _____

(IF MARRIED -- CONTINUED)

I 16. How many grades of school did your wife finish?_____

I 17. Did she have any other schooling?

☐ YES   ☐ NO (GO TO I 21)

I 18. What other schooling did she have? _____

   (IF COLLEGE)   I 19. Does she have a college degree?

                    ☐ YES   ☐ NO (GO TO I 21)

                    I 20. What degree(s) did she receive? _____

                    _____

I 21. Is this your (HEAD'S) first marriage?

☐ YES   ☐ NO

┌─────────────────────────────────┐   ┌─────────────────────────────────────┐
│ I 22. When were you married?   │   │ I 23. When were you (HEAD) married │
│   │   │   for the first time?   │
│   _____   │   │   │
│   (SPECIFY WHETHER YEAR   │   │   _____   │
│   OR AGE)   │   │   (SPECIFY WHETHER YEAR OR AGE) │
└─────────────────────────────────┘   └─────────────────────────────────────┘

I 24. (INTERVIEWER: SEE PAGE 4, Q. B2, (LISTING BOX) AND CHECK ONE)

☐ WIFE UNDER 45   ☐ WIFE 45 OR OLDER (TURN TO J1)

I 25. Do you expect to have any more children?

      ☐ YES   ☐ NO

┌─────────────────────────────────┐   ┌─────────────────────────────────────┐
│ I 26. When do you think you   │   │ I 27. How sure are you that you   │
│   might have another child?│   │   won't have any (more) children?│
│   │   │   │
│   _____   │   │   _____   │
│   _____   │   │   _____   │
│   _____   │   │   _____   │
│   (TURN TO J1)   │   │   (TURN TO J1)   │
└─────────────────────────────────┘   └─────────────────────────────────────┘

20

SECTION J: INCOME

(ASK EVERYONE)

To get an accurate financial picture of people all over the country, we need to know the income of all the families that we interview.

J1. (INTERVIEWER: CHECK BOX)

☐ FARMER   ☐ NOT A FARMER (GO TO J5)

> J2. What were your total receipts from farming in 1967, including soil bank payments and commodity credit loans? $_____ A
>
> J3. What were your total operating expenses, not counting living expenses? $_____ B
>
> J4. That left you a net income from farming of? A - B = $_____ A-B

J5. Did you (R and Family) own a business at any time in 1967, or have a financial interest in any business enterprise?

☐ YES   ☐ NO (GO TO J8)

> J6. Is it a corporation or an unincorporated business, or do you have an interest in both kinds?
>
>   ☐ CORPORATION (GO TO J8)
>
>   ☐ UNINCORPORATED
>   ☐ BOTH
>   ☐ DON'T KNOW
>
> J7. How much was your (family's) share of the total income from the business in 1967 -- that is, the amount you took out plus any profit left in? $_____

(ASK EVERYONE)

J8. How much did you (HEAD) receive from wages and salaries in 1967, that is, before anything was deducted for taxes or other things? $_____

J9. In addition to this, did you have any income from bonuses, overtime, or commissions?

☐ YES   ☐ NO (TURN TO J11)

> J10. How much was that? $_____

J11. Did you (HEAD) receive any other income in 1967 from:

a) professional practice or trade? $_____

b) farming or market gardening,
roomers or boarders? $_____

(IF "YES" TO ANY
ITEM, ASK "How   c) dividends, interest, rent,
much was it?"   trust funds, or royalties? $_____
ENTER AMOUNT
AT RIGHT)   d) ADC, ADCU ? $_____

e) other welfare? $_____

(IF "NO"   f) Social Security? $_____
ENTER "0")
g) other retirement pay,
pensions, or annuities? $_____

h) unemployment, or workmen's
compensation? $_____

i) alimony? $_____

j) help from relatives? $_____

k) anything else? _____ $_____
(specify)

J12. (INTERVIEWER: CHECK ONE)

☐ HEAD AND WIFE   ☐ SINGLE MAN OR WOMAN (TURN TO J16)

J13. Did your wife have any income during 1967?

☐ YES   ☐ NO (TURN TO J16)

J14. (IF YES) Was it income from wages, salary, a business or what?
Any other income?

_____   _____
(SOURCE)   (SOURCE)

J15. How much was it
before deductions? $_____ + $_____ = $_____

J16. INTERVIEWER: SEE PAGE 4, B2, (LISTING BOX) FOR ANYONE (OTHER THAN HEAD AND WIFE) AGED 14 AND OLDER, AND CHECK BOX

☐ NO ONE 14 OR OLDER EXCEPT HEAD AND/OR WIFE - (TURN TO J28)

☐ OTHER FAMILY MEMBERS 14 AND OLDER

↓ LIST ALL OTHER FU MEMBERS 14 AND OLDER BY RELATION TO HEAD AND AGE ⟶

J17. Did (MENTION MEMBER) have any income during 1967?	☐ YES ☐ NO (GO TO A)

(IF HAD INCOME)

J18. Was that from wages, a pension, a business, interest or what?

_____
(SOURCE)

J19. How much was that?

$ _____

J20. Did (he/she) have any other income?   ☐ YES   ☐ NO (GO TO J23)

(IF OTHER INCOME)

J21. What was that from?

_____
(SOURCE)

J22. How much was that?

$ _____

(IF ANY FROM WAGES, OR A BUSINESS)

J23. How many weeks did (he/she) work last year?

_____

J24. About how many hours a week was that?

_____

J25. (IF NOT CLEAR) Did (he/she) work more than half time?

_____

J26. Does (he/she) share in the family's expenses, or what?

_____

J27. Is (he/she) likely to stay here with you or might (he/she) move away within the next few years?

_____

_____

A REPEAT J17-J27 FOR NEXT PERSON LISTED; IF NO OTHER PERSON, TURN TO J28.

☐ YES ☐ NO (GO TO A)	☐ YES ☐ NO (GO TO A)	☐ YES ☐ NO (GO TO A)
_____ (SOURCE) $ _____	_____ (SOURCE) $ _____	_____ (SOURCE) $ _____
☐ YES ☐ NO (GO TO J23)	☐ YES ☐ NO (GO TO J23)	☐ YES ☐ NO (GO TO J23)
_____ (SOURCE) $ _____	_____ (SOURCE) $ _____	_____ (SOURCE) $ _____

INTERVIEWER: FOR ALL PERSONS AGED 18-61 LISTED IN J16:

IF ANYONE LISTED ABOVE MEETS THESE CRITERIA BELOW, CONSIDER THIS/THESE PERSON(S) SUBFAMILIES, AND ARRANGE AT END OF INTERVIEW TO TAKE INTERVIEW WITH EACH ONE. (IF HUSBAND AND WIFE, CONSIDER AS ONE SUBFAMILY). The criteria are as follows: (1) Has $2000 or more in income, (2) Answers "NO" to J26, (3) "Might move away within the next few years," or some similar response to J27. ALL THREE MUST HOLD BEFORE CONSIDERING AS SUBFAMILY.

J28. Did you get any other money in the last year -- like a big settlement from an insurance company, an inheritance, or anything?

☐ YES   ☐ NO (GO TO J30)

J29. (IF YES) How much did that amount to? $_____

J30. Did anyone here get more than $50 worth of food or clothing as a part of their pay?

☐ YES   ☐ NO (GO TO J32)

J31. (IF YES) About how much would that be worth? $_____

J32. Did you (FAMILY) get any free food, clothing, or food stamps worth $50 or more in 1967?

☐ YES   ☐ NO (GO TO J34)

J33. (IF YES) About how much did that save you last year? $_____

J34. Was your family's income a lot higher or lower than usual this past year (1967)?

☐ NO (GO TO J36)   ☐ HIGHER THAN USUAL   ☐ LOWER THAN USUAL

> J35. Why was that? _____
>
> _____

J36. Does your family's income change from month to month, stay the same over the year, or what?

☐ STAYS THE SAME -   ☐ CHANGES FROM MONTH TO MONTH
(TURN TO J38)

> J37. Why does it vary? _____
>
> _____
>
> _____
>
> (TURN TO J38)

J38. Would you say you are better off financially than you were a few years ago, or are you in the same situation?

_____

J39. Is there anything that makes your family's expenses unusually high?

☐ YES   ☐ NO (GO TO J41)

J40. (IF YES) What is that? _____

_____

J41. Is anything likely to happen over the next few years that will make things much different for your family -- like more or less earners, a better job for you, or fewer people living here?

☐ YES   ☐ NO (GO TO J44)

(IF YES)

J42. What is that? _____

_____

(IF <u>NOT</u>   J43. Will that make things better, or worse, financially?
CLEAR)

_____

J44. Are there any people that do <u>not</u> live with you who are dependent on you for more than half of their support?

☐ NO - NONE   ☐ YES
(GO TO J47)

(IF YES)

J45. How many are there? _____

J46. How much did that amount
to in the last year? $_____

J47. Do you (FAMILY) have parents or other relatives that you would feel that you had to help (more), if you had more money?

☐ YES   ☐ NO

26

SECTION K: TIME USE

K1. We're interested in how people spend their spare time. What things do you
(HEAD) usually do in your spare time?

_____

_____

_____

K2. How often do you (HEAD) go to church? _____

K3. Are you (HEAD) taking any courses or lessons?

☐ YES   ☐ NO (GO TO K5)

K4. (IF YES) What are they? _____

_____

K5. About how many hours do you (HEAD) usually watch television on an average weekday?

_____

K6. How often do you (HEAD) read a newspaper -- every day, once a week, or what?

_____   ☐ NEVER

K7. About how many people in this neighborhood do you know by name? _____

K8. Do you (FAMILY) have any relatives who live within walking distance of here?

_____

K9. Did you spend more than 40 hours helping friends or relatives last year?

☐ YES   ☐ NO (TURN TO K11)

K10. (IF YES) About how many hours was that? _____

K11. Did you get any free help with housework, baby sitting, or anything like that in the last year (1967)?

☐ YES ☐ NO (GO TO K15)

K12. Did it save you as much as $50 during the year?

☐ YES ☐ NO (GO TO K14)

K13. (IF YES) About how much did it save you? $_____

K14. Was it from someone who doesn't live here? _____

K15. How often do you (HEAD) go to social clubs or organizations? _____

K16. How often do you (HEAD) go to a bar or tavern? _____

K17. Do you (HEAD) belong to a labor union?

☐ YES ☐ NO (TURN TO L1)

K18. (IF YES) How much did your union dues amount to last year? $_____

SECTION L: FEELINGS

Here is something different -- some questions about how you feel towards things.

(INTERVIEWER: IF RESPONDENT SIMPLY REPEATS ONE OF THE ALTERNATIVES GIVEN IN A QUESTION,
CIRCLE THAT WORD OR PHRASE. "YOU" MEANS HEAD IN THIS SECTION.)

L1. Have you usually felt pretty sure your life would work out the way you want it to,
or have there been more times when you haven't been very sure about it?

_____

L2. Are you the kind of person that plans his life ahead all the time,
or do you live more from day to day?

_____

L3. When you make plans ahead, do you usually get to carry out things the way you expected,
or do things usually come up to make you change your plans?

_____

L4. Would you say you nearly always finish things once you start them,
or do you sometimes have to give up before they are finished?

_____

L5. How much do you like to do things that are difficult and challenging?

_____

L6. Would you rather spend your money and enjoy life today,
or save more for the future?

_____

L7. Would you rather have a job that you like even if the chances for a raise were small,
or a job you don't like which offers a good chance for making more money?

_____

L8. Are you more often satisfied, or dissatisfied with yourself?

_____

L9. Do you have some limitations that keep you from getting ahead as far as you would like?

_____

L10. Do you get angry fairly easily,

or does it take a lot to get you angry?

_____

L11. How much does it matter what other people think about you?

_____

L12. Do you trust most other people, some, or very few?

_____

L13. Do you spend much time figuring out ways to get more money?

_____

L14. Do you think a lot about things that might happen in the future,

or do you usually just take things as they come?

_____

L15. Do you think the life of the average man is getting better

or is it getting worse?

_____

L16. Are there a lot of people who have good things they don't deserve?

_____

30

SECTION M: THE PAST

Now, just a few questions about things you've done in the past.

M1. Where did you (HEAD) grow up?_____
      (SPECIFY STATE, IF U.S., COUNTRY IF FOREIGN)

M2. Was that on a farm, in a large city, small town, or what?_____

M3. How many grades of school did you (HEAD) finish?_____

(IF 6 GRADES OR LESS)

M4. Did you get any other training?

☐ YES   ☐ NO - (GO TO M6)

M5. What was it?_____

_____

M6. Do you have any trouble reading?

_____

(GO TO M11)

(IF 7 GRADES OR MORE)

M7. Did you have any other schooling?

☐ YES   ☐ NO - (GO TO M11)

M8. What other schooling did you have?

_____

(IF   M9. Do you have a
COL-   college degree?
LEGE)

☐ YES   ☐ NO -
                (GO TO M11)

M10. What degree(s) did you receive?

_____

(GO TO M11)

(ASK EVERYONE)

M11. Are you (HEAD) a veteran?   ☐ YES   ☐ NO

M12. How many brothers and sisters did you have?_____

M13. Were your parents poor when you were growing up, pretty well off, or what?

_____

M14. How much education did your father have?_____

(IF NONE OR
 DON'T KNOW) M15. Could he read and write?_____

<u>TURN TO PAGE 4 OF COVER SHEET</u>

SECTION N: BY OBSERVATION ONLY

N1.   Who was present during interview?_____

_____

N2.   Who was respondent (relation to head)?_____

N3.   Race? | WHITE | | NEGRO | | OTHER |_____
                                                              (SPECIFY)

N4.   Number of calls?_____

N5.   How clean was the interior of the DU?
      | VERY CLEAN | | CLEAN | | SO-SO | | NOT VERY CLEAN | | DIRTY |

N6.   How much reading material was visible in the DU?
            | A LOT | | SOME | | NONE |

N7.   About how many times did you have to repeat a question?_____

N8.   About how many times did you have to ask R to repeat a reply?_____

N9.   Does R have any obvious disfigurements or habits that could make it difficult for
      him to get a job? _____

_____

N10. What is the name of the nearest city of 50,000 population or more?

      _____
                    CITY   STATE

N11. How far is this DU from the center of that city?

      | LESS THAN | | 5-14.9 | | 15-29.9 | | 30-49.9 | | 50 OR MORE |
      | 5 MILES | | MILES | | MILES | | MILES | | MILES |

N12. TYPE OF STRUCTURE IN WHICH FAMILY LIVES:

[ ] TRAILER
[ ] DETACHED SINGLE FAMILY HOUSE
[ ] 2-FAMILY HOUSE, 2 UNITS SIDE BY SIDE
[ ] 2-FAMILY HOUSE, 2 UNITS ONE ABOVE
    THE OTHER
[ ] DETACHED 3-4 FAMILY HOUSE
[ ] ROW HOUSE (3 OR MORE UNITS IN AN
    ATTACHED ROW)

[ ] APARTMENT HOUSE (5 OR MORE UNITS,
    3 STORIES OR LESS)
[ ] APARTMENT HOUSE (5 OR MORE UNITS,
    4 STORIES OR MORE)
[ ] APARTMENT IN A PARTLY COMMERCIAL
    STRUCTURE
[ ] OTHER (Specify)_____

N13. NEIGHBORHOOD: Look at 3 structures on each side of DU but not more than 100 yards
      or so in both directions and check as many boxes as apply, below.

[ ] VACANT LAND ONLY
[ ] TRAILER
[ ] DETACHED SINGLE FAMILY HOUSE
[ ] 2-FAMILY HOUSE, 2 UNITS SIDE BY SIDE
[ ] 2-FAMILY HOUSE, 2 UNITS ONE ABOVE
    THE OTHER
[ ] DETACHED 3-4 FAMILY HOUSE
[ ] ROW HOUSE (3 OR MORE UNITS IN AN
    ATTACHED ROW)

[ ] APARTMENT HOUSE (5 OR MORE UNITS,
    3 STORIES OR LESS)
[ ] APARTMENT HOUSE (5 OR MORE UNITS,
    4 STORIES OR MORE)
[ ] APARTMENT IN A PARTLY COMMERCIAL
    STRUCTURE
[ ] WHOLLY COMMERCIAL OR INDUSTRIAL
    STRUCTURE
[ ] OTHER (Specify)_____

N14. Is this DU located in a public housing project?   [ ] YES   [ ] NO

Thumbnail Sketch

STUDY OF FAMILY ECONOMICS

Project 457680

1974

OMB#85-RO224
Exp. 2/28/75

(Interview Number)

SURVEY RESEARCH CENTER
INSTITUTE FOR SOCIAL RESEARCH
THE UNIVERSITY OF MICHIGAN

| 68 Int. | 70 Int. | 72 Int. |
| 69 Int. | 71 Int. | 73 Int. |

(Do not write in above space)

1. Interviewer's Label

2. P.S.U. _____
3. Your Interview No. _____
4. Date _____
5. Length of Interview _____

SECTION A: CHILDREN

(MAKE SURE PAGE 2 OF COVER SHEET IS COMPLETED BEFORE ASKING Q. A1)

A1. INTERVIEWER: SEE LISTING BOX, ON PAGE 2 OF COVER SHEET, AND CHECK ONE:

| 1. CHILDREN UNDER 25 IN FU DURING 1973 OR 1974 | 5. NO CHILDREN UNDER 25 IN FU DURING 1973 OR 1974 |

A2. Did any of the children stop going to school in 1973 or 1974?

1. YES   5. NO   (TURN TO B1, PAGE 2)

	Person #1	Person #2
A3. Who was that?	_____ (RELATION TO HEAD) (AGE)	_____ (RELATION TO HEAD) (AGE)
A4. What was the highest grade (he/she) finished?	_____ (GRADE FINISHED)	_____ (GRADE FINISHED)

2

SECTION B: TRANSPORTATION

(ASK EVERYONE)

B1.   Is there public transportation within walking distance of (here) your house?

    | 1. YES | | 5. NO | (GO TO B3)

    B2.   Is it good enough so that a person could use it to get to work?

    _____

    _____

B3.   Do you or anyone else in your household own a car or truck?

    | 1. YES | (GO TO B6) | 5. NO |

    ┌───┐
    │ B4.   Does not having a car cause any difficulties? │
    │ | 1. YES | | 5. NO | (TURN TO C1, PAGE 3) │
    │   B5.   What are they? _____   │
    │   │
    │   _____   │
    │   │
    │   _____   │
    │   │
    │   _____   │
    │   (TURN TO C1, PAGE 3)   │
    └───┘

B6.   During the last year how many miles did you and your family drive in
      (your car/all of your cars)?

    _____

    _____

                    (TURN TO C1, PAGE 3)

3

SECTION C: HOUSING

C1. How many rooms do you have for your family (not counting bathrooms?) _____

C2. Do you own the (home/apartment), pay rent, or what?

| 1. OWNS OR IS BUYING | 5. PAYS RENT | 8. NEITHER OWNS NOR RENTS |

                          (GO TO C4)   (GO TO C5)

(IF OWNS OR IS BUYING)

> C3. Could you tell me what the present value of your house (farm) is - I mean about what would it bring if you sold it today?
>
> $_____
>
>   (GO TO C7)

(IF PAYS RENT)

> C4. About how much rent do you pay a month? $_____
>
>   (GO TO C7)

(IF NEITHER OWNS NOR RENTS)

> C5. How is that? _____
>
> _____
>
> C6. How much would it rent for if it were rented? $_____ per _____
>
>   (GO TO C7)   (MONTH,YEAR)

(ASK EVERYONE)

C7. Have you (HEAD) moved since the spring of 1973?

| 1. YES | | 5. NO | (GO TO C9)

C8. Why did you move? _____

_____

C9. Do you think you might move in the next couple of years?

_____ | 5. NO | (TURN TO D1, PAGE 4)

(IF MIGHT MOVE
     OR
    WILL MOVE)   C10. Why might you move? _____

_____

4

SECTION D: EMPLOYMENT

D1. We would like to know about your (HEAD's) present job - are you (HEAD) working now, looking for work, retired, a housewife, or what?

1. WORKING NOW, OR ONLY TEMPORARILY LAID OFF	2. LOOKING FOR WORK, UNEMPLOYED (TURN TO E1, PAGE 8)	3. RETIRED
		3. PERMANENTLY DISABLED
		4. HOUSEWIFE
		5. STUDENT
		6. OTHER - _____ (SPECIFY)

(TURN TO F1, PAGE 10)

(GO TO D2 IF HAS JOB, OTHERWISE TURN TO F1, PAGE 10)

D2. What is your main occupation? (What sort of work do you do?)

OCC

_____

OCC   IND

(IF NOT CLEAR) ───▶ D3. Tell me a little more about what you do.

_____

_____

D4. What kind of business is that in? _____

_____

D5. Do you work for someone else, yourself, or what?

| 1. SOMEONE ELSE | 2. BOTH SOMEONE ELSE AND SELF | 3. SELF ONLY |

D6. How long have you had this job? _____

_____ (IF 1 YEAR OR MORE, TURN TO D11, PAGE 5)

(IF LESS THAN 1 YEAR)

D7. What happened to the job you had before - did the company fold, were you laid off, or what?

_____

_____

D8. Does your present job pay more than the one you had before?

| 1. YES, MORE | 5. NO, SAME OR LESS |

D9. On the whole, would you say your present job is better or worse than the one you had before?

| 1. BETTER | 5. WORSE | 3. SAME | (TURN TO D11, PAGE 5)

D10. Why is that? _____

_____

_____

D11. Did you take any vacation during 1973?

    1. YES ──────► D12. How much vacation did you take? ____ ____ ____
                                                     DAYS WEEKS MONTHS
    5. NO (GO TO D13)

D13. Did you miss any work in 1973 because you were sick, or because someone else in the family was sick?

    1. YES ──────► D14. How much work did you miss? ____ ____ ____
                                             DAYS WEEKS MONTHS
    5. NO (GO TO D15)

D15. Did you miss any work in 1973 because you were unemployed or on strike?

    1. YES ──────► D16. How much work did you miss? ____ ____ ____
                                       DAYS WEEKS MONTHS
    5. NO (GO TO D17)

D17. Then, how many _weeks_ did you actually work on your main job in 1973? _____
                                                                        (WEEKS)

D18. And, on the average, how many _hours a week_ did you work on your main job last year? _____

D19. Did you have any overtime which isn't included in that?

    [ ] YES   [ ] NO (GO TO D21)

    D20. How many hours did that overtime amount to in 1973? _____
                                                                             (HOURS)

D21. If you were to work more hours than usual during some week, would you get paid for those extra hours of work?

    1. YES   5. NO

| D22. What would be your hourly rate for that overtime?

  $ _____ per hour | D23. Do you have an hourly wage rate for your regular work?

  1. YES   5. NO (TURN TO D25, PAGE 6) |

D24. What is your hourly wage rate for your regular work time? $ _____ per hour

6

D25. Did you have any extra jobs or other ways of making money in addition to your main job in 1973?

[1. YES]   [5. NO] (GO TO D31)

OCC
[ ]

> D26. What did you do? _____
>
> _____
>
> D27. Anything else? _____
>
> D28. About how much did you make per hour at this? $_____ per hour
>
> D29. And how many <u>weeks</u> did you work on your extra job(s) in 1973? _____
>
> D30. On the average, how many <u>hours a week</u> did you work on your extra job(s)?
>
> _____

D31. Was there more work available on (your job) (any of your jobs) so that you could have worked more if you had wanted to?

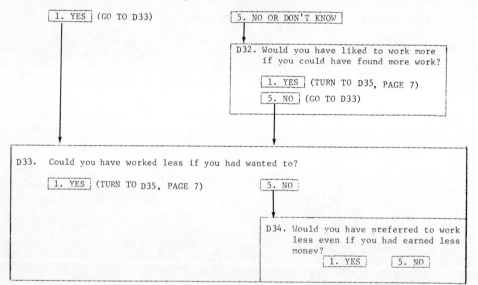

[1. YES] (GO TO D33)   [5. NO OR DON'T KNOW]

> D32. Would you have liked to work more if you could have found more work?
>
> [1. YES] (TURN TO D35, PAGE 7)
> [5. NO] (GO TO D33)

D33. Could you have worked less if you had wanted to?

[1. YES] (TURN TO D35, PAGE 7)   [5. NO]

> D34. Would you have preferred to work less even if you had earned less money?
>
> [1. YES]   [5. NO]

D35. About how much time does it take you to get to work each day, door to door?

_____(ONE WAY)   [ ]NONE (GO TO D38)

D36. About how many miles is it to where you work?   _____ (ONE WAY)

D37. Do you use public transportation to get to work, have a car pool, drive by yourself, walk, or what?

| 1. PUBLIC TRANSPORTATION | 2. CAR POOL | 3. DRIVES | 4. WALK | 7. OTHER |

D38. Have you been thinking about getting a new job, or will you keep the job you have now?

| 1. THINKING ABOUT GETTING A NEW JOB | | 5. KEEP JOB HAVE NOW |

(TURN TO G1, PAGE 11)

8

SECTION E: IF LOOKING FOR WORK, UNEMPLOYED IN Q. D1

OCC ☐

E1. What kind of job are you looking for? _____

_____

E2. How much might you earn? $_____ per _____

E3. Will you have to get any training to qualify? _____

_____

E4. What have you been doing to find a job? _____

_____ | 5. NOTHING | (GO TO E6)

E5. How many places have you been to in the last few weeks to find out about a job?

| 1. ONE | | 2. TWO | | 3. THREE | | 4. FOUR | | 5. FIVE OR MORE |

E6. What sort of work did you do on your last job? (What was your occupation?)

OCC   OCC   IND

_____ ☐☐☐ ☐☐

_____

E7. What kind of business was that in? _____

_____

E8. What happened to that job – did the company fold, were you laid-off, or
what? _____

_____

_____

E9. How many _weeks_ did you work in 1973? _____ |00. NONE | (GO TO E11)

E10. About how many _hours a week_ did you work when you worked? _____

E11. How many weeks were you sick in 1973? _____

E12. Then, how many weeks were you unemployed or laid off in 1973? _____

E13. INTERVIEWER: REFER TO E9 AND CHECK ONE:

[ ] WORKED IN 1973   [ ] DID NOT WORK IN 1973 (GO TO E17)

E14. On your last job, how much time did it take you to get to work each day, door to door? _____ [ ] NONE (GO TO E17)
(ONE WAY)

E15. About how many miles was it to where you worked? _____ (ONE WAY)

E16. Did you use public transportation to get to work, have a car pool, drive by yourself, walk, or what?

| 1. PUBLIC TRANSPORTATION | 2. CAR POOL | 3. DROVE | 4. WALKED | 7. OTHER |

E17. Are there jobs available around here that just aren't worth taking?

| 1. YES | | 5. NO | (GO TO E19)

E18. How much do they pay? $_____ per _____ (HOUR, WEEK)

E19. Would you be willing to move to another community if you could get a good job there?

| 1. YES, MAYBE, OR DEPENDS | | 5. NO |

E20. How much would a job have to pay for you to be willing to move?

$_____ per _____

E21. Why is that? _____

_____

_____

(TURN TO G1, PAGE 11)

10

SECTION F: RETIRED, HOUSEWIFE, STUDENT, PERMANENTLY DISABLED

F1. During the last year (1973), did you (HEAD) do any work for money?

| 1. YES | | 5. NO |

F2. Are you thinking about going to work?

| 1. YES | (GO TO F8) | 5. NO | (TURN TO G1, PAGE 11)

| | OCC | | OCC | IND |

F3. What kind of work did you do when you worked? (What was your occupation?)

_____

F4. What kind of business is that in? _____

_____

F5. How many <u>weeks</u> did you work last year? _____

F6. About how many <u>hours a week</u> did you work (when you worked)? _____

F7. Are you thinking of getting a new job in the next year or so?
| 1. YES | (GO TO F8) | 5. NO | (TURN TO G1, PAGE 11)

(IF YES TO F2 OR TO F7)

F8. What kind of job do you have in mind? _____

_____

F9. How much might you earn? $_____ per _____

F10. Would you have to get any training to qualify? _____

F11. What have you been doing to find a job? _____

_____ | 5. NOTHING | (GO TO F13)

F12. How many places have you been to in the last few weeks to find out about a job?
| 1. ONE | | 2. TWO | | 3. THREE | | 4. FOUR | | 5. FIVE OR MORE |

F13. Are there jobs around here that just aren't worth taking?
| 1. YES | | 5. NO | (TURN TO G1, PAGE 11)

F14. How much do they pay? $_____ per _____

(TURN TO G1, PAGE 11)

SECTION G: OTHER WORK

(ASK EVERYONE)

G1. Are you married, single, widowed, divorced, or separated?

| 1. MARRIED | | 2. SINGLE | | 3. WIDOWED | | 4. DIVORCED | | 5. SEPARATED |

(TURN TO G16, PAGE 12)

(Q's G2-G8 REFER TO WIFE's OCCUPATION)

G2. Did your wife do any work for money in 1973?

| 1. YES | | 5. NO | (GO TO G9)   OCC   OCC   IND

G3.   What kind of work did she do? _____

_____

G4. What kind of business is that in? _____

_____

G5. About how many weeks did she work last year? _____

G6. And about how many hours a week did she work? _____

G7. Was there more work available so that your wife could have worked more
     in 1973 if she had wanted to?

     | 1. YES | | 5. NO |
     (GO TO
      G11)

              G8. Would she have liked to work more if she could have
                   found more work?

     (GO TO G11) | 1. YES | | 5. NO |

G9. INTERVIEWER: CHECK ONE

     [ ] WIFE UNDER 65 AND DID NOT WORK IN 1973 | 0. | ALL OTHERS (GO TO G11)

     G10. What about the next few years? Do you think your wife will go to work
          in the near future?

          | 1. YES | | 3. DEPENDS | | 5. NO |

G11. How much education did your wife's father have? _____

_____

G12. How much education did your wife's mother have? _____

_____

12

G13. How many years has your wife worked for money since she was 18? _____

_____

_____ | 00. NONE | (GO TO G16)

G14. How many of these years did she work full time for most of the year? _____

_____

_____ | ALL | (GO TO G16)

G15. During the years that she did not work full time, how much of the time did she work?

_____

_____

G16. INTERVIEWER: CHECK ONE:

| 1. CHILDREN UNDER 12 LIVING IN FU | | 5. NO CHILDREN UNDER 12 | (TURN TO G22, PAGE 13)

G17. CHECK ONE:

| 1. SINGLE HEAD WHO WORKED IN 1973 | 3. MARRIED COUPLE WITH WIFE WHO WORKED IN 1973 | 5. ALL OTHERS WITH CHILDREN UNDER 12 |
(GO TO G18)   (GO TO G18)   (TURN TO G22, PAGE 13)

G18. How were the children (child) taken care of while (you were/ your wife was) working?

_____

_____

_____

G19. How many hours per week were they taken care of (not counting time in regular school)?
_____ PER WEEK
(Hours)

G20. How much did that cost you per week? $ _____ PER WEEK

G21. In the past year how many times did someone have to stay home from work to take care of the children (child) because these arrangements broke down?

_____

_____

_____

(TURN TO G22, PAGE 13)

(ASK EVERYONE)

G22. How many years have you (HEAD) worked since you were 18? _____

_____ | 00. NONE | (GO TO G25)

G23. How many of these years did you (HEAD) work full time for most of the year? _____

_____ | ALL | (GO TO G25)

G24. During the years that you (HEAD) were not working full time, how much of the time did you (HEAD) work?

_____

_____

G25. How much do you (FAMILY) spend on the food that you use at home in an average week?

$ _____ (PER WEEK)

G26. Do you have any food delivered to the door which isn't included in that?

[ ] YES   [ ] NO (GO TO G28)

G27. How much do you spend on that food? $ _____ per _____
                                                              (WEEK, MONTH)

G28. Did you (FAMILY) use any government food stamps (commodity stamps) in 1973?

[ ] YES   [ ] NO (TURN TO G34, PAGE 14)

G29. How much did you pay for the stamps? $_____ per _____
                                                                  (WEEK, MONTH)

G30. How much food could you buy with the stamps? $_____ per _____
                                                                  (WEEK, MONTH)

G31. You said you spent _____ on food in the average week.
                           (MENTION AMOUNT IN G25)

Did you include in that only the amount of money you actually spent or did you also include the extra value of the food you got with the stamps?

1. INCLUDES ONLY AMOUNT	5. ALSO INCLUDES EXTRA VALUE OF FOOD
OF	GOT WITH STAMPS (I.E., MONEY
MONEY SPENT	SPENT PLUS VALUE OF STAMPS

G32. Did you use food stamps regularly during all of 1973?

[ ] YES   [ ] NO
(TURN TO G34,
PAGE 14)   G33. Did you start using stamps in 1973,
                                 stop using them, or did you use
                                 them on and off?

| 1. START | 5. STOP | 7. USED ON |
| | | AND OFF |

(TURN TO G34, PAGE 14)

14

G34. About how much do you (FAMILY) spend in an <u>average week</u> eating out, <u>not counting</u> meals at work or at school?

$ _____ (PER WEEK)

G35. We're interested in the time people spend working around the house. Who does most of the housework in your family?

_____ (RELATION TO HEAD)

G36. About how much time (does he/she) (do you) spend on this housework in an average week - I mean time spent cooking, cleaning, and other work around the house?

_____ (HOURS PER WEEK)

G37. INTERVIEWER: CHECK ONE

[ ] 2 OR MORE PEOPLE IN FU | 0. ONLY ONE PERSON IN FU | (TURN TO H1, PAGE 15)

   ↓

G38. Does anyone else here in the household help with the housework?

| 1. YES | | 5. NO | (TURN TO H1, PAGE 15)

   ↓

	Person #1	Person #2	Person #3
G39. Who is that?	(RELATION- (AGE) SHIP TO HEAD)	(RELATION- (AGE) SHIP TO HEAD)	(RELATION- (AGE) SHIP TO HEAD)
G40. About how much time does (he/she) spend on housework in an average <u>week</u>?	(HOURS PER WEEK)	(HOURS PER WEEK)	(HOURS PER WEEK)
G41. Anyone else?	[ ] YES (ASK G39-G40 ABOVE)	[ ] NO (TURN TO H1, PAGE 15)	

15

SECTION H: INCOME

(ASK EVERYONE)

To get an accurate financial picture of people all over the country, we need to know the income of all the families that we interview.

H1. (INTERVIEWER: CHECK ONE)

| 1. FARMER, OR RANCHER | | 5. NOT A FARMER OR RANCHER | (GO TO H5)

H2. What were your total receipts from farming in 1973, including soil bank payments and commodity credit loans? $_____ A

H3. What were your total operating expenses, not counting living expenses? $_____ B

H4. That left you a net income from farming of? A-B= $_____ A-B

H5. Did you (R AND FAMILY) own a business at any time in 1973, or have a financial interest in any business enterprise?

| 1. YES | | 5. NO | (GO TO H8)

H6. Is it a corporation or an unincorporated business, or do you have an interest in both kinds?

        | 1. CORPORATION | (GO TO H8)
        | 2. UNINCORPORATED |
        | 3. BOTH |
        | 8. DON'T KNOW |

H7. How much was your (FAMILY's) share of the total income from the business in 1973 - that is, the amount you took out plus any profit left in?

        $_____

(ASK EVERYONE)

H8. How much did you (HEAD) receive from wages and salaries in 1973, that is, before anything was deducted for taxes or other things?

                                                    $_____

16

H9. In addition to this, did you have any income from bonuses, overtime, or commissions?

    [ ]YES   [ ]NO (GO TO H11)

H10. How much was that? $_____

H11. Did you (HEAD) receive any other income in 1973 from:

(IF "YES" TO ANY ITEM, ASK "How much was it?" ENTER AMOUNT AT RIGHT)

(IF "NO" ENTER "0")

    a) professional practice or trade? $_____ per_____

    b) farming or market gardening, roomers or boarders? $_____ per_____

    c) dividends, interest, rent, trust funds, or royalties? $_____ per_____

    d) ADC, AFDC? $_____ per_____

    e) other welfare? $_____ per_____

    f) Social Security? $_____ per_____

    g) other retirement pay, pensions, or annuities? $_____ per_____

    h) unemployment, or workmen's compensation? $_____ per_____

    i) alimony? Child support? $_____ per_____

    j) help from relatives? $_____ per_____

    k) anything else? _____ $_____ per_____
                     (SPECIFY)

H12. Did anyone (else) not living here now help you (FAMILY) out financially - I mean give you money, or help with your expenses during 1973?

    [ ]YES   [ ]NO (TURN TO H14, PAGE 17)

H13. How much did that amount to last year? $_____

H14. INTERVIEWER: REFER TO H11d AND H11e AND CHECK ONE.

[ ] INCOME FROM WELFARE OR ADC, AFDC   [ ] NO SUCH INCOME (GO TO H17)

> H15. Did welfare also help you out in any other way - like with your rent or other bills?
>
> [ ] YES   [ ] NO (GO TO H17)
>
> H16. About how much did that amount to in 1973? _____
>
> _____

H17. INTERVIEWER: DOES HEAD HAVE WIFE IN FU?

[ ] YES, WIFE IN FU   [ ] NO WIFE IN FU OR FU HAS FEMALE HEAD (TURN TO H21, PAGE 18)

> H18. Did your wife have any income during 1973?
> [ ] YES   [ ] NO (TURN TO H21, PAGE 18)
>
> H19. Was it income from wages, salary, a business, or what?
>
> _____   _____
>   (SOURCE)   (SOURCE)
>
> H20. How much was it before deductions?
>
> $_____ $_____

18

H21. INTERVIEWER: REFER BACK TO COVER SHEET AND LIST ALL PEOPLE 14 AND OLDER OTHER THAN THE CURRENT HEAD AND WIFE. LIST THOSE IN THE FU AT ANY TIME DURING 1973, INCLUDING THOSE WHO MOVED OUT! IF NO SUCH PEOPLE, TURN TO H32, PAGE 20

RELATION TO HEAD   AGE

H22. Did _____ have any
          (MENTION PERSON)

     income in 1973?

[ ]YES   [ ]NO (GO TO H22 FOR NEXT PERSON LISTED)

H23. About how much did that amount to in 1973?

$_____ in 1973

H24. Was that from wages, a pension, a business or what?

(SOURCE)

IF WAGES OR BUSINESS

H25. What kind of work did (he/she) do?

(OCCUPATION)

H26. Can you tell me about how many weeks (he/she) worked?

(WEEKS)

H27. About how many hours a week was that?

(HOURS)

H28. (IF DON'T KNOW) Was it more than half time?

H29. Did (he/she) have any other income?

[ ]YES   [ ]NO (GO TO H22 FOR NEXT PERSON LISTED)

H30. What was that from?

(SOURCE)

H31. How much was that last year?

$_____ in 1973

RELATION TO HEAD AGE	RELATION TO HEAD AGE	RELATION TO HEAD AGE
[ ]YES [ ]NO (GO TO H22 FOR NEXT PERSON LISTED)	[ ]YES [ ]NO (GO TO H22 FOR NEXT PERSON LISTED)	[ ]YES [ ]NO (GO TO H22 FOR NEXT PERSON LISTED)
$ _____ in 1973	_____ in 1973	_____ in 1973
(SOURCE)	(SOURCE)	(SOURCE)
(OCCUPATION)	(OCCUPATION)	(OCCUPATION)
(WEEKS)	(WEEKS)	(WEEKS)
(HOURS)	(HOURS)	(HOURS)
[ ]YES [ ]NO (GO TO H22)	[ ]YES [ ]NO (GO TO H22)	[ ]YES [ ]NO (GO TO H22)
(SOURCE)	(SOURCE)	(SOURCE)
$ _____ in 1973	$ _____ in 1973	$ _____ in 1973

(TURN TO H32, PAGE 20)

494

20

(ASK EVERYONE)

H32. Did anyone else living with you in 1973 have any income? (INCLUDING CHILDREN UNDER 14)

[ ] YES   [ ] NO (GO TO H34)

H33. Who was that?

_____   _____   _____
RELATION TO HEAD   AGE   RELATION TO HEAD   AGE   RELATION TO HEAD   AGE
(TURN BACK AND ASK H22-H31 FOR THESE ADDITIONAL MEMBERS)

H34. Did you get any other money in 1973 - like a big settlement from an insurance company, or an inheritance?

| 1. YES | | 5. NO | (GO TO H36)

H35. How much did that amount to? $_____ in 1973

H36. Do you help support anyone who doesn't live with you?

| 1. YES | | 5. NO | (GO TO H41)

H37. How many? _____

H38. How much money did that amount to in the last year? $_____ in 1973

H39. Were any of these people dependent on you for more than half of their total support?

     | 1. YES | | 5. NO | (GO TO H41)

     H40. How many? _____

H41. How much education did your (HEAD's) mother have? _____

_____

H42. Did you have any brothers or sisters older than you?
| 1. YES | | 5. NO |

H43. Do you (HEAD) belong to a labor union?
| 1. YES | | 5. NO |

INTERVIEWER: REMEMBER TO FILL OUT "BY OBSERVATION" SECTION FOR ALL INTERVIEWS.

21

SECTION J: NEW WIFE

J1. INTERVIEWER: REFER TO COVER SHEET AND CHECK ONE:

| 1. FU HAS NEW WIFE THIS YEAR | 5. FU HAS SAME WIFE AS IN 1973 OR FU HAS NO WIFE OR FU HAS FEMALE HEAD (GO TO K1) |

J2. How many grades of school did your wife finish? _____

J3. Did she have any other schooling?

[ ]YES   [ ]NO (GO TO K1)

J4. What other schooling did she have? _____

(IF COLLEGE)   J5. Does she have a degree?

[ ]YES   [ ]NO (GO TO K1)

J6. What degree(s) did she receive? _____

SECTION K: NEW HEAD

K1. INTERVIEWER: CHECK ONE

| 1. FU HAS A NEW HEAD THIS YEAR | 5. THIS FU HAS THE SAME HEAD AS IN 1973 (TURN TO PAGE 3 OF COVER SHEET) |

K2. Now I have some questions about your family and past experiences. Where did your father and mother grow up? (FROM BIRTH TO 18 YEARS OF AGE)

ST, CO- FA

[ ][ ][ ][ ]   Father: _____   _____
                        (State if U.S., Country if foreign)   (COUNTY OR TOWN)

ST, CO- MO

[ ][ ][ ][ ]   Mother: _____   _____
                        (State if U.S., Country if foreign)   (COUNTY OR TOWN)

22

K3. What was your father's <u>usual</u> occupation when you were growing up?

OCC ☐

_____

_____

K4. Thinking of <u>your</u> (HEAD's) first full time regular job, what did you do?

OCC ☐

_____ | 0. NEVER WORKED |
(GO TO K6)

K5. Have you had a number of different kinds of jobs, or have you mostly worked in the same occupation you started in, or what?

_____

_____

K6. Do you (HEAD) have any children who don't live with you?

[ ]YES   [ ]NO (GO TO K9)

   1st
   2nd
   3rd

K7. How many? _____ (NUMBER)

K8. When were they born? _____ _____ _____   #
(YEAR BORN)   (YEAR BORN)   (YEAR BORN)

BY 25 ☐

K9. Did you (HEAD) have any children who are not now living?

[ ]YES   [ ]NO (GO TO K11)

K10. When were they born? _____ _____ _____
(YEAR BORN)   (YEAR BORN)   (YEAR BORN)

K11. How many brothers and sisters did you (HEAD) have? _____ | 0. NONE |
(SPECIFY NUMBER)

K12. Is your religious preference Protestant, Catholic, or Jewish, or what?

[ ]PROTESTANT | 8. CATHOLIC | | 9. JEWISH | OTHER _____
(SPECIFY)

(GO TO K14)

K13. What denomination is that? _____

K14. Did you (HEAD) grow up on a farm, in a small town, in a large city, or what?

| 1. FARM | | 2. SMALL TOWN | | 3. LARGE CITY | OTHER _____
(SPECIFY)

K15. In what state and county was that (EXAMPLE: ILLINOIS, COOK COUNTY)

ST, CO- H

| | | | | |

(STATE)   (COUNTY)

(IF DON'T KNOW TO K15)────►K16. What was the name of the nearest town?

_____(TOWN)

K17. What other states or <u>countries</u> have you lived in? (Including time spent abroad while in the armed forces.)

_____

K18. Have you (HEAD) ever moved out of a community where you were living in order to take a job somewhere else?

| 1.YES | (GO TO K20) | 5. NO |

K19. Have you ever turned down a job because you did not want to move? | 1. YES | | 5. NO |

K20. Were your parents poor when you were growing up, pretty well off, or what?

_____

K21. How much education did your father have? _____

(IF LESS THAN 6 GRADES)────► K22. Could he read and write? _____

K23. How many grades of school did you (HEAD) finish? _____

(IF <u>6 GRADES OR LESS</u>)   (IF <u>7 GRADES OR MORE</u>)

| K24. Did you get any other training?
[ ]YES   [ ]NO (GO TO K31)
K25. What was it?_____

K26. Do you have any trouble
     reading?
_____
_____
                    (GO TO K31) | K27. Did you have any other schooling?
[ ]YES   [ ]NO (GO TO K31)
K28. What other schooling did you
     have?
_____
(IF COLLEGE) K29. Do you have a
                  college degree?
        [ ]YES [ ]NO (GO TO K31)
        K30. What degree(s) did
             you receive?
_____
                    (GO TO K31) |

K31. Are you (HEAD) a veteran?

| 1. YES | | 5. NO |

24

Now I have a few questions about your (HEAD's) health.

K32. Do you have a physical or nervous condition that limits the type of work, or the amount of work you can do?

| 1. YES | 5. NO | (TURN TO PAGE 3 OF COVER SHEET) |

K33. How much does it limit your work? _____

_____

K34. How long have you been limited in this way by your health? _____

_____

K35. Is it getting better, or worse, or staying about the same? _____

_____

(TURN TO PAGE 3 OF COVER SHEET)

25

COMPLETE THIS SECTION FOR <u>ALL</u> INTERVIEWS

SECTION L: <u>BY OBSERVATION ONLY</u>

L1. Who was respondent (relation to head)? _____

L2. Number of calls? _____

L3. What is the nearest city of 50,000 or more (<u>include city living in</u>)? _____

_____

L4. How far is this DU from the center of that city (CITY IN L3)?

1. LESS THAN 5 MILES	2. 5–14.9 MILES	3. 15–29.9 MILES	4. 30–49.9 MILES	5. 50 OR MORE MILES

26

THUMBNAIL SKETCH:

GLOSSARY

The following is a description of some of the technical terms used in this volume. For more details on the measures used in these analyses see the documentation, A Panel Study of Income Dynamics, 2 volumes, Survey Research Center, Institute for Social Research, University of Michigan, Ann Arbor, Michigan, 1972, A Panel Study of Income Dynamics: Procedures and Tape Codes 1973 Interviewing Year, Wave VI Supplement, A Panel Study of Income Dynamics: Procedures and Tape Codes 1974 Interviewing Year, Wave VII Supplement.

ACHIEVEMENT MOTIVATION - A personality measure from social psychology representing a propensity to derive satisfaction from overcoming obstacles by one's own efforts in situations where the outcome is ambiguous. It is believed to be developed by early independence training, to result in the taking of calculated but not extreme risks and in the raising of goals after success experiences. It was administered in the 1972 interview.

ASPIRATION-AMBITION - A seven-item index of attitudes and plans reflecting attempts to improve economic well-being; see Volume II of the documentation, p. 789. The items include the following:

> Might move on purpose
> Wanted more work, and/or worked more than 2500 hours last year
> Might quit a job if it was not challenging
> Prefers a job with chances for making more money to one more pleasant
> Is dissatisfied with self
> Spends time figuring out how to get more money
> Plans to get a new job, knows what type of job and what it might pay
> (Second and last items neutralized for those for whom they are inappropriate.)

BETA - A measure of the explanatory power of an independent variable when considered in a multivariate context. See Appendix D Regression with Categorical Predictions.

BETA WEIGHTS - When the independent and dependent variables in the regression equation $Y = a + b_1X_1 + b_2X_2 + u$ are measured in their "natural" units (e.g., in dollars, years, hours) then the parameters b_1 and b_2 reflect the effect on Y of a one unit change in X_1 and X_2, respectively. If all variables are standardized so that each has a mean of zero and a standard deviation equal to one, then the equation becomes $Y = \beta_1X_1 + \beta_2X_2 + v$ and the β's can be interpreted as the fraction of a standard deviation that Y changes as a result of a change of one standard deviation in the X's. The b's are regression coefficients (sometimes called "partial regression coefficients"), the β's are *beta weights* or standardized regression coefficients. The unstandardized and standardized coefficients are related in the following way:

$$\beta_1 = \frac{b_1\sigma_{X_1}}{\sigma_Y}$$

COGNITIVE ABILITY - See *TEST SCORE*

CONNECTEDNESS (to sources of information and help) - The following eight-item set of reported behaviors measuring the extent to which the respondent has friends or habits likely to keep him informed or provide help; see Volume II of the documentation, p. 793.

> Attended PTA meeting within the year
> Attends church once a month or more
> Watches television more than one hour a day
> Knows several neighbors by name (2 points if 6 or more)
> Has relatives within walking distance
> Goes to organizations once a month or more
> Goes to a bar once a month or more
> Belongs to a labor union and pays dues
> (First item is neutralized for families without children).

COUNTY WAGE RATE for unskilled casual labor - An estimate of the wage rate for unskilled labor in the county where the respondent lives, secured by mail questionnaires sent each year to the state official in charge of unemployment compensation.

COUNTY UNEMPLOYMENT - An estimate of the unemployment rate in the county where the respondent lives, secured by mail questionnaires sent each year to the state official in charge of unemployment compensation.

CRAMER'S V - A measure of association between two nominal scale variables when they have no natural rank order. It is similar to the Chi-square measure except it is adjusted for the number of observations and is constrained to take on values between 0 and 1. The higher Cramer's V, the greater the association between the classification.

DECILE - If all units are arranged in ascending order on some criterion such as income and each tenth marked off and identified, the ten groups formed are called deciles. The actual dividing points of incomes are given in Volumes II and III of the documentation.

DESIGN EFFECT - The effect of departures from simple random sampling in probability samples, defined as the ratio of the actual sampling variance to the variance of a simple random sample of the same size.

ECONOMIES OF SCALE - As the size of a family increases, if the costs do not increase proportionately, then we say there are economies of scale in large families.

ECONOMIZING INDEX - An index of six reported behaviors taken to indicate parsimonious use of money; see Volume II of documentation, p. 790.

> Spent less than $150 a year on alcohol
> Spent less than $150 a year on cigarettes
> Received more than $100 worth of free help
> Do not own late model car
> Eat together most of the time
> Spent less than $260 a year eating out
> (The fourth item is neutralized for those not owning cars).

EFFICACY INDEX - An index composed of six self-evaluations which reflect a sense of personal effectiveness, and a propensity to expect one's plans to work out; see Volume II of documentation, p. 787.

> Is sure life will work out
> Plans life ahead
> Gets to carry out plans
> Finishes things
> Would rather save for the future
> Thinks about things that might happen in future.

ELASTICITY - Refers to the response of the quantity of a good consumed to a change in price or in income. If the percentage change in the quantity of food consumed, for example, is greater than the percentage change in the price, then the demand for food is said to be price-elastic; if it is less than the percentage change in price, it is price-inelastic.

ETA - A measure of the explanatory power of a set of subclass means based on a one-way analysis of variance. The square of eta for a single categorical variable is analogous to the unadjusted R^2 from regression with a single independent variable. Eta is sometimes called the correlation ratio.

EXOGENOUS VARIABLE - Variables whose levels and changes are determined by forces independent of those being studied, as contrasted with endogenous variables which are interdependent with variables in the system.

EXPECTED VALUE - When a dependent variable is determined by a combination of systematic and random effects, the expected value is that part which can be predicted from the systematic relationship. In the case of regression, it is the value predicted by the regression equation.

F-TEST - A test of the significance of the proportion of the variance explained by a set of several predictors or several classifications of a single predictor; see *STATISTICAL SIGNIFICANCE*.

FAMILY - All persons living in a household who are related by blood, marriage, or adoption. In occasional cases an unrelated person has been included in the family unit if he or she shares expenses and is apparently a permanent member of the unit. The definition of family used in this study includes single person families. This contrasts with the Census Bureau convention of classifying single persons separately as "unrelated individuals."

FAMILY COMPOSITION - Contains several dimensions, most of them related to the family's position in the standard life cycle: marriage, birth of first child, youngest child reaches age six and starts school, children leave home, one spouse dies. The sex and marital status of the head, the number of children, and age of the youngest are the main components.

FAMILY MONEY INCOME - Family income, unless otherwise designated, is the total regular money income of the whole family, including income from labor, capital, and transfers such as pensions, welfare, unemployment compensation, workmen's compensation, and alimony received by all members of the family. It includes neither capital gains (realized or unrealized) nor irregular receipts from insurance settlements.

FAMILY TAPE - A data file containing all the data on that family from all six interviews. There is one record for each sample family. The final seven-year data tape includes only families interviewed in 1974 so that there are no partial records. Where there are several families derived from an original sample family, the early family information will appear on each of their records.

GINI COEFFICIENT - A measure of inequality that ranges from 0 when every family has the same income to 1 where one family has it all and the rest have none. A measure of inequality. If one orders all units (families) in ascending order on some measure (income) and plots the cumulative fraction of aggregate income against the cumulative proportion of families, the resulting curve sags below a straight diagonal line to indicate inequality. The ratio of the area between the curve and the diagonal line to the whole triangular area below the diagonal is the Gini coefficient.   It varies from zero for total equality to 1 for total inequality.   The curve is called the Lorenz curve.

HEAD OF FAMILY - In nuclear families the husband is defined as the head.   In families with a single adult, he or she is defined as the head.   In ambiguous cases of more than one adult, the head is the major earner or the one who owns the home or pays the rent.   Note that the head of the family may change due to marriage, divorce, or death.   For splitoff families, the head is similarly defined.

HORIZON INDEX - A six-item index of reported behavior indicating a propensity to plan ahead; see Volume II of documentation, p. 792.

>   Is sure whether will or will not move
>   Has explicit plans for children's education
>   Has plans for an explicit kind of new job
>   Knows what kind of training new job requires
>   Has substantial savings relative to income
>   Expects to have a child more than a year hence, or expects no more
>   children and is doing something to limit the number.

HOUSEHOLD - Probability samples usually sample occupied dwellings, which may contain more than one household, which in turn may contain more than one family. However, the term household is often used loosely to mean family, since the number of individuals living with unrelated adults is very small.   A family is a group of individuals related by blood, marriage, adoption.

HUMAN CAPITAL - The economically valued skills which result from the investment in one's self through education or other training.

IMPUTED RENT - A form of nonmoney income and consumption for home owners who can be thought of as in the business of renting a house to themselves.   It is estimated by taking six percent of the owner's net equity in his house (house value minus remaining mortgage principal).

INCOME - Unless otherwise specified, this means total family money income including regular money transfers.   (See *FAMILY MONEY INCOME*)   When a year is given, it is the year of the income, not the (later) year when the interview was taken.

INCOME/NEEDS RATIO - See *NEEDS STANDARD*

INDIVIDUAL TAPE - A data file with one record for each individual as of 1974, containing all the data for that individual over the whole period and all the data for the family that individual was in each of the seven years.   The tape contains some individuals who are not in the sample and are thus excluded from the analysis but who are necessary in order to derive family information for those in the sample. Individuals and families have separate weights; see *WEIGHT* and the documentation, Volume I.

INELASTIC - See *ELASTICITY*

INFORMATION THEORY - A substitute for the analysis of variance where what is being decomposed and analyzed is the amount of information rather than the unexplained variance.

INTELLIGENCE - See *TEST SCORE*

KENDALL'S TAU - A measure of rank correlation between two classifications.

LEAST SQUARES ESTIMATOR - That method of estimation which minimizes the squared deviations of the actual value from the predicted value of the dependent variable. Such estimators are sensitive to extreme cases and nonnormal distributions.

LINEAR REGRESSION - See *REGRESSION*

LORENZ CURVE - A curve plotting the cumulative proportion of some aggregate quantity against the cumulative fraction of families (arranged in ascending order). It is a measure of inequality--the more it sags, the greater the inequality. It depends heavily on the definition of the measure and the unit, particularly the latter.

MARGINAL PROPENSITY TO CONSUME - That fraction of an increase in income which is spent on consumption.

MOTIVATION - See *ACHIEVEMENT MOTIVATION*

MULTICOLLINEARITY - A problem arising in estimation if two or more predictors are highly intercorrelated. It thus becomes difficult to estimate the separate effects of these variables.

MULTIPLE REGRESSION - See *REGRESSION*

MONEY EARNINGS ACTS INDEX - An index of behavioral reports that the family is doing things to increase its money income including working long hours, getting to work on time, changing jobs, looking for a better job; see documentation, Volume II, p. 794.

MTR - Tables and other computer output are indexed by a Machine Tabulation Request number for checking and filing purposes. The number appears at the bottom of each table.

NEEDS STANDARD - An estimate of the annual income necessary for a family. The standard is generated in the same way as the official Federal poverty line; food needs are determined according to age and sex, as estimated and priced by the

USDA (in <u>Family Economics Review</u>), and food costs are adjusted for economies of scale; this figure is then multiplied by a factor to allow for other needs also differentially greater for smaller families. The needs standard, based on the "low cost" food plan is 1.25 times the official federal poverty standard, which is based on the "economy" food plan.

The absolute level is to some extent arbitrary and is not adjusted for inflation in later years, but the standard adjusts for differences in family size and structure so the status of families that differ in composition can be compared.

The needs standard is corrected for changes in family composition during the prior year, so that it is legitimate to compare it with that year's income. See the documentation, Volume I, for further details.

NUMBER OF CASES - The actual number of families or individuals on which the estimate is based. The number does not reflect the proportion of the population represented by that group because of the differences in sampling and response rates. See *WEIGHTS*.

NULL HYPOTHESIS - See *STATISTICAL SIGNIFICANCE*

ORDINARY LEAST SQUARES (OLS) - See *REGRESSION*

QUINTILE - If all cases are arranged in ascending order on some criterion such as income and each fifth is marked off and identified, these five groups are called quintiles.

PARTIAL CORRELATION COEFFICIENTS (partial R^2) - The partial correlation coefficient (squared) is a measure of the marginal or added explanatory power of one predictive variable or set of variables, over and above all the other predictors. It can be thought of as the correlation of two sets of residuals, after removing the effects of all other predictors from both the dependent variable and the predictor in question. It is also the fraction of the remaining distance to perfect explanation (1.00) the multiple correlation (squared) is moved by the added predictor. It is the best measure of the "importance" of a predictor or group of predictors.

PERCENT OF POPULATION - The fraction of the weight-sum represented by a subgroup is an estimate of the percent of the population (of families or of individuals) it represents. Aggregate estimates can be made by ratio-estimating procedures, i.e., multiplying the sample mean by the proportion of the population times an outside estimate of the aggregate number of families or individuals.

PLANNING INDEX - A subset of the efficacy index consisting of the following items:

> Plans ahead
> Prefers to save for future
> Thinks about the future.

REAL EARNING ACTS INDEX - A five-item index, with neutralization of the inapplicable items, reflecting ways of earning nonmoney income or investing in self; see documentation, Volume II, pp. 789-90.

> Saved more than $75 doing own additions or repairs
> Saved more than $75 growing own food
> Saved more than $75 repairing own car
> Head was taking courses or lessons with economic potential
> Head spent spare time productively.

R^2 - The fraction of variance in the dependent variable which is explained by the set of explanatory variables.

REGRESSION - A statistical technique which estimates the separate, independent effect of each of several predictors on a dependent variable. It minimizes the sum of the squared deviations from predicted values (see *LEAST SQUARE ESTIMATOR*) and assumes that the dependent variable is a linear and additive function of the predictors and a random error term.

REGRESSION COEFFICIENT - The estimated effect of a predictor on the dependent variable obtained from a regression analysis. It shows the expected effect that a unit change in the predictor would have on the dependent variable if all other predictors were held constant.

RISK AVOIDANCE INDEX - An index of six reported behaviors indicating the avoidance of undue risks; see Volume II of the documentation, p. 791.

> Car (newest if several) in good condition
> All cars are insured
> Uses seat belts (2 points if all the time)
> Has medical insurance or a way to get free care
> Head smokes less than one pack of cigarettes a day
> Have liquid savings (2 points if more than two months income in
>   savings).

SIZE OF LARGEST CITY IN AREA - The primary sampling unit is a county or (rarely) cluster of counties and the size of the largest city in that area is intended to reflect the number and variety of jobs, as well as differences in costs and standards of living. When the city is 50,000 or more, the area is a Census Standard Metropolitan Statistical Area.

SPLITOFF - A splitoff is someone who left a sample family and is living in a different household. Most splitoffs are children who left the parental home to set up their own households. When a couple is divorced, one of them is designated as the continuing family and the other is a splitoff.

SPLIT SAMPLE - In order to allow proper testing of the significance and explanatory power of the descriptive and explanatory models finally selected, we have divided the sample into independent subsamples. This requires attention to the original sample design and the allocation of whole primary sampling areas to one subsample or another, so that they are truly independent (households within a cluster in a clustered sample are more like each other than a purely random set). The sample is divided into four parts, so that some initial analysis can be done on half-sample and some on three-fourths depending on the amount of searching that may need to be done and the precision of the needed testing.

STANDARD DEVIATION - A measure of the dispersion of a distribution of observations around their average (or predicted) value. If random effects are normally distributed, roughly two-thirds of the observations fall in a range of the mean plus or minus one standard deviation. It is equal to the square root of the variance and is denoted by the symbol σ. The standard deviations presented in the tables should be considered in context of the design effect.

STATISTICAL SIGNIFICANCE - Traditional statistical inference tests the hypothesis that a finding (e.g., that some effect is greater than zero), is a chance result from the sample, not existing in the population. If the probability is sufficiently small, (e.g., less than five percent), this "null hypothesis" is rejected and it is believed that there is some effect which is "statistically significant." Tests of significance should consider the design effect.

In most initial searching of data for what matters, and in what form, the assumptions of statistical testing are violated because many alternative models are tried. In addition, there are problems of estimating sampling variance with complex samples. Hence, we have used only part of the sample for searching and have reserved an independent part of the sample for assessing significance and explanatory power.

TARGET POPULATION - Those families who were in the lowest 20 percent of the income/needs distribution in any one of the five years, 1967-1971, or eight years, 1967-1974.

TEST SCORE - A 13-item sentence completion task developed as a culture-free, sex-free, and race-free measure of "intelligence." Of course, like all such measures, it may also test acquired skills or freedom from test anxiety. For further details, see Appendix F.

510

TRUST IN OTHERS - An index composed of five self-evaluating items on trusting others, believing in the fairness of the system; see Volume II of the documentation, p. 788.

> Does not get angry easily
> It matters what others think
> Trusts most other people
> Believes the life of the average man is getting better
> Believes there are *not* a lot of people who have good things they don't deserve.

T-TEST - Under certain assumptions, estimated regression coefficients have a frequency distribution known as the t-distribution. This fact can be used to form a test of significance for the coefficients, called the t-test. See also STATISTICAL SIGNIFICANCE.

TWO STAGE LEAST SQUARES (2SLS) - A statistical technique which explicitly recognizes the simultaneity of a system in deriving estimates of the effects of predictors on a dependent variable. Ordinarily least squares is applied twice with the objective of the first stage to purge the endogenous predictor of any dependence with the error term. This is accomplished by regressing the endogenous variable on all the exogenous variables in the system. The estimated value of the endogenous variable together with the other predictors as used to estimate the separate, independent effects of each predictor.

WEIGHT - There are weights both for the file of individuals and families which make the weighted estimates representative of the national non-institutional population of the continental United States. They offset differences in sampling rates and response rates, and the extra probabilities of inclusion of those who married nonsample members. There will be more respondents in lower income and minority groups than the weighted proportions because of oversampling. The oversampling simply makes the estimates for those groups more reliable.

Weighted estimates essentially multiply each case by a number representing the number of households it represents. Each digit of the weight represents 500 households.

YEAR - Interviewing was done in the spring of 1968, 1969, 1970, 1971, 1972, 1973, and 1974, but the income questions refer to the year prior to each (1967-1973).

INDEX

Employer discrimination, 259

Family composition change
    beneficial effects of, 158
    decisions about, 10-11
    and divorce and separation, 14, 16
    economic factors in, 9-10, 17
    effects of
        on children, 18, 155-158
        on economic status, 3, 5-8
        on housing costs and income change, 225 (*see also* Housing Costs)
        on men's economic status, 16
        on "other" family members, 30, 155-156, 158-159, 162, 164
        on unmarried heads of households, 80-88
        on women's economic status, 16
    and marital stability, 15
    and marriage/remarriage, 15-16
    model of, 9-16
        price analogue in, 13
        simultaneous equations estimation for, 429-431
        supply and demand framework for, 12-13
    psychological and sociological factors in, 8, 9
    public policy factors in, 3, 9, 17-18
    and splitoffs, 14, 117-153
    types of, 3, 10
    variables of, 9, 10

Family status and life cycle stages, effects of, 413-414
Fertility
    analysis, framework of, 315-316
    economic theory of, 315
    and income, 315-330
    planned birth intentions, 325, 328
    quantity and quality aspects of, 315, 317, 319
    summary, 330-331

Five Thousand American Families - Patterns of Economic Progress
    Volume I, 55
    Volume III, 60